KIDS LOVE Guide ®

KIDS

LOVE

INTERSTATE 95

Nearly **200,000** Kids Love Books Sold

Pennsylvania

Harrisburg ★
Philadelphia
Baltimore 95 · Wilmington
Annapolis · ★Dover

Washington D.C.

Virginia

Richmond ★ · Norfolk
Roanoke 95

Greensboro · Raleigh

North Carolina
Asheville · Charlotte
Greenville 95
Columbia ★

South Carolina

Macon 95 · Charleston
Georgia
Savannah

Albany · Brunswick
Jacksonville

Tallahassee ★
Gainesville 95 · Daytona Beach

Orlando

Tampa ·
Florida · West Palm
Sarasota · Beach
95

Miami

Your Family Travel Guide to I-95

500 Kid-Tested Fun Stops & Unique Spots
from the Mid-Atlantic to Miami

Michele Darrall Zavatsky

Dedicated to the Families traveling

In a Hundred Years...It will not matter, The size of my bank account...The kind of house that I lived in, the kind of car that I drove...But what will matter is...That the world may be different Because I was important in the life of a child.

- author unknown

© Copyright 2014, Kids Love Publications

For the latest major updates corresponding to the pages in this book visit our website:

www.KidsLoveTravel.com

- **REMEMBER:** Museum exhibits change frequently. Check the site's website before you visit to note any changes. Also, HOURS and ADMISSIONS are subject to change at the owner's discretion. If you are tight on time or money, check the attraction's website or call before you visit.
- **INTERNET PRECAUTION**: All websites mentioned in KIDS LOVE I-95 have been checked for appropriate content. However, due to the fast-changing nature of the Internet, we strongly urge parents to preview any recommended sites and to always supervise their children when on-line.
- **EDUCATORS**: There are suggestions for finding FREE lessons plans embedded in many listings as helpful notes for educators.

KIDS ♥ I-95 ™ Kids Love Publications, LLC

For over a decade, author Michele Darrall Zavatsky has visited thousands of places to find the best sites kids love to visit! You'll learn from her years of experience about the unique places listed in this guide. Best of all, as a mom, she knows how to add value to each visit and gives you tools to plan day trips for your family...on a budget!

TABLE OF CONTENTS

Over _1,200 miles_ of America awaits you...

Why we wrote this book?

For over 10 years, we've had the privilege of traveling 300,000 miles as a family visiting over 5,000 places to kid-test them for our book series, "KIDS LOVE TRAVEL GUIDES". Our family is known as the "Family that Vacations for a Living." Hundreds of thousands of those miles were along I-95. We doubt any other family has spent that much time on one interstate road!

Over the years, folks who use our individual state travel guides have asked us to map out an action plan for traveling up and down a major interstate. A quick conversation or e-mail reply could not possibly cover the wealth of knowledge we have from personally stopping at 1,000s of exits to eat, rest and most importantly, visit attractions nearby. So, this book is the ultimate answer to how to keep any family happy on a two hour trip or a twenty hour trip traveling along an interstate! All of the listings are within 10 miles of I-95, most are just minutes from an exit. The best part –

THIS IS THE STUFF A GPS UNIT DOESN'T TELL YOU!

Do KIDS LOVE I-95?

Who Can Benefit from this Book... A new way to travel - Sidetripping

Every year, thousands of families load up their minivans and drive I-95 to visit family and friends or vacation destinations. I-95 has also become a "driveway" to Florida, the most visited vacation area in the United States.

While most kids would agree they can't wait to get to their destination, many feel boredom or cause stress on the way there. But, road trips don't need to be tense or difficult to plan. "Getting there" can be half the fun - if you know what family-friendly places are along the way. And, you can trust our advice as the best-selling "Family Travel Parents" who have been there, done that - wrote the books. We don't just do internet research, we actually kid-test most every site we list, weeding out the bad and highlighting favorites. We also share clues on how to make the visit more valuable...even on a budget. We did the busy work so you don't have to...

HOW TO USE THIS BOOK

Here are a few hints to make your adventures run smoothly:

BEFORE YOU LEAVE:

- Each chapter represents a state that I-95 traverses through. The chapter begins with an introduction and **Quick Tour** of favorites within the chapter. The listings are by Exit Number and then by proximity to the exit (places closest listed first). Each listing has tons of important details (pricing, hours, website, etc.) and a review noting the most engaging aspects of the place. Our popular **Activity Index** (at the beginning of each state/chapter) is helpful if you want to focus on a particular type of attraction (i.e. History, Tours, Outdoor Exploring, Animals & Farms, Suggested Lodging and Dining, etc.).

- Begin by assigning each family member a different colored highlighter (for example: Daniel gets blue, Jenny gets pink, Mommy gets yellow and Daddy gets green). At your leisure, begin to read each review and put a highlighter "check" mark next to the sites that most interest each family member or highlight the features you most want to see. Now, when you go to plan a quick trip - or a long van ride - you can easily choose different stops in one day to please everyone.

BEFORE YOU LEAVE *(cont.)*

▣ Know directions and parking. Use a GPS system or print off directions from websites.

▣ Most attractions are closed major holidays unless noted.

▣ When children are in tow, it is better to make your lodging reservations ahead of time. Every time we've tried to "wing it", we've always ended up at a place that was overpriced, in a unsafe area, or not super clean. We've never been satisfied when we didn't make a reservation ahead of time.

▣ Campers? The best reference you may find to make campsite reservations is: www.i-95-rv-guide.com.

▣ If you have a large family, or are traveling with extended family or friends, most places offer group discounts. Check out the company's website for details.

▣ For the latest critical updates corresponding to the pages in this book, visit our website: www.kidslovetravel.com. Click on **Updates.**

EASILY REMEMBER YOUR TRIP:

▣ Make a family "treasure chest". Decorate a big box or use an old popcorn tin. Store memorabilia from a fun outing, journals, pictures, brochures and souvenirs. Once a year, look through the "treasure chest" and reminisce. "Kids Love Travel Memories!" is an excellent travel journal and scrapbook template that your family can create (available on www.kidslovetravel.com).

Trip Notes:

WAYS TO SAVE MONEY:

- <u>MEMBERSHIPS</u> - many children's museums, science centers, zoos and aquariums are members of associations that provide FREE or Discounted reciprocity to other such museums across the country. AAA Auto Club cards offer discounts to many of the activities and hotels in this book. If grandparents are along for the ride, they can use their AARP card and get discounts. Be sure to carry your member cards with you as proof to receive the discounts.
- <u>SUPERMARKET CUSTOMER CARDS</u> - national and local supermarkets often offer good discounted tickets to major attractions in the area.
- <u>INTERNET HOTEL RESERVATIONS</u> - if you're traveling with kids, don't take the risk of being spontaneous with lodging. Make reservations ahead of time. We don't use non-refundable, deep discount hotel "scouting" websites (ex. Hotwire) unless we're traveling on business - just adults. You can't cancel your reservation, or change them, and you can't be guaranteed the type of room you want (ex. non-smoking, two beds). Instead, stick with a national hotel chain you trust and join their rewards program (ex. Choice Privileges) to accumulate points towards FREE night stays.
- <u>STATE TRAVEL CENTERS</u> - as you enter a new state, their welcome centers offer many current promotions.
- <u>HOTEL LOBBIES</u> - often have a display of discount coupons to area shops and restaurants. When you check in, ask the clerk for discount pizza coupons they may have at the front desk.
- <u>ATTRACTION ONLINE COUPONS</u> - check the websites listed with each review for possible printable coupons or discounted online tickets good towards the attraction.

Trip Notes:

ON THE ROAD:

- Consider the child's age before you stop at an exit. Some attractions and restaurants, even hotels, are too formal for young ones or not enough adventure for teens. Read our trusted reviews first.

- Estimate the duration of the trip and how many stops you can afford to make. From our experience, it is best to stop every two hours to stretch your legs or eat/snack or maybe visit an inexpensive attraction. Some of our favorite stops on the way are little BBQ or ice cream diners that keep the kids looking forward to the journey, not just the final destination. We also indicate **Playlands, Rest Areas and Welcome Centers** when available at most exits.

- Pace yourself. Each map is <u>20 miles long</u> and gives you a sense of "traveling with the book" in small increments which breaks up the monotony of long journeys. It's also great for estimating how far you've come and how much farther you have to go.

- Allow kids to bring their favorite music and personal electronics. Bring along a small portable DVD player, too. Decide family rules for how much time you allow electronics on while traveling BEFORE you leave.

- Bring along travel books and games for "quiet time" in the van. (see tested travel products on www.kidslovetravel.com) As an added bonus, these "enriching" games also stimulate conversation - you may get to know your family better and create memorable life lessons.

- In between meals, we offer the family snacks like: pretzels, whole grain chips, nuts, water bottles, bite-size (dark) chocolates, carrots, grapes, dried fruit, string cheese and apples. None of these are messy and all are healthy. Keep these in a small cooler or backpack near the front of the vehicle.

- Plan picnics along the way. Many Historical sites and State Parks are scattered along the highway. Kids can run around outside and release some energy. Allow time for a rest stop or a scenic byway to take advantage of these free picnic facilities.

- Safety - we indicate Hospital or major Health Care facility exits.

A QUICK TOUR OF THE MAPS

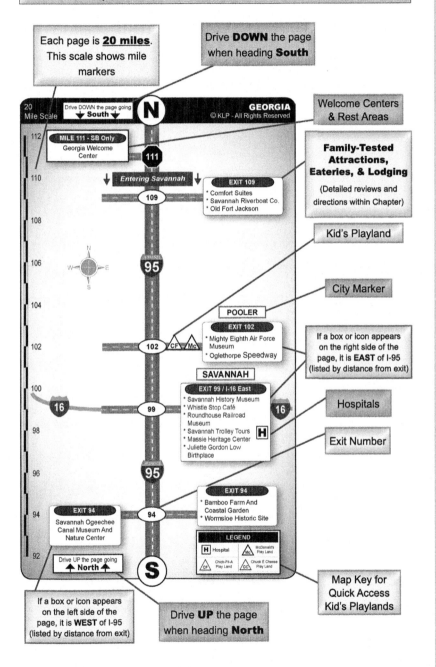

Each page is **20 miles**. This scale shows mile markers

Drive **DOWN** the page when heading **South**

Welcome Centers & Rest Areas

Family-Tested Attractions, Eateries, & Lodging

(Detailed reviews and directions within Chapter)

Kid's Playland

City Marker

If a box or icon appears on the right side of the page, it is **EAST** of I-95 (listed by distance from exit)

Hospitals

Exit Number

Map Key for Quick Access Kid's Playlands

If a box or icon appears on the left side of the page, it is **WEST** of I-95 (listed by distance from exit)

Drive **UP** the page when heading **North**

Map detail

20 Mile Scale

Drive DOWN the page going ↓ South ↓

N GEORGIA

MILE 111 - SB Only
Georgia Welcome Center

111

↓ *Entering Savannah* ↓

EXIT 109
* Comfort Suites
* Savannah Riverboat Co.
* Old Fort Jackson

109

95

POOLER

EXIT 102
* Mighty Eighth Air Force Museum
* Oglethorpe Speedway

102 CF Mc

SAVANNAH

EXIT 99 / I-16 East
* Savannah History Museum
* Whistle Stop Café
* Roundhouse Railroad Museum
* Savannah Trolley Tours
* Massie Heritage Center
* Juliette Gordon Low Birthplace

16   99   16   **H**

95

EXIT 94
* Bamboo Farm And Coastal Garden
* Wormsloe Historic Site

94

EXIT 94
Savannah Ogeechee Canal Museum And Nature Center

LEGEND
| **H** Hospital | McDonald's Play Land |
| Chick-Fil-A Play Land | Chuck E Cheese Play Land |

Drive UP the page going ↑ North ↑

S

Travel Journal & Notes:

Chapter 1
PENNSYLVANIA

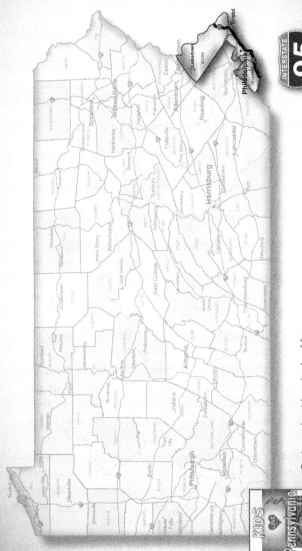

Curious about hundreds of fun places in the lighter gray areas? See *Kids Love Pennsylvania*

PENNSYLVANIA - PHILADELPHIA & ITS COUNTRYSIDE

Begin where battles raged – Trenton, NJ and **Washington's Crossing** the Delaware on cold winter mornings. Can you imagine the conditions that soldiers had to endure? Find out if you have what it takes.

In November of 1682, William Penn sailed from Great Britain to the new world on the Welcome and landed in Upland, near what is now Chester (south of Philadelphia). Penn named his colony Pennsylvania and began to plan the city that is known as Philadelphia, a Greek word meaning City of Brotherly Love. Philadelphia is affordable, accessible, educational and fun – especially closer to I-95!

Begin your adventure on a **Ride The Ducks** quacking tour through Old Town. On board, you'll learn about all there is to see and do – from a humorous perspective! After grubbing on some delicious Philly Cheesesteaks from a street vendor, head east to the Historic District, where you'll find **The Liberty Bell, Independence Hall** and **Franklin Court**. First check in at the **Independence Visitor Center** to get your free timed tickets (or order them online for a small fee before you arrive) before heading off to see the sights. Scattered throughout this area are several "Once Upon a Nation" storytelling benches, where you can rest your feet and hear a tale about Colonial Philadelphia. In the evening, be sure to make reservations for the imaginative **Lights of Liberty** tour. You won't believe how magical the night sky brings historic figures back to life.

Once you've gotten your fill of history, other options like the **Insectarium** (north of town) and Art, Children's (younger set) or Science museums (older kids) like Franklin Institute prevail. This city allows you to look under a microscope at bugs, crawl like bugs and even eat bugs!

Now, you're off to Penn's Landing, where you take a short trip on the ferry across the Delaware River to Camden, New Jersey's Riverfront. From here, it's a quick walk to the **Adventure Aquarium**, home to more than 5,000 marine animals. Next, tread over to **Camden Children's Garden**, a four-acre horticultural wonderland featuring a host of interactive habitats including the Dino Garden, Storybook Garden or the Treehouse. Children can even take a train ride around the grounds or hop on the Garden's beautiful carousel. Nearby is a **Battleship** you can board and tour.

Travel Journal & Notes:

_____

_____

_____

_____

_____

_____

_____

_____

_____

_____

_____

_____

_____

_____

_____

_____

_____

_____

_____

_____

_____

_____

_____

_____

_____

_____

_____

_____

_____

ACTIVITIES AT A GLANCE

AMUSEMENTS

Exit - 46 - *Sesame Place*
Exit - 22 - *Franklin Square*

ANIMALS & FARMS

Exit - 22 West / I-676 To I-76 N Exit 342 - *Philadelphia Zoo*
Exit - 22 / I-676 South - *Adventure Aquarium*
Exit - 6 - *Linvilla Orchards*

HISTORY

Exit - 46 - *Pennsbury Manor*
Exit - 46 - *New Jersey Statehouse*
Exit - 46 - *New Jersey State Museum*
Exit - 46 - *Old Barracks Museum*
Exit - 31 - *Washington Crossing Historic Park*
Exit - 22 - *Independence Visitor Center (For The National Historical Park)*
Exit - 22 - *Liberty Bell*
Exit - 22 - *Independence Hall*
Exit - 22 - *National Constitution Center*
Exit - 22 - *Lights Of Liberty*
Exit - 22 - *Declaration (Graff) House*
Exit - 22 - *Atwater Kent, Museum Of Philadelphia*
Exit - 22 - *Franklin Court*
Exit - 22 - *Christ Church*
Exit - 22 - *Betsy Ross House*
Exit - 22 - *Fireman's Hall*
Exit - 22 / I-676 South - *Battleship New Jersey*
Exit - 20 - *Carpenter's Hall*
Exit - 20 - *Todd House*
Exit - 20 - *Thaddeus Kosciuszko National Memorial*
Exit - 20 - *Independence Seaport Museum*
Exit - 15 - *Fort Mifflin*

MUSEUMS

Exit - 22 / I-676 To I-76 N Exit 342 - *Please Touch Museum*
Exit - 22 West / I-676 To I-76 S Exit 346 - *University Of Pennsylvania Museum Of Archaeology & Anthropology*
Exit - 22 - *Federal Reserve Bank Money In Motion*
Exit - 20 - *Mummers Museum*

OUTDOOR EXPLORING

Exit - 49 - *Tyler State Park*
Exit - 37 - *Neshaminy State Park*
Exit - 22 / I-676 To I-76 N Exit 342 - *Fairmount Park*
Exit - 22 East / I-676 South - *Camden Children's Garden*
Exit - 10 - *Heinz National Wildlife Refuge*
Exit - 7 - *Ridley Creek State Park*

SCIENCE

Exit - 30 - *Insectarium*
Exit - 22 West / I-676 North - *Franklin Institute Science Museum*
Exit - 22 / I-676 North - *Academy Of Natural Sciences*

SPORTS

Exit - 17 - *Philadelphia Phillies Baseball*

SUGGESTED LODGING & DINING

Exit - 22 / I-676 North - *Doubletree Hotel Philadelphia*
Exit - 20 - *City Tavern*
Exit - 22 / I-676 North - *Reading Terminal Market*
Exit - 22 - *Shanes Candies*
Exit - 22 - *Franklin Fountain*
Exit - 22 - *Philly Cheesesteak*
Exit - 20 - *Jones Restaurant*

ACTIVITIES AT A GLANCE

THE ARTS

Exit - 22 / I-676 North - *Philadelphia Museum Of Art*
Exit - 20 - *National Liberty Museum*

TOURS

Exit - 51 - *New Hope And Ivyland Railroad*
Exit - 51 - *New Hope Boat Rides*
Exit - 22 / I-676 North - *Philadelphia City Hall Observation Deck*

TOURS *(cont.)*

Exit - 22 West / I-676 North - *Eastern State Penitentiary*
Exit - 22 - *Philly Transportation & Tours*
Exit - 22 - *Ride The Ducks Tours*
Exit - 22 - *U.S. Mint*
Exit - 17 - *Wells Fargo Center Tours*

GENERAL INFORMATION

Contact the services of interest. Request to be added to their mailing lists.

- Biking Directory of PA. (717) 787-6746. Free through PENN DOT.
- PA Historical: www.ExplorePAHistory.com
- PA State Association of County Fairs. www.pafairs.org or (717) 365-3922
- PA Tourism. (800) VISIT-PA or www.visitpa.com
- PCOA. PA Campground Owners Association Directory. www.pacamping.com or (888) 660-7262.
- PA Fish and Boat Commission. (717) 657-4518 or www.fish.state.pa.us. Information on FISH FARMS/HATCHERIES is here. Fun place to tour.
- PA Snowmobile Hotline. (717) 787-5651.
- PA State Forests. (717) 783-7941 or www.dcnr.state.pa.us/forestry/stateforests/
- PA State Parks. (888) PA-PARKS or www.dcnr.state.pa.us/stateparks/. Junior Naturalist Program and Cabin/Camping Rentals.
- Statewide Fall Foliage Hotline. (800) FALL-IN PA or www.fallinpa.com
- Philadelphia, PA, www.visitphilly.com or Visitors Center at Independence Historical Park Center. Follow them on their online blog site: www.uwishunu. com. Check out their FAMILY PHILADELPHIA packages that are truly an economical way to explore some of Philly's best sites while staying at "kid-friendly" hotels in town.

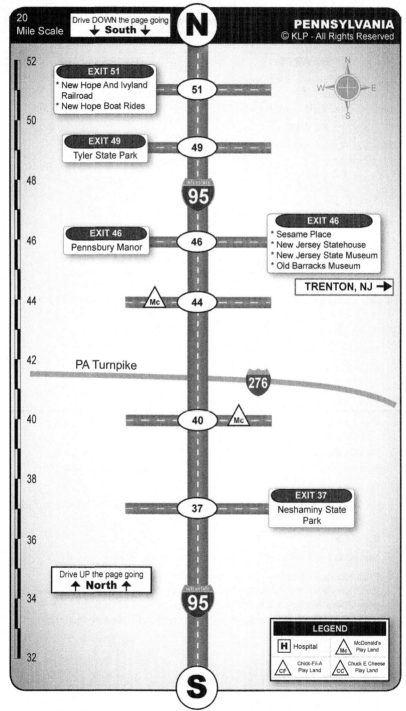

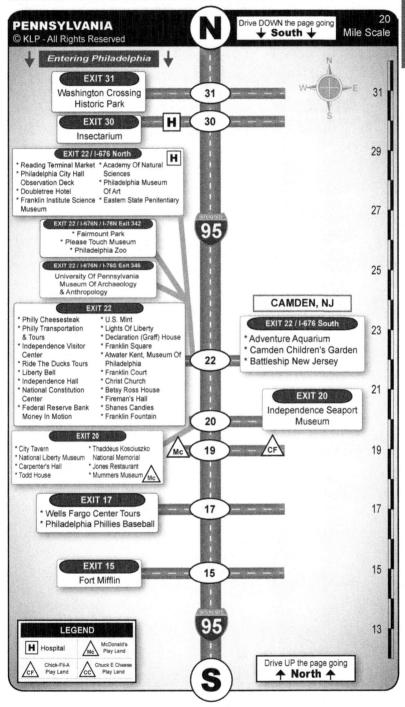

PENNSYLVANIA

Drive DOWN the page going ↓ **South** ↓

20 Mile Scale

↓ **Entering Philadelphia** ↓

EXIT 31
Washington Crossing Historic Park — 31

EXIT 30
Insectarium — [H] — 30

EXIT 22 / I-676 North — [H]
* Reading Terminal Market
* Philadelphia City Hall Observation Deck
* Doubletree Hotel
* Franklin Institute Science Museum
* Academy Of Natural Sciences
* Philadelphia Museum Of Art
* Eastern State Penitentiary

EXIT 22 / I-676N / I-76 Exit 342
* Fairmount Park
* Please Touch Museum
* Philadelphia Zoo

EXIT 22 / I-676N / I-76S Exit 346
University Of Pennsylvania Museum Of Archaeology & Anthropology

EXIT 22
* Philly Cheesesteak
* Philly Transportation & Tours
* Independence Visitor Center
* Ride The Ducks Tours
* Liberty Bell
* Independence Hall
* National Constitution Center
* Federal Reserve Bank Money In Motion
* U.S. Mint
* Lights Of Liberty
* Declaration (Graff) House
* Franklin Square
* Atwater Kent, Museum Of Philadelphia
* Franklin Court
* Christ Church
* Betsy Ross House
* Fireman's Hall
* Shanes Candies
* Franklin Fountain

CAMDEN, NJ

EXIT 22 / I-676 South — 23
* Adventure Aquarium
* Camden Children's Garden
* Battleship New Jersey

EXIT 20
Independence Seaport Museum — 21

EXIT 20
* City Tavern
* National Liberty Museum
* Carpenter's Hall
* Todd House
* Thaddeus Kosciuszko National Memorial
* Jones Restaurant
* Mummers Museum

[Mc] — 19 — [CF]

EXIT 17 — 17
* Wells Fargo Center Tours
* Philadelphia Phillies Baseball

EXIT 15 — 15
Fort Mifflin

Drive UP the page going ↑ **North** ↑

LEGEND
[H] Hospital
[Mc] McDonald's Play Land
[CF] Chick-Fil-A Play Land
[CC] Chuck E Cheese Play Land

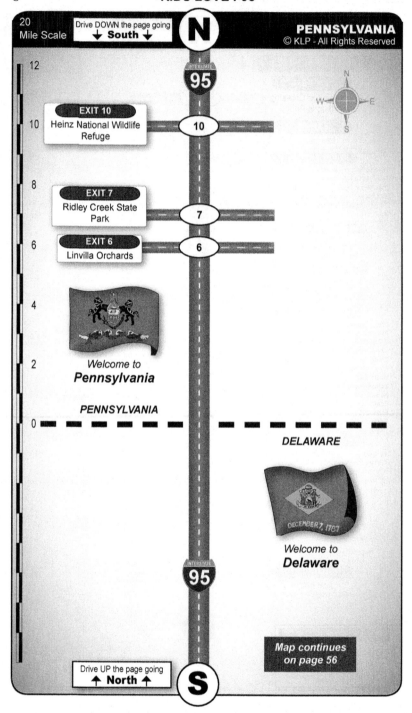

Sites and attractions are listed in order by Exit Number (North to South) and distance from the exit (closest are listed first). Symbols indicated represent:

 Restaurants    Lodging

Exit - 51 (west of I-95)

NEW HOPE AND IVYLAND RAILROAD

New Hope - *32 West Bridge Street (Taylorsville Rd 5 miles. Rte. 32 north 5 miles. Depot at West Bridge and Stockton Street) 18938. www.newhoperailroad. com. Phone: (215) 862-2332. Hours: Daily (April-Holidays). Admission: Generally $17.95-$19.95 per ticket. Toddlers $3.95. Special trains more. Tours: Departure times vary, phone or visit website for schedule. 9 miles round trip - 45 minutes.*

Climb aboard the New Hope & Ivyland passenger train and travel into a scene from the past. Relax and leave your cares behind as you journey into history, learning what rail travel was like for your parents, grand parents and great-grand parents. This ride is famous for the trestle called "Pauline" upon which actress Pearl White was bound to in the 1914 silent film "The Perils of Pauline". It might be the best way to expose young kids to the silent movies era (pictures available at the depot, too).

NEW HOPE BOAT RIDES

New Hope - *18938*

☐ **CORYELL'S FERRY HISTORIC BOAT RIDES**. 22 South Main Street at Gerenser's Ice Cream. (215) 862-2050. A Mississippi-style paddlewheel boat, the Coryell's Ferry offers trips on the Delaware River near New Hope. The boat departs daily at 11:00am from May to September. A Seniors special is offered on Tuesday, and Kids Day is Wednesday. Buy your tickets at Gerenser's Exotic Ice Cream on Main Street. Learn about the history of the region and enjoy the scenery of the area. 1/2 hour tours on path once used to commute passengers by canoe (now they use paddleboats). Make sure to ask the driver about the area's importance as a colonial ferry crossing (Coryell's Ferry has been operating in the area since 1733), including the story about General George Washington's crossing.

☐ **WELLS FERRY** - Ferry Street and River Road. (215) 862-5965. Today, you can ride in comfort and savor the gentle river breezes on the 37-foot "Star of New Hope," a pontoon boat which departs New Hope at exactly the same spot as the original ferry, the end of Ferry Street. Guided tour on a 36 passenger boat highlighting history of river and canal plus famous homes and wildlife. Admission. Departs on the hour, from the end of May to mid-October, every day except Tuesday.

Exit - 49 (west of I-95)

TYLER STATE PARK

Langhorne (Newtown) - *101 Swamp Road (I-95 at the Newtown/Yardley Exit 49, then drive west on the four-lane bypass around Newtown) 18940. Phone: (215) 968-2021.   www.dcnr.state.pa.us/stateparks/findapark/tyler/index.htm. Admission: FREE.*

The meandering waters of Neshaminy Creek flow through the park along with 10 miles of paved bicycling trails, a playhouse--Spring Garden Mill (www. langhorneplayers.org), and several children's play areas. Maze Picnic Area: This area is especially popular with families with young children because of the Children's miniature play barn and maze, Sand box, and Large play field. Gravel hiking trails to the east of Neshaminy Creek link each picnic area. Anglers may fish along the banks of Neshaminy Creek or from a canoe. A 27-hole Disc Golf course begins by the Upper Plantation Picnic Area. Neshaminy Creek offers calm, easy boating (electric motors only) upstream from the canoe rental. Horseback Riding, Trails, Winter Sports like Ice Skating, Ice fishing, Sledding & Tobogganing.

Exit - 46 (west of I-95)

PENNSBURY MANOR

Morrisville - *400 Pennsbury Memorial Lane (Rte. 1 north, Morrisville to Rte 13 south. Exit onto Tyburn Road East. on the Delaware River) 19067. Phone: (215) 946-0400. www.pennsburymanor.org. Hours: Tuesday-Saturday 9:00am-5:00pm, Sunday Noon-5:00pm (open Summer holidays). Closed January. Admission: $9.00 adult, $7.00 senior (65+), $5.00 child (3-11) . Tours: 90 minutes long - a little difficult for pre-schoolers. Miscellaneous: Best for kids to visit (April - October) Sundays for living history days. Picnic areas.*

A quaint, Quaker, simple homestead of

William Penn, the founder of Pennsylvania. In 1682, William Penn sailed to Pennsylvania with one hundred other passengers on The Welcome. See a replica of the boat Penn used to "commute" to Philly. Horses, cattle, sheep and even a few peacocks roam the grounds as 17th century costumed interpreters demonstrate crafts and activities of the day. They may be baking bread (up to 30 loaves at one time!) in the bake house or check out the farm where sheep and geese roam. Inside the Visitor's Center try writing with the original "pen" - a quill pen. You can also learn about Colonial James writing style here.

Exit - 46 *(east of I-95)*

SESAME PLACE

Langhorne - 100 Sesame Road (I-95 to US1 north to Oxford Valley exit. Next to Oxford Valley Mall) 19047. Phone: (215) 752-7070. www.sesameplace.com. Hours: Daily 10:00am-8:00pm (mid May - Labor Day Weekend), Weekends (early May, September & October) - Call for current schedule. Admission: ~$53.00 general admission. Parking $10.00. Discounts up to $10 are available at several online & retail partners and can be redeemed at front gate ticket windows. Note: Late afternoon and family discounts. Bathing suits required for water attractions. We'd recommend staying all day to get your money's worth. Eateries, cafes and a bistro for sit down eating or set up a character meal.

While your kids continue to peek over their shoulders for a glimpse of a Sesame Street character like Big Bird (great photograph opportunities),

they'll be pulling your hand in every direction so they won't miss anything. Big Bird, Elmo and the other stars of Sesame Street come out and play at Sesame Place, the only theme park in the nation featuring the popular TV show's most lovable characters. Catch a show like "Rock Around the Block", then jump on Ernie's Bed Bounce (that even sounds like fun to adults, doesn't it?) or scale "Cookie Mountain". Mechanical rides include: A roller coaster called "Vapor Trail", or, a 40-foot high balloon tower ride carries you up in one of eight balloon baskets - providing a bird's eye view of the park, and, also a character themed tea cup ride turns you "round and round" - as fast or as slow as you want to go. Everybody's favorite character hosts the new Elmo's World ride area. There's also 14 refreshing water attractions. As you float, zoom or chute through Big Bird, Ernie's and Slimey's Rides, you'll be splashed or trickled by a giant rubber ducky. Toddlers can be water trickled in Teany Tiny Tidal Waves. Bet your kids just can't wait to walk down a full-sized replica of Sesame Street and take pictures to show their friends back home!

Exit - 46 (east of I-95)

NEW JERSEY STATEHOUSE

Trenton, NJ - *125 West State Street (head east on Rte.1. Take Route 29 north toward Lambertville. Exit right at Memorial Drive. Follow signs for the Capitol Complex. NOTE: This attraction is from a Pennsylvania Exit, but is located just across the state line in New Jersey). 08625. Phone: (609) 633-2709. www.njleg. state.nj.us/legislativepub/statehousetour.asp. Hours: Generally 9:30am-4:30pm weekdays. Admission: FREE. Tours: Hourly Tours, Monday through Friday, 10:00am-3:00pm & Saturday, 12:00pm-3:00pm. Closed Sunday and State holidays. Educators: Teacher Resources - State House Express, Vote 2009 Mock Election, and Learning Materials. FREEBIES: Kids' Page - Coloring Books, Puzzles, and other Fun Pages Just for Kids!*

The second-oldest capitol in continuous use in the U.S. The Governor's wing dates from 1792. The legislative quarters have been restored to their turn-of-the-century splendor. Most visits to the New Jersey State House begin in the historic Rotunda space where guests learn about our Capitol's evolution from a simple rubble-stone structure built in 1792 to the grand architectural monument of today. Impressive stained glass windows surround portraits of early Governors. Where's the Painted Ceiling Room and why is it called that? Next, tour the Senate & Assembly Rooms. You'll want to browse around the Welcome Center to get the skinny on NJ government. Just in Jersey is a series of interactive exhibits which includes multiple levels of learning so that both children and adults can enjoy it. The centerpiece is Making Laws -- Debate, Negotiation and Compromise, where a ball rolls on a track representing the path of legislation. Treasures and Trivia uses touch-screen monitors to quiz visitors on State trivia. A large display monitor enables guests to Discover New Jersey by showing legislative district, major attractions, and fun facts. Nearby, a rotating mobile represents our Democracy in Balance. For I Have a Voice, visitors hear short debates on public policy issues and cast votes. Large blocks representing portions of the State House help visitors construct The Building of Government. Tour reservations required.

NEW JERSEY STATE MUSEUM

Trenton, NJ - *205 W. State Street (head east on Rte.1. Take Route 29 north toward Lambertville. Exit right at Memorial Drive. Follow signs for the Capitol Complex NOTE: This attraction is from a Pennsylvania Exit, but is located just across the state line in New Jersey) 08608. Phone: (609) 292-6464. Hours: Tuesday – Saturday 9:00am to 5:00pm, Sunday, noon to 5:00pm. Closed Mondays & State Holidays Admission: General admission is FREE.*

From fossils to fine art, from Native American tools to the finest silver, from quilts to comets, from prehistory to the future, the New Jersey State Museum is four museums in one and offers a galaxy of experiences for every member of the family. Treasures, collected since the early 1800's, are housed in a modern main building overlooking the Delaware River in Trenton and are enhanced by exciting programs offered in an adjoining 150-seat planetarium and an adjacent 400-seat auditorium. Ranging from ceramics produced by Trenton potteries to flags carried into battle by New Jersey Civil War regiments to utilitarian artifacts reflecting the rich maritime and agricultural heritage of the Garden State, the Cultural Gallery displays implements used in everyday life. The archeological collection encompasses over 2 million prehistoric and historic specimens from nearly 100 years of excavation. Streetside, they often have a display of recent Fossil Mysteries using CSI-type science to determine the source of found objects. And, if your kids like animals, the Natural History portion of the museum is all about that - even some live animals are represented.

OLD BARRACKS MUSEUM

Trenton, NJ - *(The Old Barracks is located in downtown Trenton, next to the New Jersey State House) 08608. Phone: (609) 396-1776. www.barracks.org. Hours: Monday-Saturday 10:00am-5:00pm. Closed Thanksgiving, Christmastime, New Years & Easter. Admission: $6.00-$8.00 per person (age 6+).*

The only original French & Indian War Barracks still standing in the US. Also famous for its role in Washington's victory over Hessian troops during the Revolutionary War. The museum offers a peek into the daily life of an American Colonial person. Site of the famous day-after-Christmas battle during the Revolutionary War (Battle of Trenton which is re-enacted Saturday after Christmas). Open daily year round.

Exit - 37 (east of I-95)

NESHAMINY STATE PARK

Bensalem - *3401 State Road (follow PA 132 signs towards Delaware River @ State Road and Dunks Ferry Road) 19020. Phone: (215) 639-4538. www.dcnr.state. pa.us/stateparks/findapark/neshaminy/index.htm. Admission: FREE. Pool and camping require fees. Note: The Playmasters Theatre Workshop: The playhouse, on State Road, offers entertainment throughout the year. Visit www.playmasters.org.*

Can you feel the ocean's tides in Pennsylvania? You can at Neshaminy State Park. Waves won't knock you down, but if you watch the river, you'll see it rise or fall an inch a minute. When the tide comes in at a New Jersey beach, the water rises here also. Because tides affect this part of the river, it's called an estuary. Neshaminy State Park provides boating access to the Delaware River. The picnic areas and seasonal swimming pool are the most popular park attractions. River Walk Trail: follows the shoreline and gives views of the river with its boating traffic, and also explores the tidal marsh. The River Trail Inner Loop explores the interior of the park and is a great way to discover animals and plants. The River Walk Brochure compares the past to the present, and describes some of the river inhabitants like sturgeon, shad and eel. Puzzles help children explore the estuary, river and tidal marsh. A self-guiding brochure is available at the park office. Fishing, Boating (unlimited HP motors permitted), and Cross-Country Skiing.

Exit - 31 (west of I-95)

WASHINGTON CROSSING HISTORIC PARK

Washington's Crossing - *SR32 and SR532 (off I-95, exit 31, head northwest on Rte. 532) 18977. Phone: (215) 493-4076. www.ushistory.org/washingtoncrossing. Hours: Thursday-Sunday 10:00am-4:00pm. Hill Tower open Tuesday-Sunday. Closed some holidays. Admission: $6.00 (age 3+) for tours for each site. Combo tickets $11.00. Park charges $1.00 per vehicle at entrance. Cash & check only. Tours: Tours begin on the hour. During winter months, tours may conclude earlier in the day due to low light levels in the historic structures. The Thompson-Neely grist mill is open seasonally for tours. Allow additional time to tour the grist mill. Note: Events occur each month on the weekends, especially Sundays. Every Christmas (at 1:00pm) the park re-enacts Washington's crossing and special events also occur on his birthday. Also on grounds is the Bowman's Hill and Wildflower Preserve. FREEBIES: click on FOR KIDS icon to browse thru several games and FAQ. Be sure to print a copy of the Washington Crossing Scavenger*

Hunt to complete while you're on site.

It's December 25, 1776. Washington planned his attack on the British, first crossing the Delaware River by boat. In the Durham Boat House, you can see the boats that were actually used. A larger than life copy (20 ft. X 12 ft.) of the painting "Washington's Crossing" creates the best image of this

historic Christmas Day for freedom. A total of 13 historic buildings are on site and your tour ticket includes Bowman's Hill Tower observation point, Thompson-Neely House (where Washington ate and slept), The Ferry Inn (where Washington dined before crossing the icy Delaware) and the Memorial Building where the giant painting stands. All of this, plus a short historical film is shown of the event. It'll give you goosebumps!

Exit - 30 *(west of I-95)*

INSECTARIUM

This is the largest insect museum in the nation !

Philadelphia - *8046 Frankford Avenue (1-95 Cottman Avenue exit thru to right on Frankford for several blocks) 19136. www.myinsectarium.com. Phone: (215) 335-9500. Hours: Monday-Saturday 10:00am-4:00pm. Admission: $9.00 (ages 2+)*

While in Philly, maybe add a creepy trip over to the INSECTARIUM, north of downtown. Philadelphia's only all-bug museum exhibits thousands of live and mounted insects from Africa, Tanzania and other exotic locations, as well as interactive displays and movie room. Did you know we eat bugs every day? They're ground up in plants as they are harvested. See a glow in the dark scorpion or bugs with noses. There's giant bugs and little bees (do you know what honey really is?). Pet live bugs like Martin the cockroach or Harry the millipede (yes, Mommy actually pet them!). Interact as you climb thru a spider web, eat fried worms, or push buttons.

The highlight has to be the Cockroach Kitchen & Bathroom! How do they keep them inside the room? They live here and are welcome! Great photo ops and their gift shop has inexpensive craft kits and bug food and toys. You will learn so much here and the guides really add the "magic". Outside, there's a learning garden where you can go on bug hunts.

George, "calmly" holding a scorpion...yikes!

Exit - 22 (west of I-95) / I-676 North

READING TERMINAL MARKET

Philadelphia - *12th and Arch Streets (neighborhood: Convention Ctr/Chinatown/ Market East-Broad St. exit south, follow signs) 19107. Phone: (215) 922-2317. www.readingterminalmarket.org. Hours: Monday through Saturday: 8:00 am–6:00 pm Note: Some of the Market's restaurants close after 4:00pm. Sunday: 9:00am– 5:00pm. Weds-Saturday only hours for Pennsylvania Dutch vendors. Wednesday 8:00am-3:00pm, Thursday-Saturday 8:00am-5:00pm. Sunday 9:00am-4:00pm.*

Begin your historic adventure with an early lunch at the Reading Terminal Market, the nation's oldest continuously operating farmers' market. Family-run vendors sell virtually every type of farm-fresh cuisine, as well as prepared food ready to eat there. The northwestern corner of the market is primarily devoted to Amish merchants from Lancaster County, who bring their farm-fresh products and distinctive prepared dishes to the Market four days a week. Watch as Amish bakers twist and bake soft pretzels right in front of your eyes — then try one while it is still warm from the oven. You can get a traditional Amish-style meal at the counter of the Dutch Eating Place (Famous blueberry pancakes, egg sandwiches, apple dumplings, fresh cut fries, deli sandwiches and scrapple) - or get an authentic Philadelphia cheesesteak. But those are just two options at this foodie paradise — look around and see what you like!

PHILADELPHIA CITY HALL OBSERVATION DECK

Philadelphia - *Broad & Market Streets (Broad St. exit south about 4 blocks) 19107. Phone: (215) 686-2840. Hours: Daily 9:30am-4:15pm. Admission: $4.00-$5.00 per person (age 3+). Tours: Tower tours every 15 minutes from 9:00am-2:00pm. A full tour of City Hall, including the tower, starts at 12:30. Separate tower tours resume at 3:00 until 4:15.*

Every city has one building that stands as one of the tallest in town and usually it has a lot of history behind it. Most noted is the courtroom (available to view on the tour only) where a motion picture film was made and the 548 foot tall tower that has a statue of William Penn on top. At the base of the statue is the observation deck. Its observation deck,

Arguably the most popular sculpture in Philadelphia, LOVE, by artist Robert Indiana, debuted in John F. Kennedy Plaza during the 1976 Bicentennial Celebration.

which is open to the public, provides a panoramic view of the city. This building is so breathtakingly beautiful and stands in the center of downtown...believe us, you can't miss it!

DOUBLETREE HOTEL PHILADELPHIA CENTER CITY

Philadelphia - *237 S. Broad Street (neighborhood: Convention Ctr/Chinatown/Market East-Broad St. exit south about 5 blocks) 19107. Phone: (215) 893-1600. www.doubletree.com.*

Guests who want to stay in the middle of the action check in to the Doubletree Hotel Philadelphia, located on the Avenue of the Arts. Families can spend some time at the rooftop pool, sundeck and racquetball courts, and kids get a free cookie at check-in. Especially nice if you want to stay in between the Science Museums and the Historic Area. The views of the city are pretty cool, too. Some packages offer free parking, which is a good value here as parking is $22.00 per day or more. You could walk to everything (or take the Phlash) but that means a minimum of 10 blocks each way.

FRANKLIN INSTITUTE SCIENCE MUSEUM

Philadelphia - *222 North 20th Street (Center City) (to the "Ben Franklin Parkway/ Museum Area" exit, follow signs) 19103. Phone: (215) 448-1200. www.fi.edu. Hours: Daily 9:30am-5:00pm. Closed November/December major holidays only. Admission: $18.50 adult, $14.50 child (3-11). Sci-Pass includes museum, science demos, and planetarium. IMAX and special exhibits extra. Note: Ben's Bistro - Lunch, Café, Museum Stores. Special exhibits change in the Mandell Center. IMAX Theatre (additional charge).*

If you have older kids, you may want to check out the Franklin Institute instead of the children's museum. The Franklin is the area's premier science museum, housing a planetarium, IMAX movie theater, several permanent exhibits and rotating special exhibits (advanced tickets are typically required for the special exhibits). What began as a national memorial to Ben Franklin is

now a hands-on exhibit and demonstration complex.

At the entrance are displays of some of Franklin's personal effects and a famous statue by James Earle Fraser. Some exhibits have been there forever. Walk through a "Human Heart" - hear a heart beating as "blood" races through the arteries. Also, see a full-size train or airplane cockpit!

Learn how Sports and Physics mix or how Art & Physics collide. Highlights include The Sports Challenge, which uses virtual-reality technology to illustrate the physics of sports; The Train Factory's climb-aboard steam engine; Space

Command's simulated earth-orbit research station; a fully equipped weather station; and exhibits on electricity. Our favorite area is Space Command where you visit a research station right here on Earth! Locate your house using a satellite home-tracking device. Travel through time to uncover what our ancestry thought about

Did you know the Franklin Institute is Pennsylvania's most visited museum?

space. Embark on a mission to discover a lost, unmanned space probe. Check out equipment used by real astronauts to explore space.

Films like "Everest" and "The Lion King" assume grand proportions on the Tuttleman

IMAX Theater's 79-foot domed screen; galaxies are formed and deep space explored in North America's second-oldest planetarium sporting the continent's most advanced technology. Don't miss the 3D Theater and the indoor SkyBike.

ACADEMY OF NATURAL SCIENCES

Philadelphia - *1900 Benjamin Franklin Parkway (exit Ben Franklin Pkwy exit off I-676 & follow signs, one block from Franklin Instit) 19103. Phone: (215) 299-1000. www.acnatsci.org. Hours: Monday-Friday 10:00am-4:30pm, Saturday, Sunday & Holidays 10:00am-5:00pm. Closed Thanksgiving, Christmas, and New Year's Day. Admission: $15.95 adult, $13.95 senior (65+), $13.95 child (3-12). Butterflies! Exhibit extra $2.00 per person. Part of CityPass discount card. Note: Ask for Scavenger Hunts sheets (age appropriate) when you enter. The kids stay focused this way. Films shown daily. Academy Café and gift shop.*

The oldest dinosaur and natural science exhibit in the world is here. Actually peer into, or walk under, dinosaurs. You're greeted by a roaring robotic dinosaur at one entrance. A giant dinosaur skeleton hangs over the information desk at the main entrance. Most families' favorite area is the Dinosaur Hall. This is hands-on paleontology including a fossil dig (child equipped with goggles and tools), fossil prep lab, and Time Machine (get your picture image appearing with dinosaurs!). You'll also meet T-Rex, plus 11 friends, and even get to climb into a dinosaur skull. The North American Hall has some stuffed large animals that are almost 200 years old. Butterflies!, a completely redesigned permanent exhibit, features a lush, tropical garden filled with colorful plants and a multitude of exotic butterflies from around the globe. Educational demos and computer interactives add to this Metamorphysis space ($2.00 extra admission). There are live animals shows and "Outside In"... hands-on, touching mice, snakes, frogs, and huge bugs. Touch a real meteorite, view a stream from underneath, crawl through a fallen log,

"Friendly" dinosaurs everywhere...

look for fossil footprints, pan for shark teeth, watch a working beehive, build a sandcastle or read a book on Lucy's Back Porch. There's also a crystals and gems exhibit that features a 57 pound amethyst and "Living Downstream" - a showcase of life in a watershed.

Exit - 22 (west of I-95) / I-676 North

PHILADELPHIA MUSEUM OF ART

Philadelphia - *26th Street and Ben Franklin Parkway (follow I-676 west. Get off at "Art Museum/Benjamin Franklin Parkway" Exit. Turn right) 19130. Phone: (215) 763-8100. www.philamuseum.org. Hours: Tuesday-Sunday, 10:00am-5:00pm. Wednesday & Friday evening until 8:45pm. Admission: $20.00 adult, $18.00 senior (65+), $14.00 child & students (age 13+). FREE child (12 & under). First Sunday of each month: Pay what you wish all day. Note: Museum restaurant.*

The 3rd largest museum in the country. 2000 years of fine and applied arts (crafts, interiors, architecture) with 200 galleries. Many rooms have themes that transport you back to when the works were created. Let your creativity soar at the Splash Studio, a family destination where people of all ages can drop in and create art together. Build with blocks, curl

The famous steps from famous movies...

up with a book, or just chill out in a bean bag chair in our Art Splash Playspace. Plus, Museum educators are out and about in the galleries all summer with stories to tell, games to play, and tricks up their sleeves for our Pop up Mini Tours.

Outside, your kids (or parents!) will love running up the numerous steps to the top like Rocky (from the movie by the same name). Pretend you hear the crowd cheer as you step onto the brass glazed imprints of Rocky's shoes!

EASTERN STATE PENITENTIARY

Philadelphia - *2124 Fairmount Avenue (follow I-676 west. Get off at "Art Museum / Benjamin Franklin Parkway" Exit. Turn right and go five blocks past the Museum of Art) 19130. Phone: (215) 236-3300. www.easternstate.org. Hours: Daily 10:00am-5:00pm. Closed Thanksgiving, Christmas Eve, Christmas Day and New Year's Day. Admission: $14.00 adult, $12.00 senior (62+) and $10.00 student, $10.00 child (7-12). Children under the age of 7 cannot be admitted to the site.*

Let's go to jail. This Penitentiary introduced Americans to a new- and a supposedly more humane-form of housing criminals: solitary confinement. Kids are fascinated by the massive cellblocks, dark cells, and stories of punishment and escape at Eastern State Penitentiary. There are special guided tours on the subjects of daily life, escapes, prison uprisings and artifacts available several times a day, every day April-November. These tours are hands-on, interactive experiences, designed for visitors age seven and up. Tours include: The central rotunda, restored cells, the solitary confinement yards, the baseball diamond, death row and Al Capone's Cell. A "Voices of Eastern State" audio tour is available during all hours. Although the subject matter is family friendly, it's recommended for kids 12 and up. Special Guided Tours with themes on Escape! Or Prison Life are highlighted versions of the audio tour. These tours are hands-on, interactive experiences, designed for visitors to engage in the spaces more.

Exit - 22 (west of I-95) / I-676N to I-76N - exit 342

FAIRMOUNT PARK

Philadelphia - *Benjamin Franklin Parkway, Fairmount Park (info at Visitor's Center at Memorial Hall. Follow signs off exit) 19131. Phone: (215) 685-0000. www.fairmountpark.org or www.smithplayhouse.org. Hours: Open daylight hours. Centers open for programs and special events.*

Along both sides of Schuylkill River, one of the world's largest city park's features include:

- SMITH PLAYGROUND & PLAYHOUSE - (215) 765-4325. Emphasis on playhouse (3 story) for preschoolers with trains, foam blocks and comfortable reading rooms. Pick up a Cozy Car and drive along the play roads with stop signs and traffic lights. This 100 year old playground has a Giant Wooden Slide that four generations have slid down.

- ENVIRONMENTAL EDUCATION CENTERS: Come check out Fairmount Park's two environmental education centers and its 112-acre working livestock farm. The Pennypack and Wissahickon Environmental Centers are open year-round. Experience their interpretive exhibits, wildlife viewing areas, picnic areas and miles of trails. Fox Chase Farm is an enjoyable place for children and adults to visit and explore. Open House the first Saturday of each month. Come experience Maple Sugar Day, Sheep Shearing or Apple Fest too.

-

- <u>FAIRMOUNT WATER WORKS INTERPRETIVE CENTER</u>: 640 Water Works Drive (215) 685-0723 or www.fairmountwaterworks.org. Who cares that you don't know the difference between a watershed and a woodshed? At the Fairmount Water Works Interpretive Center you and your family can learn about watersheds and have a ton of fun doing it. Fly a helicopter simulation from the Delaware Bay to the headwaters of the Schuylkill River. Or visit Pollutionopolis, America's most contaminated and disgusting town, to see how a city can really mess up its water supply. The Water Works is a pumping station from 1815 to 1909 where visitors can create rain, view historic photos and play with high-tech exhibits.

- <u>WISSAHICKON CREEK GORGE</u> - hiking trails.

PLEASE TOUCH MUSEUM

Philadelphia - *4231 Avenue of the Republic, Fairmount Park (Memorial Hall, GPS - Use 4231 North Concourse Drive for directions) 19131. Phone: (215) 581-3181. www.pleasetouchmuseum.org. Hours: Monday-Saturday 9:00am-5:00pm, Sunday 11:00am-5:00pm. Closed New Years, Thanksgiving and Christmas. Themed Shows presented several times each day. Admission: General $17.00 (over age 1). Parking fee $5.00. Miscellaneous: Please Taste Café. The Kids Store - take ideas from the museum home as souvenirs or projects. Nature's Pond and Fairy Tale Garden toddler areas for kids 3 and under.*

PLEASE TOUCH MUSEUM has moved and improved! The museum space is divided into six learning-through-play environments – based in the real world and fantasy themes. Here are some highlights: * Real Victorian era carousel &

model of the Statue of Liberty's torch made of toys. * Kid-scaled city-scape * Road-side attractions section where "kid mechanics" can work on real Toyota Scion or "ride/drive" a real SEPTA bus. * Kid-scaled supermarket with shopping carts and food packages for kids to stock up. * Exploration of space where kids can pedal a propeller bike, play hopscotch on clouds or spin inside a giant hamster wheel. * Nature-inspired instruments that play music   *

Collection of 12,000 toys and games from 1945 to the present. OR *River Adventures - race sailboats in water currents, play with bubbles, and rainbows.This hands-on museum for kids 8 and under also kept our favorite:

- ALICE IN WONDERLAND - The tale is explained in miniature (little doors to peek through) and then full size. Try on cover ups and pretend you're the Queen of Hearts ready for a tea party with Mad Hatter & rabbit (great photo op).

Although the setups are classic in here, the fresh aspects of creativity through role playing are really different. It's pricier than most kid's museums we've been to in our travels, but its uniqueness is often worth it.

Exit - 22 (west of I-95) / *I-676N to I-76N - exit 342*

PHILADELPHIA ZOO

Philadelphia - *3400 West Girard Avenue (I-76, exit 36) 19104. Phone: (215) 243-1100. www.philadelphiazoo.org. Hours: Daily 9:30am-5:00pm (March-October). Daily 9:30am-4:00pm (November-February). Closed Thanksgiving, December 24, 25 and 31 plus New Years Day. Admission: $20.00 adult, $18.00 child (2-11) Zoo. $15.00 Zooballoon Ride. Parking $10.00. Seasonal Zoo Trolley transport from Independence Visitor Center is only $2.00. Winter season discounts. Educators: click on FOR SCHOOLS & SCOUTS, then Educational Lessons. Note: Zoo shop. Varied dining opps. Victorian picnic groves. Stroller and wheelchair rentals. Camel, elephant and pony rides and "Treehouse" interactive areas have additional fees. Behind-the-Scenes tours available occasionally. Kids and grownups can climb inside one of the award-winning Dodge Wild Earth Durango adventure simulators for a thrilling 3-D ride through the plains of Africa.*

The first zoo in the country - now has 1800 animals on 42 acres of beautiful landscape. Favorites include the famous white lions, Jezebel and Vinkel, the first white lions ever to be exhibited in North America. Presently, there are no white lions in the wild. Big Cat Falls! - home to endangered big cats from around the world, including three new playful snow leopard cubs, three adorable new puma kittens and a beautiful new black jaguar cub. Carnivore Kingdom has the country's only giant otters. Bear Country allows you to interact (viewing, that is) with playful bears that love to show off. Check out the new primate habitat. The Children's Zoo has your typically petted animals plus cow-milking and other live demonstrations in the pavilion. The first passenger carrying balloon in the world to be located at a zoo is available for rides (Zooballoon). Zooballoon rises 400 feet above the treetops and overlooks giraffes, zebras and the Philadelphia skyline.

Exit - 22 (west of I-95) / I-676N to I-76S - exit 346

UNIVERSITY OF PENNSYLVANIA MUSEUM OF ARCHAEOLOGY & ANTHROPOLOGY

Philadelphia - 3260 South Street (Spruce & 34th Sts) (I-76 to South Street exit to 33rd and Spruce Streets) 19104. www.penn.museum. Phone: (215) 898-4001. Hours: Tuesday-Saturday 10:00am-4:30pm, Sunday 1:00-5:00pm (Closed Mondays, Holidays, and summer Sundays from Memorial Day to Labor Day) Admission: $15.00 adult, $13.00 senior (62+) and $10.00 student (age 6+). Reduced admission times each month - $10.00. Tours: Guided on Weekends at 1:30pm during the school year. Miscellaneous: Snack café. Pyramid Gift Shop. Most fun to come during a Family Fun Day Event (215) 898-4890.

Exhibits outstanding findings from Ancient Egypt, Asia, Central America, North America, Mesopotamia, Greece, and Africa, uncovered by University staff and student expeditions. See a giant Sphinx and real mummies. Gaze at an Apache tipi or a Navajo walk-in sky theater. On

> The Penn Museum is the only museum in the world to exhibit such a significant portion of an Egyptian royal palace.

one side of each gallery the exhibition focuses on the use of objects to display status and to transfer laws and traditions to upcoming generations, and on the ways in which some cultures have used objects to influence and communicate with the forces that control people's lives. The other side of the gallery displays objects of everyday life and invites you to compare the lifestyle of a group of hunter-gatherers with the lifestyle of subsistence farmers by looking at the objects each uses. The stories of the archeologists' thoughts and accompanying pictures of "digs" might inspire a budding career.

Exit - 22 (west of I-95)

PHILLY CHEESESTEAK

Philadelphia - (various locations)

People usually come to Philadelphia for two things: the history and the cheesesteak. So what is an authentic cheesesteak and how do you order it? Here's the lowdown on this region's

favorite sandwich:

- A cheesesteak is a long, crusty roll filled with thinly sliced sautéed ribeye beef and melted cheese. Originally, the cheese of choice was Cheez Whiz, but American and provolone are common substitutions. Other toppings include fried onions, sautéed mushrooms, ketchup and hot or sweet peppers. The onions, cheese and beef are the most common. You'll find Cheesesteaks sold on every corner of historic and south Philly...mostly at small, family-owned pizza shops or delis. Some of the best we've had were from food carts stationed around the Liberty Bell. When ordering, there are two critical questions to answer: First, what kind of cheese do you want? (Whiz? Provolone? American?) Second, do you want onions? Be forewarned: Lines are often long at lunchtime and if you don't have your order and money ready to go, you might be asked to step back to the end of the line until you decide. This isn't your mall variety cheesesteak - these babies are dripping with juices (ask for extra napkins) and filled with meat!

Here's some of our favorites to try:

- More famous for its creative menu of hoagies, **CAMPO'S DELI** cooks up a respectable traditional cheesesteak. It's a small place but fun. Great for lunch. 214 Market Street. (215) 923-1000.

- **JIM'S STEAKS** has multiple locations, but the classic smell of fried onions wafting down South Street makes that location the most memorable. 400 South Street. (267) 519-9253 or www.jimssteaks.com.

PHILLY TRANSPORTATION & TOURS

Philadelphia - *(Downtown). Admission: Call for rates. Pay as you board.*

Parking can be difficult and pricey around downtown Philly. During their spring/ summer and fall season they offer the PHLASH, a Visitors' loop bus, as a great option for visitors. The rates are very reasonable. Many parking garages give significant discounts to guests who park in their garage (all day) and then transport to museums and sites via Phlash. Street parking is available for around $4.00 per two hours at kiosk meters but you must return every two hours to add time. For a full day downtown, budget $20.00 for parking and enjoy as many free attractions as you can!

- Philadelphia's subway system is part of **SEPTA** (Southeastern Pennsylvania Public Transportation Authority.) Visitors can purchase a One Day Independence Pass for unlimited rides on all of the subways and buses for a whole day. The pass is also accepted on the Phlash (in season). This year's prices were $25 for a family up to five. More details are available at www.SEPTA.org/fares or by calling (215) 580-7800. This pass can purchased at the Independence Visitor Center at 6th and Market Streets at all SEPTA Sales Office and Regional Rail Ticket Offices or online at www.shop.septa.org.

- **PHILADELPHIA TROLLEY WORKS** www.phillytour.com. ('76 Carriage Company): This longtime Philadelphia company offers several exciting options for touring town, including Victorian Trolley Tours, Horse Drawn Carriage Tours, LandShark Tours and Double Decker Bus Tours. Entertaining staff will treat you to a fun and informative trip around the city. $10-$27.00 each.

- **PHILLY PHLASH** - (215) 4-PHLASH or www.phillyphlash.com. Look for Philadelphia Trolley Works Purple Phlash Trolleys for a quick, cheap and easy way to get around Center City Philadelphia. Phlash is the quick and easy connection between Penn's Landing and the Philadelphia Museum of Art, with stops at 21 key destinations covering most downtown hotels. $5.00 for an individual all-day pass, $10.00 family. Runs May thru end of October.

- **RIVERLINK FERRY** - (215) 925-LINK. Passenger ferry across the Delaware River between Penn's Landing and the Camden waterfront sites. Seasonal

- **BIG BUS TOURS** - www.bigbustours.com. Now you can experience the unique history and beauty of Philadelphia from an authentic London-style double-decker bus. An open-top tour of the city offers you spectacular views and make sure your ears are tuned in to the entertaining live commentaries from fully-trained and friendly guides. $10-$27

INDEPENDENCE VISITOR CENTER (FOR THE NATIONAL HISTORICAL PARK)

Philadelphia - 525 Market Street (follow signs to northeast corner of 6th & Market Sts - across from the Liberty Bell) 19106. www.nps.gov/inde. Phone: (215) 597-8974. Hours: Daily 8:30am-5:00pm. Extended summer hours. Admission: FREE. Parking garages in downtown Philadelphia are very steep ($4.00 per half hour up to $22.00). Cheaper alternatives: Philly Phlash buses, 2-3 hour parking meters *(esp. open on Walnut & Chestnut sts). Tours: sign up for programs or walking tours (daily summers, weekends only rest of year). All ranger guided tours are free. Cell Phone Audio Tours are available using special code numbers attained at various stops or thru maps at the Center. Miscellaneous: This is where to park (below center) and purchase tickets or schedule times for tours. Plan to spend 5-8 hours in the Independence Historical Park. Secure areas (I. Hall & Liberty Bell) Do Not have restrooms so use them here. Educators: click on FOR TEACHERS link and download Lesson Plans. On that same page is a link to tour worksheets for students. FREEBIES: you can download the Junior Ranger Activity booklet on the FOR KIDS link or pick one up at the Center. Search for the stamps found in the park, complete some activities and you'll earn a Ranger Badge. Coloring pages, too. This Junior activity book is one of the best ever!*

Start here before you explore the well-known sites. See award winning historical and tourism films shown throughout the day. Ben Franklin, George Washington, John Adams and others come back to life to tell the Independence story. Older children will want to sign up for the walking tour here (little ones up to grades 1 or 2 will want to wander at their own pace and usually aren't interested enough to stay with the group). To keep attention spans high, we noticed they create a theme (seasonally) of historical significance. Actors called "Town Criers" present impromptu conversations and "street stage" presentations along with that theme. They admired our "carriage" (known to you and me as a wagon) and our "horse" that was pulling it (Daddy!) Most events are daily in the summer and weekends the rest of the year.

Exit - 22 *(west of I-95)*

RIDE THE DUCKS TOURS

Philadelphia - *6th & Market Street depot (Exit at Callowhill St. Turn left onto 6th Street) 19106. Phone: (877) 887-8225. www.phillyducks.com. Tours: Daily, Daylight hours, mid-March thru December. Tickets for sale near depot or Independence Visitors Center. Admission: $29.00 adult, $19.00 child (3-12). AAA, senior & military plus online discounts.*

This fun tour provides passengers with an 80 minute entertaining, historically accurate, land and water sightseeing adventure aboard amphibious WWII Duck vessels. Each tour features a scenic "bus" tour past Philly's historical and cultural sites, then splashes down into the Delaware River for a floating tour along Penn's Landing (the kids, and kids-at-heart, get to try driving the boat on the water, too). You'll find yourself quacking (with provided official quackers) at interesting people as the captain commentates w/ theme music – party music – that really gets you in the mood! Learn about different ethnic eateries or some history "with a twist" – just little funny tidbits that never bore the kids (i.e.. What happened if you didn't have fire insurance? Who is famous for cake and ice cream?). Don't worry, the Duck Trucks look silly but you feel great as you travel this fun way...the new, hip way to see historic old Philadelphia!

LIBERTY BELL

Philadelphia - *526 Market Street (across from Independence Hall, I-95 exit 22, Phila/Indep.Hall/Callowhill) 19106. www.nps.gov/inde. Phone: (215) 597-8974. Hours: Daily 9:00am-5:00pm. Extended summer & many weekend hours. Admission: FREE. Tours: Given by park rangers, relates the bell's history. Long lines (for security checks) - but they move fast. Miscellaneous: Glass encased bell is viewable 24 hours a day. Interpretive kiosk displays explain details of the Bell.*

What does a cracked bell sound like? Try clanging the sample cracked bells that show how a bell sounds before and after repairs.

Standing inches from the Liberty Bell is surreal....

Made a few blocks away by two crafters who only made pots and pans (usually), its famous "crack" has many folklore stories associated with it. It would be nice to believe that each crack was the result of zealous ringing; however, it just wasn't cast properly to withstand its large size and temperature variances. Initially, it was just a bell ordered to be placed in the tower of the meeting hall (now called Independence Hall). Later, abolitionists used it as a symbol of freedom for slaves and proclaimed it the Liberty Bell (not until 1840 though!) - and the name stuck!

X-rays give an insider's view, literally, of the Bell's crack and inner-workings. In quiet alcoves, a short History Channel film, available in English and eight other languages, traces how abolitionists, suffragists and other groups adopted the Bell as its symbol of freedom. It'll give you goosebumps to stand inches from it. Be sure to take advantage of the photo opportunity time provided by park rangers.

Exit - 22 (west of I-95)

INDEPENDENCE HALL

Philadelphia - *520 Chestnut Street (5th & 6th Streets on Chestnut - across from Liberty Bell) 19106. Phone: (215) 965-7676. www.nps.gov/inde. Hours: Daily 9:00am-5:00pm. Weekends 9:00am-6:00pm. Admission: FREE. Tours: Guided tours only throughout the day. Long lines move pretty fast. You must reserve a free timed ticket from the Visitor Center or http://reservations.nps.gov. ($1.50 handling fee per ticket if order in advance) to enter spring, summer and fall. Arrive early — during the busy season, tickets are often gone by 1:00pm. Note: Congress Hall (where the first US Congress met and inaugurations of Presidents occurred) and Old City Hall (Supreme Court original house) are across the street.*

Hours vary but it is a must see for kids studying the setup of the United States Government.

Hey…this is the place that we see in countless movies and pictures. You will get a patriotic chill as you enter the hall where the Declaration of Independence was adopted and the U.S. Constitution was written. They risked everything — "their lives, their fortune and their sacred honor." During the blistering summer of 1776, 56 courageous men gathered at the Pennsylvania State House and defied the King of England. George Washington's "rising sun" chair dominates the Assembly Room which is arranged as it was during the Constitutional Convention. The Assembly Room looks just as it did in 1776 (you'll feel like you're in a movie) and you can see the original inkwell the Declaration signers dipped quills in to sign the famous freedom document.

NATIONAL CONSTITUTION CENTER

Philadelphia - *525 Arch Street Follow signs for Callowhill Streets to Independence National Park area 19106. Phone: (215) 923-0004. www.constitutioncenter.org. Hours: Monday - Friday 9:30am-5:00pm, Saturday 9:30am-6:00pm, and Sundays Noon - 5:00pm (except Thanksgiving Day, Christmas Day, and New Years Day) Admission: $8.00 - $14.50 (age 4+). Active Military w/ID are FREE. Parking garage under the museum runs $8.00-$18.00. Educators: click online on RESOURCES page, then Bill of Rights game or civics lesson plans for all grades. FREEBIES - click on EDUCATION, then Students, then Studying the Constitution for resources, games and puzzles just for you.*

The first-ever national museum honoring and explaining the U.S. Constitution and the Constitution's relevance to our daily lives so that all of us -- "We the People" -- will better understand and exercise our rights and our responsibilities. It's only four pages long, but the U.S. Constitution is among the most influential and important documents in the history of the world. Wandering a "street scene" in 1787 Philadelphia, you can eavesdrop on fellow citizens and discover the forces that inspired the creation of the document. You then enter a theater-in-the-round, where you view The Founding Story, a dramatic multi-media production which orients you to the major themes of the Center and the basic historical context of the Constitution. "Signers Hall," is where visitors are invited to play the role of Signer amidst life-size statues of the Founding Fathers. Place notes or sign a modern Constitution book and then hang out taking pictures with famous folks present at the 1st signing. High-tech, interactive exhibitions let everyone-even those under 18-vote on legislative bills, weigh in on court cases and take the Presidential Oath of Office. Kids get to dress up in robes and push buttons and play games.

Exit - 22 (west of I-95)

FEDERAL RESERVE BANK MONEY IN MOTION

Philadelphia - 100 N. 6th Street, ground floor of Federal Reserve (next to National Constitution Center) 19106. www.philadelphiafed.org/education/money-in-motion/. Hours: Monday-Friday 9:30am-4:30pm. Additional summer weekend hours. Admission: FREE. FREEBIES: Besides the souvenir pack of $$$, ask the hostess for a Scavenger Hunt worksheet.

This permanent exhibit explains the way our financial system works. The exhibit's 16 different stations offer artifacts ranging from wampum, the original colonial money, to a $100,000 bill, which was produced for one year (1934). Kids will gasp at the giant tube stuffed with $100 million in shredded cash and giggle at the "Match wits with Ben" game. At the end of the exhibit, visitors get a packet of shredded money worth $100.

U.S. MINT

Philadelphia - 5th & Arch Streets (Take I-95 to Exit 22 for "Central Phila/I-676". Follow signs for Phila/Independence Hall/Callowhill Streets) 19106. Phone: (215) 408-0112. www.usmint.gov/mint_tours/. Admission: FREE. Tours: Weekdays 9:00am-4:30pm, except Federal holidays. (Open Saturdays in Summer). If the Department of Homeland Security level is elevated to CODE ORANGE, the United States Mint at Philadelphia will be CLOSED to the public unless otherwise noted. All tours are free and self-guided; no reservations are necessary. Note: The United States Mint does not provide parking.

While in the historic district of Philadelphia, be sure to take your family to the world's largest coinage operation (seen through a glass enclosed gallery). They make a million dollars worth of coins per day! (29 million coins!). See them start with blanks that are cleaned and then stamped, sorted, and

So many types of coins are minted here...

bagged. To see coins in large bins or spilling out of machines is mesmerizing! Even little kids eyes sparkle. A "Stamp Your Own Medal" machine (press a big red button to operate) is located in the Gift shop. Great souvenir idea!

LIGHTS OF LIBERTY

Philadelphia - *Liberty Center, PECO Energy (Independence Hall exit. Left on N. 6th to the corner of Chestnut) 19106. Phone: (215) LIBERTY or (877) GO-2-1776. www.lightsofliberty.org. Hours: At Dark on Fridays & Saturdays (mid-April-early September). See website additional scheduled days during peak or seasonal events. Admission: $19.50 adult, $16.50 senior (65+) and student (w/ID), $13.00 child (6-12). Discount promotions on their website. Tours: 60 minute tours depart every 10 minutes. Note: The Liberty Center is also home to Ben Franklin's Ghost - a free exhibit where kids (and adults) can use a touch-screen computer "book," to query Ben with their own questions or choose from two hundred pre-formed questions, answered by Dr. Franklin, who appears as a dramatic, large screen image. Liberty 360 3D Show - $5.00-$6.00 per person.*

One evening during a visit, be sure you reserve a spot for the LIGHTS OF LIBERTY. The Lights of Liberty Show leads visitors on an evening journey to relive the American Revolution. Using headsets with 3D sound, visitors follow the drama of the American Revolution as it happened, where it happened. The sound system and enormous five-story images projected on buildings immerse visitors into events leading up to the Colonists' fight for freedom from the British. Mom and dad can tune in to hear Walter Cronkite  and Ossie Davis narrate the adult version of the tour while kids can listen to Whoopi Goldberg recite the children's version. Start in Franklin Court, end at Independence Hall where the battle rages with swirling smoke and flashes from imaginary musket blasts. Hear the hurried sound of horses' hoofs on cobblestone streets. You'll find yourself cheering for the Patriots and clapping on several occasions. The ending "God Bless America" is very moving. Our six year old really got engaged! Although anyone can see the giant projected images, only those wearing the high tech headsets hear the stories. Ask for the youth show (a fictional family, the Warren children, serve as headset hosts). Recommended ages: 6+. So unique and what an adventure!

Exit - 22 (west of I-95)

DECLARATION (GRAFF) HOUSE

Philadelphia - 7th & Market Streets (I-95 to Exit 22 for "Central Phila/I-676". Follow signs for Phila/Independence Hall/Callowhill Streets. Independence National Park) 19106. Phone: (215) 597-8974. www.nps.gov/inde/declaration-house.htm. Admission: FREE. Currently by tour only, tours are at 10:00 a.m. to 4:00 p.m. Tours are limited to 15 people.

Catch the short video and then see the rooms that Continental Congress delegate, Thomas Jefferson rented in this building where he penned the actual Declaration of Independence. The bedroom and parlor that Jefferson occupied have been recreated and contain period furnishings. Also included are reproductions of Jefferson's swivel chair and the lap desk he used when he wrote the Declaration.

FRANKLIN SQUARE

Philadelphia - 6th and Race Streets (close to the National constitution Center) 19106. http://historicphiladelphia.org/day/franklin-square/. Hours:Daylight hours. Admission: Carousel $3.00 per person (age 3+). Mini-Golf $7.00-$9.00.

Franklin Square is one of Philadelphia's five original squares - and the only one dedicated just to fun. A day outside around Franklin Square could include a ride on an old-fashioned carousel, a game of mini-golf, a romp on a modern playground and a family picnic. A concession called SquareBurger sells burgers, hot dogs, fries, drinks and frozen treats. The 18-hole Philadelphia-themed course allows Guests to putt through favorite icons including Elfreth's Alley, Benjamin Franklin Bridge, Philadelphia Museum of Art, LOVE statue, Chinatown Friendship Gate, and on the 18th hole, putt through the crack in the Liberty Bell and land in front of Independence Hall. Plus, holes celebrating Philadelphia Sports teams and Philadelphia Music legends.

PHILADELPHIA HISTORY MUSEUM @ ATWATER KENT

Philadelphia - 15 South 7th Street (Callowhill exit follow to 6th Street. Right on Ranstead and go one block to 7th) 19106. www.philadelphiahistory.org. Phone: (215) 685-4830. Hours: Tuesday-Saturday 10:30am-4:30pm. Admission: $10 adult, $8 senior, $6 student, FREE child (12 and under).

Whatever history you don't catch visiting buildings in the area, you'll get a touch of here. Included are: the wampum belt received by William Penn from the Lenni Lenape at Shakamaxon in 1682, the first German Bible in North America printed by Christopher Saur in 1743, personal items from Benjamin Franklin, and Phillies' Mike Schmidt's game-worn jersey. You'll also see Norman Rockwell's America showcasing all 322 magazine covers created by the country's most admired 20th-century illustrator for The Saturday Evening Post. Family Programs - toys of the past, hat making, children of the past.

FRANKLIN COURT

Philadelphia - *314-321 Market Street (I-95 exit 22, Phila/Indep.Hall/Callowhill to 6th & Race Sts) 19106. Phone: (215) 597-8974. www.nps.gov/inde. Hours: Usually daily 10:00am-5:00pm but can vary. Post Office closed Sundays. Admission: FREE for court bldgs. $2.00-$5.00 for Museum.*

Benjamin Franklin is accredited with being the first American to invent a musical instrument? He invented the "glass armonica" in 1761 after seeing wine glasses being used to make musical sounds.

Today the site contains a steel "ghost structure" outlining the spot where Franklin's house stood and features an underground museum with a film and displays about his personal life. "Bump into" Mr. Franklin as you roam his court and he'll invite you to gather around to hear stories of his life. What a wonderful way to study this amazing historic man!

Once owned by Ben Franklin who lived in Philadelphia from 1722-1790, the complex of buildings also includes:

*   PRINTING OFFICE - Working reproduction of 1785 printing press and bindery.

*   BEN FRANKLIN MUSEUM - Check out Franklin's numerous inventions, then walk and talk in the Phone Room where dozens of phones can call famous friends of Franklin. Hear "voices" of historic men such as Thomas Jefferson and Mark Twain talk about Franklin and how they felt about his character. In the courtyard, peek in the pits below to see actual excavations of rooms of Franklin's home.

*   POST OFFICE - In 1775, Ben Franklin was appointed as the first Postmaster General. The name "Free Franklin" was used as the hand cancellation signature because Mr. Franklin was referring to America's struggle for freedom. See actual hand-canceled letters, then, purchase a post card & send it from this working post office!

Exit - 22 (west of I-95)

CHRIST CHURCH

Philadelphia - *20 North American Street (take historic area/Indep. Hall exit & follow signs to 2nd Street (between Arch & Market Streets) 19106. Phone: (215) 922-1695. www.christchurchphila.org. Hours: Monday-Saturday 9:00am-5:00pm, Sunday 1:00-5:00pm (March-December). Wednesday-Sunday (Rest of year). Admission: Suggested Donation of $2.00-$3.00 to help maintain the church. Note: Services (Episcopal) held on Sunday mornings and Wednesday at 12:00pm.*

Christ Church is bordered by a tree-lined brick path, small park and a cobblestone alley, which provide the perfect setting for this historic treasure. The tower and steeple made it the tallest building in America until 1856. Fifteen signers of the Declaration of Independence worshiped here including George Washington and Benjamin Franklin. A brass plaque marks each pew of famous Colonists including Betsy Ross. Families and groups can visit the church and burial ground to gain a deeper understanding of our early history and the importance of religious freedom. Tours given throughout the day. The church was built in 1727 and originally had dirt or wood floors. Ask a guide what those marble rectangles are in the floor. Careful - though they won't mind...you may be stepping on the memory of a notable patron of the church!

BETSY ROSS HOUSE

Philadelphia - *239 Arch Street, Historic area (take Historic District/Indep Hall exit. Follow signs. Between 2nd & 3rd Streets) 19106. Phone: (215) 686-1252. www.betsyrosshouse.org. Hours: Tuesday-Sunday & Monday Holidays 10:00am-5:00pm. Also open summer Mondays. Closed Thanksgiving, Christmas and New Years. Tours: Self-guided audio tours are $6-$7.00 (includes admission). Self-guided tour lasts about 25 minutes. Note: Hot dogs, drinks and snacks are offered in the courtyard from Thursday through Sunday in March and April and daily each summer. FREEBIES: Ask for the "house hunt" sheet for kids.*

The nation's most famous seamstress, credited with the creation of the first American flag, stitched her way into history in the small workroom on display at this house. In 1777, the first American flag made by Colonial Mrs. Ross was sewn here. Betsy, who made a living as a furniture upholsterer, rented the 1740 home, and the teeny-tiny rooms and tight little staircases give a good portrayal of a working class woman's life in colonial America. You can tour her modest, working class home. Each room has a description, in Betsy's words (in old English), of what led up to her sewing the flag. She and the fellas that made the Liberty Bell were just ordinary folks who had a skill needed to enhance the cause of Independence. What was considered a routine job lead to national recognition many years later! After you tour the house, make sure to meet Betsy Ross and plan to spend some time relaxing in the shady courtyard where you'll enjoy free family friendly programming, hear storytelling and see colonial crafters at work (seasonally).

FIREMAN'S HALL

Philadelphia - 147 North 2nd Street (take Historic District/Indep Hall exit. Follow signs. Historic district near Elfreth's Alley) 19106. Phone: (215) 923-1438. www.firemanshallmuseum.org. Hours: Tuesday-Saturday, 10:00am-4:30pm. Admission: FREE.

Future firefighters get a head start at this restored 1902 firehouse that holds some of the nation's earliest blaze-fighting equipment and important historical artifacts. See memorabilia, films, and early equipment. Did your kids know Benjamin Franklin founded the first Philadelphia Fire Department in 1736? See old-fashioned leather buckets, fire wagons and an "around the world" display of firefighter helmets. Play pretend in the re-created living quarters or steer a fireboat. Taped firemen's stories recall high level exciting moments on the job. The Spider Hose Reel (1804) has a chariot look with brass bells and shiny mirrors. Also be on the lookout for the fire pole and injured firemen's hats (charred & broken).

SHANES CANDIES

Philadelphia - 110 Market Street (between 2nd & Front Sts.) (exit Indep. Hall/ Callowhill, bottom of ramp turn left onto 2nd st, then left onto Market. 19106. Phone: (215) 922-1048. www.shanecandies.com.

America's oldest candy store still makes candy the old-fashioned way. Handmade, hand-dipped chocolates in traditional and novelty shapes have been tempting palates since 1876. It claims to be the oldest candy store in the country and the place hasn't changed much. Shane's Candies famous creamy buttercreams are slowly cooked the old-fashioned way in a copper kettle while being stirred with a wooden paddle. These irresistible delicacies are super creamy. The ladies behind the counter try and stuff you with vanilla cream samples. They love kids!

Exit - 22 (west of I-95)

FRANKLIN FOUNTAIN

Philadelphia - *116 Market Street (exit Indep. Hall and follow signs to Market St. Head east (left) on Market) 19106. Phone: (215) 627-1800. www.franklinfountain.com. Hours: Noon to Midnight every day.*

The Franklin Fountain, in Old City Philadelphia is an authentic early 20th century soda shop with tin walls and ceiling, original marble counters and mosaic floors. Servers dressed as old-fashioned soda jerks serve homemade hard ice cream, banana splits, thick shakes, egg creams, sundaes and flavored soda water creams. Ok, so because Franklin is in the name, you know the namesake has to follow in naming the sundaes... The Franklin Mint (mint chip ice cream, crème de menthe topping) or The Lightning Rod (dark chocolate brownie, espresso, choco espresso beans, coconut and pretzel rod), for example. Plain Janes will still love the basic Homemade Hot Fudge (PA made, Wilbur's dark chocolate creamed smooth into hot fudge). Adventuresome foodie - ever thought of ordering Green Tea or pink Teaberry Gum flavors? Wonderful on their own or in ice cream sodas. Most sundaes run $8.00-$10.00 and are generally 3 scoops of ice cream (very sharable portions). With the menu's use of words like covered, glazed, suffocated, surmounted, bathed, finished, peppered, mountain, cascading, blanketed, doused, and ruffled...how can you go wrong?

Exit - 22 (east of I-95) I-676 South

ADVENTURE AQUARIUM

Camden, NJ - *1 Aquarium Drive (across Ben Franklin bridge to exit 5 or take seasonal RiverLink ferry from Penns Landing on Philly side. NOTE: This attraction is from a Pennsylvania Exit, but is located just across the state line in New Jersey) 08103. Phone: (866) 451-AQUA. www.adventureaquarium.com. Hours: Daily 9:30am-5:00pm. Avoid lines by buying and printing your tickets online. Best times to visit are posted online (beat crowds). Admission: $25.95 adult, $18.95 child (2-12). CityPass included in this attraction. 4D shows extra*

$3.00. Ferry extra. Waterfront Connections bus $2.00 roundtrip (summers only) Note: 4D Theater riders must be at least 36" tall. No babies in arms. Note: Swim w/the Sharks - So, you think you've got guts? Well, why not go for a swim with their sharks. Sharks love guts. $185 per person w/ reservation. Other Adventures w/ Penguins.

Take a short trip on the ferry across the Delaware River to Camden, New Jersey's Riverfront. From here, it's just a quick walk to the Adventure Aquarium, home to more than 8,400 marine animals. From the moment you walk in you'll hear it: the unmistakable rumble of a massive rainforest waterfall or celestial music around the jellyfish. Some 500 species, including sharks, penguins, stingrays and hippos are

The hippos were amazing to watch

there plus a 4D theater, dive shows, live animal talks, performances and a giant 760,000-gallon tank. Ask the trainers why penguins are such good swimmers or watch how smart and sassy seals are. Can you believe their hippos frolic and jump out of the water and press their snouts against the glass, going eye-

A VIRTUAL shark experience...well done!

to-eye with visitors? It's almost like they were trying to sneak a kiss! After you've made it through the shark tunnel, try your courage in Cage Match - a virtual Shark Cage experience. Movement and clanking noise allow you to feel vibrations of sharks approaching and pounding your cage. All pretend, of course. A

little scary - but, you'll come out alive! The aquarium offers equal measures of entertainment and education with additional attractions including the Touch-a-Shark tank and the Caribbean beach, home to tropical fish and birds. Don't just look. Touch.

Exit - 22 (east of I-95) I-676 South

CAMDEN CHILDREN'S GARDEN

Camden, NJ - *3 Riverside Drive (follow signs to exit 5, adjacent to Aquarium. NOTE: This attraction is from a Pennsylvania Exit, but is located just across the state line in New Jersey) 08103. www.camdenchildrensgarden.org. Phone: (856) 365-TREE. Hours: Wednesday-Friday 10:00am-4:00pm (July & August),*

Weekends 10:00am-5:00pm. Closed January-March. Admission: $6.00 per person (age 3+). Admission per person at Aquarium/Garden Gate is $4 per person. Note: 2 times/month they hold a Family Festival with a different theme each time. Festival of Lights in December.

A visit to Camden Children's Garden features a host of interactive habitats and exhibits — including the Dinosaur Garden, Storybook Garden, Tree House and Picnic Garden. Children can even take a train ride around the grounds or hop on the Garden's beautiful carousel. You might try one of the seasonal shows in the Piney Woods Amphitheatre, then hop on the Spring Butterfly ride. Or, when the weather's warm, you may just choose to splash around in the Violet Plaza Fountain. In addition to the Butterfly, Railroad, Dinosaur and Storybook gardens, the four-acre horticultural wonderland has added a new Fitness Garden where kids can crawl, climb and learn about healthy living. In the Burrowing Maze, act like a creature going through soil tunnels. By the way, why is Ben Franklin's Garden secret?

BATTLESHIP NEW JERSEY

Camden, NJ - *62 Battleship Place (take Ben Franklin Bridge over to exit 5 or take RiverLink Ferry over from Penn's Landing) 08103. www.battleshipnewjersey. org Phone: (856) 877-6262. Hours: Daily 9:30am-3:00pm. Extended hours May thru early September. Closed early January thru April. The Battleship is closed Thanksgiving, Christmas Day and New Years Day Admission: 3 different tours offered: $21.95 adult, $17.00 seniors and child (5-11), FREE for Children < 5/ Active*

Military /BB62 Vets. Combo Fish N Ship passes available for discount (combined w/Aquarium). FREEBIES: Print off your copies of the Battleship's Scavenger Hunt Enlisted Version on the EDUCATION icon online. Note: The tours of the Battleship New Jersey are interactive. You will be going up and down on ladders, stepping through passageways and sometimes maneuvering in tight spaces - just like the officers and the crew of the USS New Jersey did. We strongly recommend you wear comfortable flat shoes. If you do not feel comfortable with a complete tour, you can enjoy a main deck tour, which does not have any ladders. They also offer video tours of the Battleship in the Wardroom Lounge on the Main Deck. If you are bringing a toddler or baby, you cannot bring a stroller aboard the ship. We recommend that you wear a baby carry-on across your front to carry babies aboard.

Wannabe sailors can tour the nation's most decorated battleship, the Battleship New Jersey. Be sure to ask for the Kids Audio Tour as a young crew member gives you funny details of the officers' and

The "ferocious" main guns...

crew's mess halls, communications center and high-tech command center. Winding through tight, narrow companionways, visitors even get to see the sleeping quarters, which range from small private rooms for senior officers to even smaller cots stacked atop each other for enlisted men. Not only do you

see exhibits of artifacts from the ship's past, but you are put into the exhibit as you go through the tour route. Sit in the chair from which Admiral Halsey commanded the fleet. Stretch out on the bunks where the sailors slept. Climb into the 16" gun turret and learn how the projectiles were loaded. Answer questions like: what is a coffin box bed and why can't enlisted men walk on blue tiles? Between climbing and sneaking peeks inside small spaces and trying to look for answers to the scavenger hunt - your kids

Not much room to "spread out" here... will be totally occupied!

Exit - 20 (west of I-95)

CITY TAVERN

Philadelphia - *138 South 2nd Street at Walnut St. (Columbus Blvd. Past 6 lights to left on Dock to right on Front St, left on Walnut) 19106. Phone: (215) 413-1443. www.citytavern.com. Hours: Lunch is served from 11:30am daily. Dinner is served from 4:00pm Monday through Saturday, from 3:00pm Sundays.*

This is an authentic Colonial tavern faithfully recreated to 18th century colonial America. Servers are dressed in colonial garb and the restaurant uses historic recipes like Turkey Pot Pie, Cornmeal Fried Oysters, and Grilled Ham & Asparagus (served on City Tavern's Sally Lunn bread, baked from the 18th century recipe, accompanied with pomme frites - potato fries). Honestly, the Turkey Pot Pie is the best ever! The City Tavern features an award-winning children's menu, high chairs and booster seats so even the little colonists can eat Olde-style in comfort. The children's menu ($8.00-$13.00 per entrée) are just smaller portions of the adult menu. Staying with the theme, they offer a fun drink called the Colonial Shrub - an 18th century beverage made from fruit juice, sugar, fizzed w/ ginger ale and soda (like a fancy Shirley Temple). A spiked version is available for adults. And parents, when was the last time you saw duck sausage, Roquefort salad dressing, pork schnitzel or beef pie on a menu (lunch average $17.00). City Tavern bakes a variety of bread and pastries daily that may include such unique offerings as Sally Lunn, Anadama loaves or sweet potato and pecan biscuits - Thomas Jefferson's favorite.

NATIONAL LIBERTY MUSEUM

Philadelphia - *321 Chestnut Street (Washington Ave. exit, left on Columbus. Follow signs to Market & Second St) 19106. www.libertymuseum.org. Phone:*

(215) 925-2800. Hours: Daily 10:00am-5:00pm (Memorial Day - Labor Day). Closed Mondays the remainder of the year. Admission: $7.00 adult, $6.00 senior, $5.00 student, $2.00 child (5-17). "Family Admission" $15.00, includes two adult family members and all of their children. Educators: Lesson plans and activities/follow up questions are under EDUCATION, then PRE-VISIT MATERIALS.

This museum is home to more than 100 works of glass art by Dale Chihuly. The exhibits celebrate heroes who fight for freedom around the world. From the stories of thousands of heroes of all walks of life... to awesome glass art... to lively discussions on youth-oriented topics, try to stop in and see some of the spaces that really engage questions because the art is so fun! Parents love the interactive themes including anti-bullying and non-violence, pride in oneself, civic responsibility, character education and more. The Jelly Bean People and Flame of Liberty are must sees!

CARPENTER'S HALL

Philadelphia - *320 Chestnut Street, Historic area (exit for Indep. Hall. Follow signs for 6th St to Chestnut, left on 2nd) 19106. www.ushistory.org/carpentershall/. Phone: (215) 925-0167. Hours: Tuesday-Sunday 10:00am-4:00pm (Closed January & February Tuesdays). Admission: FREE. Educators: Lesson Plans online by clicking TEACHERS icon. FREEBIES: icon marked FUN has interactive and downloadable quizzes, puzzles and coloring books.*

Displays of early carpenter's chairs and tools used by the First Continental Congress in 1774. A 10 minute video chronicles the history of the carpenter's company (they still own and operate the hall). Because the site is dedicated to the craft of carpenters and master builders, supplementing with lesson plans and puzzles is the best way to try and engage the kids. That, and the model of Carpenter's Hall which looks like a colonial "doll house" illustrating 18th century construction methods.

TODD HOUSE

Philadelphia - *4th & Walnut Streets (just west of Carpenters Hall) 19106. Phone: (215) 597-8974. www.ushistory.org/tour/todd-house.htm. Hours: Open house daily from 4:00pm-5:00pm. Admission: $2.00 adult.*

This was the home of Dolley Todd before her marriage to James Madison (Dolley Madison pastries will get the kids on the same page). While John Todd who dwelled in the house for two years would succumb to yellow fever in 1793, has become more or less a footnote on your Philadelphia tour, his wife Dolley remains a beloved historical figure and is the reason we are here. Dolley, by most accounts, was a fabulous and spirited hostess. Here fish, meat, fruit, and baked bread all purchased fresh daily from vendors at the High Street headhouse (now Market Street) would be prepared for the Todds, their two children, Dolley's younger brother and sister, and two law clerks who worked under Barrister Todd. Add to that a pet bird and a dog named Pointer and one has a lively household. Representing a middle-class Quaker home, she became quite a First Lady when she moved from this house and married James Madison, fourth President of the United States.

Exit - 20 (west of I-95)

THADDEUS KOSCIUSZKO NATIONAL MEMORIAL

Philadelphia - *301 Pine Street & 3rd St. (I-95 Independence Hall exit/ Columbus Blvd. Follow signs to Society Hill) 19106. www.nps.gov/thko. Phone: (215) 597-9618. Hours: Wednesday-Sunday Noon-4:00pm. Admission: FREE.*

Visit the house where wounded Polish freedom fighter Thaddeus Kosciuszko lived and hear how this brilliant military engineer designed successful fortifications during the American Revolution. See the room where he received notable visitors such as Chief Little Turtle and Thomas Jefferson, who said he was "as pure a son of liberty, as I have ever known..." Exhibits & audiovisual displays (English & Polish language) describe the help Thaddeus gave to the American Revolution. Learn why he was loved and then kicked out of his native Poland, why he carried a crutch and how his skills helped Americans strategically beat the British. He was a genius engineer!

JONES RESTAURANT

Philadelphia - *700 Chestnut Street at 7th Street (follow signs for Independence Hall, then go one block west) 19106. www.jones-restaurant.com. Phone: (215) 223-5663. Hours: Lunch Monday-Friday starting at 11:30am. Saturday/Sunday brunch starts at 10:00am. Dinner starts daily at 4:00pm until late.*

With a setting right out of the Brady Bunch, Jones restaurant puts a modern spin on comfort foods, such as macaroni and cheese and meatloaf. The talented kitchen staff created a menu of affordable comfort food, which is available seven days a week, from lunchtime through late night. Down-home dishes such as Baked Macaroni and Cheese (w/ crumb topping-be sure someone in your party orders this to sample!), Beef Brisket, Deviled Eggs, Meatloaf and Mashed Potatoes, and Thanksgiving Turkey Dinner with all the Trimmings are some of the all-American specialties on the list, with eclectic variations on more worldly treats such as Cheese Pierogies with Caramelized Onion. Jones' signature entree would be a hefty plate of Fried Chicken and Waffles, served with chicken gravy. For dessert, diners choose from Apple Pie and Duncan Hines Chocolate Layer Cake served with cold milk. For drinks, order something fun like Purple People Eater (grape juice, lemonade, sprite) or Rum Punch. Appetizer portions (avg.$8.00) were just right sized for smaller appetites.

MUMMERS MUSEUM

Philadelphia - *1100 South 2nd Street & Washington Avenue (Washington Avenue. Turn left on to Columbus Blvd. Take first left onto Washington Avenue. 2 lights up on the left) 19147. Phone: (215) 336-3050. www.mummersmuseum.com. Hours: Wednesday-Saturday 9:30am-4:00pm (October - April). Closed Sundays, Mondays, Tuesdays & all Holidays. Admission: $2.50-$3.50.*

What is a mummer? Opened in 1976, the museum is dedicated to the Philly celebration of the new year. Audio and interactive displays, musical instruments, costumes, and artifacts from the traditional New Year's Day parade. Some of the spectacular costumes date back to the turn of the 20th Century. See videos of past parades or watch how those colorful sparkly costumes are made.

Exit - 20 (east of I-95)

INDEPENDENCE SEAPORT MUSEUM

Philadelphia - *211 South Columbus Blvd, Penns Landing (I-95 exit 20, follow signs to Penns Landing) 19106. Phone: (215) 925-5439. www.phillyseaport.org. Hours: Daily 10:00am-5:00pm. Closed major winter holidays. Admission: $13.50 adult, $10.00 senior (65+) and child (5-12). Small additional fee for touring the cruiser Olympia and submarine Becuna. Educators: an excellent Teacher's Activity Packet is downloadable to print by clicking on: EDUCATION, then TEACHER RESOURCES. Note: The Museum Store. Ask about the Philadelphia Citypass - it's a great value if you're seeing more than just historic area. Seafarin' Saturdays is a program where kids craft while pretending to be a pirate or ship captain.*

With historic vessels to board, a ship's hull to rivet, and cargo to unload with miniature cranes, Philadelphia's maritime museum conveys what the Delaware and Schuylkill Rivers have meant to the city over the years. "Climb in, Pull this, Please"…are common signs here (hands on area). For example, ride a waterbed boat, blow a fog horn, play the Crane Game or Climb aboard bunks on a ship. In clever dioramas, hear and see immigrant and crew

"Everyone remain calm", screams
Capt. William...

stories. Take a few moments to watch and talk to boat builders as they build skiffs, then head outdoors to the walk-on battleship Olympia and submarine Becuna. This is what the kids really come for! The Olympia is the nation's oldest floating steel warship (1892) and most famous for being Admiral

Dewey's flagship during his Spanish-American war victory in Manila Bay. The Becuna is a classic World War II submarine that fought battles in the South Pacific. Self-guided tour lets kids "feel" like sailors, captains, or pirates. The kids will move quickly following the self-guided arrows so try to keep up!

Be prepared, they may want to tour again, and again. If parents don't want to tour the ships all afternoon, the Workshop on the Water working boat shop can be a nice diversion. Watch artisans building and restoring traditional wooden boats.

History and physics lessons are woven between this additional exhibit:

- WHAT FLOATS YOUR BOAT? - Put weights in different places on a model boat to study its center of gravity, or pull different shapes through a ten-foot tank of water to examine how drag affects speed. Assemble a four-foot wooden boat puzzle. And further on, the curious can walk or crawl through a full size replica of a 22-foot 19th century Delaware River Shad Skiff.

Exit - 17 (west of I-95)

WELLS FARGO CENTER TOURS

Philadelphia - 3601 South Broad Street (South Broad Street & Patterson Avenue) 19148. Phone: (215) 389-9543. www.wellsfargocenterphilly.com/tours. aspx. Tours: Groups of 15+ (may be added to another group if less than 15 in party). Weekdays (provided no events are scheduled). By reservation. $4.00-$5.00 per person.

Guided tours of the home of the Philadelphia 76ers & Flyers In your personal guided tour through the Wachovia Center, you will be given an exclusive chance to visit and explore the private luxury seating levels, the press box, Arena Vision studio control room, Comcast SportsNet, and the official NBA and NHL locker rooms. See playing floors and learn great inside scoops on the history of favorite players and teams.

PHILADELPHIA PHILLIES BASEBALL

Philadelphia - *Citizens Bank Park (south Philadelphia) (off exit onto Broad St. and follow signs) 19148. http://philadelphia.phillies.mlb.com/phi/ballpark/index.jsp. Tour Pricing: Tickets are $10.00 for adults, and $6.00 for children (3-14 years) and senior citizens. Tour Times: Tours are offered year round, during the season, on non-game days,*

- GAMEDAY: National League East MLB team. Take a romp in the Phanatic Phun Zone, the largest Softplay area for kids in Major League Baseball. Take a stroll through Ashburn Alley, an outdoor entertainment area. Features include the All-Star Walk, Citizens Bank Games of Baseball, Memory Lane, Rooftop Bleacher Seats, Wall of Fame, Alley Store, and more! Opens 2 1/2 hours prior to game time so fans can watch batting practice. Look out for the long lines waiting for an order of delicious crab fries at Chickie's and Pete's, the famous cheesesteaks at Campo's, sinfully amazing roast pork sandwiches at Tony Luke's, authentic Philadelphia hoagies at Planet Hoagies, and the creative cheesesteak variation from Chestnut Hill's McNally's that is the Schmitter.

- BALLPARK TOURS: Come get an inside look at the Phillies home. Tour Guests will be treated to a brief audio/visual presentation of Citizens Bank Park, followed by an up-close look at the ballpark. Tour stops include the Phillies dugout, Diamond Club (which features the glass-enclosed batting cages), Cooperstown Gallery (which features 32 original oil paintings by artist Dick Perez) and the unique Hall of Fame Club. Tours last approximately 90 minutes and start and end at the Majestic Clubhouse Store.

Exit - 15 (west of I-95)

FORT MIFFLIN

Philadelphia - *Fort Mifflin Road (I-95 to Island Avenue Exit - follow signs) 19153. Phone: (215) 685-4167. www.fortmifflin.us. Hours: Wednesday-Sunday 10:00am-4:00pm. (March-December 1) Admission: $6.00 adult, $5.00 senior (65+) and $3.00 child (6-12) and veterans. Note: Sundays suggested as there are military drills and craftspeople demonstrating their skills. Check out their educational Treasure Hunts for group tours.*

"What Really Happened at Fort Mifflin?"... you'll find out that a lot happened here. Starting in 1772, it was built by the British to protect the colonies. Ironically, in 1777, it was used by Americans trying to protect the Philadelphia and Delaware River from the British (7 long, grueling weeks of siege). It also protected the city of Philadelphia during the War of 1812 and was active as a Confederate and Union prison camp during the Civil War. Until 1954, it was still used to store ammunition for the United States military. A great place to check out and study several wars all in one spot.

Exit - 10 (west of I-95)

HEINZ NATIONAL WILDLIFE REFUGE

Philadelphia - Lindbergh Blvd. & 86th Street (left onto Bartram Ave, left onto 84th St, left onto Lindbergh Blvd) 19153. http://heinz.fws.gov/. Phone: (215) 365-3118.

The refuge was established by an act of Congress in 1972 to protect the last 200 acres of freshwater tidal marsh in Pennsylvania. Hiking trails to explore butterflies, muskrats, frogs, flying geese, and loads of wildflowers is open dawn to dusk. Observation tower. The Cusano Environmental Education Center is open daily from 8:30am-4:00pm, free of charge.

Exit - 7 (west of I-95)

RIDLEY CREEK STATE PARK

Media (Newtown Square) - 351 Gradyville Road (entrances on PA3, PA 252 or PA352) 19073. www.dcnr.state.pa.us/stateparks/findapark/ridleycreek/. Phone: (610) 892-3900. Admission: FREE into park. Fee charged for Plantation tours.

Shaded equestrian, hiking and bicycling trails lace the woodlands and old meadow. Within the park is the Colonial Pennsylvania Plantation (www.colonialplantation.org) that depicts a Delaware County Quaker farm prior to the American Revolution. On weekends from April to November, visitors can observe the farm family cooking over the open hearth, preserving foods, processing textiles, tending field crops and performing other chores necessary for survival in the 18th century world. There are hundreds of picnic tables in 14 picnic areas. Each area is equipped with restrooms and charcoal grills. Several of the areas have large fields suited to sports activities. Fishing and Winter Sports.

Exit - 6 (west of I-95)

LINVILLA ORCHARDS

Media - 137 W. Knowlton Road (Rte 352 north 3.5 miles. Left onto Knowlton Rd.) 19063. Phone: (610) 876-7116. www.linvilla.com. Hours: Regular hours are 9:00am-6:00pm daily with longer fall hours and shorter winter hours. Open every day of the year except December 25 and January 1. Fees for tours.

Once everyone has had their fill of Longwood Gardens, you'll be heading to Linvilla Orchards, one of the last working farms in the Delaware Valley. With more than 300 acres, Linvilla hosts a variety of family-friendly events throughout the year. This is the oldest working farm in Delaware Valley where families can pick their own seasonal fruit, hop on a hayride and buy fresh-baked pies. Hayrides, tours, swimming and fruit and vegetable picking are offered in season. Try a Hayride to Bunnyland and Carolings Hayrides. Go out to look at the blossoms in spring and the autumn leaves each fall. After getting a nice lunch at the food stands, head out into the fields to pick some blue- or blackberries — they'll make a nice Philly-style souvenir for your ride back home!

- AUTUMN HAYRIDE AND TOUR – After a hayride, a tour guide will lead your group through a series of educational displays that teach about Johnny Appleseed, the Native Americans that lived on this site, the different varieties of apples and squash, and the process of making cider. The harvest is emphasized.

- SPRING/SUMMER HAYRIDE AND TOUR – After a hayride, a tour guide will lead your group through a discussion of planting and growing the food, how the Lenni Lenape planted in the spring, and show you some of the equipment we use today. The emphasis is on spring planting.

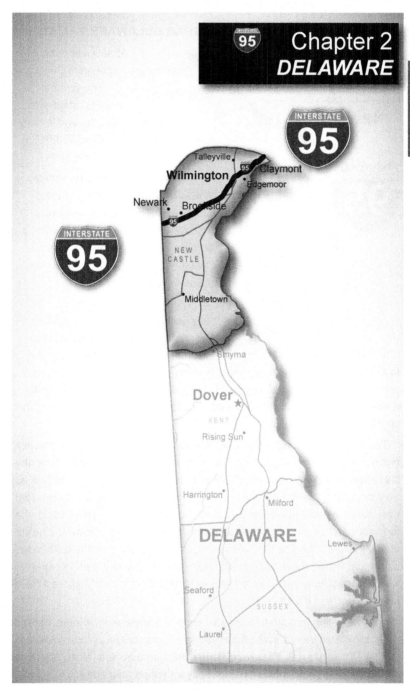

DELAWARE

DEAR DELAWARE TRAVELER:

Talleyville

Wilmington   95   Claymont

Edgemoor

Newark   Brookside

INTERSTATE

95   NEW CASTLE

Middletown

First, it's important to know who Delaware is. The second smallest state in the Union – and the first to ratify the U.S. Constitution (Dec. 7, 1787) is rightfully known as "The First State."

In Delaware, I-95 is also designated as the Delaware Turnpike and the John F. Kennedy Memorial Highway. Along with its outerbelts, I-95 is the only Interstate Highway in the state! Only two other states- Maine and Rhode Island- share this distinction.

Wilmington is located half way between New York City and Washington DC, 35 minutes to Center City Philadelphia, and 90 minutes to Baltimore. Wilmington is the gateway to the Brandywine River Valley with its world-class museums, attractions, accommodations and restaurants. So, it forms a great stopping ground for a side trip or two – even an overnight outside of the hustle and bustle of the big cities.

There are three forts along the Delaware River that formed a defense against invasion. The best one to visit is **Fort Delaware**. Take the **Delafort Ferry** to Pea Patch Island. Kids build a sense of adventure as they approach the fort by water. Ferry is the only way to get to the fort! Completed in 1859 to protect Delaware, new Jersey and Pennsylvania, the fort was used as a major prison for Confederate soldiers and sympathizers during the Civil War. The fort is five-sided and kids notice that it is surrounded by a moat. Have conversations with authentically dressed park interpreters who can teach your kids how to hammer at the blacksmith or prepare a meal for the officers in the kitchen.

Imagine rolling through forests, past historic homes and mill sites, aboard a vintage steam train, just like those your great-grandparents rode. Welcome to the **Wilmington & Western Railroad**. Come aboard. Most train rides offer a scenic trip with narration especially for young railroaders.

Heading west several miles off exit 7, a treasure (mostly under glass) awaits at **Longwood Gardens**. Here, you'll find the Children's Garden, featuring an ever-changing water curtain and leaping water "glow worm," comprised of a maze and flower-shaped water jets. It's kind of like a botanical slip 'n' slide.

Experience Delaware in the Early Republic (1790-1830) at a 300-year-old gristmill, textile mill and farm site with heritage sheep. **Greenbank Mill** is fun on weekends but many of the famous DuPont heritage homes are open weekdays, too, for touring. **Winterthur** has its **Enchanted Garden** where the wood fairies have left stories and play areas aside just for the young at heart to explore. **Hagley** is actually the original home of the famous DuPont Company. The Visitors Center details this and provides areas for the kids to "play" with DuPont company inventions: from spacesuits to a working small scale of a water-wheel mill.

They survived a stormy winter's crossing of the Atlantic Ocean from Sweden. The sturdy vessel that carried a group of 24 settlers now majestically floats - at anchor in Wilmington -- the **Kalmar Nyckel**. What a treat to walk cobblestone streets lined with Swedish storefronts and old churches as you make your way towards the waterfront. Climb aboard the ship and take the helm.

Visit unique museums or bike, hike, kayak or canoe on the beautiful Brandywine Creek or the revitalized **RiverWalk**. Try a peak at wildlife along the **DuPont Environmental Center**'s boardwalk. You can take the **River Taxi** from here or you can enjoy strolling the RIVERWALK that starts a block downstream from the park and proceeds upstream to the Shipyard Shops, Frawley Stadium, and the Riverfront Arts Center. It's your choice. And remember that shopping, dining and entertainment are all tax-free in Delaware!

Almost immediately before crossing the state line into or out of Delaware, there is a toll plaza for both the northbound and southbound lanes.

ACTIVITIES AT A GLANCE

ANIMALS & FARMS

Exit - 8 - *Brandywine Zoo*

HISTORY

Exit - 8 - *Hagley Museum*
Exit - 8 - *Brandywine Battlefield Park*
Exit - 6 - *Delaware History Museum*
Exit - 6 - *Kalmar Nyckel & New Sweden*
Exit - 5B - *Greenbank Mill*
Exit - 5B - *Auburn Heights Preserve*
Exit - 4A - *Fort Delaware State Park*
Exit - 4A - *Fort DuPont State Park*
Exit - 1 - *Iron Hill Museum*

MUSEUMS

Exit - 6 - *Delaware Children's Museum*

OUTDOOR EXPLORING

Exit - 9 - *Bellevue State Park*
Exit - 8 - *Alapocas Run State Park*
Exit - 8 - *Brandywine Creek State Park*
Exit - 7 - *Winterthur Museum*
Exit - 7 - *Longwood Gardens*
Exit - 6 - *Riverfront Park & Riverwalk*
Exit - 1 - *White Clay Creek State Park*
Exit - 1 - *Lums Pond State Park*

SCIENCE

Exit - 7 - *Delaware Museum Of Natural History*
Exit - 6 - *DuPont Environmental Education Ctr.@ Russell W. Peterson Wildlife Refuge*

SUGGESTED LODGING & DINING

Exit - 8 - *Best Western Brandywine Valley*
Exit - 7 - *Buckley's Tavern*

THE ARTS

Exit - 7 - *Delaware Art Museum*
Exit - 7 - *Brandywine River Museum*

TOURS

Exit - 6 - *River Taxi*
Exit - 5B - *Wilmington & Western Railroad*

WELCOME CENTERS

Exit - 5 - *Delaware House Service Area*

GENERAL INFORMATION

Contact the services of interest. Request to be added to their mailing lists.

- ☐ Delaware Department of Natural Resources: www.dnrec.delaware.gov
- ☐ Delaware State Parks: www.destateparks.com
- ☐ Greater Wilmington Convention & Visitors Bureau: www.visitWilmingtonDE.com
- ☐ Delaware Campgrounds: http://koa.com/where/de/

Travel Journal & Notes:

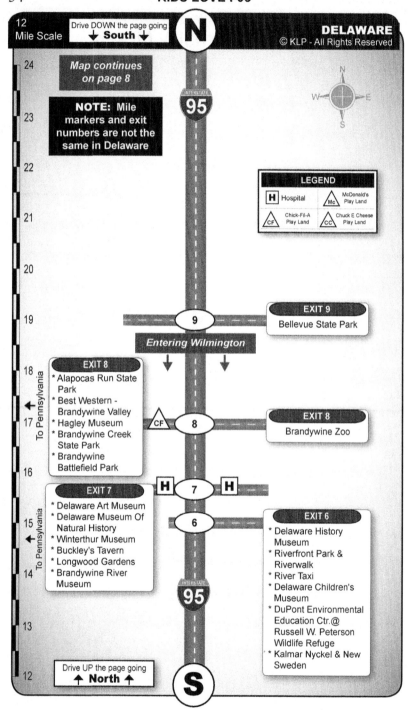

DELAWARE

12 Mile Scale

Drive DOWN the page going
↓ **South** ↓

N

Map continues on page 8

NOTE: Mile markers and exit numbers are not the same in Delaware

LEGEND

| H Hospital | Mc McDonald's Play Land |
| CF Chick-Fil-A Play Land | CC Chuck E Cheese Play Land |

INTERSTATE 95

EXIT 9
Bellevue State Park

Entering Wilmington

EXIT 8
* Alapocas Run State Park
* Best Western - Brandywine Valley
* Hagley Museum
* Brandywine Creek State Park
* Brandywine Battlefield Park

To Pennsylvania ←

CF 8

EXIT 8
Brandywine Zoo

H 7 H

EXIT 7
* Delaware Art Museum
* Delaware Museum Of Natural History
* Winterthur Museum
* Buckley's Tavern
* Longwood Gardens
* Brandywine River Museum

To Pennsylvania ←

6

EXIT 6
* Delaware History Museum
* Riverfront Park & Riverwalk
* River Taxi
* Delaware Children's Museum
* DuPont Environmental Education Ctr.@ Russell W. Peterson Wildlife Refuge
* Kalmar Nyckel & New Sweden

INTERSTATE 95

Drive UP the page going
↑ **North** ↑

S

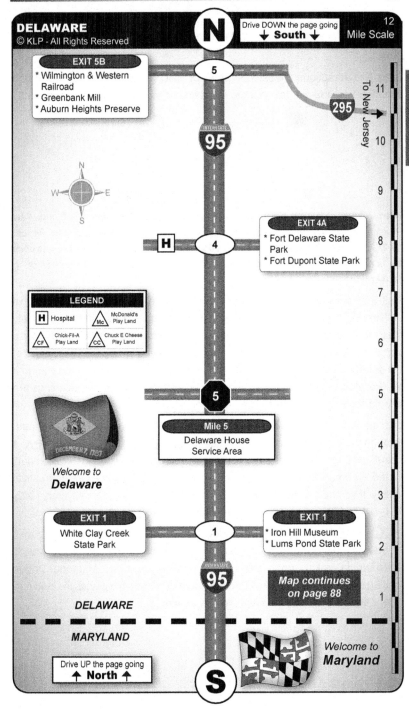

DELAWARE

12 Mile Scale

N

Drive DOWN the page going
↓ **South** ↓

DELAWARE

EXIT 5B
* Wilmington & Western Railroad
* Greenbank Mill
* Auburn Heights Preserve

5

INTERSTATE 95

To New Jersey

295

11

10

9

N
W—E
S

EXIT 4A
* Fort Delaware State Park
* Fort Dupont State Park

H 4

8

7

LEGEND
H Hospital
Mc McDonald's Play Land
CF Chick-Fil-A Play Land
CC Chuck E Cheese Play Land

6

5

Mile 5
Delaware House Service Area

4

Welcome to **Delaware**

DECEMBER 7, 1787

3

EXIT 1
White Clay Creek State Park

1

EXIT 1
* Iron Hill Museum
* Lums Pond State Park

2

INTERSTATE 95

Map continues on page 88

1

DELAWARE

MARYLAND

Drive UP the page going
↑ **North** ↑

S

Welcome to **Maryland**

> *** NOTE:** Mile markers and exit numbers **are not the same** in Delaware

Sites and attractions are listed in order by Exit Number (North to South) and distance from the exit (closest are listed first). Symbols indicated represent:

 Restaurants    Lodging

Exit - 9 (east of I-95)

BELLEVUE STATE PARK

Wilmington - *800 Carr Road (DE 3 east at Marsh Road exit ramp, left onto Carr Road, follow signs) 19809. www.destateparks.com/park/bellevue/index.asp. Phone: (302) 761-6963. Hours: Open Daily 8:00am-sunset. Admission: A park entrance fee is charged daily from March 1 to November 30. Resident: $3.00 Non-resident: $6.00 per vehicle.*

Visit the mansion and grounds of Bellevue State park, the former home of William H. duPont, Jr. The estate includes tennis courts, stables, a lovely catch-and-release pond stocked with fish, a former racetrack that is now a popular walking/jogging track. Hiking trails allow you to explore other parts of the estate. If you prefer cycling, both paved and unpaved paths lead you on a leisurely tour. Full Moon Hikes and Concerts offered on summer evenings are popular programs. There's also a disc golf course.

Incidentally, it's an easy 20--minute walk from Bellevue on a paved path through the woods and along the creek to **ROCKWOOD MANSION PARK**, a beautiful county park that is the home of a Victorian Rural gothic mansion built in 1851. Thousands come to the county's annual two-day Ice Cream Festival in July. If you have a little time, you can have lunch in the Butler's Pantry (302-731-4340). Afterwards, walk back to your car to work off the extra calories...

FOX POINT STATE PARK: A window on the River. And what a window it is! You can stand at any of the park's new overlooks and see all the way to Philadelphia looking north and well beyond the Delaware Memorial Bridge looking south. There just aren't that many easily accessible places in Delaware where such a spectacular view is readily available.

Exit - 8 (west of I-95)

ALAPOCAS RUN STATE PARK

Wilmington - *1914 West Park Dr. (Rte. 202 north to exit Rte. 141 south. Left on West Park Drive) 19803. www.destateparks.com/park/alapocas-run/. Phone: (302) 577-1164. Hours: Daily 8:00am-sunset. Admission: A park entrance fee is charged daily from March 1 to November 30. $3.00 per vehicle (instate) $6.00 out-of-state.*

The newest state park, Alapocas Run, just off I-95 and Route 202, offers wooded trails, the unique Can-Do Playground, the innovative Blue Ball Barn and many recreational opportunities. The innovative CAN DO PLAYGROUND (www.candoplayground.org), the first Boundless Playground™ in Delaware gives children of all abilities a place to play together. On a Boundless playground you'll find: every child can reach the highest play deck, play structures configured to support children's development, universally accessible pathways and surfacing, cozy spots where everyone can gather, equipment like swings and bouncers with back support, and elevated sand tables and activity panels where children of all abilities can play together. Trails through fields and forest will take you to the rock-climbing area, nestled in one of the area's most serene spots. Along the way, you will pass the Blue Ball Barn. The once-abandoned dairy barn built by Alfred I. du Pont has been transformed into a showcase that is the permanent home of the Delaware Folk Art collection.

BEST WESTERN BRANDYWINE VALLEY

Wilmington - *1807 Concord Pike (Route 202 North) 19803. Phone: (302) 656-9436. www.brandywineinn.com.*

This comfortable hotel offers a variety of room configurations to suit your lodging needs. All of the guest rooms are 100% brand new and include breakfast by Einstein Bros. Bagels, in-room microwave ovens, refrigerators, free local calls, voicemail, in-room coffee, and a daily complimentary copy of USA Today. Take a refreshing dip in the courtyard, outdoor pool (with kiddie pool) and Jacuzzi (in season), or keep yourself in shape in the state-of-the-art Nautilus-Lifecycle Fitness Room. Most rooms run well under $100/night. Two major shopping malls, three movie multiplexes and a variety of restaurants are all within minutes of the Inn. There's even an old-fashioned diner in front of the hotel for late night comfort food snacking.

Exit - 8 (west of I-95)

HAGLEY MUSEUM

Wilmington - *200 Hagley Road (West Chester exit. Follow Rte 202 north-Concord Pike for 1.3m. Left onto Rte 141 south. Follow signs) 19807. Phone: (302) 658-2400. www.hagley.org. Regular Hours - Open daily from 9:30am-4:30pm (mid-March thru early January). The last bus for a tour of the DuPont residence leaves at 3:30pm. Winter Hours - Open daily from 9:30am-4:30pm, Guided tours at 10:30am & 1:30pm. Admission: $11.00 adult, $9.00 senior and student, $4.00 child (6-14). Under 6 yrs. Old FREE. Free parking and picnic areas. Bus transport included in admission from lower property to higher properties. Note: Creek Kids programs on summer Sundays adds music, games, crafts, and leisure play activities. Educators: Mill Times Video & Activity Guide. The activity guides are free and available upon request. The video can be borrowed from the Hagley Museum for 2 weeks. A downloadable .PDF of African American Schools in Delaware is available free online on the Teacher Resources tab.*

Two hundred and thirty acres along the banks of the Brandywine River, is a lovely museum, which surprises everyone who thinks anything having to do with the Industrial Revolution has to be grimy. A parade of stone buildings house exhibits showcasing the important role Wilmington and the Brandywine Valley have played in American history - first with innovations in the milling of grain and the making of textiles and paper, and then in the manufacture of gunpowder. The campus is closed to traffic so families can feel safe walking by the river and up Workers Hill or wandering paths through the woods.

Hagley is actually the original home of the famous DuPont Company. The Visitors Center details this and provides areas for the kids to "play" with DuPont company inventions: from spacesuits to a working small scale of a water-wheel mill. Sit in Jeff Gordon's #24 DuPont NASCAR or don a lab coat & goggles as you invent new fibers. Additionally, on weekends, students will learn about levers, pulleys, gears, and the wheel and axle by exploring "Easy Does It: How Machines Make Life Easier," an interactive exhibit that includes examples of simple machines. Along with trying out things like a car transmission and a sluice gate, students will explore the powder yards to find more simple machines and to see machinery demonstrations. A lighted/narrated

3D map in the Henry clay Mill gives you an overview of the development of the Brandywine Valley. A tour of the Powder Yard offers an in-depth look at the making of the DuPont Company's original product, gunpowder. There are exhibitions of stone cutting, making and testing gunpowder, leather belt-driven machinery, various types of waterwheels, and a steam engine. Models inside portray the exact workings of the giant machinery outside. Amidst whirring belts and grinding wheels, machinists will explain what they do while they work. After you answer questions like: why wooden shovels or why did workers wear stockings instead of shoes?, your

See and Hear a firing test of DuPont's "famous black powder"

guide asks you to stand back for a real-life "firing test" of DuPont's famous black powder. Finally, on the Workers Hill, the focus is on the social and family history of the workers who operated the powder mills. These buildings answer the questions about what home life was like in the late nineteenth century. Families can sit in a school room and try writing with a quill pen or solving problems on lesson boards.

Hagley's <u>BELIN HOUSE RESTAURANT</u> is located on Workers' Hill. Once home to several generations of company bookkeepers, today the Belin House provides a panoramic view for visitors to enjoy while dining. Visitors may enjoy selections from the menu daily from mid-March through November and on weekends in December. The chicken salad is their specialty.

Exit - 8 (west of I-95)

BRANDYWINE CREEK STATE PARK

Wilmington - *41 Adams Dam Rd. (start on US202, keep right on DE261, then left. Take 1st left onto W Park Drive. Follow signs) 19807. Phone: (302) 577-3534. www.destateparks.com/park/brandywine-creek/. Hours: Daily 8:00am-sunset. Admission: A park entrance fee is charged daily from March 1 to November 30. $3.00 per vehicle (instate) $6.00 out-of-state.*

Delaware's first two nature preserves are located within Brandywine Creek State Park: Tulip Tree Woods, a majestic stand of 190-year-old tulip poplar, and Freshwater Marsh. An extensive meadow management program, active bluebird population program, and variety of habitats make Brandywine Creek State Park an outstanding place to see wildflowers, songbirds, deer, and other flora and fauna. Many species of hawks can be seen migrating over the valley from mid-September to mid-November. The modern Brandywine Creek Nature Center offers interpretive nature programs for visitors, school groups, and organizations. Inside, a gift shop features environmental books, field guides, shirts, Frisbees, and other items. Disc Golf, picnicking and a few trails round out the offerings here.

BRANDYWINE BATTLEFIELD PARK

Chadds Ford, PA - *(take US 202 north to US1. Turn left. 1 mile east of SR100 NOTE: This attraction is from a Delaware Exit, but is located just across the state line in Pennsylvania) 19317. www.ushistory.org/brandywine. Phone: (610) 459-3342. Hours: Wednesday - Saturday 9:00am-4:00pm, Sunday Noon-4:00pm (March-November). Open Thursday - Sunday (January-February). Closed most federal holidays. Admission: Grounds FREE. General admission $5.00 adult, $3.50 senior (65+), $25.50 youth (6-17). Parking free. Tours: Maps for self-guided tour at Visitor's Center. House Tours daily except in March. Note: Museum shop. Plenty of picnic areas. Battle re-enactment every September. Educators: click on History Articles for some great material for research reports on characters of the battle. FREEBIES: click on KIDS CORNER for several fun activities to play.*

The peaceful nature of the Brandywine Valley was shattered in the summer of 1777, when British and Hessian forces fought American Continentals and local militia under George Washington and the young Marquis de Lafayette in the largest land battle of the Revolutionary War. This giant park and museum are focused on actual Revolutionary War events. Watch the audiovisual introduction to the park first, then drive along a tour that includes 28 historic points taking you back to 1777. Remember, this defeat of American forces (led by George Washington) left the Philadelphia area open to attack and conquest by the British.

Exit - 8 (east of I-95)

BRANDYWINE ZOO

Wilmington - *101 North Park Drive (along the Brandywine River, downtown in Brandywine Park) 19802. Phone: (302) 571-7788. www.brandywinezoo.org. Hours: Daily 10:00am-5:00pm. Admission: $5.00-$7.00 per person (age 3+). Slightly reduced in winter. FREE parking.*

Open since 1905, Delaware's only zoo is located a few steps from the Brandywine River. The 12-acre zoo features big cats, condors, and other animals. The monkeys in natural settings are a favorite - goofy, aren't they?

Exit - 7 (west of I-95)

DELAWARE ART MUSEUM

Wilmington - *2301 Kentmere Parkway (follow Delaware Ave. to N. Bancroft Pkwy. Right on Bancroft, left onto Kentmere Pkwy) 19806. Phone: (302) 571-9590. www.delart.org. Hours: Wednesday-Saturday 10:00am-4:00pm, Sunday Noon-4:00pm. Admission: FREE on Sundays. Other days, $12.00 adult, $10.00 senior (60+), $6.00 youth (7-18) and students w/ID. $25.00 max for families (2 adults and 4 kids). Note: delART café; Museum store.*

Because you're in the Brandywine Valley, it's appropriate that this art museum predominately displays captivating American (Brandywine) painting and illustration (Howard Pyle, N.C. Wyeth, etc.). It also has the largest collection of Pre-Raphaelite art objects outside the U.K., our favorite: blown-glass by Dale Chihuly, as well as other artists and traveling displays. Outdoors in the Copeland Sculpture garden, the 13-foot-tall Crying Giant is a kid favorite. A sound sculpture by Joe Moss manipulates the voices of those nearby, while Three Rectangles Horizontal Jointed Gyratory III moves with the slightest breeze. Toward the back of the sculpture garden is the Fusco Reservoir, which has been recast as a labyrinth. Follow the single, folded path to arrive in the center.

But the interactive Kids Corner is the unique area within the Museum where children have the freedom to touch the art on the walls and even design their own artwork. And the art is kind of quirky. A gigantic white wall is covered in pegs for hanging colored pieces of foam. Think of the wall as the canvas and the foam pieces as paint. Use as many pieces as you want. The elements of Art allows for direct interaction with three repros of the Museum's priceless works. By feeling a painting's texture and changing its colors and line patterns, kids identify tools artist's use to create things like movement or depth. The Story Station provides couches, chairs, and a small library of children's books - all related to art in some way. Adults can relax, too, as they share quiet stories with their kids.

Exit - 7 (west of I-95)

DELAWARE MUSEUM OF NATURAL HISTORY

Wilmington - *4840 Kennett Pike (Rte. 52, five miles. Across from Winterthur) 19807. Phone: (302) 658-9111. www.delmnh.org. Hours: Monday-Saturday 9:30am-4:30pm, Sunday Noon-4:30pm. Admission: $7.00-$9.00 per person ages 3+.*

Real dinosaur fossil

Please touch!

As the only natural history museum in the state, DMNH welcomes visitors each year to experience an African watering hole, gaze up at a giant squid, encounter a jaguar face-to-face, and marvel at the diversity of nature. The museum houses a world-renowned collection of seashells and the second-largest collection of birds' eggs in

Touch a REAL dinosaur fossil...

North America. Gallery highlights also include the only permanent dinosaur collection in Delaware, a simulated coral reef (that you walk over!), and a Science in Action real-life paleontology lab. Kids have a blast in the Discovery Room where they can dress in field scientists' garb, handle specimens, look under the microscope, and enjoy books and puzzles. Outdoors, a one-mile trail is a great place to experience nature. In addition, nature films are shown in the Auditorium.

WINTERTHUR MUSEUM

Pretend you "live in a mansion..."

Winterthur - *5105 Kennett Pike (SR 52, six miles northwest of town) 19735. Phone: (302) 888-4600. www.winterthur.org. Hours: Tuesday-Sunday 10:00am-5:00pm. Last tour ticket sold at 3:45pm. Closed Mondays (except holidays and during Yuletide), Thanksgiving Day, and Christmas Day. Closed February thru early March for maintenance. Admission: General $18.00-*

$20.00, $5.00 child (2-11). Includes Intro Tour of house, galleries, garden tram tour and gardens, enchanted woods. Educators: click on Educational Programs tab, School Programs and then For Teachers to download .PDF Pre-and Post visit materials including suggested literature, vocabulary and activities.

A bit further out Rte. 52 past Hagley Museum is Winterthur, An American Country Estate. Although many large homes may be boring to tour for kids, this collection grew so large, the house grew, too until it reached 175 rooms! Just asking the kids to count them all occupies them for a while. Be sure to reserve the Family Tour (only 45 minutes long). Their Touch-It Room is where history fits into the palm of your hand. The Touch-It Room is a popular stop, providing children with the opportunity to dress up in period costumes; role-play in the colonial kitchen, parlor, and general store; and explore toys and books from a bygone era. The tea set, puzzles, dress-up clothes, and basket of

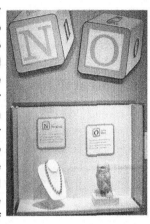

wooden toys provide a playful way to learn about early American life. Your kids will be amazed they get to touch everything AND move it around to their liking! Go back in time with the "K is for Kids" exhibition in the Winterthur Galleries, an alphabetic exploration of the museum's collections. Special "touchables" in the Galleries also provide hands-on contact for all ages.

The Tulip Tree House

Ok, but we label this attraction as "Outdoor Exploring" for a reason - mostly, the gardens. You can walk or ride the tram for the narrated tour. If you walk the trails, your kids may disappear from time to time in the trees. Notice how many trees are great for climbing or hiding - especially the "playhouse" golden conifers. Watching the giant fish in the mansion's coy pond is a playful spot, too.

The ENCHANTED WOODS are by far "for children of all ages." The wood fairies have a letter (you can get a copy at admission desk or print one off ahead of time online) to the children inviting them into the garden with cutesy narratives of each space. Find storyteller stones. Look down. Are you standing on the S-s-serpentine Path? If you step inside the fairy ring - you might just see magic mist appear. When you cross over the Troll Bridge, please be careful. At Water's Edge, you can hug Harvey, their enchanted frog. Lark, the music fairy, needed a safe home, so she built a Bird's Nest big enough so friends could visit. Tuck your kids into a huge bird's nest for a memorable photo. Climb up into the Nest or over the Fallen Oak to reach the Tulip Tree House. If you carefully go through the open door, you'll be inside a tree. Peek behind the tree to spy the Pixie Fire

See a bird's nest big enough to climb into...

Pit. Another fairies' cottage is now a playhouse. A working pump provides a cooling splash, and there are spaces to climb into, hide behind, and explore.

Exit - 7 (west of I-95)

BUCKLEY'S TAVERN

Centreville - *5812 Kennett Pike (take Rte. 52 west several miles thru town, almost to the PA border) 19807. Phone: (302) 656-9776. www.buckleystavern.org. Hours: Lunch daily. Brunch Sundays 10:00am-2:30am. Dinner daily beginning at 5:00pm.*

"This casual roadside restaurant set in the quaint little borough of Centreville has been in the business of feeding people since the 1800s. But the menu today is up to date with trendy small plates, lots of hearty sandwiches, salads, and intriguing entrees." Being in an historic place is the real fun but this place isn't "old school" cooking. Very modern and local flavors are presented and their Pajama Brunch is the cutest idea ever. If you wear pajamas to brunch on Sunday, you get your meal 50% off! We hear folks really dress extreme with bunny slippers, night caps, blankees and all! While they don't really have a kids menu, their burgers and Mac & Cheese are big hits with the kiddos. We highly recommend the Tobacco Onions (onion straws) for the family to munch on and the Shrimp & Grits for parents to order (with plenty to share - but you may not want to :). Meals range $13-$18.00+.

LONGWOOD GARDENS

Kennett Square, PA - *US Route 1 (take SR 52 northwest to US 1. Left on US 1. Follow signs. NOTE: This attraction is from a Delaware Exit, but is located just* *across the state line in Pennsylvania) 19348. www.longwoodgardens.org. Phone: (610) 388-1000. Hours: Daily 9:00am-5:00pm (open later during peak Spring / Summer & Holiday seasons). Admission: $18.00 adult, $15.00 senior (62+), $8.00 student (5-18). Note: Stop by the Terrace Restaurant for Kids Value Meals (offered daily). Breakfasts with the Easter Bunny and Santa, and Family Fireworks BBQs are featured seasonally by reservation. Go online to find out more about how you make your visit to the Gardens more enjoyable and worth the admission.*

See exotic plants from around the world, examine insect-catching plants up close, enjoy dancing fountains that shoot water 130 feet in the air, and be  dazzled by 40 colorful indoor and outdoor displays every day of the year. Daily activities feature fun and educational adventures and activities for kids and families. Special children's programs like Peter Rabbit and Friends, Christmas and Mazes.

Is Longwood Gardens a place for family fun? Yes, if you look for it. Explore three awesome tree houses, have your picture taken next to animal-shaped topiaries and be amused by colorful indoor and outdoor floral displays. The Indoor Children's Garden is an whimsical space of ramps, mazes, grottoes, and lots of running water (30 water features in all). A shooting jet that rings a bell, a spitting fish, a pond with rising steam, a cave with dripping walls, and a gigantic drooling dragon are just a few of the water wonders visitors will enjoy. Two mazes - one square accented by story tiles and shooting jets of water - and one Bamboo offering a jungle of tree-size bamboos for children to explore. Kids will enjoy frolicking in the Bee A-mazed garden designed especially for them. The Garden features three major areas: the Honeycomb Maze, Flower Fountain, and Buzz Trail. All the children's areas are accessible for kids of any age. We noticed lots of moms pushing strollers on the pathways. Within reason, kids can romp and squeal to their hearts content.

Exit - 7 (west of I-95)

BRANDYWINE RIVER MUSEUM

Chadds Ford, PA - *US 1 & SR 100 (Creek Road) (head northwest on Rte. 52 to Rte. 1. Left on Rte. 1. Follow signs. NOTE: This attraction is from a Delaware Exit, but is located just across the state line in Pennsylvania) 19317. Phone: (610) 388-2700. www.brandywinemuseum.org. Hours: Daily 9:30am-4:30pm. Closed Christmas. Admission: $12.00 adult, $8.00 senior (65+), $6.00 student/child (age 6+). $3.00 for Children's Audio Tours (highly recommended in addition to, or replacing the Game Sheets). Tours: Kuerner Farm Tours (April through November). For more than 70 years, the historic Kuerner Farm has been a major source of inspiration to Andrew Wyeth. Since his earliest painting of the farm in 1932 at the age of 15, Wyeth has found subjects in its people, animals, buildings and landscapes for more than 1,000 works of art. Educational tours departing from the museum are offered at timed intervals. Wednesday through Sunday. $5 per person in addition to museum admission. Due to uneven walking surfaces, the Kuerner Farm is not accessible to disabled individuals. Read-Aloud Tours w/Storytimes are offered occasionally. Note: Restaurant open daily 10:00am-3:00pm except Mondays & Tuesdays and winters. FREEBIES: go on a gallery hunt and see if you can find items on the Discovery Game Sheets.*

American art in a 19th century gristmill. Known for collections by three generations of Wyeths. The house where N.C. Wyeth raised his extraordinarily creative children and the studio in which he painted many of his memorable works of art have been restored to reflect their character in 1945, the year of the artist's death ($5.00 more per person to tour, April-November). On the house tours, find out which window Wyeth looked out to "see" the painting he made - was it real life or dramatized? Two life-size sculptures are on the riverside path - a cow named Miss Gratz and a pig named Helen - create a "bronze petting zoo" outside. The art museum tours are best for budding artists studying art styles and effect (using the Discovery Game Sheets as your tool), or during a festival or special event.

Exit - 6 (east of I-95)

DELAWARE HISTORY MUSEUM

Wilmington - *CLOSED FOR RENOVATIONS BEGINNING JUNE 15, 2014.*

505 N. Market Street (exit onto Maryland Avenue. Right onto MLK Blvd. Left onto Orange. Right onto Sixth St. to King. Look for arch) 19801. Phone: (302) 295-2388. www.dehistory.org. Hours: Museum: Wednesday-Friday 11:00am-4:00pm,

Saturday 10:00am-4:00pm. Read House: Open Tuesday thru Sunday until 4:00pm. Weekends only each winter. Admission: Museum: $2.00-$4.00 per person (age 3+). Read House: $2.00-$5.00 per person (age 6+). Note: they also have a very good gift shop that features Delaware items.

Delve into the First State at The Delaware History Museum of the Delaware Historical Society. Located in a renovated Art Deco Woolworth's store, the Museum features three galleries of changing interactive exhibits - 400 years of history that you can see, touch, and hear. Every area has hands-on fun like: feel furs and sit in an Indian longhouse; ride in a stagecoach; try on clothes of Swedes first founding these new lands (even wooden shoes); or see if you can turn the train wheel on the track (warning, it's heavy). Dress up, play games, run the corner store, and have old-fashioned fun in "Grandmas Attic". At every turn interactive multimedia, audio, and video bring new adventures to Delaware's past.

Families have lots to talk about after touring the restored 22-room **READ HOUSE AND GARDEN** (42 The Strand, New Castle, 302-322-8411), located in Delaware's Colonial capital, Old New Castle. Notice the contrast between spacious family bedrooms and cramped servants' quarters, see how the colonists grew their own medicinal plants, and don't miss the 19th-century cutting-edge technology: hot-air roasting ovens and steam tables in the kitchen.

Exit - 6 (east of I-95)

RIVERFRONT PARK & RIVERWALK

Wilmington - *3 South Orange (exit east and follow signs to Riverfront @ the Christina River) 19801. www.riverfrontwilm.com. Hours: Tuesday-Saturday 9:00am-6:00pm (Market) and dawn to dusk (Park).*

On the left side of Market Street are the Amtrak Station, Tubman-Garrett Riverfront Park and the B&O Railroad Station. Wilmington was the "Last Stop to Freedom" on the important middle line of the eastern branch of the pre-Civil War Underground Railroad. The park, which is the site of many festivals and concerts, honors Harriet Tubman and Thomas Garrett, world-famous conductor and stationmaster, respectively. Garrett lived here and both he and Tubman used Wilmington extensively in combating slavery.

You can take the River Taxi from here (see separate listing) or you can enjoy strolling the RIVERWALK that starts a block downstream from the park and proceeds upstream to the Shipyard Shops, Frawley Stadium, and the Riverfront

Arts Center. Along the Riverwalk you will enjoy 21 interesting historical panels, gardens, covered overlook areas, and benches. The walk is lighted and patrolled at night. Look for rowers from the Wilmington Rowing Center on the Christina. Rowing is big here and a major regatta is held in October, attracting high school, college and adult teams from significant distances.

A short walk and you're at **FRAWLEY STADIUM** (801 South Madison, 302-888-2015), home of the **WILMINGTON BLUE ROCKS** minor league baseball team. The 6500-seat stadium is a great place to go for a low-cost evening of sports. Many Wilmington players have gone on to the majors and have a devoted local following from their days here.

The **RIVERFRONT MARKET** features a variety of food, flower and restaurant stations. It's a fun place to grab a bite to eat (Tuesday-Saturday). There's a Butcher, a Baker (both Amish) and a Salad maker plus a Fish Market, fresh produce, and exotic specialty foods and trinkets.

RIVER TAXI

Wilmington - *815 Justison Street (exit east and follow signs to Riverfront @ the Christina River) 19801. Phone: (302) 530-5069. www.riverfrontwilm.com. Tours: 36-passenger boat runs hourly during high season (except Mondays). $$5.00-$7.00 per person.*

People get much more than a boat ride aboard Capt. Lionel Hynson's 42-foot pontoon, as it plies the river at the historic Wilmington Riverfront. This one-man water-shuttle operation has become such an attraction because of the personality and storytelling of its captain. The boat makes hourly runs from Dravo Plaza to the Brandywine. As Capt. Hynson steers from dock to dock, he talks about the river's history - in between handing out lollipops to the children. When he motioned to the log cabin, he shared that the Swedes were the first settlers to build such cabins, not American pioneers heading into western territories. What famous people worked at the shipbuilding companies? Every trip, he hopes to point out wildlife on it. Maybe you'll get to see mink, a falcon, muskrat, otters, red-tailed fox or eagles in the barren treetops. Make sure your kids are ready to take turns being captain (steering) the boat.

DELAWARE CHILDREN'S MUSEUM

Wilmington - *550 Justison Street (MLK exit, follow signs to Riverfront) 19801. Phone: (302) 654-2340. www.delawarechildrensmuseum.org. Hours: Tuesday-Sunday 9am-4:30pm. Admission: General $12.00 per person. Educators: The Kids Room tab takes you to rainy day projects and coloring pages you can print.*

A three-story jungle gym that looks like Saturn? A forest kids create pressing their bodies against walls to make virtual trees? Got your kids interested yet?

The giant jungle gym that looks like a space module is actually The Stratosphere, which is the museum's centerpiece. This 3-story climber accessible to kids of all abilities will allow children to play 20 feet above their parents' heads, negotiating space with other children along the way. The virtual forest uses digiwalls to create "trees" and then divert water to keep the trees alive. These "wow" exhibits are complemented by an ever-popular water table with boats and waterwheels, an auto shop with a mini-car, a toddler-sized train and a paddle boat, and Studio D for exploring artistic media, including weaving, printmaking, sculpture and painting. Bank on It, a nod to the state's banking and financial industry, features an ATM kids can operate, a shop they can run and even oversized checks they can write. Each exhibit includes elements that will appeal to both toddlers - who may simply be interested in climbing, stacking and touching things - and older kids, who can begin to figure out how things work.

Exit - 6 (east of I-95)

DUPONT ENVIRONMENTAL EDUCATION CTR. @ RUSSELL W. PETERSON WILDLIFE REFUGE

Wilmington - *1400 Delmarva Lane (follow signs for Riverwalk, south end of Riverwalk) 19801. Phone: (302) 656-1490. www.duponteec.org. Hours: Center: Tuesday-Friday 11:00am-3:00pm, Saturday 10:00am-3:00pm, Sunday Noon-4:00pm. Refuge open dawn to dusk. Admission: Charged for some programs. Note: The Riverwalk connects to the new pedestrian bridge that leads to the facility.*

This new four-story Riverfront facility is located on the edge of the 212-acre Peterson Refuge on the tidal Christina River, where the city, river and marsh meet. The center showcases the many species of amphibians, birds, mammals, fish, reptiles and native plants that make their home in the refuge. Some of the exhibits are to look at (natural settings), others can be touched. Each season, guided tours and free or low-cost programs for families are offered. For example, visitors may be able to enjoy canoe trips, guided bird walks, a river cruise, or marsh walks with cast and dip net exploration. Flashlight-guided night hikes and dinner plus scavenger hunts are available some evenings.

Outside, various wildlife nesting structures were installed in the marsh and surrounding upland habitats to enhance the site for wildlife. This includes osprey nesting platforms, wood duck boxes, mallard nesting structures, waterfowl nesting platforms, bluebird/tree swallow boxes and bat houses. Head to the center's boardwalk, which encircles a marsh pond, for a ringside seat on any day of the seasonal migrations. And when the ospreys return each year, an Osprey Cam is ready to give Educations Center visitors a real-time look inside the huge pile of sticks that makes up an osprey nest. Images from the Osprey Cam are shown on a screen on a "touch table" in the lobby inside the center. Before you leave, be sure you've visited the snapping turtles - "living relics," which once shared their world with dinosaurs. Raccoons are abundant, too. Did you know a raccoon is known for its intelligence? They can remember the solution to tasks for up to three years.

KALMAR NYCKEL & NEW SWEDEN

Wilmington - 815 Justison Street (Dravo Plaza at Riverfront) 19801. www. kalmarnyckel.org. Phone: (302) 429-7447. Hours: Park is open daylight hours. Tours of ship and New Swedes Centre open when ship is in port or during special events held each season. The Kalmar Nyckel offers a wide array of sailing opportunities—from May through October - for up to 49 passengers, including three-hour sails, and hour-and-a-half cruises. Admission: $20.00-$35.00 fee for sailings (Family or Pirate). Museum open for events and by appointment. Donations are strongly suggested. Public Dockside Tours: You can see her 10-story high mainmast, 7,800 square feet of sails, 9 miles of rigging, and the 4 cannons. Tours describe the daily life onboard a 17th Century ship, including topics such as: Food, Drink, Sleep, Sanitation, Daily Routines, Entertainment, Punishment, Navigation, and Dangers. Admission is charged based on amount of activities offered. Note: In addition to tours of the Hendrickson House and Old Swedes Church, tour guides often offer activities that duplicate lifestyles in the 17th century. These activities include butter making, soap making, household spinning and stained glass work. During the Christmas holiday period, they run Swedish ornaments making sessions.

The Swedish colony - the first permanent Old World settlement in the entire Delaware Valley - eventually grew into Wilmington, the State of Delaware and nearby Pennsylvania and New Jersey.

They survived a stormy winter's crossing of the Atlantic Ocean from Sweden on the KALMAR NYCKEL. That same sturdy vessel that carried a group of 24 settlers now majestically floats - at anchor. This is the home of the full-size recreation of the armed, ornately carved tall ship that brought settlers to the Delaware Valley in 1638 - and made three more roundtrip crossings of the Atlantic, more than any other "settlers' ship." The Kalmar Nyckel Foundation offers guided tours of the ship, the shipyard and a small museum. When the Kalmar is in port, you can't miss her tall mast reaching 100 feet into the air. Most comment that it looks like a ship that you're drawn to sail on - and, you can. Come Aboard! See her cannons, massive timbers and ornate wood carvings plus nine miles of rigging.

NEW SWEDEN CENTRE, CHURCH & HOUSE: Experience New Sweden at the shipyard in the Hands-on History New Sweden Centre (colonialnewsweden. org or 302-429-0464). Once the kids learn HOW colonists came over, they then can learn WHAT they had to do to set up a settlement. See a scale model of Fort Christina, life-size and miniature figures from history, including the Lenape, early Swedish and Finnish settlers and the first African in the Colony. Kids can dress in character with fun clothes that make them look like the real deal. The guide may ask questions like, "Why didn't Swedish boys wear underwear?" Want to play? Colonial games like hoops are fun to play outside. What did they eat? Grind corn and learn how long it took to prepare food to eat.

Go over to 4th Street, go under the railroad overpass and turn right onto Church Street. In two blocks you will see a cobblestone parking area and an old stone house on the right. This original tract of land was about 300 acres which was deeded to a pair of New Sweden colonists in the 1650's. When the Grandfather and Father died, the land was divided between two sons, one of whom built Hendrickson House to impress his fiancée. Pull in and visit the **HENDRICKSON HOUSE** (a Swedish farmhouse built in 1690) and **OLD SWEDES CHURCH** (Holy Trinity - 606 Church Street). It is the nation's oldest church building still standing as originally built (1698) and in regular use for worship. It took 9 months to build the church and they went through 3 carpenters. The tour focuses on the use of the early church. Tours are offered Wednesday-Saturday 10:00am-4:00pm but call first (302-652-5629)

FORT CHRISTINA PARK: as you come to the end of East 7th Street, turn right and go about a half block to the brick walls with wrought iron gates. Here the Swedes, Finns, Dutch and Germans landed on March 29, 1638, met with local Native American chiefs and made arrangements to colonize land along the Delaware River. They founded the Colony of New Sweden, built Fort Christina (named in honor of their six-year-old queen) and built the first log cabins in the New World. The park features a number of interesting historical markers. At the river end of the park are "The Rocks," the natural wharf the first settlers used when they came ashore.

Exit - 5B (west of I-95)

WILMINGTON & WESTERN RAILROAD

Wilmington - 2201 Newport Gap Pike (exit 5 head north on DE141, then northwest on DE41, just past intersection of Route 2) 19808. www.wwrr.com. Phone: (302) 998-1930. Hours: Friday, Saturday, Sunday plus special trains (April-December). Meet Santa Claus or the Easter Bunny or come on Pufferbelly Days. Admission: Fares range from $8.00-$15.00 adult, $6.00-$12.00 child, with some special events costing slightly more.

Imagine yourself riding on a real railroad through the Red Clay Creek Valley. Imagine that you are rolling through forests, past historic homes and mill sites,

aboard a vintage steam train, just like those your great-grandparents rode. Welcome to the railroad. Come aboard. Most train rides offer a scenic trip with narration especially for young railroaders. Learn about the men and machines that built this country, chug across spectacular bridges, clickety-clack through narrow rock cuts and hear the whistle blow as it approaches a station.

GREENBANK MILL

Wilmington - 500 Greenbank Road (head north on DE 141 to Rte 2 west. Right onto Rte 41 north. Just past WWRR.) 19808. www.greenbankmill.com. Phone: (302) 999-9001. Hours: Saturdays 10:00am-4:00pm (April-October). Open through the week for reserved group tours. Open one Saturday in December for Family Christmas and Candlelight Tours. Admission: $5.00-$7.00 per person (age 3+).

Experience Delaware in the Early Republic (1790-1830) at this 300-year-old gristmill, textile mill and farm site with heritage sheep. Step into the past and experience the day-to-day lives of the men, women and children of Greenbank. History

comes alive with the 18-foot water wheel and hands-on activities. Visitors are invited to join the millers, textile workers, wives and children who live and work at Greenbank Mill. Meet the people who lived and worked at Greenbank Mill during the Early Republic (1790-1830). Discover how people in the new nation coped with military threats, economic challenges, and changing technology while defining what it meant to be an "American." Economic freedom came from the mills and factories. In the Philips farmhouse, lie on a rope bed, perform simple tasks using period lighting, and discover what Miller Philips kept under the floorboards. Experience the work required to grow and prepare food in Feeding the Republic. Discover the role of plants in everyday life by exploring the heirloom gardens (Kitchen, Specimen, Medicinal, and Dye).

Learn about cooking techniques and recipes. On baking days make bread in a wood-fired oven. In Amusements, join the Philips Family during their leisure activities including games, dancing, and crafts. On 18th century dance afternoons, join the Heritage Dancers. They will happily instruct beginners, or you may just observe the graceful dancing of the 18th century. Merino sheep are king here

See the giant waterwheel that made it all happen...

(and, so cute) and their long wool is highly prized. Next, visit the mill. Why is the creek called" That Never Failing Stream" and why is that important to milling? Delaware inventor Oliver Evans patented the revolutionary milling system that uses bucket elevators and screw conveyors automating the milling process. Watching the waterwheel is like a live study of the Industrial Revolution.

Exit - 5B (west of I-95)

AUBURN HEIGHTS PRESERVE

Hockessin - *3000 Creek Road (head north on Rte. 141/41 to right on Rte 82) 19707. Phone: (302) 239-5687. www.auburnheights.org. Hours: Seasonal & Special Events only. Usually Sundays from 12:30pm-4:00pm. Admission: $11.00 adult, $8.00 child (ages 2-12) for museum, operating steam cars/train rides and grounds. Educators: Steam engine FAQs answer multiple questions for student research on the age of steam.*

Visit Delaware State Parks' newest attraction to experience life at the dawn of the automotive age. Home to the three generations of the Marshall family, the Auburn Heights mansion is fully furnished with exquisite antiques. The Marshall Steam Museum features model and scale trains as well as the

largest collection of steam automobiles in the world!

The Auburn Valley Railroad is a 1/8 size coal-burning steam locomotive taking passengers on a 5/8 mile trip around the estate. It's miniature size appeals to the kids. You can also take a "bus" tour

of the property. Hop aboard the "First Bus" in Delaware - A Stanley Mountain Wagon - for a spin around the property in a fully restored 1915 Model 820 Mountain Wagon. Pssssst! Don't tell anybody else but....there's free popcorn courtesy of their steam powered popper!

Exit - 5 MILE

DELAWARE HOUSE SERVICE AREA

Wilmington - *(left exit; located in center median)* . *Phone: (843) 784-3275. Hours: Daily 9:00am-5:00pm.*

Directions and mapping information, and informative brochures to help you discover the treasures of Delaware. The centers also offer discount coupons for attractions and accommodations. Traffic information is readily available as well as weather information for the state. Food and Gas Stations. Bathrooms, a pet walk, and picnic areas are also available.

Exit - 4A (east of I-95)

FORT DELAWARE STATE PARK

Delaware City - *Access to the fort is only by Ferry (exit 4A southeast on SR 1 to SR 72 east towards Delaware City) 18796. Phone: (302) 834-7941.*

www.destateparks.com/park/fort-delaware/index.asp. Hours: Fort Delaware is always closed on Mondays and Tuesdays. Download a PDF of the season schedule as it changes each year. The first Ferry leaves at 10:00am from Delaware City. The last tram leaves at 5:30pm from Fort Delaware back

to Delaware City. The Fort's season runs only from mid-June through Labor Day with May and early June long weekends included. Admission: Fort is FREE. However, you must take the ferry over the one mile crossing & then a tram to fort entrance. Ferry Fees: $6.00-$11.00 per person (ages 2+). Note: Private boats are not permitted to dock on the island. Hands-On and Premium Programs (additional small fee) capacity is limited, and they can sell out quickly. Be sure to stop in the Visitors' Center as soon as you arrive to purchase your tickets.

BATTERY PARK along the Delaware River provides a scenic panorama of the river, Pea Patch Island and the New Jersey shoreline. A diving bell (can you imagine what this archaic object is?) is located in the park and you can visit the restored stonewall lock that was part of the C&D Canal when it went through the town until 1927.

From Battery Park you can take the DELAFORT FERRY to FORT DELAWARE on Pea Patch Island. Completed in 1859 to protect Delaware, New Jersey and Pennsylvania, the fort was used as a major prison for Confederate soldiers and sympathizers during the Civil War. The fort is five-sided and kids love that it is surrounded by a moat. During the war, some 16,000 people lived in the fort. Have conversations with authentically dressed park interpreters who can offer insights on the history of Fort Delaware. Be on hand when the 8-inch Columbiad gun fires a live gunpowder charge! See

> Fort Mott, Fort Delaware, and Fort DuPont were part of a three-fort defense system designed for the Delaware River during the post Civil War modernization period.

a replica of Pea Patch Island as it appeared in 1864 and artifacts from the Island's past. For a small fee, you may also register for special hands-on activities while on the island. Help the blacksmith hammer out new parts for a cannon or work with the laundress. Help out in the Officers' Kitchen to prepare Civil War era meals for the soldiers, officers, and families. Better yet, exchange

your 21st -century dollars for Civil War era script, including greenbacks and stamps. Then, while you are on the island, if you see someone making something you like, you can try to negotiate a deal with them. Just be careful, the people on Pea Patch need as much money as they can get, so most are shrewd hagglers. (BTW, if you don't find anything you like, feel free to keep the repro script as a souvenir, or return it for your modern greenbacks. Make a day of it - there is a food concession stand on the island. And if you like, you can bring a picnic lunch to enjoy in their picnic area - tables and grills are provided. The island is also a nesting ground for nine species of birds, including herons, egrets and ibis. An overlook provides excellent views of the 90-acre rookery and the thousands of adult and juvenile birds. The Delafort Ferry also takes visitors to FORT MOTT in New Jersey. http://www.stateparks. com/fort_mott.html.

Exit - 4A (east of I-95)

FORT DUPONT STATE PARK

Delaware City - *(Rte 1 south to Rte 72 east/Rte 9 south, across the canal on the grounds of the Governor Bacon Health Center) 19706. Phone: (302) 834-7941. www.destateparks.com/park/fort-dupont/. Hours: Open Daily 8:00am-sunset. Admission: A park entrance fee is charged daily from March 1 to November 30. Resident: $3.00 Non-resident: $6.00 per vehicle.*

Located in Delaware City at the northern foot of the Reedy Point Bridge, Fort DuPont State Park is currently under development. Fort DuPont (1863) is part of the three forts along the Delaware River once supporting attacks of DC or Philadelphia. Delaware's newest state park features a self-guided trail and periodically-scheduled walking tours that detail the Fort's military history from the Civil War through the First World War. Other facilities include tennis courts, a basketball court, and a ball field. A popular fishing area, the park provides a beautiful view of the Delaware River.

Exit - 1 (west of I-95)

WHITE CLAY CREEK STATE PARK

Newark - *750 Thompson Station Road (head north on Rte. 896, thru town to park entrance) 19702. www.destateparks.com/park/white-clay-creek. Phone: (302) 368-6900. Hours: Daily 8:00am-sunset. Admission: A park entrance fee is charged daily from March 1 to November 30. $3.00 per vehicle (instate) $6.00 out-of-state.*

Hiking is one of the most popular activities in the park. Thirty-seven miles of trails lead explorers to historic sites and scenic vistas overlooking lush valleys and impressive rock outcrops. Hikers and mountain bike riders can travel through the Middle Run Valley Natural Area to Possum Hill, follow the Lifecourse Fitness Trail in Carpenter Recreation Area, or hike the Pomeroy

Rail-Trail to the pedestrian bridge over White Clay Creek. There are plenty of year-round activities available at White Clay Creek. The Nature Center hosts fun and interesting public programs (hawk count, owl prowls), and visitors can enjoy outdoor activities such as fishing, birdwatching or disc golf. Families may take advantage of the large picnic area followed by an evening concert or other special event throughout the summer. Sledding and cross-country skiing are among the many winter activities available at the park.

Exit - 1 (east of I-95)

IRON HILL MUSEUM

Newark - *1355 Old Baltimore Pike (east on Rte. 896 to right turn on Old Baltimore Pike) 19702. Phone: (302) 368-5703. www.ironhill-museum.org. Hours: Tuesday - Friday 10:00am-3:00pm, Saturday Noon-4:00pm. Admission: $2.00 per person (age 6+). FREEBIES: online, printable puzzles & trivia games by clicking on: Kids page.*

Wonder how this hill got its name? Did you realize iron ore looks very different before it's melted into Pig Iron. Find out what it was like to be an iron miner or a Lenni Lenape Indian as both inhabited the area and used its resources. See what material they used and how they used them to live a life without electricity, telephones, televisions, or any of our modern conveniences. Stop by the Please Touch Wall and touch a turtle shell or a piece of petrified wood. Although Delaware never had dinosaurs, they did have many varieties of monosaurs. What's a monosaur? Find out what other types of creatures were crawling along the sea floor that would eventually become Delaware. One room has a colorful rocks and minerals collection, another has rocks that glow. These fluorescent minerals turn bright red, green, purple, and much more! See the radioactive marbles and gum plates.

LUMS POND STATE PARK

Bear - *1068 Howell School Road (exit and head south on Rte 896/US 301 to park) 19701. Phone: (302) 368-6989. www.destateparks.com/park/lums-pond/. Hours: Daily 8:00am-sunset. Admission: A park entrance fee is charged daily from March 1 to November 30. $3.00 per vehicle (instate) $6.00 out-of-state.*

Lums Pond State Park is built around the largest freshwater pond in Delaware. The park features excellent fishing, sports facilities, hiking trails and more on its 1790 acres on the north side of the Chesapeake and Delaware Canal. Lums Pond itself covers 200 acres, and although there is no swimming allowed, boat rentals and fishing provide water-bound recreation in the summer months. A boat launching ramp and two piers allow easy access to the water. Hikers have the opportunity to explore a variety of habitats along the 7.5 mile Swamp Forest Trail circling the pond. Lums also features over 10 miles of multi-purpose trails (horses, bikes, hikers, and snowmobiles). The Whale Wallow Nature Center hosts a variety of programs for visitors during the summer season (Nature Center will be open daily from noon-6:00pm - Memorial Day to Labor Day.). For outdoor dining, picnic areas are scattered throughout the park.

Chapter 3
MARYLAND & D.C.

Curious about hundreds of fun places in the lighter gray areas? See *Kids Love Maryland*

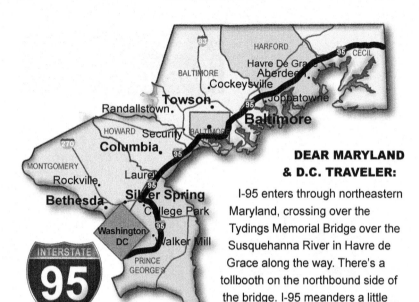

DEAR MARYLAND
& D.C. TRAVELER:

I-95 enters through northeastern Maryland, crossing over the Tydings Memorial Bridge over the Susquehanna River in Havre de Grace along the way. There's a tollbooth on the northbound side of the bridge. I-95 meanders a little and then travels diagonally through the middle of the state, through Baltimore (see Interstate 95 in Baltimore). South of Baltimore, the interstate soon becomes the Capital Beltway. I-95 follows the Capital Beltway around Washington, D.C. Interstate 95 exits Maryland on the Woodrow Wilson Bridge over the Potomac River heading to Alexandria, Virginia.

The first family-friendly town you hit on your way south through the state is **Havre de Grace** (pronounced hav-er da grace). Maybe try an overnight at a B&B, and then walk to any waterfront museum, skipjack tour or quaint restaurant – each with their specialties clearly presented on the menu. Because this is a walkable town, we consider all of Havre de Grace one big attraction.

Maryland is a kid-friendly state and the perfect place for some serious sidetripping. A logical choice is a trip to Baltimore, where you can explore the acclaimed **Inner Harbor** museums and shops…especially the big ship, the **USS Constellation** in port. Audio players allow you to listen as a young girl's grandpa shares stories about the Constellation's magnificent power on the waters of combat. Surrounding Inner Harbor are some pretty historic sites. Baseball great **Babe Ruth's Birthplace** is just down the street from Camden Yards and the truly interactive **Sports Legends Museum**. Or, visit the actual spot where the "Star Spangled Banner" originated at **Ft.**

McHenry or the **Flag House** where a small group of women created the famous flag.

What kids don't love trains at some point in their childhood? Remember the Monopoly game you played at home and one property marked the **B&O Railroad**? What about visiting the original huge trains, miniature trains, trains you can ride – all here and all presented in short presentations inside and outside. Haven't had enough? Travel a little ways off the connecting outerbelt and you'll find another quaint railroad station: the **Ellicott City B&O Railroad**. The surrounding little town has dozens of whimsical shops, too.

When it comes to offbeat, Maryland is home to some bizarre, yet amusing attractions like the **Museum of Dentistry** in Baltimore, which includes George Washington's dentures and crazy people who use their teeth to lift things! We found another extremely unique and a little creepy museum at Fort Meade Military base. The **National Cryptologic Museum** is all about secret codes and deciphering them. Talk about stories that make you wonder who's watching (or listening to) you!

Maryland gets a lot of attention for their succulent blue crabs, plucked from the Chesapeake Bay and transformed into pink crustaceans that you can dissect for dinner. It seems silly to don a bib and "tools" for a meal but the reward is the yummy meat in the middle. We found the best crab at Crab/BBQ joints not far from the interstate. Just follow the signs…

Maryland is a generous state; so generous, in fact, that in 1791 they donated the land that became Washington, D.C. To try to name favorites in D. C. is pretty near impossible as the entire area is one small place packed with dozens of historical attractions one must see in their lifetime to truly feel American. Before you fill your day with museum visits, here are some tips to make the visit easier:

Overnight in nearby Virginia suburbs close to a Metro Station so once you get up in the morning - you can easily navigate the Metro into town. We've suggested a couple different places in Alexandria. If you like to picnic, the National Mall and West or East Potomac Park have dozens of lawn sites to spread out a picnic blanket. You'll be dining, al fresco, by a view of famous monuments. As the sun started setting, we especially enjoyed walking the perimeter of the Tidal Basin in Potomac Park with a view of the **FDR Memorial** & the **Jefferson Memorial**, as they are backlit towards nightfall. Also, surrounding the White House are oodles of vendors offering the best prices in town on souvenirs and sandwiches.

MD & D.C.

How To Do Attractions - every family is different but honestly you can "do" as many as your family desires if you work the 10:00am-7:00pm full day. Maybe devote an entire day to the FREE **Smithsonian Museums** & National Mall buildings. DC by Foot, a walking tour company, gives FREE, kid-friendly tours infused with games, fun facts and trivia. Or, just wander from one building to the next. Be sure to go online first and print off any "Hunts" (scavenger hunts) that interest you (ways to engage, not overwhelm young guests). Play pilot in a mock cockpit at America by Air, an exhibition on permanent display at the Smithsonian **National Air and Space Museum**. Teach kids about history at the newly renovated **National Museum of American History** for a rare look at the original "Star-Spangled Banner," the flag that inspired Francis Scott Key to write the national anthem. The museum's Spark!Lab uses fun activities to help kids and families learn about the history and process of invention through games and conducting experiments plus there's an Under 5 Zone just for preschoolers. Walk among the butterflies or witness a view of the blinding Hope Diamond at the **National Museum of Natural History**.

Maybe following a thread of your favorite President is the best way to tour. **Fords Theatre Museum & Tour** is a newly renovated museum using 21st century technology to transport visitors to 19th-century Washington, DC. The museum's collection of historic artifacts (including the derringer that John Wilkes Booth used to shoot Lincoln and a replica of the coat Lincoln wore the night he was shot) is supplemented with a variety of narrative devices. As you sit in the theatre for the park ranger presentation, chills run up your spine! After lunch, go to our favorite wax museum, **Madame Tussauds**. DC's wax museum has a distinctly "Washington" feel, and gives parents the perfect opportunity to give kids a taste of politics without the crowds on the Mall. We interacted with the figures for some amazingly realistic photo ops like: Sitting with Lincoln in Ford's Theatre, Dad discussing decisions of the day in the Oval Office or taking photos with famous presidents. They look so real (in the digital pics) that folks on the Metro thought we had actually met the President that day!

ACTIVITIES AT A GLANCE

AMUSEMENTS

Exit - 53 / I-395 N - *Harborplace*
Exit - 19 - *Madame Tussauds Wax Museum, D.C.*
Exit - 15 - *Six Flags America*
Exit - 15 - *Watkins Regional Park*

ANIMALS & FARMS

Exit - 53 / I-395N / I-83N - *Maryland Zoo In Baltimore*
Exit - 53 / I-395N - *National Aquarium In Baltimore*
Exit - 43 - *Enchanted Forest & Clark's Elioakfarm*
Exit - 27 / I-495 West - *National Zoo*

HISTORY

Exit - 89 - *Susquehanna Museum Of Havre De Grace Lock House*
Exit - 89 - *Havre De Grace Maritime Museum*
Exit - 89 - *Concord Point Lighthouse*
Exit - 85 - *U.S Army Ordnance Museum*
Exit - 64 / I-695W - *Baltimore Streetcar Museum*
Exit - 64 / I-695W - *Hampton National Historic Site*
Exit - 64 / I-695S - *Maryland Aviation Museum, Glenn L Martin*
Exit - 56 - *Douglass - Isaac Myers Maritime Park*
Exit - 55 - *Fort McHenry National Monument & Historic Shrine*
Exit - 55 - *Baltimore Museum Of Industry*
Exit - 53 / I-395N - *USS Constellation*
Exit - 53 / I-395N - *Baltimore Maritime Museum*
Exit - 53 / I-395N - *World Trade Center "Top Of The World"*
Exit - 53 / I-395N - *Reginald F. Lewis Museum Of Maryland African American History & Culture*

Exit - 53 / I-395N - *Flag House & Star Spangled Banner Museum*
Exit - 53 / I-395N - *Maryland Historical Society Museums*
Exit - 53 / I-395N - *National Great Blacks In Wax Museum*
Exit - 53 / I-395N - *B & O Railroad Museum*
Exit - 52 - *National Museum Of Dentistry*
Exit - 49 / I-695S - *Ellicott City B&O Railroad Station Museum*
Exit - 47 / I-195S / Rt.295N - *Historical Electronics Museum*
Exit - 38 - *National Cryptologic Museum*
Exit - 28A - *National Capital Trolley Museum*
Exit - 27 / I-495 West - *President Lincoln's Cottage*
Exit - 23 - *College Park Aviation Museum & Airport*
Exit - 19 - *Ford's Theatre*
Exit - 11 - *Capitol Building, United States*
Exit - 11 - *Library Of Congress*
Exit - 11 - *National Archives*
Exit - 11 - *Newseum*
Exit - 7A - *Surratt House Museum*
Exit - 3A - *Fort Washington Park*
Exit - 3 - *Frederick Douglass NHS*
Exit - 3 - *Oxon Hill Farm At Oxon Cove Park*
Exit - 2 / I-295 North - *U.S. Navy Museum*
Exit - 2 / I-295 North - *Smithsonian Institution*
Exit - 2 / I-295 North - *Holocaust Memorial Museum, United States*
Exit - 2 / I-295 North - *Washington Monument*
Exit - 2 / I-295 North - *Jefferson Memorial*

MD & D.C.

ACTIVITIES AT A GLANCE

HISTORY *(cont.)*

Exit - 2 / I-295 North - *Franklin D. Roosevelt Memorial*

Exit - 2 / I-295 North - *Lincoln Memorial*

MUSEUMS

Exit - 89 - *Havre De Grace Decoy Museum*

Exit - 53 / I-395N - *Port Discovery, The Children's Museum*

Exit - 52 - *Geppi's Entertainment Museum*

Exit - 19 - *International Spy Museum*

OUTDOOR EXPLORING

Exit - 89 - *Susquehanna State Park / Rocks State Park*

Exit - 74 - *Gunpowder Falls State Park / Jerusalem Mill*

Exit - 47 / I-195S - *Patapsco Valley State Park*

Exit - 27 / I-495 West - *Rock Creek Park And Nature Center*

Exit - 2 / I-295 North - *National Mall*

SCIENCE

Exit - 55 - *Maryland Science Center*

Exit - 23 - *NASA Goddard Space Flight Center*

Exit - 22 - *National Wildlife Visitor Center (Patuxent Refuge)*

SPORTS

Exit - 85 - *Ripken Stadium / Ironbirds*

Exit - 53 / I-395N - *Lacrosse Museum And National Hall Of Fame*

Exit - 52 - *Sports Legends @ Camden Yards*

Exit - 52 - *Babe Ruth Birthplace*

SUGGESTED LODGING & DINING

Exit - 89 - *MacGregors Restaurant*

Exit - 89 - *Laurrapin Grille*

Exit - 89 - *Vandiver Inn*

Exit - 53 / I-395N - *Hyatt Regency*

Exit - 41 - *Hilton Columbia*

Exit - 19 - *Clyde's At The Gallery*

Exit - 17 - *Radisson Hotel Largo*

THE ARTS

Exit - 55 - *American Visionary Art Museum*

Exit - 55 - *Baltimore Museum Of Art*

Exit - 53 / I-395N - *Walters Art Museum*

Exit - 2 / I-295 North - *National Gallery Of Art*

TOURS

Exit - 100 - *Day Basket Factory*

Exit - 89 - *Skipjack Martha Lewis*

Exit - 57 - *Urban Pirates, Baltimore City*

Exit - 53 / I-395N - *Baltimore Spirit Cruises*

Exit - 52 - *Oriole Park At Camden Yards*

Exit - 19 - *DC Ducks Tours*

Exit - 19 - *Old Town Trolley Tours*

Exit - 2 / I-295 North - *White House*

Exit - 2 / I-295 North - *Bureau Of Engraving And Printing Tour*

WELCOME CENTERS

Exit - 97 Mile - *Chesapeake House Welcome Center*

Exit - 82 Mile - *Maryland House Welcome Center*

GENERAL INFORMATION

Contact the services of interest. Request to be added to their mailing lists.

- ☐ State Park Camping & Cabin Reservations: http://reservations.dnr.state.md.us. or (888) 432-CAMP.
- ☐ Maryland Association Of Campgrounds: (301) 271-7012. http://www.gocampingamerica.com/stateOverview.aspx?id=MD&state=Maryland
- ☐ Maryland Department Of Natural Resources: www.dnr.state.md.us. or (877) 620-8DNR
- ☐ Maryland Bicycle Maps And Publications: (410) 545-5656 or www.sha.state.md.us/SHAservices/mapsbrochures/maps/oppe/maps.asp
- ☐ Maryland Scenic Byways: (877) 632-9929 or www.sha.state.md.us/exploremd/oed/scenicbyways/scenicbyways.asp
- ☐ U.S. Fish & Wildlife Service, Maryland Fishery Resources Office: (410) 263-2604 or http://marylandfisheries.fws.gov
- ☐ Chesapeake Bay Gateways Network: (866) BAY WAYS or www.baygateways.net
- ☐ Maryland Tourism: www.visitmaryland.org
- ☐ Baltimore Area Tourism: www.baltimore.org and HARBORPASS: www.baltimore.org/harborpass
- ☐ Havre De Grace Tourism: www.havredegracemd.com
- ☐ Howard County Tourism / Ellicott City: http://www.howardcountymd.gov/hct/hct_homepage.htm

MD & D.C.

Travel Journal & Notes:

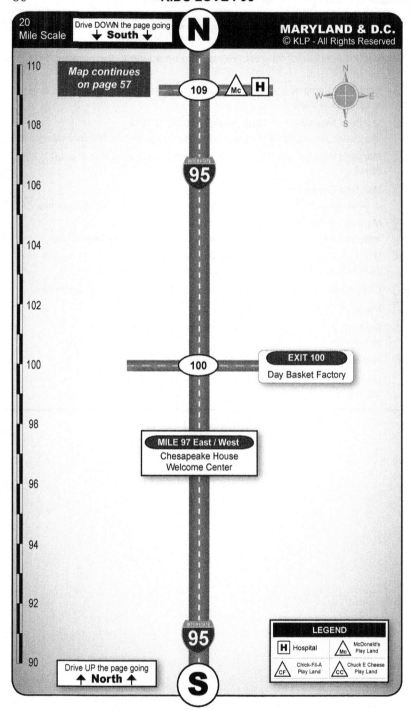

Map continues on page 57

For updates & travel games visit: **www.KidsLoveTravel.com**

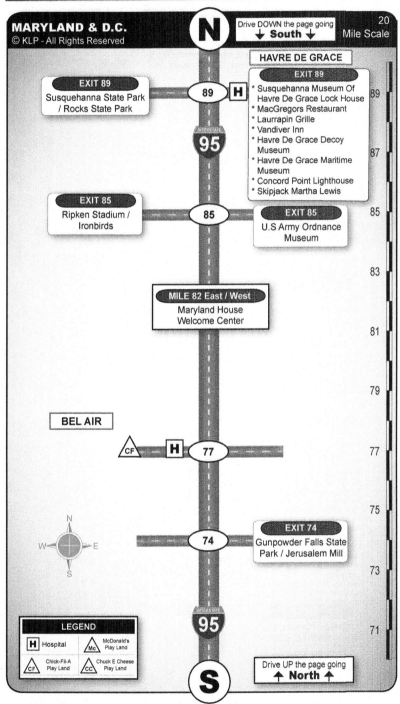

MARYLAND & D.C.

N

Drive DOWN the page going
↓ South ↓

20 Mile Scale

HAVRE DE GRACE

EXIT 89
Susquehanna State Park / Rocks State Park

89 H

EXIT 89
* Susquehanna Museum Of Havre De Grace Lock House
* MacGregors Restaurant
* Laurrapin Grille
* Vandiver Inn
* Havre De Grace Decoy Museum
* Havre De Grace Maritime Museum
* Concord Point Lighthouse
* Skipjack Martha Lewis

INTERSTATE 95

MD & D.C.

EXIT 85
Ripken Stadium / Ironbirds

85

EXIT 85
U.S Army Ordnance Museum

MILE 82 East / West
Maryland House Welcome Center

BEL AIR

CF H 77

EXIT 74
Gunpowder Falls State Park / Jerusalem Mill

74

N
W E
S

INTERSTATE 95

LEGEND

| H Hospital | Mc McDonald's Play Land |
| CF Chick-Fil-A Play Land | CC Chuck E Cheese Play Land |

Drive UP the page going
↑ North ↑

S

89
87
85
83
81
79
77
75
73
71

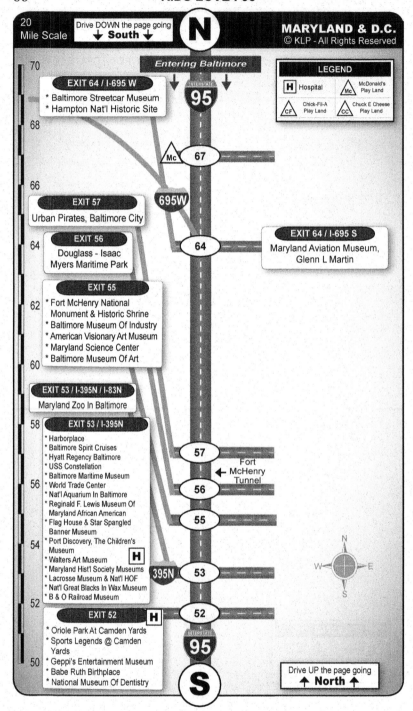

20 Mile Scale

Drive DOWN the page going
↓ **South** ↓

N

MARYLAND & D.C.
© KLP - All Rights Reserved

70

Entering Baltimore

INTERSTATE **95**

EXIT 64 / I-695 W
* Baltimore Streetcar Museum
* Hampton Nat'l Historic Site

68

LEGEND

H Hospital	**Mc** McDonald's Play Land
CF Chick-Fil-A Play Land	**CC** Chuck E Cheese Play Land

Mc **67**

66

695W

EXIT 57
Urban Pirates, Baltimore City

64

64

EXIT 64 / I-695 S
Maryland Aviation Museum, Glenn L Martin

EXIT 56
Douglass - Isaac Myers Maritime Park

62

EXIT 55
* Fort McHenry National Monument & Historic Shrine
* Baltimore Museum Of Industry
* American Visionary Art Museum
* Maryland Science Center
* Baltimore Museum Of Art

60

EXIT 53 / I-395N / I-83N
Maryland Zoo In Baltimore

58

EXIT 53 / I-395N
* Harborplace
* Baltimore Spirit Cruises
* Hyatt Regency Baltimore
* USS Constellation
* Baltimore Maritime Museum
* World Trade Center
* Nat'l Aquarium In Baltimore
* Reginald F. Lewis Museum Of Maryland African American
* Flag House & Star Spangled Banner Museum
* Port Discovery, The Children's Museum
* Walters Art Museum **H**
* Maryland Hist'l Society Museums
* Lacrosse Museum & Nat'l HOF
* Nat'l Great Blacks In Wax Museum
* B & O Railroad Museum

56

54

52

395N **53**

57

Fort
McHenry
← Tunnel

56

55

EXIT 52 **H**
* Oriole Park At Camden Yards
* Sports Legends @ Camden Yards
* Geppi's Entertainment Museum
* Babe Ruth Birthplace
* National Museum Of Dentistry

50

52

INTERSTATE **95**

S

N
W ✦ E
S

Drive UP the page going
↑ **North** ↑

For updates & travel games visit: **www.KidsLoveTravel.com**

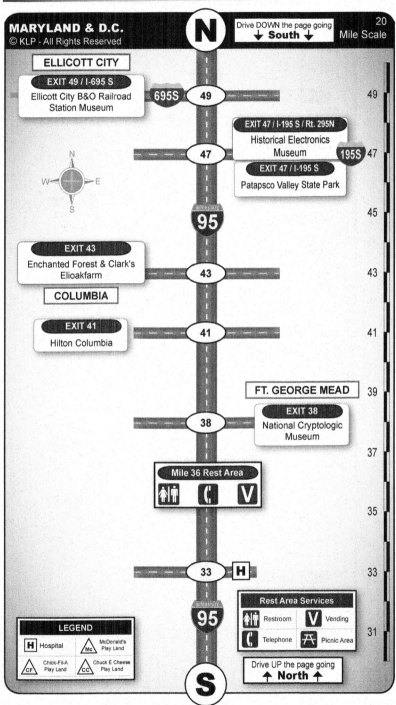

MARYLAND & D.C.

N

Drive DOWN the page going
↓ **South** ↓

20
Mile Scale

ELLICOTT CITY

EXIT 49 / I-695 S
Ellicott City B&O Railroad
Station Museum

695S 49

49

EXIT 47 / I-195 S / Rt. 295N
Historical Electronics
Museum

47

195S 47

EXIT 47 / I-195 S
Patapsco Valley State Park

45

95

EXIT 43
Enchanted Forest & Clark's
Elioakfarm

43

43

COLUMBIA

EXIT 41
Hilton Columbia

41

41

FT. GEORGE MEAD 39

EXIT 38
National Cryptologic
Museum

38

37

Mile 36 Rest Area

🚻 📞 V

35

33 **H** 33

95

Rest Area Services

🚻 Restroom V Vending

📞 Telephone 🎋 Picnic Area

31

LEGEND

H Hospital Mc McDonald's Play Land

CF Chick-Fil-A Play Land CC Chuck E Cheese Play Land

Drive UP the page going
↑ **North** ↑

S

MD & D.C.

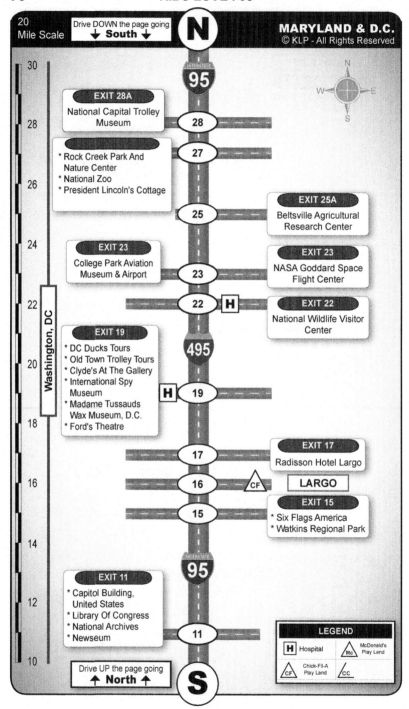

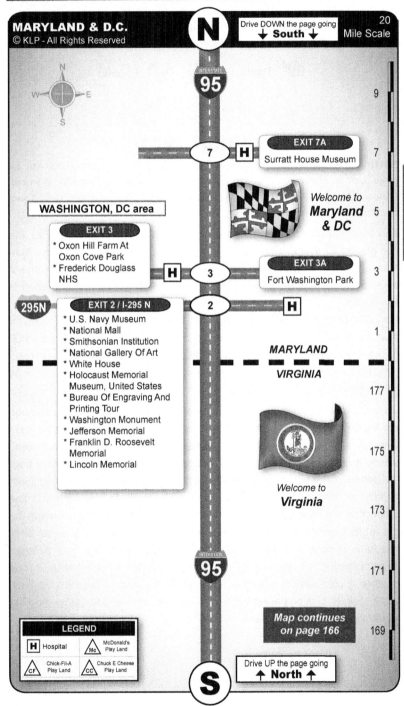

Drive DOWN the page going
↓ South ↓

20
Mile Scale

N

INTERSTATE **95**

9

7

EXIT 7A
Surratt House Museum

7

H

MD & D.C.

Welcome to
Maryland
& DC

5

WASHINGTON, DC area

EXIT 3
* Oxon Hill Farm At
  Oxon Cove Park
* Frederick Douglass
  NHS

H

3

EXIT 3A
Fort Washington Park

3

295N

EXIT 2 / I-295 N
* U.S. Navy Museum
* National Mall
* Smithsonian Institution
* National Gallery Of Art
* White House
* Holocaust Memorial
  Museum, United States
* Bureau Of Engraving And
  Printing Tour
* Washington Monument
* Jefferson Memorial
* Franklin D. Roosevelt
  Memorial
* Lincoln Memorial

2

H

1

MARYLAND

VIRGINIA

177

175

Welcome to
Virginia

173

171

INTERSTATE **95**

*Map continues
on page 166*

169

Drive UP the page going
↑ North ↑

S

LEGEND

| **H** Hospital | McDonald's Play Land (Mc) |
| Chick-Fil-A Play Land (CF) | Chuck E Cheese Play Land (CC) |

Sites and attractions are listed in order by Exit Number (North to South) and distance from the exit (closest are listed first). Symbols indicated represent:

 Restaurants   Lodging

Exit - 100 (east of I-95)

DAY BASKET FACTORY

North East - *714 South Main Street (I-95 North, to Exit 100, MD-272 South 2.4 miles. Left on Irishtown). Proceed 2.4 miles) 21901. www.daybasketfactory.com. Phone: (410) 287-6100. Hours: Wednesday-Saturday 11:00am-5:00pm. Daily hours Summer and Christmastime.*

This local industry makes hand-made white oak baskets. Shortly after the end of the Civil War in 1876, Edward & Samuel Day came to North East from Massachusetts. Edward was an experienced basket maker. The brothers, who had been supplying the southern market with baskets, set-up shop in North East - partly to save on transportation costs, also because the forests along the Susquehanna River were full of White Oak, the best kind of wood for baskets. Business boomed - during World War I the factory produced 2,000 baskets weekly. Craftsmen carefully select and split each piece of oak used by skilled weavers, who produce baskets using techniques passed down by generations for over 128 years.

On tour: After the sides are woven, the weaver wraps an outside hoop around the inside hoop and nails through both hoops with brass nails. These nails automatically crimp themselves when they strike the steel band on the form, saving an extra step. Next, yokes if needed, are laced under the fillers from the bottom of the basket for reinforcement. Some baskets are also fitted with handles of different types. How do they get the wood to bow like that? The production of a basket is a three to four day process. After drying overnight the basket its trimmed, sanded and finished. The completed Day Baskets have hundreds of uses and come in a variety of sizes and styles. Four different sizes of market baskets, round farm baskets with bentwood handles or rope handles, picnic baskets with lids, laundry baskets, fish or firewood baskets, berry baskets, picking baskets with drop handles, and eel pots (yes, a popular waterman activity around these parts!).

Exit - 97 MILE

CHESAPEAKE HOUSE WELCOME CENTER

Chesapeake House offers food, fuel, auto repair services, and a traveler information center to motorists. It also includes a full-service business center including phone jacks for portable computers and postal service. Find brochures, maps and other information. Of course, plenty of restrooms inside and areas to relax outside.

Exit - 89 (west of I-95)

SUSQUEHANNA STATE PARK / ROCKS STATE PARK

Havre de Grace - *4122 Wilkinson Road (off Rte. 155 west to Rte. 161. Turn right on Rte 161 and then right on Rock Run Rd.) 21078. Phone: (410) 557-7994. http://dnr2.maryland.gov/publiclands/Pages/central/susquehanna.aspx Note: the Rocks State Park portion (most scenic & hiking possibilities) is further west*

Located along the Susquehanna River valley with its heavy forest cover and massive rock outcroppings, Susquehanna State Park offers a wide variety of outdoor recreational opportunities as well as historical significance. The park is home to some of the most popular mountain biking trails in Maryland and the river itself beacons fishermen and boaters alike. Susquehanna State Park also contains a very family friendly campground with traditional campsites and cabins. History buffs will be drawn to the restored Rock Run Historical Area with its working grist mill, the Archer Mansion, Jersey Toll House and the remains of the Susquehanna Tidewater Canal. A freshwater pond is on site and is ideal for the novice angler. The Susquehanna State Park campground contains two loops with a total of 69 sites, six of which are electric, and six camper cabins.

The Falling Branch area of ROCKS STATE PARK is located about 5 miles north of the main part and features a 17-foot scenic free-falling waterfall - the second highest vertical falls in the state. Historical sites include the ROCK RUN GRIST MILL, Archer Mansion and Jersey Toll House. The stone mill is open on weekends all

summer operating using a 12-ton water wheel, which runs on a limited basis.

STEPPINGSTONE MUSEUM: visitors can spend the afternoon touring the sites of a once working Harford County farm. The farmhouse, furnished as a turn-of-the-century home, charms the visitor as a guide invites you to share the daily life of the period. With no electricity, what did kids do for fun? Tours include the formal sitting room, sleeping quarters, and kitchen with its wood burning stove and ice box. Can you find the toaster? In the other buildings, maybe watch a woodworker, blacksmith or weaver. Our favorite building is the recreated tomato cannery. Kids did this as a summer job. They begin

by scalding the fruit to loosen the skin and peel. Then they pack (on a giant wheel conveyor!), cap, cook, label and store the canned product. They even have equipment to make Catsup. Very interesting and well displayed processes in here! 888-419-1762 or www.steppingstonemuseum.org. (May thru September weekends 1:00-5:00pm & special events, $3.00 - ages 13+).

Exit - 89 (east of I-95)

SUSQUEHANNA MUSEUM OF HAVRE DE GRACE LOCK HOUSE

Havre de Grace - *817 Conesteo Street (corner of Erie) (follow signs into town) 21078. Phone: (410) 939-5780. www.thelockhousemuseum.org. Hours: Friday-Sunday 1:00-5:00pm (mid April-October). Admission: Donations accepted.*

Why is a lockhouse right next to a river? The canal was built as a water staircase because the river was too shallow for large cargo boats. Why did they use a leather scoop on board. Where was the parking lot for boats ready for shipping? Listen to a 160 year old xylophone and secret birthday music box. In the kitchen, learn how to make an old fashioned snow ball

Help move a 4000 lb. pivot bridge.. with just a push...

treat. Look for the high chair that turns into a stroller. Why is it better to have rounded travel trunks vs. a flattop. At the end of the tour, make sure the kids help move the pivot bridge. You just moved 4000 pounds! Fun things to learn in every room - and you get to touch most items.

MACGREGORS RESTAURANT

Havre de Grace - *331 Saint John Street (follow Rte. 155 east into town, then follow signs to riverfront, downtown) 21078. www.macgregorsrestaurant.com. Phone: (410) 939-3003.*

Originally a bank built in 1924, all tables here have a water view. The two-tiered all glass upscale casual dining room features lunch ($8.00-$12.00), dinner (around $20.00), lite fare and Sunday Brunch. We have to highly recommend the award-winning Rockfish and their garlic chive mashed potatoes! Mild gourmet sauces are served and fit each entrée perfectly. Children's Menu (everything from crab pretzels to sliders to spaghetti - most around $7.00-$10.00), balloons and coloring books.

LAURRAPIN GRILLE

Havre de Grace - *209 North Washington Street (take Rte. 155 east into downtown) 21078. Phone: (410) 939-3663. www.laurrapin.com.*

Where Northern California meets the Chesapeake Bay. Items like spring rolls, pizza, muffalattas or crab on the same menu. The newbie kid gourmet will enjoy their meatloaf and steak and potatoes, too. Lunch around $10 and dinner around $20. Daily (except Mondays) for lunch and dinner. Sunday brunch only.

Exit - 89 (east of I-95)

VANDIVER INN

Havre de Grace - *301 South Union Avenue (corner of Fountain) (take Rte.155 into town, hard left onto Juniata, hard left onto Otsega, another left onto Union) 21078. Phone: (800) 245-1655. www.vandiverinn.com.*

The Vandiver Inn is an 1886 Victorian mansion located two blocks from the Chesapeake Bay in historic Havre de Grace, Maryland. What a nice treat! The owner greeted us on the front porch where we later sat during a heavy rainstorm. The kids were apprehensive at first - being in such an old mansion - but soon eased and began exploring all the nooks and crannies. One night, our family, some staff and the owner's son, Jack watched a movie in the parlor - "Movies at the Mansion." All the staff are gracious but not at all pretentious. Breakfast and the amenities weren't so "foo-foo" that our kids wouldn't enjoy - no mile-high, lime infused cheese French toast here - more like homemade eggs or pancakes with oodles of blueberries.

The Vandiver Mansion has eight elegant rooms, many with fireplaces. The adjacent Murphy & Kent Guest Houses provide an additional nine rooms. This Country Inn really tries to cater to family getaways, family reunions (take over the mansion!) and weddings or corporate meetings. Girls love that every room is decorated differently. All rooms are air conditioned and four of their new suites feature luxury Jacuzzi tubs. ALL of their rooms offer private in-room baths, full breakfast every morning, cable TV, phones w/data ports, high speed wireless internet, voice mail, hair dryers, irons and many other amenities. (rates around $100-$150 per night).

The Inn is surrounded by historic homes, museums, golf, shopping, antique stores, marinas and water-oriented activities. As you walk towards downtown - you'll notice many other friendly neighbors wave from their adorable restored homes. Since the "downtown" is only one mile long, you can walk to everything. You'll love the charming streets and people. So many "pictures" captured in our memory bank…

HAVRE DE GRACE DECOY MUSEUM

Havre de Grace - *215 Giles Street (on the waterfront near Tydings Park) 21078. Phone: (410) 939-3739. www.decoymuseum.com. Hours: Monday-Saturday 10:30am-4:30pm, Sunday Noon-4:00pm Admission: $6.00 adult, $5.00 senior (65+), $3.00 youth (9-18). Note: Each Saturday and Sunday, local carvers provide carving demonstrations to the public in the R. Madison Mitchell Shop, located behind the museum's main facility. Stop by to observe some of the techniques involved in the traditional folk art of decoy-making. This exhibit is included in the price of admission.*

A "please touch" exhibit greets you...

Located on the banks of the historic Susquehanna Flats, the Havre de Grace Decoy Museum houses one of the finest collections of working and decorative Chesapeake Bay decoys ever assembled. Not only exhibits, but

tours and demonstrations are regularly scheduled. The newer areas, by the entrance, have many hands-on exhibits for kids. The museum's main gallery features "What is a Decoy?" A look at the dozens of decoys in this gallery demonstrates that the appearance of any decoy depends upon the species of animal being imitated, the purpose of the

A "coffin box" duck hunter

decoy, the region in which the decoy is carved, and the unique approach of the carver. "What is a Decoy?" also

features a popular diorama that freezes in time a gathering of prominent carvers during an afternoon in the early 1940s. Look for the two-headed duck decoys (part of the scavenger hunt sheet kids can ask for). Compare different styles

Why a two-headed decoy?

and see a recreated workshop setting. "Gunning the Flats" explores the history of waterfowling on the Susquehanna Flats, an area long noted for its bounty of waterfowl. Please touch decoy heads display greets you. What is a body Booting? Or a sinkbox? The town's waterfowling traditions truly make Havre de Grace the "Decoy Capital of the World!"

"Trust me Jenny...
I've got a good aim?"

Exit - 89 (east of I-95)

HAVRE DE GRACE MARITIME MUSEUM

Havre de Grace - *100 Lafayette Street (follow signs to the waterfront, near Tydings Park) 21078. Phone: (410) 939-4800. www.hdgmaritimemuseum. org. Hours: Wednesday-Saturday 10:00am-5:00pm (April - mid October); weekends only (rest of year). Admission: $2.00-$4.00 per person (ages 8+).*

The museum tells the story of the region's rich maritime heritage. Changing exhibits on boating are the mainstay. They have a boat building school on the premises you can observe or tour (Tuesday night is live boat building). Ring the ships' bell or play with real 19th century boating tools. Try using these 200 year old tools to "caulk" the boat cracks yourself. Try casting nets, too. On the North side of the Yacht Basin are the entries to the city's Promenade, a half-mile boardwalk that follows the shoreline and overlooks the confluence of the Susquehanna River and the Chesapeake Bay.

CONCORD POINT LIGHTHOUSE

Havre de Grace - *(follow Rte 155 into town towards riverfront museums. Lafayette & Concord Streets) 21078. Phone: (410) 939-1498. www.concordpointlighthouse. org Hours: Weekends 1:00-5:00pm (May-October).*

The Concord Point light is one of the oldest lighthouses in continual use on the East Coast. It was part of a navigational improvement effort to enhance the safe flow of goods down the Susquehanna River to the ports of Baltimore and Philadelphia. Kids love the giant iron key used to open the lighthouse door. There are only about 35 steps up to the top. Up top is a great view of the Chesapeake Bay. Wander around the light keepers house on the property. Learn about the first keeper who was also a quirky hero of a self-prompted "battle" between British ships and one man, John O'Neill, on shore. When he ran out of cannon balls, he began to use potatoes instead - the first potato gun! On the grounds behind the lighthouse is one of the cannons used by John O'Neill in his near solitary-attempt to defend town.

SKIPJACK MARTHA LEWIS

Havre de Grace - *121 N Union Avenue (boat berthed at Tydings Park) 21078. Phone: (410) 939-4078. www.skipjackmarthalewis.org. Admission: $10.00-15.00 per person. Special themed cruise run $10.00-$30.00 per person. Tours: Public cruises on Thursday, Saturday and Sunday afternoons, including sunset. Theme cruises scheduled each month with a popular kids character on board for Miscellaneous: Martha's Treasure Hunters: There's treasure in them their waters! Children 6-10 will read a map and help find sunken treasure in the Susquehanna Flats. Each camper will be given the opportunity to take the helm as the Marta Lewis is navigated around the Flats in*

All together now...hoist up the sails...

search of the prize. Captain, crew along with the other mates will be on a constant watch for pirates lurking to steal the bounty. Cost $15.00. CRUISES ON HOLD UNTIL SPRING 2015

MARTHA LEWIS is a V-bottom, two sail bateau (skipjack). She is one of the few remaining working dredge boats, that make up the Chesapeake Bay oyster fleet -- the last to fish commercially, under sail, in the United States of America. There was a time when hundreds of wind driven vessels called "Skipjacks" sailed the Chesapeake Bay in search of oysters. Crews were hard working men, pushed to the limits of their endurance, competing for a share of the harvest-challenging the elements while dredging under sail. Those days are gone, some say never to return! However, a rare opportunity exists to experience life aboard a WORKING skipjack. On the public cruises, help the crew as you hear calls like: "Ready on Deck?", "Heave!", and "Helm's A-lee." On Thursday evening cruises, watch the sailboat races. Learn about how fast they dredge, the oyster harvesting peak years, and what a spat is. Even the Chesapeake Bay had Pirates - Oyster Pirates!

Exit - 85 (west of I-95)

RIPKEN STADIUM / IRONBIRDS

Aberdeen - *873 Long Drive (take the MD-22 exit number 85 - towards Aberdeen / Churchville. Keep LEFT at the fork in the ramp. Turn LEFT onto MD-22) 21001. Phone: (410) 297--9292. www.ironbirdsbaseball.com.*

Home of baseball's best known family. Tours of the stadium, which includes the Ripken Museum exhibit, are offered during the Aberdeen Ironbirds off-season (October-May). The New York-Penn League affiliate for the Orioles plays seasonal home games, has a Kids Club, and hosts the Cal Ripken World Series and All-Star Games for the league. The name "IronBird" is a product of two distinct tie-ins that Cal wanted to incorporate into the team's image. "Iron" is a reference to Cal's streak of 2,632 consecutive games played, surpassing the record previously held by Lou Gehrig. Ripken is now known as baseball's all-time "Iron Man." The "Bird" part of the name refers to Cal playing his entire 21-year career in an Orioles uniform.

Exit - 85 (east of I-95)

U.S ARMY ORDNANCE MUSEUM

Aberdeen - *(I-95 exit onto Rte. 22 going towards Aberdeen. Exit Rte. 40 west to Rte. 715 south) 21005. Phone: (410) 278-3602. www.ordmusfound.org. Hours: Daily 9:00am-4:45pm. Closed National Holidays except for Armed Forces, Memorial, Independence and Veterans Days. Admission: Free Day Pass will be issued only at the "Maryland Ave. Gate". This gate is on Rt. 715. The Rt. 22 gate will not issue any passes.*

You can now visit the Ordnance Museum at Aberdeen Proving Ground as a civilian. Inside the museum, you'll find a collection of small arms, artillery, combat vehicles and ammunition. Outside is more impressive at the Proving Ground. Drive the "Mile of Tanks" at the 25 acre Tank & Artillery Park. A park full of real tank trucks is pretty eye-popping for little (and big) guys.

Exit - 82 MILE

MARYLAND HOUSE WELCOME CENTER

Maryland House offers food, fuel, auto repair services, and a traveler information center to motorists. It also includes a full-service business center including phone jacks for portable computers and postal service. Find brochures, maps and other information. Of course, plenty of restrooms inside and areas to relax outside.

Exit - 74 (east of I-95)

GUNPOWDER FALLS STATE PARK / JERUSALEM MILL

Kingsville - *2813 Jerusalem Road (follow state park signs) 21087. Phone: (410) 592-2897. http://dnr2.maryland.gov/publiclands/Pages/central/gunpowder.aspx.*

Gunpowder Falls State Park features numerous scenic areas on 18,000 acres in the Gunpowder River Valley. The park features over 100 miles of trails, trout streams and the historic Village of Jerusalem, an 18th century grist mill company town. A Visitors Center Museum in the town displays artifacts and there's a blacksmith shop and gun factory on the premises. Seasonal Revolutionary and Civil War era living history demonstrations and encampments are held here (www.jerusalemmill.org or 410-877-3560). Nearby

NORTH POINT STATE PARK (in Fort Howard, off Rte. 20, 410-477-0757) features the Defenders' Trail used during the War of 1812. Other park areas include a rail trail, swimming beach, and a marina. Guided trips with local outfitters are available for flatwater and moving water kayaking, canoeing, fishing, catamaran sailing, windsurfing and natural history walks.

Exit - 64 (west of I-95)/ I-695 W

BALTIMORE STREETCAR MUSEUM

Baltimore - *1901 Falls Road (exit I-695 exit 32. Take US 1 south past Penn Station to Falls Road) 21211. Phone: (410) 547-0264. www.baltimorestreetcar. org. Hours: Sunday Noon-5:00pm. Open Saturdays (June-October). Admission: $7.00 adult, $5.00 senior and child (4-11). Family max = $24.00.*

Admission includes: Unlimited rides on original Baltimore streetcars and a guided carhouse tour. Visit Trolley Theatre and view our new 10 minute orientation video, Baltimore and Streetcars, about trolleys and how they built our cities, including, of course, Baltimore. The Trolley Theatre, is a 3/4 scale trolley model that you can sit in,

HAMPTON NATIONAL HISTORIC SITE

Towson - *535 Hampton Lane (I 695) eastbound or westbound: Take Exit 27B, Dulaney Valley Road northbound) 21286. www.nps.gov/hamp. Phone: (410) 823-1309. Hours: VISITOR CENTER OPEN: 10:00am-4:00pm Thursday-Sunday except Thanksgiving, Christmas, and New Year's Day. Admission: FREE. Tours: Explore the farm with a Ranger. A forty minute presentation including visit to worker's quarters. Tours offered several times per day. Educators: lesson plans - www.nps.gov/hamp/forteachers/index.htm*

The self-guided tour of this farm and grounds includes original slave quarters that tell the story of the family who lived here for more than 150 years, as well as slaves and indentured servants. Scenes from Hampton's past include a colonial merchant shipper amassing thousands of acres of property along Maryland's Chesapeake shore; indentured servants casting molten iron into cannons and ammunition for the Revolutionary army; and enslaved people loading barrels of grain, iron, and timber onto merchant ships bound for Europe that would return with luxury goods.

Exit - 64 (east of I-95)/ I-695 S

MARYLAND AVIATION MUSEUM, GLENN L MARTIN

Baltimore - 701 Wilson Point Road, Hanger 5 at Martin Airport (exit 36 Southeast Blvd to Eastern Blvd. Heading northeast to airport) 21220. Phone: (410) 682-6122. www.mdairmuseum.org. Hours: Wednesday-Saturday 11:00am-3:00pm. It is always best to confirm open dates in advance in case of changes. Admission: $1.00-$3.00 (age 6+).

The site is dedicated to the promotion, preservation, and documentation of aviation and space history in the state of Maryland. Outside planes with names like Thunderchief, Thunderflash, Phantom, Sabor and Voodoo entice the kids to look around some

Exit - 57 (west of I-95)

URBAN PIRATES, BALTIMORE CITY

Baltimore - 913 S Ann Street, Thames Street, Fells Point (follow O'Donnell St and merge onto Boston St. Slight left on Aliceanna St. Left on Ann Street to pier) 21224. Phone: (410) 327-8378. www.urbanpirates.com. Admission: $22.00 general. $12.00 children 2 and under. Tours: tours take place during the weekends in May, September & October and everyday from Memorial Day through Labor Day. Reservations are required.

Dress, talk and tie ropes like a pirate; fight enemies with water cannons; navigate treacherous waters; and discover hidden treasures during an interactive excursion around the Inner Harbor on Fearless. The 48' long ship with a 17-foot beam and 3-foot draft can accommodate up to 49 passengers. Arrive 30 minutes before your cruise to check in and allow the crew to transform you into pirates with costumes, tattoos and face painting. Remember, pirates are not afraid to get a little wet. If you prove yourself worthy being a member of the crew, you get a share of the booty and take home a few trinkets from the treasure chest. Dance a jig and sing sea shanties all the way home…

Exit - 56 (west of I-95)

FREDERICK DOUGLASS - ISAAC MYERS MARITIME PARK

Baltimore - 1417 Thames Street, Fells Point (near the intersection of Caroline St)

21231. Phone: (410) 685-0295. www.douglassmyers.org. Hours: Monday-Friday 10:00am-4:00pm, Saturday-Sunday Noon-4pm. Admission: $2.00-$5.00 (age 6+).

This park features a re-creation of the first marine shipyard and marine railway operated by African Americans, as well as the Sugar House, the oldest remaining industrial building on the waterfront. Frederick Douglass lived in Baltimore for a time and worked in the maritime trades (before he became a famous abolitionist) and Isaac Myers founded the shipyard and the first black maritime unions. Baltimore was home to one of the largest populations of free blacks before the Civil War, many of whom worked here. After the Civil War, other ethnic workers asked not to work with Blacks and so many were fired - they needed work and new, black owned shipyards were established for a time. Wander through a once busy shipyard railway and a deep-water pier; monuments to Douglass and Myers; and exhibits concerning African American maritime history including "pretend" stations where the kids are put to work.

Exit - 55 (west of I-95)

FORT MCHENRY NATIONAL MONUMENT & HISTORIC SHRINE

Baltimore - *End of E. Fort Avenue (Exit 55 Key Highway and follow Fort McHenry signs on Key Highway to Lawrence Street) 21230. www.nps.gov/fomc. Phone: (410) 962-4290. Hours: Daily 8:00am-5:00pm. Closed: Thanksgiving Day, December 25 and January 1. Admission: Entrance fee to the historic fort is $7.00 for adults 16 and over. Children 15 and under are admitted free of charge. Educators: a new, and wonderfully organized, Lesson Plan is available at this link: www.nps.gov/history/nr/twhp/wwwlps/ lessons/137FOMC/137FOMC.htm. It sets the stage with coordinated readings, images and activities that delve into the "Theme of our Nation."*

This is The Birthplace of the American National Anthem!

Fort McHenry National Monument and Historic Shrine, a star-shaped fort best known for its role in the War of 1812, when its successful defense against the British bombardment inspired Francis Scott Key to write the words that became our national anthem. "O say can you see, by the dawn's early light," a large red, white and blue banner? "Whose broad stripes and bright stars...were so gallantly streaming!" over the star-shaped Fort McHenry during the Battle of Baltimore, September 13-14, 1814. Watch the orientation film and look at the day's calendar of interpretive programs (in season). The movie is wonderfully done with a grand interactive patriotic

just like GIANT
bottle rockets...

finish! See the long stick rockets that glared red in the sky or the huge cannonball bombs designed to explode in air. Regardless of the "rockets red glare, the bombs bursting in air" the defenders of Fort McHenry stopped the British advance on Baltimore and helped to preserve the United States of America – "the land of the free and the home of the brave." Within the actual fort you may enter some rooms that have visuals and audio plays or an electric map. The most special kid-friendly Defenders Room has unique hands-on activity. Because soldiers here were so close to the harbor and town, they could purchase seafood, chocolate and spices. Touch and smell everything they ate and then try on some very authentic looking apparel and be a soldier for a moment. Following the Battle of Baltimore during the War of 1812, the fort never again came under attack. However, it remained an active military post off and on for the next 100 years.

BALTIMORE MUSEUM OF INDUSTRY

Baltimore - 1415 Key Hwy, Inner Harbor (take Key Hwy to 1400 block) 21230. Phone: (410) 727-4808. www.thebmi.org. Hours: Tuesday-Sunday 10:00am-4:00pm, Admission: $12.00 adult, $9.00 senior, $7.00 student/child.

Step back in time to the Industrial Revolution at the Baltimore Museum of Industry, with its vividly recreated workshops on machining, printing, garment-making and metalworking. Walk through an 1886 bank building; step into the 1910 Bunting Pharmacy where Noxzema was invented and experience the local innovations that touched the world - from the world's first disposable bottle cap to America's first umbrella company. Students become garment workers and hand sewers and learn about life in a turn-of-the-century garment shop. As they work, they hear about labor activist "Mother Jones" and her crusade to rid the world of abominable working conditions for children. Learn Baltimore's role as one of the busiest and most important ports in America. See a replica of an early dock and dockmaster's shed. Walk through the original 1865 Platt

Oyster Cannery structure, the only surviving cannery building. Look outside and see the coal-fired S.S. Baltimore, the only operating steam tugboat on the East Coast. To get the best value it is better to visit on weekends or part of a group tour so the kids can actually dress up and participate in the re-enacting areas like the cannery and clothing factory.

Exit - 55 (west of I-95)

AMERICAN VISIONARY ART MUSEUM

Baltimore - 800 Key Hwy, Inner Harbor (Key Hwy for 1.5 miles to corner of Covington & Key) 21230. Phone: (410) 244-1900. www.avam.org. Hours: Tuesday-Sunday 10:00am-6:00pm. Admission: $15.95 adult, $13.95 senior (60+), $9.95 student/child (age 7+). Metered parking nearby.

This museum only exhibits art produced by folks who have no formal training (farmers, housewives, doctors, auto mechanics...you get the picture). Between the four week themed temporary installations, you can gain access to the permanent collection on Level 1 for $2.00 a person (vs. much more for special exhibits) or just go in and shop around the Eye Shop for artsy gifts. The Giant Whirligig & Sculpture Plaza is Baltimore's most beloved outdoor sculptural landmark. Fifty-five feet tall, this brilliant, multicolored wind-powered sculpture was created in the central plaza as a salute to Federal Hill and "Life, Liberty & The Pursuit of Happiness" by 76 year-old mechanic, farmer and visionary artist, Vollis Simpson. Free to visit anytime. The Sculpture Plaza functions as the ground level connector to Federal Hill and Baltimore's Inner Harbor.

MARYLAND SCIENCE CENTER

Baltimore, Inner Harbor - 601 Light Street (Key Hwy north towards downtown. a couple of blocks from Inner Harbor at corner of Key Hwy & Light St) 21230. Phone: (410) 545-5927. www.mdsci.org. Hours: Monday-Friday 10:00am-5:00pm, Saturday 10:00am-6:00pm, Sunday 11:00am-5:00pm. Extended summer hours. Closed Mondays in the fall and winter. The IMAX theater is open after hours for evening shows; the Observatory is open after hours on Fridays for Stargazing Fridays; and the Kids Room closes one hour prior to museum closing Saturdays through Thursdays and two hours prior to close Fridays. Admission: $19.00=$21.00 (ages 3+). Note: Beakers Café & Science Store. IMAX theater and Planetarium shows extra fee.

Dinosaurs. Planet Earth. The Human body. Outer space. Chesapeake Bay life. The Kids Room (under age 8 play area). Science Sir Isaac Newton never imagined. At the Maryland Science Center you'll find three floors of demonstrations to exercise your imagination and challenge your mind. See exciting combustible reactions, eye-boggling optical illusions and learn about lasers. Hands-on exhibits include a voyage through the human body and learning how microbes work for us. Traveling exhibits abound, so there's always something new see and learn. Real time connections to real time science. So much to see and do—all in a Please Touch environment. Live Maryland crustaceans and their fellow Chesapeake citizens inhabit the Blue Crab water exhibit. A kinetic, energetic, hands-on exhibit powered by you and looking at space by 3-D or satellite image.

BALTIMORE MUSEUM OF ART

Baltimore - Art Museum Drive at N Charles and 31st Sts. (head north on Key Hwy. Right onto Charles heading north of downtown) 21218. Phone: (410) 396-7100. www.artbma.org. Hours: Wednesday-Friday 10:00am-5:00pm, weekends 11:00am until 6:00pm. Admission: FREE.

Home to a wonderful collection of Matisse, Picasso and 19th century and contemporary art, plus a scenic sculpture garden. Three different self-guided kits invite kids to dress up, sketch, or sing their way through the galleries; available Thursdays, Saturdays, and Sundays 11:00-3:00pm. A Grand Legacy Family Guide will help you explore five centuries of European art. Matisse for Kids Guide is a fun way to discover the Museum's renowned Cone Collection. During extended evening hours, enjoy family-friendly activities including music, performances, guided tours, hands-on workshops, and more.

Exit - 53 (west of I-95)/ I-395 N/ I-83 N

MARYLAND ZOO IN BALTIMORE

Baltimore - Druid Hill Park (Continue straight on I-83 North. Take Exit 7 (West) to Druid Park Lake Drive - follow signs to the Zoo) 21217. Phone: (410) 366-LION. www.marylandzoo.org. Hours: Daily 10:00am-4:00pm. Extended summer weekend hours. Closed only Thanksgiving and Christmas. Admission: $12.50-$17.50. Reduced winter pricing. Parking is free.

Journey from Africa to the Arctic on this wooded, 180-acre setting in Druid Hill Park. Otters, polar bears, bats and even skunk are here. Plus the regular lions, tigers and bears. A free tram system transports visitors from the main gate to the zoo's central plaza. Another highlight is the Polar Bear Watch, a state-of-the-art exhibit about life on the edge of the Arctic, featuring an area where guests can watch Alaska and Magnet, the zoo's polar bears cavorting in and out of the water. Children will create lifelong memories as they hop across lily pads, perch in an oriole's nest, play on a giant barn silo slide, a tree slide or groom friendly goats at the hands-on Children's Zoo. Look for baby chimps or maybe a new elephant. There's also giraffe feeding stations and the return of the Zoo's flamingos.

Exit - 53 (west of I-95)/ I-395 N

HARBORPLACE

Baltimore, Inner Harbor - *200 East Pratt Street, Inner Harbor (Light Street and Pratt Street) 21202. Phone: (410) 332-4191. www.harborplace.com.*

Indoor and outdoor eateries, shopping (many souvenirs related to Crabs and sports) and live entertainment on the waterfront.

Try PHILLIPS SEAFOOD on the edge of the harbor serving extensive seafood menus, plus sandwiches, beef and chicken entrees. A wide variety of offerings and friendly staff make this busy Baltimore institution a great place for first-time visitors to get acquainted with the city's number one culinary attraction: the Blue Crab. The tasty crustaceans are served in many forms: Crab Imperial, crab dip, crab cakes. Authentic Maryland Style Seafood is tradition at Phillips so come prepared to feast! Festival Buffet. (www.phillipsfoods.com).

Either that, or BALTIMORE'S WATER TAXI (www.thewatertaxi.com) can provide water transport to more than 30 attractions and neighborhoods. Look for the blue and white boats. One price for all-day unlimited on-off service. $5.00-$10.00 per person.

BALTIMORE SPIRIT CRUISES

Baltimore, Inner Harbor - *561 Light Street (follow signs for HarborPlace, waterside) 21202. www.spiritcruises.com/baltimore. Phone: (410) 727-3113 or (800) 695-LADY. Tours: 75-minute interactive tour, the only Inner Harbor sightseeing cruise from the Inner Harbor past Ft. McHenry and back. Kick-back and relax as you take in the sites and enjoy an animated narration of Baltimore's rich history. They will give you an insider's view of Baltimore's historic places and the world-famous Inner Harbor. $16.00-$18.00 (May-October). Lunches run around $43.00-$45.00, Dinners around $60.00-$70.00. Children under 11 are about half price.*

They cruise just about everyday with lively lunch, dinner and special event cruises. Also, an one-hour scenic, narrated tour is offered. An original Baltimore cruise line, they offer the most themed tours in Maryland. If you love Maryland blue crab, try their weekend Crab Fest cruises. Or, for the kids, Easter Brunch with Bunny or Christmas Brunch with Santa.

HYATT REGENCY BALTIMORE

Baltimore - *300 Light Street, Inner Harbor (follow signs to HarborPlace/Inner Harbor. Directly across street from HarborPlace) 21202. Phone: (410) 528-1234. www.hyattregencybaltimore.com.*

Perfectly located, this Four-Diamond Inner Harbor hotel offers a luxurious haven in the midst of the city's premier attractions with many rooms providing an excellent Harbor View. Stroll to Camden Yards, the National Aquarium or a skywalk to HarborPlace, and then return to the downtown Baltimore harbor hotel to enjoy features like pillow top beds, flat screen TVs, summer sundeck and outdoor pool, tennis, or shoot some hoops on a rooftop deck. Several styles of restaurants are on the premises. This property is often part of Baltimore Inner Harbor family packages.

USS CONSTELLATION

Baltimore, Inner Harbor - *301 E. Pratt Street, Pier 1, Inner Harbor (follow signs to HarborPlace, just on other side, waterside) 21202. www.constellation.org. Phone: (410) 539-1797. Hours: Daily 10:00am-4:30pm. Extended to 5:30pm (May-October). Admission: $11.00 adult, $9.00 senior (60+) and military, $5.00 child (6-14). Add just a few dollars on to see all of the maritime ships in the Inner Harbor piers.*

Built in 1854, this is the last all-sail warship built by the U.S. Navy and the only Civil War era naval vessel still afloat. History comes "alive" with hourly hands-on demonstrations and self-guided audio tours. Before you head up the stairs to the ship, be sure to get a complimentary audio tour wand. This will help guide you and help you to learn more about what life was like on

Nearly 200' long and 300 crew aboard... it was a 19th Century floating city!

board. Using a "Youth" or "Adult" number system, you follow a modern girl through the ship. Discover how sailors lived on board - officers in their own cubbies and shipmen on hundreds of hammocks hanging from the ceiling - no, not for naps - for good, swaying sleep before the next watch. What's a Powder Monkey? Learn how this mighty sailing machine was powered, propelled and controlled. What technology did they have and what did they eat? Interactives include steering the ship or ringing the loud ship's bell to tell time. Listen for the cannon firings!

Exit - 53 (west of I-95)/ I-395 N

BALTIMORE MARITIME MUSEUM

Baltimore, Inner Harbor - *802 S. Caroline Street (follow signs to Inner Harbor & Piers 3 & 5) 21231. www.historicships.org. Phone: (410) 783-1490 or (877) NHCPORT. Hours: Daily 10:00am - 5:00pm. Extended Hours in the Summer. Admission: $11.00 adult, $9.00 senior (60+), $5.00 youth (age 6-14). Best to combine (a few extra dollars) with two - four ships in the Inner Harbor piers... including the USS Constitution.*

The US Coast Guard Cutter Taney, US Submarine Torsk, Lightship

Chesapeake, and the Seven Foot Knoll Lighthouse tell a story of American power and technology. Over sixty years ago, two of the ships of the Baltimore Maritime Museum were involved in events

that changed the history of the world. US Coast Guard Cutter Taney was an amphibious command ship for the Battle of Okinawa, one of the bloodiest battles in US Naval history. Taney was called to battle stations ninety-nine times in forty-five days and was at the center of the some of the fiercest action in this crucial campaign. By virtue of her 50 year career, she is the last surviving warship afloat today from the 7 December 1941 Japanese attack on Hawaii. Many can sense the somberness of an event that occurred on the other side of the nation

A lighthouse ship?

- just looking at it.

On August 14th 1945, the USS Torsk fired a torpedo which hit home, sinking a Japanese coastal patrol vessel. This dramatic moment was to become the last naval action of World War II, as the Cease Fire was declared the next day.

The US Lighthouse Service first assigned Lightship 116 to the Fenwick Island Shoal (DE) Station from 1930-33; after that assignment she marked the entrance to Chesapeake Bay. Crew accommodations included two-man staterooms for the enlisted men, a crew's mess, and an electrically powered galley and refrigerator unit (a major advancement for 1930).

The Seven Foot Knoll Lighthouse, the oldest surviving screw-pile lighthouse, was built as an aid to navigation on the Chesapeake Bay. All of these actual pieces of history are docked together at the Inner Harbor - a convenient way to witness early 1900s sea life on the Chesapeake and American ocean waters.

WORLD TRADE CENTER "TOP OF THE WORLD"

Baltimore, Inner Harbor - *401 E. Pratt Street (follow signs for HarborPlace exits to World Trade Center, 27th floor) 21202. www.viewbaltimore.org. Phone: (410) 837-VIEW.   Hours: Daily 10:00am-6:00pm(spring, summer). Some longer summertime hours. Wednesday-Sunday hours (mid September thru mid-November). Friday-Sunday only (winter). Admission: $3.00-$5.00 (ages 3+).*

Start your visit to the city at the Top of the World Observation Level, where the beauty of the resurgent city will unfold before you - from all sides - harbor and downtown. Enjoy a spectacular panoramic view of Baltimore's skyline, as well as photo-map guides featuring local attractions, hotels and neighborhoods.

Baltimore's World Trade Center is a must-see for anyone visiting Charm City. Its a good place to get a sense of the city. The observation level also contains exhibits about Baltimore and its economic renaissance. The World Trade Center is the tallest pentagonal building in the world. You will have a wonderful view of the city from an elevation of 423 feet.

"Top of the World" to ya...

Exit - 53 (west of I-95)/ I-395 N

NATIONAL AQUARIUM IN BALTIMORE

Baltimore, Inner Harbor - *501 East Pratt Street, Pier 3, Inner Harbor (I-95 to I-395 to Pratt Street, turn right) 21202. Phone: (410) 576-3800. www.aqua.org. Hours: Open daily 9am-6:30pm and Fridays until 8:00pm with seasonal extended morning and evening hours. Admission: $34.95 adult, 29.95 senior (60+) and $21.95 child (3-11). Dolphin Show and 4D Immersion Theater extra. Note: for safety, strollers must be checked; free front-and backpacks are available to carry babies. Educators: Click Teachers icon, then educators booklets for .PDF versions of activity sheets on dozens of grade appropriate topics. Doing a report on water creatures? Download fact sheets under Students icon.*

Take a short walk across the promenade from the World Trade Center to the National Aquarium where stingrays (look for butterfly rays), sharks and sea turtles will greet you on the first level to start your adventure...up close! You

might visit during a feeding of sharks. Each exhibit brings new surprises, including a blackwater Amazon River forest with schools of dazzling tropical fish, giant river turtles, dwarf caimans, and pygmy marmosets - the smallest species of monkey in the world. And in the Upland Tropical Rain Forest, keen observers may spot colorful birds, golden lion tamarins (monkeys), two-toed sloths, red-bellied piranhas, iguanas and even poison dart frogs, as they wander on pathways through the dense tropical foliage. The 8-minute intro film in Australia Animal Planet is very helpful for kids to learn differences in extreme geography. Australia Wild Extremes has fish that shoot water from their mouths, an encounter with the Outback's deadliest snake or the sound of the 35-foot cascading indoor waterfall. And don't forget the shark ring and giggling at the dolphin show at the adjoining Marine Mammal Pavilion. Trek across Maryland's varied terrain in the Waterfront Park outdoors.

REGINALD F. LEWIS MUSEUM OF MARYLAND AFRICAN AMERICAN HISTORY & CULTURE

Baltimore - *830 East Pratt Street, just east of Inner Harbor (follow signs for Inner Harbor-corner to World Trade Center. 21202. www.AfricanAmericanCulture.org. Phone: (443) 263-1800. Hours: Wednesday-Saturday 10:00am-5:00pm, Sunday Noon-5:00pm. Admission: $6.00-$8.00 (age 6+).*

See 400 years of progress in one day. The African American experience, from tobacco and ironworking to education and law, there is not an industry or profession that has not been touched by the accomplishments of African Americans. . . Often against incredible odds. Discover how ancient-African skills influenced laborers here. Try your hand at some of the most difficult occupations, including caulking and the art of oystering. Meet several families and follow their lives from slavery to freedom and equality. Listen to historical music. Get to know famous African Americans including Frederick Douglass and Harriet Tubman. Follow Benjamin Banneker, Eubie Blake, Joyce Scott and others as they guide you through understanding African American traditions of music, art, sculpture, storytelling and invention.

FLAG HOUSE & STAR SPANGLED BANNER MUSEUM

Baltimore - *844 E Pratt Street (Little Italy, 2 blocks east of Inner Harbor) 21202. Phone: (410) 837-1793. www.flaghouse.org. Hours: Tuesday-Saturday 10:00am-4:00pm. Admission: $6.00-$8.00 per person. Tours: Guided tours last approximately 45 minutes but they are happy to adapt to your schedule. Just let them know when you arrive.*

Mary Pickersgill's flag still survives and now hangs at the Smithsonian Institution's National Museum of American History

A museum dedicated to the story of Mary Young Pickersgill who made the enormous 30 x 42-foot Star-Spangled Banner that flew over Fort McHenry during the War of 1812 and inspired Francis Scott Key to write the poem that became our National Anthem. The new Star-Spangled Banner Museum, adjacent to the Flag House, houses an orientation theatre film and exhibits on the American Flag, Mary and the War of 1812. The unique feature of the museum is the Great Flag Window, a glass wall the same size, color and design of the original Star-Spangled Banner!

Visitors to the Flag House are given a personalized tour of the 18th-century home of Mary Young Pickersgill. You'll learn how Mary Pickersgill, a widowed flag maker and mother, made the flag. How do you hand sew a flag so large? The 90 pound flag made of wool bunting was recreated by local ladies and laid on display in the parlor to help you imagine the task these 1800 era women undertook. As you tour, you'll realize how contemporary Mary

and her family were for their time. Who would guess their large commissioned project would inspire patriotism even now! An American must visit.

Discovery Gallery is a hands-on room where the kids dress up and then color their own Star Spangled flag to take home. Cook for your family at a replica of the Flag House kitchen, design your own flag and fly it on the gallery's flagpole, tell a story at the puppet stage or try games and toys from long ago.

Exit - 53 (west of I-95)/ I-395 N

PORT DISCOVERY, THE CHILDREN'S MUSEUM

Baltimore - *33 Market Place (MLK Blvd. To right on Pratt. Follow signs to corner of Lombard Street and Market Place) 21202. www.portdiscovery.org. Phone: (410) 727-8120. Hours: Tuesday-Friday: 9:30am-4:30pm, Saturday: 10:00am-5:00pm, Sunday: Noon-5:00pm. Summertime open Mondays, too. The Museum is closed Thanksgiving Day, Christmas Day, and on Mondays during the months of October through May, except during select Maryland Public School holidays. Admission: $14.50 (age 2+). Note: Unlike most kids museums, this one is stroller accessible throughout. Concerned about safety? The treehouse structure is clear and steps surround it so you can follow your kids with your eyes or feet. Exits have family check-out station bracelets, too.*

Port Discovery, the Children's Museum in Baltimore, offers three floors of interactive, educational exhibits and programs for children ages 2-10 years old. Use your problem solving and critical thinking skills to climb, slide and glide your way through this three-story urban treehouse. Visit the farm area and look under interactive hanging signs to learn all about life on the farm, including how milk is made, or what a fowl is. Barter, sell or trade your new crops at the roadside market. Shop for farm-fresh fruits and vegetables and then use the giant crane to move hay bales from the market to the train for transport. Every kid enjoys the Wonders of Water as they pump, squirt or float objects through a maze of streams, dams and waterfalls (rain coats and crocs are provided). Creative? Act, puppet or design skits or artwork. Step right up to a realistic gas station where you can pack the car, check the tires' air-pressure and fill the tank. Uncover secret hieroglyphics that provide clues to solving the mystery inside the tomb. Use giant sized MegaLogs to build anything or take some quiet time to read a story. Play hostess, waitress, cook or cashier in a realistic diner. Pick up clues using your detective-sharp research, literacy and problem solving skills to find out what happened to the missing members of the Baffled family. P.S. Don't forget to crawl through the sink, it could lead you to clues on the other side!

WALTERS ART MUSEUM

Baltimore - *600 N Charles Street, entrance on Centre St. (MLK Blvd., right onto Druid Hill which becomes Centre St to Cathedral) 21201. Phone: (410) 547-9000. www.thewalters.org. Hours: Wednesday-Sunday 10:00am-5:00pm. Admission: FREE for Permanent Collection. FREEBIES: Waltee's Quest game online. Waltee Club Card kids club. Look for ArtCarts games and books on weekends and during school breaks.*

The Walters Art Museum offers a variety of extraordinary programs where you can make cool art, see live performances, play dress up, or tour the museum with a kid-friendly passport designed to foster discovery and engagement (scavenger hunt or audio tours). Listen to lively storytelling in the galleries during festivals, watch a family-friendly video in the cozy Family Art Center, create a piece of original artwork during drop-in hours, celebrate your birthday, and earn a scout patch. Their permanent collection includes Egyptian Mummies and medieval armor. The Palace of Wonders features paintings, artifacts and furniture all arranged as they might have been in the home of wealthy European collector during old time periods.

MARYLAND HISTORICAL SOCIETY MUSEUMS

Baltimore - *201 W Monument (MLK Blvd. Right on Druid Hill. Left on Park Ave. Left on Monument) 21201. Phone: (410) 683-3750. www.mdhs.org. Hours: Wednesday-Saturday 10:00am-5:00pm, Sunday Noon-5pm. Admission: Varies by museum, generally $6.00-$9.00 per person (ages 3+). On the first Thursday of every month, the MdHS offers free museum admission.*

Discover the people and events that shaped the state of Maryland. The bombardment of Fort McHenry, Francis Scott Key's original manuscript of the "Star Spangled Banner", hear the stories of civil rights activists, and the difficulties and successes of colonists. Don't miss Tench Tilghman's Revolutionary War uniform and Eubie Blake's eyeglasses.

MARITIME EXHIBIT: The museum tells the story of the notorious Privateer Clipper ships of the War of 1812 and the rich history of the town's ports. Privateers, shipbuilders, immigrants, merchants, and sailors sought their fortunes in this waterfront community, home to the world-famous Baltimore clipper schooners. These vessels, known then as pilot-boat schooners, were the fastest in the world and carried cargoes both legal and illegal. On a single voyage in 1814, one of the most famous captains, Thomas Boyle, captured 14 British vessels and 48 prisoners, and returned with cargo worth over $100,000.

BALTIMORE CIVIL WAR MUSEUM: 601 President St. (410) 385-5188. Daily 10:00am-5:00pm. The Baltimore Civil War Museum, housed in the 1849 train station - one of the oldest in the nation - examines the events of that day and highlights Maryland's divided loyalties and critical role as a border state during the war. Learn the story of the first deaths of the Civil War at the Pratt Street Riot. In addition, visitors will hear the story of the stations important role in the escape of enslaved African Americans via the Underground Railroad.

LACROSSE MUSEUM AND NATIONAL HALL OF FAME

Baltimore - *113 W. University Pkwy. (stay left past Ravens Stadium & Oriole Park. Right onto Pratt. Left onto Charles. Left onto Univ.) 21210. Phone: (410) 233-6882. www.uslacrosse.org. Hours: Weekdays 10:00am-2:00pm. Admission: $2.00-$3.00 per person (age 5 +).*

This modern museum spans the history of lacrosse from Native American origins to modern times. Relive the origins of America's oldest sport. View the all-time greats of lacrosse in the beautiful Hall of Fame Gallery and study their outstanding accomplishments through state-of-the-art computer interactives, striking sculptures, vintage equipment and uniforms, and ancient artifacts. Capture the thrill of playing lacrosse during the multimedia show "Lacrosse: The Spirit Lives" and historical documentary "More than a Game: A History of Lacrosse."

MD & D.C.

NATIONAL GREAT BLACKS IN WAX MUSEUM

Baltimore - *1601-03 E North Avenue (395 north onto South MLK Blvd. East onto E. Baltimore St and quickly north onto SR-2. East onto US1) 21213. Phone: (410) 563-7809. www.greatblacksinwax.org. Hours: Tuesday-Saturday 9:00am-5:00pm, Sunday Noon-5:00pm. Summers open Monday also. Open until 6:00pm (March thru mid-October). Admission: $11.00-$13.00 (age 3+).*

This unique museum is the first one of wax in Baltimore, Maryland and the first wax museum of African American history in the nation. The museum houses more than 100 life-size and lifelike wax figures presented in dramatic and historical scenes, and takes you through the pages of time with wax figures featuring special lighting, sound effects and animation. Harriet Tubman, Benjamin Banneker and Billie Holiday, as well as many other national figures, chronicle the history of African people from around the globe. The experience is highlighted by a dramatic walk through a replica of a slave ship complete with Middle Passage history. Visitors enter the cramped hold of a slave ship replica to witness a story of struggle, survival, and triumph. Be sensitive to your kids response to this moving exhibit as it is very realistic and heart-wrenching.

Exit - 53 (west of I-95)/ I-395 N

B & O RAILROAD MUSEUM

Baltimore - *901 West Pratt Street (I-395 exit to ML King St. to Pratt St, west a couple of blocks) 21223. Phone: (410) 752-2490. www.borail.org. Hours: Monday-Saturday 10:00am-4:00pm, Sunday 11:00am-4:00pm. Train rides are offered Wednesday through Sunday, April through December and weekends in January. Admission: $16.00 adult, $14.00 senior (60+), $10.00 child (2-12). Train rides $2-$3.00 extra. Note: A café is on the premises as well as a delightful, large gift shop.*

The world's first telegraph line was erected between Baltimore and Washington, D.C., in 1844. Baltimore's Mount Clare Station, which was built in 1830 as the first railroad station in the country, was the receiving point of Samuel Morse's famed "What hath God

Baltimore & Ohio Railroad Pioneers

wrought" message. Today the station is the B&O Railroad Museum, a great place to learn about the history of the railroad that brought fame and fortune to Baltimore and which earned immortality on the Monopoly board! Ride the FIRST MILE of track in America, see them restoring old trains, learn the simple science of locomotion, get caught up in railroad flicks, and get a great view of the newly restored giant Roundhouse (the slumber house). The 20-minute train ride (just the right length for antsy kids) has interesting narrative accompanied by travel folk music. Younger kids marvel at the operating 60 foot HO gauge model railroad outside. The model railroad is a cute way for little engineers to push buttons to hear train whistles and horns or hearing the conductor shout "all aboard." There are several trains you can board. Some are unusual - how was the spiked Clearance Car used? What a wonderful and incredibly historical train attraction!

Exit - 52 (west of I-95)

ORIOLE PARK AT CAMDEN YARDS

Baltimore - *333 W Camden Street (follow Russell Street to Camden Yards signs) 21201. http://baltimore.orioles.mlb.com/bal/ballpark/tours.jsp. Phone: (410) 685-9800.*

The famous park is home to the American League Orioles. Take A Stroll Through Oriole Park at Camden Yards On A Ballpark Tour! (by appointment, $6.00-$9.00) Daily times during regular season - schedule varies for game days. Come see Camden Yards from a whole new perspective! Enjoy the charm of the ballpark from club level suites, the press levels, and even the Orioles dugout!

SPORTS LEGENDS @ CAMDEN YARDS

Baltimore - *301 W Camden Street (follow Russell St. to Oriole Park) 21201. www.baberuthmuseum.org. Phone: (410) 727-1539. Hours: Daily, except Mondays 10:00am-5:00pm. Open later in the summer and Oriole or Raven game nights. Admission: $8.00 adult, $6.00 senior, $4.00 child (3-12). Discount combo tickets with Babe Ruth BP. Educators: Pre-visit Activities downloads click on Education, then Educational Programs online.*

Sports Legends is located in historic Camden Station passenger terminus at the gateway to Oriole Park. Every fan has favorite memories from attending sporting events, and in these videos and exhibits, fans remember the great plays, great games, and great players of Maryland sports, plus what makes going to a game such a special part of the sports experience. Walk through

a simulated rail station terminal into the theatre. The comical "Lucky Harry" intro video is really cute. Then, Babe welcomes you to his gallery and famous "point" game. Interactives throughout include: Make a call to the Bullpen; sit on the bus to a game in the Negro Leagues; sit on the bench watching a Little League game; check your stance; listen to a post-game pep talk; try on actual official uniforms; radio call a game; go behind the scenes of a ball field pre-game; block

"Photo ops" with sports heros...

the shot; catch like Berry; and get the "call" up for Johnny Unitas. The Colts, the Ravens, the Orioles and college teams are all here in spirit to learn about. Probably the most interactive sports museum we've ever seen!

Exit - 52 (west of I-95)

GEPPI'S ENTERTAINMENT MUSEUM

Baltimore - *Camden Station (take Russell St north towards signs for Camden Yards) 21201. Phone: (410) 427-9438. www.geppismuseum.com. Admission: $10.00 adult, $9.00 senior(55+), $7.00 student (5-18). Special game Day reduced admission. Hours: Tuesday - Sunday 10:00am-6:00pm.*

On TV and radio, in the papers and comic books - even toy stores - pop culture has performed magic for years. This new museum features colorful, chronologically arranged displays that explore 230 years of American life. From rare toys and antique advertising to comic books, movie posters and animation, the journey through history takes visitors from the late 1700s right up to today. Look for famous characters like Superman, Spiderman and Batman. Each chronological period highlighted in the museum is anchored by a centerpiece exhibit representing a historically significant character in pop culture.

BABE RUTH BIRTHPLACE

Baltimore - *216 Emory Street (Russell St. north. Left on Portland, right on Emory) 21230. Phone: (410) 727-1539. www. baberuthmuseum.org. Hours: Daily, except Mondays 10:00am-5:00pm. Open later summers and nights of Oriole or Ravens games. Admission: $3.00-$6.00 (age 3+). Discount combo tickets with Sports Legends.*

The Babe Ruth Birthplace is located just three blocks west of Camden Station (follow the 60 painted baseballs along the sidewalk). George Herman "Babe" Ruth was born February 6, 1895 on Emory Street, a Baltimore row house that is now just a long fly ball from Oriole Park at Camden Yards. The property was leased by Babe's grandfather, Pius Schamberger, who made his living as an upholsterer. The Baltimore Orioles signed Ruth to his first pro contract. Some of the priceless artifacts the Babe Ruth Museum holds in its collections: a nearly-complete team set of 1914 International League Baltimore Orioles baseball cards (including the rookie card of a 19-year-old pitcher named George Ruth, Jr.) or a baseball bat given to Ruth by Shoeless Joe Jackson sometime between 1915 and 1916. This thick-handled, 38 3/4 ounces of baseball history is the only one known to exist — a game-used bat shared by Shoeless Joe and the Babe.

NATIONAL MUSEUM OF DENTISTRY

Baltimore - *31 S Greene Street (MD 295 to downtown, exit ML King Blvd. Right on Baltimore, right on Greene) 21201. Phone: (410) 706-7461. www.dentalmuseum.org. Hours: The museum is open to visitors by appointment only. If it's just your family, ask to tag along with a group tour. Admission: $7.00 for Admission and Audio Tour. $3.00-$5.00 each for Seniors (60+), college students, and children (ages 3-18).*

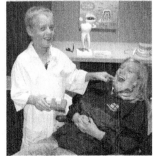

This won't hurt a bit Jenny...?

Discover the power of a healthy smile at this Smithsonian affiliate. The infamous Doc Holliday was a student at the Baltimore College of Dental Surgery, founded in 1840 as the first dental school in the world. An appropriate place, then, for the National Museum of Dentistry, a fabulous interactive facility that showcases the evolution of dentistry. Interactives include: Guess the Smile, Amazing Feats - using teeth to write, to waterski, to pull, to paint; Mouth Power - meet Mouthy and take up a tooth chair to pretend dentistry. Want to know the history of the tooth fairy? What about a whole room devoted to Spit? Modern-day forensics feature the section explaining how DNA in teeth can be used to identify missing persons and solve criminal cases. Among the pieces in its collection are George Washington's dentures (no, they weren't wooden; they were ivory) and a set of dental instruments used by Queen Victoria. We loved this museum!

Exit - 49 (west of I-95)/ I-695 S

ELLICOTT CITY B&O RAILROAD STATION MUSEUM

Ellicott City - *2711 Maryland Avenue (I-675 exit 13 on MD 144 toward Catonsville. Travel 4 miles, cross over the Patapsco River bridge and into town. Museum is corner of Main and Maryland 21043. Phone: (410) 461-1944. www.ecborail.org. Hours: Wednesday-Sunday 11:00am-4:00pm. Admission: $4.00-$6.00. Closed most holidays. Note: The Thomas Isaac Log Cabin is nearby on the corner of Main Street and Ellicott Mills Drive. This is one of the earliest dwellings in Ellicott City and the site of various living history events.*

This 19th-century museum profiles the oldest terminus for the first 13 miles of track of the first commercial railroad in America! Walk through history from the 1830s thru the Civil War up to the great flood. See the cluttered Agent's Living Quarters as the first items transferred by rail were product, not people. People came later. Notice the ladies and gents had separate waiting rooms upstairs. Folks dressed in period costume inform you about each room. Exhibits include the fascinating 40-foot HO scale teaching railroad and audio-visual presentation. Only ten minutes long, the movie quickly tells you who and why the railroad was built and this is followed by a light show of the path the B&O rails took. The climb aboard outside caboose is fun for play and photos.

The adorable old downtown of Ellicott City just footsteps away - with quaint shops and cafes makes this stop a perfect day trip for every member of the family. Kids will love the Museum gift shop and the toy stores downtown.

Exit - 47 (east of I-95)/ I-195S / Rt.295N

HISTORICAL ELECTRONICS MUSEUM

Linthicum - 1745 W Nursery Road (Rte. 295 north (Baltimore Washington Parkway) to W. Nursery Rd exit. Left at light) 21090. www.nationalelectronicsmuseum.org. Phone: (410) 765-0230. Hours: Monday-Friday 9:00am-4:00pm, Saturday 10:00am-2:00pm. Admission: $1.00-$3.00.

You can learn about TVs, radios, cell phones, and even see a working original Edison cylinder phonograph. The museum houses the first American radar ever built (used in Pearl Harbor to detect incoming Japanese planes), a lunar camera just like the one used to photograph Neil Armstrong's moon landing, and the SCR 584 - a giant radar unit that visitors can enter and explore! Use their hands on equipment to generate electricity and experiment with magnetism. Learn how electromagnetic waves power our cell phones, cook our food, and help us see into space. Become part of a human battery. Take a look at an operational amateur radio station capable of worldwide communications by voice, Morse code, digital modes, and television. Go under the sea in an Interactive demonstration of passive and active underwater sounds and then go to a room where you can see yourself in infrared.

Exit - 47 (east of I-95)/ I-195 S

PATAPSCO VALLEY STATE PARK

Ellicott City - 8020 Baltimore National Pike (I 95 take I-195 to Rt. 1 (Exit 3) toward Elkridge to South St. Turn right) 21043. Phone: (410) 461-5005. www.dnr2. maryland.gov/publiclands/pages/central/patapsco.aspx Hours: Daily 9:00am-dusk.

The park extends along 32 miles of the Patapsco River, with 14,000 acres and five developed recreational areas. The Avalon Visitor Center houses exhibits spanning over 300 years of history along the Patapsco River. Housed in a 19th century stone dwelling in the Avalon Area, the center includes a re-creation of a 1930's forest warden's office. View the Thomas Viaduct – world's longest multiple-arched stone railroad bridge or hike the Grist Mill Trail – A 1.5 mile paved and accessible trail for the disabled along the river. (Avalon Area) Walk across the Swinging Bridge – a 300 foot suspension walkway over the river or hike to Bloede's Dam – world's first internally housed hydroelectric dam. (Orange Grove Area) Visit the Daniels Area fish ladder to learn about Maryland's first barrier free river to shad and herring migrations. Recreational opportunities include hiking, fishing, camping (primitive and cabins), canoeing, horseback and mountain bike trails, as well as picnicking for individuals or large groups in the park's many popular pavilions.

Exit - 43 (west of I-95)

ENCHANTED FOREST & CLARK'S ELIOAKFARM

Ellicott City - *10500 Rte. 108, Clarksville Pike (exit Rte. 100 west to end. Exit onto Rte. 29south to Rte.108 west 2 miles) 21042. www.clarklandfarm.com. Phone: (410) 730-40409. Hours: Tuesday-Sunday 10:00am-4:00pm (April-early November). Admission: Petting Zoo and Enchanted Forest $5.00 per person. Additional $2.00 for hayrides or pony rides.*

Once upon a time, there was a wonderful storybook park in Ellicott City called The Enchanted Forest. Opened in 1955, it thrilled and delighted generations of families from far and wide throughout the next 30 years. Sadly, it closed to the public in the late 1980's. The folks on this farm are slowly finding and restoring many of the Storybook characters back to display park quality. Look for Mother Goose and her Gosling, the Black Duck, the six Mice that pulled Cinderella's Pumpkin Coach (and the big pumpkin coach!), Papa Bear,

The Enchanted Forest lives on...

the giant Mushrooms, the bell-shaped Flowers, two giant Lollipops, a number of Gingerbread Men, a large Candy Cane, the Little Red Schoolhouse, the Crooked House and the Crooked Man, the Easter Bunny's House, the Beanstalk with the Giant at the top and the beautiful Birthday Cake. You can now also see Snow White, Sleeping Beauty, Robin Hood, the Three Little Pigs' straw, stick and brick houses, the Rainbow Bridge, and Little Boy Blue, the Old Woman's Shoe and the Three Bears House. Once finished, it will feel like you're walking thru the Nursery rhymes from childhood. The scenes are weaved throughout the petting farm area and into a forested area.

The Clark family has been farming in Howard County since 1797. Come and visit the 540-acre farm and see a wide variety of animals - goats, sheep, donkeys, pigs, alpacas, calves, horses, ponies, turkeys, ducks, chickens, bunnies, and turtles. You can feed the animals and visit the Barnyard area where you can touch and pet them. They offer hay rides through the storybook farm fields and a number of play areas for the children. Pony rides are available all day, every day that they are open. Too cute!

Exit - 41 (west of I-95)

DOUBLETREE HOTEL COLUMBIA

Baltimore (Columbia) - *5485 Twin Knolls Road (On Rte. 175 for 4 miles. Left onto Thunder Hill Rd. 1st right onto Twin Knolls) 21045. Phone: (443) 539-1119. http://doubletree1.hilton.com.*

Situated in a park-like setting, this place offers standard guest rooms that are welcoming with warm, yet vibrant color scheme and modern decor. All rooms include complimentary high-speed wireless internet service, complimentary use of the indoor pool, jacuzzi, exercise facilities and sauna. Morgan's restaurant serves great chicken (Frangelico) and steak (Cajun) dishes as well as Maryland crab. The children's menu runs $4.00-$5.00 and offers so many well-portioned kids foods.

Exit - 38 (east of I-95)

NATIONAL CRYPTOLOGIC MUSEUM

Fort George G. Meade - *Colony Seven Road (I-95 to Rte. 32 east/Ft. Meade, exit Canine Rd. Turn left at Colony Seven Road) 20755. Phone: (301) 688-5849. www.nsa.gov/about/cryptologic_heritage/museum/index.shtml.* Hours:

Monday-Friday 9:00am-4:00pm. Admission: FREE. Note: Vigilance Park outside is home to actual spy planes used for secret missions. Once home, follow the CryptoKids characters with online stories and games. FREEBIES: Ask the attendant for a decoder and Picture Scavenger Hunt to make the visit even more engaging.

Codemakers and Codebreakers. Located adjacent to NSA Headquarters, the Museum collection contains 1000s of artifacts of the cryptologic profession. The most secret organization in the United States. Catch a glimpse of some of the most dramatic moments in history, using cryptology machines and techniques. Learning past secrets, some events in American and world history may take on a new meaning. Peek into a once secret world - the cracking of enemy

ssshhhh...it's all a "<u>secret</u>" here!
Figure it all out here...

codes and the protection of American communications. Look at Union code books and Confederate cipher cylinders. Learn about Code Talkers - Native Americans who used their own language and terms in radio transmissions - they NEVER made mistakes and codes were NEVER broken! Check out the world's only remaining Enigma - the German encrypting machine that Allied intelligence cracked to glean knowledge that assisted in winning the Battle of the Atlantic and facilitated the ending of WWII. And, look at everyday life applications. Government and top security level companies use Biometrics - human fingerprints or eye scans as password IDs - machines and technology developed from military security needs. Even the post office uses cryptology. Metered mail uses a 2D bar code encryption system. There are several areas where parents might want to watch movies while the kids use their free cipher disk and activity book to try to decode messages and win a small prize. This place is so secretive and so interesting!

Exit - 28A (west of I-95)

NATIONAL CAPITAL TROLLEY MUSEUM

Colesville - *1313 Bonifant Road (New Hampshire Avenue North (Route 650) and go for 5.7 miles to Bonifant Road. Turn Left onto Bonifant Road, and go 1.6 miles) 20905. Phone: (301) 384-6088. www.dctrolley.org. Hours: Saturday & Sunday*

Noon-5:00pm. Holly Trolley Festival in December evenings. Admission: $7.00 adult, $5.00 child (2-17). Educators: go online to For Teachers and download Lesson Plans for a variety of subjects.

The collections consist of 17 streetcars from Washington D.C. and other cities. Many of these are operated on a one-mile demonstration railway. Check out the O-scale model layout representing a Washington streetscape from the 1930s, a video or various street railway artifacts. Trolley rides.

Exit - 27 (west of I-95) / I-495 WEST

ROCK CREEK PARK AND NATURE CENTER

Washington - *5200 Glover Road, NW 20008. www.nps.gov/rocr/naturecenter/. Phone: (202) 426-6829. Hours: Wednesday-Sunday 9:00am-5:00pm. Closed most national holidays. FREE. Educators: click on: For Teachers and then Curriculum for lesson plans and scavenger hunts.*

This 2,000-acre park provides a perfect setting for an urban escape or a family outing. Explore a woodland trail. Discover other planets. Touch live animals. Visit a historic flour mill. Visit a 17th century colonial home (Old Stone House). The park has a golf course, tennis courts, picnic tables, bike trails, jogging trails, and horseback riding. The Rock Creek Nature Center is home to the only planetarium in the National Park system and the Discovery Room has a live beehive viewing area. Visitors can watch the bees at work in the hive, visible through glass panes. The hive is connected to the outdoors by a plastic tube. Guided nature walks and curriculum based environmental education programs take place daily.

Exit - 27 (west of I-95) / I-495 WEST

NATIONAL ZOO

Washington - *3001 Connecticut Avenue, NW (I-395 north to exit 8B, Washington Blvd. To Arlington Bridge. Cross Bridge, veer to left. Turn right on Constitution, left on 17th. Metro: Zoo) 20008. http://nationalzoo.si.edu. Phone: (202) 633-4800. Hours: Daily 10:00am-4:30pm. Open until 6:00pm (April-October). Closed Christmas Day. Admission: FREE. Educators: Curriculum guides, Wildlife Explorer Kits and Activity Sheets are all online on the "Education" icon.*

Most of you are thinking Giant Pandas at the National Zoo. See Bao Bao, the Zoo's newer panda, on the web cams. Information on viewing the cub during your visit can be read there. Like babies? Popular areas are: Asian elephants,

MD & D.C.

Cheetah cubs, Tiger cubs or animals in the Kids' Farm. It wouldn't be the National Zoo without a Bald Eagle Refuge. While many animals are always or usually in indoor exhibits, many others, including giant pandas, other bears, seals, sea lions, and great cats, are usually outdoors. To make your walk around the Zoo more enjoyable, comfortable shoes are recommended. The Zoo is set on hilly terrain and some paths are steep. You can expect to see more animals early in the morning. Print off a scavenger hunt sheet before you visit (on the Info for Visitors web page).

PRESIDENT LINCOLN'S COTTAGE

Washington - *Armed Forces Retirement Home campus (Metro-Georgia Ave-Petworth. Head northeast) 20408. www.lincolncottage.org. Phone: (202) 829-0436. Hours: Visitors Center: Daily 9:30am-4:30pm, opens at 10:30am Sundays. The site is closed Thanksgiving, Christmas, and New Year's Day. Admission: $15.00 adult, $5.00 child (6-12). Tours: One hour, guided tours are offered of the Cottage and a portion of the Soldiers' Home grounds. Reservations online are highly suggested. This tour is suitable for children 6 years or older.*

Located on a picturesque hilltop in Washington, DC, President Lincoln's Cottage is the most significant historic site directly associated with Lincoln's presidency aside from the White House. During the Civil War, President Lincoln and his family resided here from June to November of 1862, 1863 and 1864. In part, the Lincolns were seeking privacy to grieve after the death of 12-year-old son Willie. Until recently, little was known about the home. Much has been pieced together from diaries, letters and newspaper stories. While you may be thinking you'll get to see the chair or bed Lincoln's family sat on - this museum instead focuses on the person. "Historical" voices and images illuminate the compelling stories of Lincoln as father, husband, and Commander in Chief. In "Lincoln's Cabinet Room" (Visitors Center) visitors can participate in an innovative interactive experience exploring Lincoln's Toughest Decisions. Students can play the roles of rival cabinet secretaries and debate the emancipation. We especially like that, before touring the Cottage, visitors first gather in the theater for an introduction to the site. An interactive audio-visual presentation sets the context for the Lincolns' move here.

Exit - 23 (west of I-95)

COLLEGE PARK AVIATION MUSEUM & AIRPORT

College Park - *1985 Corporal Frank Scott Drive (exit onto Rte 201 south, then right onto Paint Branch Park, right again onto Frank Scott Drive) 20740. Phone: (301) 864-6029. www.collegeparkaviationmuseum.com. Hours: Daily 10:00am-5:00pm.*

Closed major holidays. Admission: $2.00-$4.00 per person. Note: Notice the "ghost" screens of the first flights here, outside, near the parking lot. Educators: click on visit, then For Educators, then Teachers guides for activities and worksheets.

The College Park Aviation Museum is located on the grounds of the world's oldest continuously operating airport. The Museum tells the story of flight from the Wright Brothers to today. An animatronic Wilbur Wright welcomes visitors to the exhibits. The museum gallery contains historic and reproduction aircraft associated with the history of the airfield, as well as hands-on activities and experimentation areas for children. Create your own Air Mail postcard using rubbings and stamps. Be an Air Mail pilot, work the controls, test the drag and lift, or air flow. While you're a test pilot, look the part and try on some bomber jackets and caps. Next, hop in the Imagination Plane and pretend you're the pilot of a 1939 Taylorcraft Airplane...a real plane. Next, write a short story about your "first flight." For the little guys, there is a mini-airport outside with small planes the kids can sit on and ride. The newer 1911 Model B Flight Simulator allows a visitor to fly over the airport with cockpit hand controls and state-of-the-art visuals in the simulator Wright Brothers Experience. (the 3 minute "ride" is $1.00 additional). The airport runway is just outside the glass windows of the museum - be sure to watch for a take-off or landing as today's pilots fly. The airport was founded in 1909 for the Wright Brothers' instruction of the first military aviators.

Exit - 23 (east of I-95)

NASA GODDARD SPACE FLIGHT CENTER

Greenbelt - *Visitor Center, Soil Conservation Road, 8800 Greenbelt Road (I95/495 Capital Beltway- exit 23 to Greenbelt Rd., Rte. 193 east) 20771. Phone: (301) 286-8981. www.nasa.gov/centers/goddard/visitor/home/index.html#.U7_8yJRdX6c. Hours: Tuesday-Friday 10:00am-3:00pm and Saturday, Sunday Noon-4:00pm. Open weekdays until 5:00pm (July, August). Admission: FREE. Educators: NASA educator resources: http://search.nasa.gov/search/edfiltersearch. jsp?empty=true.*

The hub of all NASA tracking activities, Goddard is also responsible for the development of unmanned sounding rockets, and research in space and earth sciences including the Mission to Planet Earth. Through interactive exhibits, families explore the Flight Center with a focus on 1958 to the present. Collections include space flight artifacts and photographs. Check the website for the schedule of model rocket launchings. Science on a Sphere (SOS) is a large, mesmerizing 'earth ball' that uses computers and video projectors to display animated data on the outside of a suspended, 6-foot diameter, white sphere. Four strategically placed projectors work in unison to coat the sphere with data such as '3-D surface of the earth and Nighttime Lights,' 'moon and Mars' and 'X-Ray Sun.' To further enhance the experience, catch the movie, "Footprints." The movie consists of a visually rich presentation where the earth appears in a variety of guises, from depictions of the biosphere to planetary views of city lights at night to dramatic examinations about the science of hurricane formation. In the Science Center, students use the Hubble Telescope computer to "hit" Jupiter with a comet, attempt to put star clusters in order of age, use the Hubble Deep Field image to estimate the number of galaxies in the universe, match before and after images of colliding galaxies, and also learn about the different wavelengths of light by taking pictures of their hand in visible and infrared light. Numerous videos will be shown including, Shoemaker-Levy (a comet collision with Jupiter), Star Life Cycle Animations, Age of the Universe and the Hubble Deep Field. Outside, The Center features a full-size rocket garden located outside of the facility that features many types of rockets, mock-ups, and old flight hardware. This collection is 100% real NASA artifacts. Ask to see the tree that went to the moon.

Exit - 22 (east of I-95)

NATIONAL WILDLIFE VISITOR CENTER (PATUXENT REFUGE)

Laurel - *10901 Scarlet Tanager Loop (off of Powder Mill Rd. between the Baltimore-Washington Parkway and Rt. 197 south of Laurel) 20708. Phone: (301) 497-5760. www.pwrc.usgs.gov/. Hours: Daily 10:00am-4:30 EXCEPT Federal Holidays. Trails open at sunrise. Admission: Events are held at the National Wildlife Visitor Center unless otherwise noted and are FREE. Tram Tours are $1.00-$3.00 per person. Tours: Wildlife Conservation Tram Tours are Mid-March through Mid-November, Saturday & Sunday, 11:30am-3:30pm. Weather permitting. The tram tour offers a ride through woodland and wetland areas guided by an interpreter. A variety of wildlife and evidence of ongoing research here can be seen along the way. Tickets can be purchased in the bookstore.*

The National Wildlife Visitor Center is the largest science and environmental education center in the Department of the Interior. It highlights the work of professional scientists who strive to improve the condition of wildlife and their habitats. Be a field researcher and travel through five life-scale habitat areas. Learn through hands-on interactive exhibits how wildlife research has led to important discoveries. See dramatic dioramas of gray wolves, whooping cranes, canvasback ducks and sea otters displaying true-to-life behavior - up close and in their own environment. If the weather is unkind, stay indoors and peer out their giant Pond Window.

The Visitor Center also offers hiking trails. The Loop Trail - (0.5 km/0.3 mi.) is a paved and fully accessible trail. It leaves the visitor center gallery door and offers views of both Lake Redington and Cash Lake. Goose Pond Trail - (0.3 km/0.2 mi.) parallels the woods' edge as it wanders first through a forested wetland area as it leads to Goose Pond. Laurel Trail - This woodland trail (0.6 km/0.4 mi.) was named for the many Mountain Laurels found along the trail. Visitors have the opportunity to see woodland songbirds and mammals (especially deer). Cash Lake Trail - (2.3 km/1.4 mi.) travels along the edge of Cash Lake. This trail offers many opportunities to view the lake and its waterfowl, as well as a beaver lodge and evidence of their activity. There is also a seasonal fishing program at Cash Lake, with fishing by permit from the accessible pier and along parts of the shoreline.

Exit - 19 (west of I-95)

DC DUCKS TOURS

Washington - *(Tours depart Union Station) 20018. www.dcducks.com. Phone: (202) 966-DUCK. Tours: 90 minutes. Daily every 30 minutes starting at 10:00am-4:00pm, (mid-March thru October). $39.00 adult, $29.00 child (4-12). Discounts online.*

DUCKS come from DUKW, a military acronym that designated the vehicle as amphibious military personnel carriers. D stands for the year built, 1942; U for its amphibious nature; K for its all-wheel drive; and W for its dual rear axles. This is the most unusual tour of our nation's capital you'll ever take. . . Land and water in the same vehicle. From Union Station you'll "waddle" down to the mall where you'll see the inspiring monuments and pass the Smithsonian Museums. Then, just after you reach the Potomac River, you'll splash down for a duck's view on the river. The Ducks return to land at National Airport under the approach pattern. Hold your ears as incoming aircraft pass over just feet from where you're sitting . . . giving new meaning to "sitting duck"! The wise-quacking captains will entertain you with anecdotes, sneak in some interesting historical facts & tell corny jokes.

OLD TOWN TROLLEY TOURS

Washington - *50 Massachusetts Ave NE (departs at Union Station & the Welcome Center) 20001. Tours: $39.00 adult, $29.00 child (4-12). Online discounts. "Hop on - Hop off" privileges at 16 conveniently located stops. Trolleys will come by each stop at least every 30 minutes. No Reservations Required.*

A one-of-a-kind fully narrated tour of Washington DC covering over 100 points of interest. The popular Old Town Trolley tour covers Washington's major attractions such as the Lincoln Memorial, Georgetown, Washington National Cathedral, the White House, the museums of the Smithsonian Institution, and the Vietnam Veteran's Memorial. The licensed and professional tour guides share colorful anecdotes, humorous stories and well researched historical information.

CLYDE'S AT THE GALLERY

Washington, DC - *707 7th St. NW (take US 50 into town. Follow Metro: Gallery Place/ Chinatown) 20004. www.clydes.com.*

Sit down lunch option in Washington, D.C.: Clyde's at the Gallery offers a great Kids Menu for $6.00. Ten entrees to choose from with basics plus something new: Finger Food Platter – string cheese, apple wedges, celery, carrot sticks and peanut butter. Every Kids Meal is served with a toy, activity sheet & crayons, milk or soft drink, and ice cream or seasonal fruit dessert. Teens will love the Margarita Pizza...adults, be sure to try their seafood – oysters or their meaty crab cakes maybe? Reasonable for D.C. pricing!

INTERNATIONAL SPY MUSEUM

Washington - 800 F Street, NW (Metro: Gallery Place/ Chinatown) 20004. Phone: (202) 393-7798. www.spymuseum.org. Hours: Daily 9am-7pm. (hours vary October-March). Last Admission: 2 hours before closing. Closed major winter holidays. Admission: $20.95 adult (12-64), $15.95senior (65+), $14.95 child (ages 7-11). Children age 4 and under FREE. All admission tickets are date and time specific and are subject to availability. Advance Tickets are highly recommended. Note: The exhibit spaces are tight (maybe for effect-spies hide in small, hidden passages). The Permanent Exhibition is most appropriate for ages 12+. Be sure to watch the "Briefing Room" video intro before you begin the tour (to orient).

Packed with high-tech, interactive displays and activities, visitors can take on a spy's cover and test their skills of observation and surveillance, while learning about the history and the future of espionage. Examine over 200 spy gadgets, weapons, bugs, cameras, vehicles, and technologies. Look for the Bond car and a Buttonhole Camera. Learn about the earliest codes--who created them and who broke them. A spy must live a life of lies. Adopt a cover identity and learn why an operative needs one. See the credentials an agent must have to get in - or out.

The first half of the museum is interactive but kids may get bored with the second, historical half.

Exit - 19 (west of I-95)

MADAME TUSSAUDS WAX MUSEUM, D.C

Washington - 1001 F Street NW (take US 50 for 9 miles to the corner of 10th and F Street) 20004. Phone: (888) WAX-IN-DC. www.madametussaudsdc.com.

Hours: Daily 10:00am-6:00pm (last ticket sold at 6:00pm). During peak season the attraction will stay open later or open earlier as needed. Fall weekdays may open at Noon instead. Admission: $21.50 adult, $17.00 child (3-12). Discounts for online purchases and Membership Cards savings.

DC's wax museum has a distinctly "Washington" feel, and gives parents the perfect opportunity to give kids a taste of politics without the crowds on the Mall. If you still have time and money left, you have to go to our new favorite wax museum, Madame Tussauds. We've never been to one like

Hanging out with President Lincoln...

this. DC's wax museum has a distinctly "Washington" feel, and gives parents the perfect opportunity to give kids a taste of politics without the crowds on the Mall. We interacted with the figures for some amazingly realistic photo ops like: Sitting with Lincoln in Ford's Theatre, Dad discussing decisions of the day in the Oval Office, getting arrested sitting next to Rosa Parks on the bus, or taking photos with famous presidents. They look so real (in the digital pics) that folks on the Metro (who overheard us talking...) thought we had actually met the President that day!

FORD'S THEATRE

Washington - *511 10th Street, NW (between E and F Streets) 20004. Box Office: (202) 347-4833. NPS Phone: (202) 426-6924. www.fordstheatre.org. Hours: for museum & tours the site is open daily from 9am-5pm. Final entry into the theatre is at 4:30pm. Visits to Ford's Theatre NHS are FREE but do require a ticket. Tickets can be reserved online for a small fee. Tours: Extend that feeling with History on Foot tours lead by an actor in costume ($18.00 per person). The Peterson House, where Lincoln died, is open for tours too. Educators: click on Education icon for Printable Resources/Educational Resources. Click on "Explore Lincoln" for background material for reports.*

<u>ACT I</u> - Ford's Theatre museum preserves and displays over 8,000 artifacts relevant to the assassination of Abraham Lincoln. The museum uses 21st century technology to transport visitors to 19th-century Washington DCThe museum's collection of historic artifacts (including the Derringer pistol that John Wilkes Booth used to shoot Lincoln and the replica coat Lincoln wore the night he was shot) is supplemented with a variety of narrative devices.

Interactive, self-guided exhibits set the stage for guests by painting a social and political picture of Washington, DC, and the United States during the 1860s.

<u>ACT II</u> - Visitors move into the theatre itself for a presentation—either of a one act play or a National Park Service ranger talk—that illuminates the dramatic events of April, 1865. See the Presidential Box (notice how the view from here is almost like being on stage), the inner door (notice how mangled it is) to the box, and many historical artifacts such as the evenings program (notice it announced Lincoln's attendance that was publicized as a long awaited appearance of the Commander and Chief) and the Notice of Reward for the killer. Who was supposed to be a guest in the box with the President and Mrs. Lincoln that night? Why didn't they come?

As you sit in the theatre for the presentation, chills run up your spine!

Standing under the VIP box where President & Mrs Lincoln sat...

ACT III

The journey continues across the street at the Petersen House, where visitors will learn more about President Lincoln's final hours, the vigil at his deathbed and the subsequent hunt for his assassin.

Exit - 17 (east of I-95)

RADISSON HOTEL LARGO

Largo - 9100 Basil Court (head east on SR 202 following signs for hotel - set back in corporate park area) 20774. www.radisson.com/largomd. Phone: (301) 773-0700.

The Largo Hotel features 184 perfectly designed guest rooms featuring all of the amenities to make your stay enjoyable. Guest rooms feature the exclusive Sleep Number® Bed, well lit work desk and Complimentary Wireless High-Speed Internet Access. Just 4 miles from Six Flags and 12 miles from DC. When it's time to relax, guests at the Largo Hotel can enjoy an indoor swimming pool and fully equipped, 24 hour fitness center. The Radisson Hotel Largo features a full service restaurant and lounge (breakfast buffet, Kids Menu - around $4.00). The Grill, open daily until 10:00pm. For your convenience they also offer a lobby shop with light snacks, beverages and microwavable meals available. Micro and Frig in each room. Value rates start around $125.00.

Exit - 15 (east of I-95)

SIX FLAGS AMERICA

Largo - *13710 Central Avenue (I-95 to Largo exit #15A Central Avenue. Head east 5 miles) 20775. Phone: (301) 249-1500. www.sixflags.com/america. Hours: Summer Break, daily 10:30am opening, closing near dark. Weekends only in May and September. Admission: Begins around $40.00 for little ones up to $60.00 for most riders. Discount tickets online. Parking additional $15.00.*

Thrilling theme and water-park featuring more than 100 rides, shows and attractions, headlined by the constantly spinning Penguin's Blizzard River raft ride and eight exciting coasters. Younger families enjoy the Pirate themes at Buccaneer Beach and the classic amusement park rides at Looney Toons Movie Town (kiddie rides are plentiful and cute). Parents will like that the music and noise is not loud here. There are plenty of shade trees - especially the entire area of rides near the entrance (right off Main Street). We also liked the fact that many rides were mild enough for many family members to enjoy. Gotham City and the Southwest Territory contained more "thrill" roller coasters although the Batman Thrill Show wasn't too scary for kids to watch as you cheer Batman on. For a classic wooden roller coaster, try the Wild One. And don't forget the price includes Hurricane Harbor water park with the same combo of mild to max rides for all ages.

WATKINS REGIONAL PARK

Upper Marlboro - *301 Watkins Park Drive (take Rte 214 east for three miles, right on Watkins Park Drive) 20774. Phone: (301) 218-6700. www.pgparks.com. Hours: Daytime park hours vary each season.*

The park is 3 minutes from Six Flags and is a must see. It includes the Old Maryland Farm with farm animals petting zoo, Watkins Nature Center, miniature train that runs through the park, miniature golf, an antique carousel, walking and biking trails and the like. Most activities only require $1.00-3.50 per person. It's a good complement for Six Flags and a wonderful cost-friendly option for families.

Exit - 11 (west of I-95)

CAPITOL BUILDING, UNITED STATES

Washington - *(east end of the National Mall) 20540. Phone: (202) 737-2300 or (800) 723-3557. www.visitthecapitol.gov Hours: Monday-Saturday 8:30am-4:30pm. Admission: FREE. Visitors must obtain free tickets for tours on a first-come, first-served basis, at the Capitol Guide Service kiosk located along the curving sidewalk southwest of the Capitol (near the intersection of First Street, SW, and Independence Avenue). Ticket distribution begins at 9:00am, daily. Tours: Guided tours of the U.S. Capitol Building are free of charge and are conducted Monday through Saturday, 8:50 a.m. to 3:20 p.m. Tours must be booked in advance and schedules can fill up quickly (particularly in spring), so it is advisable that you book your tour well in advance. Note: A limited number of free passes to the House and Senate galleries are available by contacting your representative's office, in advance or reserving a tour at the Visitors Ctr. An underground tunnel connects to the Library of Congress too.*

The Capitol is one of the most widely recognized buildings in the world. It is a symbol of the American people and their government, the meeting place of the nation's legislature, an art and history museum, and a tourist attraction visited by millions every year. The bright, white-domed building was designed to be the focal point for DC, dividing the city into four sectors and organizing the street numbers. Begun in 1793, the Capitol has been built, burnt, rebuilt, extended, and restored. An 180-foot dome is adorned by the fresco Brumidi painting (took him 20 years to complete). The Rotunda, a circular ceremonial space, also serves as a gallery of paintings and sculpture

depicting significant people and events in the nation's history. The Old Senate Chamber northeast of the Rotunda, which was used by the Senate until 1859, has been returned to its mid-19th century appearance. The third floor allows access to the galleries from which visitors to the Capitol may watch the proceedings of the House and the Senate when Congress is in session...learning firsthand how a bill becomes a law. The Visitors Center, an underground facility, includes an exhibition gallery, orientation theatres, a large cafeteria, gift shops, and restrooms. Another feature is a walking tunnel connected to the Library of Congress.

Exit - 11 (west of I-95)

LIBRARY OF CONGRESS

Washington - 101 Independence Ave, SE (Metro: Capitol South) 20540. Phone: (202) 707-8000. www.loc.gov. Hours: Monday-Saturday 10:00am-5:30pm. Admission: FREE public tours. Tours: Docent-led scheduled public walking tours are offered Mondays through Saturdays in the Great Hall. Ask at either of the information desks in the Visitors' Center of the Jefferson Building (west front entrance). You may enter this building on the ground level under the staircase at the front of the building, located directly across from the U.S. Capitol. Educators: Kids and Families - Log on, play around, learn something. Teachers - More than 10 million primary sources online.

The world's largest library is home to much more than just books. At the Library of Congress, kids can see a perfect copy of the Gutenberg Bible, personal papers of 23 presidents, a collection of Houdini's magic tricks, the Wright Brothers' flight log books and more. Equipped with new information desks, a visitors' theater features a 12 minute award winning film about the Library and interactive information kiosks. The Visitors' Center enhances the experience of approximately one million visitors each year.

NATIONAL ARCHIVES

Washington - 700 Pennsylvania Avenue, NW (Metro Archives station - The Rotunda entrance, which includes the Exhibit Hall, is on Constitution Avenue) 20408. Phone: (202) 357-5000. www.archives.gov. Hours: Daily 10:00am-5:30pm. Open later each spring and summer. Admission: FREE. Educators: Lesson Plans and great biographical writings can be used for teachers and kids' reports.

The Rotunda of the National Archives Building in downtown Washington, DC, contains the permanent exhibit of the Constitution, Bill of Rights, and the Declaration of Independence. A new exhibit called the Public Vaults displays over 1,000 fascinating records (originals or reproductions) from the National Archives holdings. Often, the wait may be long, but most say worth it, to enter the Charters of Freedom.

NEWSEUM

Washington - *555 Pennsylvania Ave., NW (6th Street and Pennsylvania Avenue, NW) 20001. Phone: (888) NEWSEUM. www.newseum.org. Hours: Daily 9:00am-5:00pm. Closed winter holidays. Admission: $22.95 adult, $18.95 senior (65+), $13.95 youth (7-18). Summer Fun Deal discounts. Tours: 2 hour Tour Guide Print out and take this guide with you on your next visit and, if you walk fast, you can discover some of the most compelling, revealing and fun exhibits and activities the Newseum has to offer. Educators: Many students in 8th grade study US Government and the Constitution, spend some time getting inspiration for a report. Note: Food Court, two-level Newseum Store.*

The world's only interactive museum of news. The exhibits take you behind the scenes to see and experience how and why news is made. Visitors here can act as editors and put together newspaper front pages. They can also step into a reality ride to the scene of a breaking news story and test their skills as investigative reporters or photographers. Learn about some history from a journalist's point of view - how the media have covered major historical events such as the fall of the Berlin Wall and the Sept. 11, 2001, terrorist attacks. Other great works on display include the Magna Carta, Thomas Paine's "Common Sense," and a 1787 first pamphlet printing of the U.S. Constitution. A major storyline of the World News gallery is the dangers reporters face around the globe while reporting the news. Dramatic icons — including a bullet-riddled, armor-reinforced pickup truck used by reporters and photographers in the Balkans — illustrate the dangerous conditions in which journalists often work. In the broadcast studio, visitors can watch "in person" a live TV newscast (most folks never get this chance). Try your hand at being a TV news reporter or photographer in the "Hot Seat" exhibit. A long news bar displays news from around the world. Below the wall are the front pages of daily newspapers from every state and many countries - all diversely covering the same stories. The theater presents great moments in news history or another theater offers a glimpse of vintage newsreels.

Exit - 7A (east of I-95)

SURRATT HOUSE MUSEUM

Clinton - *9118 Brandywine Road (Beltway exit 7A, Branch Ave. South (MD 5), right onto Woodyard Rd. (Rte.223W), left on Brandywine) 20735. Phone: (301) 868-1121. www.surrattmuseum.org. Hours: Wednesday - Friday 11:00am-3:00pm, Saturdays*

and Sundays Noon-4:00pm (mid-January thru mid-December). Closed Easter Sunday and 4th of July. Last tour of the day begins one-half hour before closing. Admission: $3.00 adult, $2.00 senior and groups, $1.00 child (5-18).

Study the escape route on an electric map...

The 1800s middle-class farm home, tavern and post office with special emphasis on the crucial years from 1840 to 1865. It explores the impact of this period on our national history as well as on the family of John and Mary Surratt who became entangled in the web of conspiracy surrounding the assassination of President Abraham Lincoln. Today much of the structure of the House & Tavern is original. Very engaging, entertaining costumed guides share little stories in every room. On a tour, you can see a reproduction of the original attic of the kitchen wing and look down a shaft where a rifle was hidden by Lloyd after Booth and Herold left the premises. The museum's permanent exhibit displays family artifacts, such as Surratt's wire-rim spectacles, pocket watch and a handkerchief with the family name embroidered on it. Want to follow the trail John Wilkes Booth followed to escape being caught? The visitors center map is a great start. The kids really liked this tour and the costumed guides, especially.

Probably not a coincidence that a rifle was hidden in the wall...

Exit - 3A (east of I-95)

FORT WASHINGTON PARK

Fort Washington - *13551 Fort Washington Road (I-95 exit 3A. Indian Head Hwy south 4 miles to Fort Washington Rd) 20744. www.nps.gov/fowa/. Phone: (301) 763-4600. Hours: Daily 9:00am-4:30pm. Admission: $5.00 per vehicle. Note: Civil War artillery demonstrations, first Sunday of the month from April to October.*

Picturesque Fort Washington sits on high ground overlooking the Potomac River and offers a grand view of Washington and the Virginia shoreline. Today, only one silent gun stands behind the masonry wall-the last armament of the powerful fort that once guarded the water approach to our Nation's Capital. The old fort is one of the few U.S. seacoast fortifications still in its original form. Exhibits inside the Visitors Center include information and artifacts describing the history of Fort Washington as the Capital's Guardian.

The old **FORT FOOTE** is just down the road in Oxon Hill. (301-763-4600 or www.nps.gov/fofo) Open 10:00am to dark, the fort was designed in the 1860s to protect the river entrance to the surrounding sea ports. The National Park Service has cleared paths around the ruins of what is considered the best preserved Civil War fort in the region.

Exit - 3 (west of I-95)

OXON HILL FARM AT OXON COVE PARK

Oxon Hill - 6411 Oxon Hill Road (I-95/495 Capital Beltway exit 3 heading just northwest off the highway) 20745. Phone: (301) 839-1176. www.nps.gov/oxhi/. Hours: Daily 8:00am-4:30pm. Admission: FREE. Note: Venture beyond the hilltop and explore part of Oxon Cove Park's 512 acres by strolling along the lower fields or riding the bike path along Oxon Cove. The Woodlot Trail is a steep 1/2-mile trail, marked with yellow blazes on trees, from just below the farm house to the parking lot. Find out how this wooded ravine benefited early farmers.

Oxon Hill Farm operates as an actual working farm, representative of the early 20th century. You can see a farm house, barns, a stable, feed building, livestock buildings and a visitor activity barn. It exhibits basic farming principles and techniques as well as historical agricultural programs for urban people to develop an understanding of cropping and animal husbandry. The most unique story about this place is the early farmers of the wheat crops. From the 1890's until the 1950's, Oxon Hill Farm was operated by patients from St. Elizabeth Hospital. It provided therapy as well as food for the patients at the institution. Interesting.

> An average dairy cow weighs about 1,400 pounds and can drink an average of 35 gallons of water a day - the equivalent of a bathtub full of water! There are six cattle that live on Oxon Hill Farm.

Each month offers a variety of programs, such as crafts, walks to observe plants and wildlife, wagon rides, and talks about farm life and the animals. Call ahead for reservations. Farming is a year-round business directed by the seasons. In spring, catch some planting corn or sheering sheep. June is dairy month with cows a milking. Fall brings the harvest season and cider pressing or sorghum syrup. Winter is a quiet time for walks, hayrides and tracking.

FREDERICK DOUGLASS NHS

Washington - *1411 W Street SE 20020. www.nps.gov/frdo/. Phone: (202) 426-5961. Admission: FREE. Hours: 9am-4:30pm. Tours: Ranger-led tours of the home are available daily at 9:00am, 12:15pm, 1:45pm, 3:00pm, and 3:30pm. Tour tickets are available by reservation or on a first-come first-served basis. Tours of the home last approximately 30 minutes. Note: The historic home is set high atop a hill. There are approximately 85 steps between the Visitor Center and the house.*

The Frederick Douglass National Historic Site is dedicated to preserving the legacy of the most famous 19th century African American. This restored home to a former slave is where you can begin to learn about his efforts to abolish slavery and his struggle for rights for all oppressed people. Begin with the 17-minute film "Frederick Douglass: Fighter for Freedom." Look for his original piano and documents he published.

Exit - 2 (west of I-95) / I-295 NORTH

NATIONAL MUSEUM OF U.S. NAVY

Washington - *805 Kidder Breese Street, SE (Washington Navy Yard) 20374. Phone: (202) 433-6897. www.history.navy.mil/branches/org8-1.htm   Hours: 9:00am-5:00pm Monday-Friday, Saturday-Sunday Holidays 10am-5pm. Display Ship Barry is open to the public Thursday-Sat from 22 May to 30 August. Educators: Lesson plans & activities on the Teacher Resources icon.*

Opened in 1963, the Navy Museum is housed in the former 600-foot long Breech Mechanism Shop of the old Naval Gun Factory. Exhibits offer a look at the traditions and contributions of the Navy throughout American history. Popular attractions include the fully rigged fighting top from the frigate Constitution, a submarine room with operating periscopes and a variety of large guns which can be elevated and aimed by the visitor. There is no admission charge.

NATIONAL MALL

Washington - *(stretches from 3rd St., NW and the Capitol grounds to 14th St., between Independence and Constitution Aves.) 20024. Visitor Information: (202) 426-6841. www.nps.gov/nama/. Hours: Rangers on duty 9am-10pm.*

Officially, the National Mall is green space that begins at 3rd Street and stretches to 14th Street. Visitors and locals, however, widely use the term to refer to the entire expanse of monuments and museums, from the grounds of the Capitol to the Lincoln Memorial. Pierre L'Enfant's original plans for the city called for this open space and parklands, which he envisioned as a grand boulevard to be used for remembrance, observance, and protest. Today, it serves this purpose, hosting concerts, rallies, festivals, as well as Frisbee matches, family outings, picnics and memorials: The Presidential Memorials; Vietnam Veterans Memorial (the Wall); U.S. Navy Memorial and Naval Heritage Center (701 Pennsylvania Ave., NW); Korean War Veterans Memorial (West Potomac Park, Independence Ave., beside the Lincoln Memorial); and the National World War II Memorial (East end of the Reflecting Pool, between the Lincoln Memorial and the Washington Monument). Call a veteran from a Memorial to thank him/her for their service.

If you like to picnic, the National Mall and West or East Potomac Park have cheap parking spaces (if you can find one) and dozens of lawn sites to spread out a picnic blanket. You'll be dining, al fresco, by a view of famous monuments. Also, near the White House & Washington Monument are oodles of vendors offering the best prices in town on souvenirs and sandwiches. It's a block or two walk to lawn space between the Lincoln & Washington Monuments. As the sun started setting, we especially enjoyed walking the perimeter of the Tidal Basin in Potomac Park with a view of the FDR Memorial & the Jefferson Memorial, as they are backlit towards nightfall.

Exit - 2 (west of I-95) / I-295 NORTH

SMITHSONIAN INSTITUTION

Washington - *(I-295N to I-395N located on the National Mall exit and may be entered from many directions. Follow signs.) 20560. Phone: (202) 357-2700 or (202) 633-1000 (voice). www.smithsonian.org Hours: All museums are open from 10:00am-5:30pm, daily. Admission: FREE. Educators: Click on "Educators" button and you'll find a wealth of exciting approaches to curriculum and related crafts or projects! Have your kids go to the Smithsonian Kids pages to explore before they go - their pages are whimsical and short - meant to pique interest, not destroy it. Note: Docents are available in many popular galleries daily to answer visitor questions between 10:30am and 2:30pm, Mondays through Saturdays and Sundays from noon to 4:00pm.*

Walt Disney Pictures has filmed in the space, and in many other Library enclaves, for its hugely popular and successful "National Treasure" movies.

MD & D.C.

A visit to Washington, DC is not complete without experiencing at least one of the 14 Smithsonian museums. The Castle is the original building, completed in 1855, which provides an overview of the entire offering to help your family determine which museums interest you the most (you probably can't do them all). Be sure you have on your walking shoes. DC by Foot, a walking tour company, gives FREE, kid-friendly tours (gratuity recommended) infused with games, fun facts and trivia. Or, just wander from one building to the next. Be sure to go online first and print off any "Hunts" (scavenger hunts) that interest you (ways to engage, not overwhelm young guests). The following are highlights of the myriad of exhibits and activities offered especially for children. Maybe only choose two to explore each visit.

- **ON THE MALL**: Outside the National Air and Space Museum, a scale model of the solar system entitled Voyage: A Journey through our Solar System helps children grasp the magnitude of the world around them. During the summer months, a ride on the world's oldest carousel, near the Arts and Industries Building, is a sure treat.

- **AMERICAN ART MUSEUM**: (Gallery Place Metro station at 8th and F Streets N.W. Open 11:30am-7:00pm). The Smithsonian American Art Museum is dedicated exclusively to the art and artists of the United States. All regions, cultures, and traditions are represented in the museum's collections, research resources, exhibitions, and public programs. The collection features colonial portraits, nineteenth-century landscapes, American impressionism, twentieth-century realism and abstraction, There's a neat display of license plates from every state that write out the Preamble to the Constitution (clever). You may especially like the Washington and Lincoln studies (ever study Lincoln's eyes?). The Civil War space is good, too.

- **HIRSHHORN GALLERY**: The Smithsonian's modern art museum's "Young at Art" program introduces young visitors to different artistic disciplines through hands-on activities. Participants can act in a play, create portraits in chocolate, make clay sculptures, and more. The museum also offers regularly-scheduled guided family tours.

NATIONAL AIR & SPACE MUSEUM: Play pilot in a mock cockpit at America by Air, an exhibition on permanent display at the Smithsonian National Air and Space Museum. The large space provides a world-renowned collection of flying machines from the Wright Brothers' Kitty Hawk Flyer to the Apollo 11 Command

See the <u>ACTUAL</u> Wright Brother's famous airplane...WOW...

Module. Kids can see a moon rock, Lindbergh's Spirit of St. Louis and a variety of special films. The museum's IMAX theatre provides large format and 3-D glimpses of space and beyond. (fee for IMAX shows AND Planetarium shows). Enclosed within the Museum is the Albert Einstein Planetarium. Not only does the planetarium have a spectacular star field instrument, but it has been upgraded to include a first-of-its-kind, Sky Vision™ dual digital projection system and six-channel digital surround sound. For the first time, you'll feel the sensation of zooming through the cosmos with a blanket of color and sound. Infinity Express: A 20-Minute Tour of the Universe; Cosmic Collisions, or Stars Tonight (free) program.

Early Americans hauled 25 pails of water (at 21 lbs each!) just to do a load of laundry...

• **NATIONAL MUSEUM OF AMERICAN HISTORY**: Also known as "America's Attic," this popular museum houses such treasures as the First Ladies' inaugural gowns, Dorothy's Ruby Red Slippers, Mr. Roger's sweater, Abraham Lincoln's top hat, Lewis and Clark's compass, Custer's buckskin coat, Thomas Jefferson's bible, Edison's light bulb and the flag that inspired "The Star-Spangled Banner." Your mouth will drop when you first turn the corner and see it! The museum's Spark!Lab uses fun activities to help kids and families learn about the history and process of invention through games and conducting experiments plus there's an Under 5 Zone just for preschoolers. A transportation exhibition, America on the Move, explores the world of transportation, including real artifacts from historic Route 66.

• **NATIONAL MUSEUM OF NATURAL HISTORY**: Walk among the butterflies or witness a view of the blinding Hope Diamond at the National Museum of Natural History. After seeing a digitally-restored Triceratops or dining in the special dinosaur café, check out the famous Insect Zoo. Kids can learn all about these creatures and non-squeamish types are allowed to handle them for an up-close look. The renovated Mammal Hall shows some of the museum's specimens in lifelike, realistic settings. The Ocean Hall is the largest exhibit - exploring the ancient, diverse, and constantly changing nature of the ocean, the long historical connections humans have had with it, and ways in which we are impacting the ocean today.

The "priceless" Hope Diamond..

- **NATIONAL MUSEUM OF THE AMERICAN INDIAN**: (4th Street & Independence) Experience culture at the National Museum of the American Indian, where FREE programming from storytelling and dance festivals to music performances by Native composers is available based on changing monthly performance schedules. The four story brilliantly lighted atrium captures your senses to explore the simple chronicle of people's courageous survival to present day accomplishments.

- **NATIONAL POSTAL MUSEUM**: Located next to Union Station, the National Postal Museum offers its young visitors insights into the interesting world of mail service. Children can create a souvenir postcard, learn about the history of the Pony Express and the legend of Owney the Postal Dog, and participate in a direct mail marketing campaign. Climb up into the cab of an Interstate Mail Truck and blow the bell and whistle. 2 Massachusetts Ave., NE. Metro: Union Station.

- **SACKLER GALLERY** @ The National Museums of Asian Art: Through the Sackler Gallery's ImaginAsia, kids visit a featured exhibition with a special guide written for children and create an art project to take home. Other special family programs include Asian dance and music lessons, storytelling, and more.

Exit - 2 (west of I-95) / I-295 NORTH

NATIONAL GALLERY OF ART

Washington - *6th Street & Constitution Avenue, NW (Metro: Archives/Navy Memorial, on the National Mall between Third and Seventh Streets) 20565. Phone: (202) 737-4215. www.nga.gov. Hours: Monday-Saturday 10:00am-5:00pm, Sunday 11:00am-6:00pm. Closed Christmas and New Years. Admission: FREE.*

This fine art museum contains a collection of European and American works in chronological order with recognizable names including da Vinci, Renoir, Monet and Whistler. The new NGAkids Still Life interactive encourages young artists to explore the world around them by arranging artistic elements and everyday objects into works that mirror those of the old masters. But there are surprises in store, as some of the objects unexpectedly spring to life! Experiment with spatial arrangements, size variables, and perspective angles, then switch modes and add layers of textured "brushstrokes" to create a more abstract image. This Art Zone activity is suitable for all ages. Visitors with children can also participate in drop-in workshops, take several postcard tours of the collection using a packet of cards with pictures of objects and questions for discussion or rent a family-oriented audio tour. Ask for the "Great Picture Hunt" at the info desk which lists paintings of special interest to kids.

Exit - 2 (west of I-95) / I-295 NORTH

WHITE HOUSE

Washington - 1600 Pennsylvania Avenue, NW (Metro: Metro Center, McPherson Square) 20500. Phone: (202) 456-7041. www.whitehouse.gov. Hours: Visitors Center: Daily 7:30am-4:00pm. Tours: The White House is currently open only to groups (of 10 or more) who have made arrangements through a congressional representative. These self-guided tours are available from 7:30am-11:30pm. Tuesday through Thursday and 7:30am-1:30pm Fridays&Saturdays (excluding federal holidays), and are scheduled on a first come, first served basis. You are given a specific entry time. Educators: Life in the White House, a presentation of the rich history of the White House and West Wing by video online.

WHITE HOUSE VISITOR CENTER: All visits are significantly enhanced if visitors stop by the White House Visitor Center located at the southeast corner of 15th and E Streets, before or after their walking or White House group tour. The Center features many aspects of the White House, including its architecture, furnishings, first families, social events, and relations with the press and world leaders, as well as a thirty-minute video. Allow between 20minutes to one hour to explore the exhibits.

WHITE HOUSE TOUR: You are given a specific entry time. There are many items you can't bring onto the property. The tour is self-guided with guards and Secret Service people in every room. You aren't rushed through and they willingly answer questions. The entry has lots of interesting displays and artifacts. Some of the rooms you can peak into are the East Room, Green Room, Blue Room, Red Room, State Dining Room and then out through the North Portico. It is definitely an impressive place to visit.

The guided OUTSIDE tour combined with the Visitor Center and online video presentations give you the best "feel" for the White House without actually going inside. I think they realize citizens still want to know about the President's house but can't always go through the "hoops"

America's most famous address...
1600 Pennsylvania Avenue

necessary to secure an inside visit these days. Please note that restrooms are available, food service is not.

MD & D.C.

HOLOCAUST MEMORIAL MUSEUM, UNITED STATES

Washington - *100 Raoul Wallenberg Place, SW (I-295N to I-395N exit Smithsonian, near the National Mall, just south of Independence Ave., SW, between 14th Street and Raoul Wallenberg) 20024. www.ushmm.org. Phone: (202) 488-0400 or (800) 400-9373. Hours: Daily 10:00am-5:20pm, except Yom Kippur and Christmas. Extended hours in the summer. Admission: FREE. Timed tickets required for permanent exhibition; available same day or in advance on their website. Usuallysold out by Noon.*

Our teen-aged daughter had just studied WWII so she had interest in the Holocaust Memorial Museum. There are two "exhibit tracks" to follow: the General Exhibit and Daniel's Story (a softer version for tender hearts and kids). We'd recommend walking through Daniel's Story to everyone BEFOREHAND to prepare you for the intensity to follow in the main exhibit. The permanent collection of the U.S.

We recommend the "kid's version" of the museum FIRST to prepare for learning more...

Holocaust Memorial Museum tells the moving story of the persecution of the Jewish people. The exhibition is divided into three parts: "Nazi Assault," "Final Solution," and "Last Chapter." The narrative begins with images of death and destruction as witnessed by American soldiers during the liberation of Nazi concentration camps in 1945. Most first-time visitors spend an average of two to three hours in this self-guided exhibition. Parents and pre-teens or teenagers - be prepared to be changed.

Exit - 2 (west of I-95) / I-295 NORTH

BUREAU OF ENGRAVING & PRINTING TOUR

Washington - *Department of the Treasury, 14th and C Streets, S.W. 20228. www.moneyfactory.com. Phone: (202) 874-2330 (local) or (866) 874-2330. Hours: Public Tour: 9:00am-10:45am & 12:30pm-2:00pm (every 15 minutes). Extended Summer Hours (May-August): 5:00-6:00pm (every 15 minutes). Tours are about 40 minutes long. Visitors Center: Weekdays 8:30am-3:30pm and summer early* *evenings. The Bureau is CLOSED on weekends, federal holidays and the week between Christmas and New Years. Tours: Tickets are required for all tours from the first Monday in March through the last Friday in August, on a first-come, first-served basis. The ticket booth is located on Raoul Wallenberg Place (formerly 15th Street). They offer same day tickets only. The Ticket Booth opens at 8:00am - Monday through Friday, and closes when all tickets have been distributed. Lines form early and tickets go quickly, most days' tickets are gone by 9:00am. Many are in line by 7:00am. No tickets required (September-February). Note: Please be advised that strollers are not allowed on the tour.*

You'll see millions of dollars being printed during a tour of the BEP. The tour features the various steps of currency production, beginning with large, blank sheets of paper, and ending with the paper money we use every day! The BEP designs, engraves and prints all U.S. paper currency. Did you know they also produce postage stamps and White House invitations? Established in 1862, the Bureau, at that time, used just six people to separate and seal notes by hand in the basement of the Treasury building. The Bureau moved to its present site in 1914. Though new printing, production and examining technologies have brought us into the 21st century, the Bureau's engravers continue to use the same traditional tools that have been used for over 125 years - the graver, the burnisher, and the hand-held glass. At any given time, you may see millions of dollars roll off the presses in a flash!

WASHINGTON MONUMENT

Washington - *15th & Jefferson Drive (National Mall area, Tourmobile stop, Metro Smithsonian stop) 20228. Phone: (202) 426-6841 or (877) 444-6777 reservations. www.nps.gov/wamo/. Hours: Washington Monument are from 9:00am-4:45pm, closed December 25 and July 4th. Admission: Free tickets are distributed for that day's visit from the kiosk on the Washington Monument grounds on a first-come first-served basis. All visitors 2 years of age or older must have a ticket to enter the Monument. Hours for the ticket kiosk are 8:00am-4:30pm, but tickets run out early. While tickets to the Washington Monument are free of charge, pre-sale callers will incur a $1.50 service charge and a $.50 shipping and handling fee. Note: Bookstore, restrooms and concessions on site.*

What is an Obelisk?
A tapering 4-sided stone shaft with a pyramid on top!

Take the fast elevator ride to the top of the Monument for a panoramic view of the city. Most rides make stops to allow viewing of the commemorative stones set along the inside walls of the elevator shaft. Many folks like to start here as Washington was our first President and the view gives you a good feel for the lay of the land in D.C. The 555-foot tall obelisk is marble and is the tallest free-standing obelisk in the world. Why are there two different colors of marble used? The immense structure represents Washington's enormous contribution to the founding of our republic.

Exit - 2 (west of I-95) / I-295 NORTH

JEFFERSON MEMORIAL

Washington - *East Potomac Park, South end of 15th St., SW on the Tidal Basin 20024. Phone: (202) 426-6822. www.nps.gov/thje/. Hours: The public may visit the Thomas Jefferson Memorial 24 hours a day. However Rangers are on duty to answer questions from 9:30am to 11:30pm daily. Admission: FREE.*

Easily recognizable to Jeffersonian architects, the colonnade and dome memorial reflect Jefferson's love of this architectural style. The graceful, beautiful marble design pays tribute to the third president and primary author of the Declaration of Independence. Inside, there is a large bronze statue and excerpts from his writings on the walls. Jefferson stands at the center of the temple, his gaze firmly fixed on the White House, as if to keep an eye on the institution he helped to create. A museum is located in the lower lobby of the memorial.

FRANKLIN D. ROOSEVELT MEMORIAL

Washington - *900 Ohio Drive, SW (West Potomac Park at West Basin and Ohio Drive) 20024. Phone: (202) 426-6841. www.nps. gov/fdrm/. Hours: Park ranger in attendance 9:30am-11:30pm. Closed Christmas. Admission: FREE. Note: The memorial did not originally feature any renderings of the president in his wheelchair. FDR did not wish to be portrayed in his wheelchair, and designers honored this request. Many people with and without disabilities were angered by this omission, and a statue of FDR in his wheelchair was installed*

in 2001.

"The only thing we have to fear is fear itself". These are the words of our 32nd President, a man who truly knew the meaning of the word courage. Despite, at age 39, being stricken with polio and paralyzed from the waist down, he emerged as a true leader, guiding our country through some of its darkest times: the Great Depression and World War II. The rambling FDR Memorial (it spans 7.5 acres) consists of four "rooms" arranged chronologically to represent the 32nd President's unprecedented four terms in office. A fountain in the first room flows peacefully, representing the healing effect water had on the president during his term in the Navy and while at Warm Springs, GA. The second room addresses the Great Depression and the hope FDR cultivated with his extensive social programs. The third room represents the war years, 1940-1944 with choppy, unsettling stonework and water. In a stark contrast, the final room projects peace and optimism. Acknowledging FDR's own physical difficulties, his memorial was the first creation of its kind designed with easy access for people with disabilities. Of all the presidential memorials, this is the most "open" to wander and take many pictures "with" the statues.

LINCOLN MEMORIAL

Washington - *900 Ohio Drive, S.W. (west end of Mall, 23rd St. and Constitution Ave., NW) 20024. Phone: (202) 426-6841. www.nps.gov/linc/. Hours: Visitors Center 8:00am-midnight. Park ranger in attendance 24 hours, However Rangers are on duty to answer questions from 9:30am-11:30pm daily. Admission: FREE.*

Note: New! Free Interpretive Ranger Talks via your telephone. Dial (202) 747-3420 to hear new Lincoln Memorial programs organized around more than ten themes.

The most famous of the monuments, this site was used for several of history's greatest moments. The artist opted to portray Lincoln seated, much larger than life, a symbol of mental and physical strength. Lincoln faces the US Capitol. Murals sculpted by Jules Guerin adorn the temple's inner walls. Emancipation is on the south wall and hangs above the inscription of the Gettysburg Address. Unification is on the north wall, above Lincoln's Second Inaugural Address. The view of the National Mall from this vantage point is spectacular. It gives you chills every time you visit.

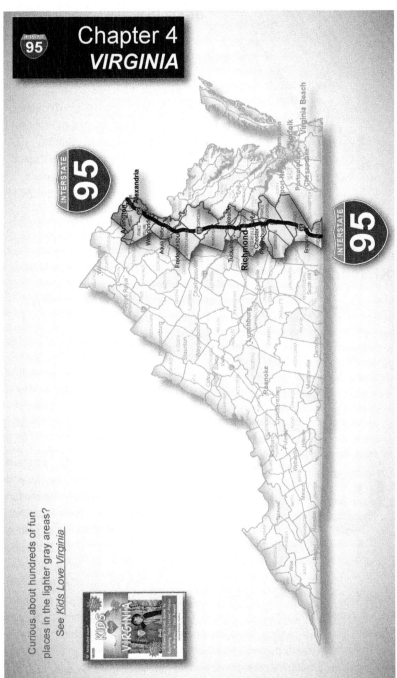

Chapter 4
VIRGINIA

Curious about hundreds of fun places in the lighter gray areas? See *Kids Love Virginia*

VIRGINIA

DEAR VIRGINIA TRAVELER:

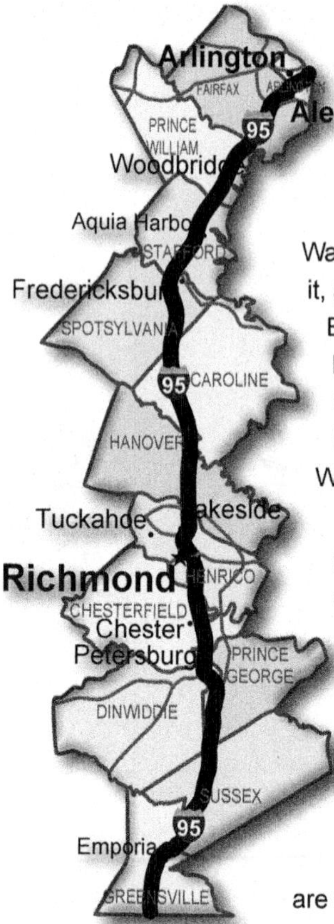

In the Commonwealth of Virginia, Interstate 95 runs 179 miles through the state. Though Interstate 95 was originally planned to go straight through Washington, DC, it was instead routed around it, along the eastern portion of the Capital Beltway. The point where it enters the Capital Beltway is one of the busiest interchanges in the U.S. (daylight hours). I-95 continues into Maryland along the Beltway over the Woodrow Wilson Bridge.

On the Virginia side of the D.C. area, take a moment to journey back to an 18th-century **Old Town Alexandria** tavern, apothecary or church where famous historical figures and everyday people dined and slept. Pick up an **Old Town Scavenger Hunt** to guide you on your adventure. There are centers on modern art, inventions and old archeology to visit, too. Weaved in (especially near King Street) are some of our favorite family-owned eateries serving kid-friendly pizza and ice cream.

Just south of Alexandria is **Mount Vernon Estate** and Gardens, beloved home of George and Martha Washington. The Kids' Adventure Map is a fun way to experience Washington's Estate for families. This colorful map is free with admission and guides kids around the estate in a quest to solve nine puzzles by exploring outbuildings and the Mansion. And, what concerns newbie moms out there – where do the young kids (ages 3-8) go for fun? ...the Hands on History Room area. What we liked best about the Education Wing was how it draws kids in: start with Washington's eyes following you to CSI-style forensics on how they "reconstructed" George's face from childhood through old age. Youth, love stories, war drama, touching, smelling, even spying? Most kids will want to move at a good pace through the actual house, linger a while outdoors at the farm, but save time and energy for the newer Education Wing.

Encounter the richness of the American experience at every turn in the **Fredericksburg Area** and walk in the footsteps of Presidents and Generals. Start with a wonderful **Fredericksburg Trolley Tour** of the old town. You'll pass many sites you may want to visit later. Several historic national battlefields are just outside of Old Town.

Any family who likes a variety of museums will be fond of **Richmond**, Virginia. They have a huge **science museum** and a **children's museum** next door. See the place where Patrick Henry exclaimed: "Give me liberty or give me death!" Condense the state's history at the **Virginia Historical Society**. Discover the entire "Story of Virginia" through videos, story phones, computer games and other interactive devices that make learning fun for the whole family. Tired of being cooped up in the vehicle or museums? Take a thrilling canoe or kayak trip through the nation's only urban setting for class IV rapids - right through downtown Richmond! Or find a calmer section for fishing or swimming in the magnificent James River.

Ever wonder what it was like to be a Civil War soldier? **Pamplin Historical Park** lets you travel back 140 some years and become a buck private. The kids get to use their personal MP3 players (or borrow one on site) to participate in drills, experience being fired upon (with air bursts), and play period games. Sleep in a platform tent, eat the Civil War era meals (hardtack, yuk!), or learn military codes and communications. Think you can cut it as a soldier in the 1860s?

Travel Journal & Notes:

ACTIVITIES AT A GLANCE

AMUSEMENTS

Exit - 174 - *Great Waves At Cameron Run Regional Park*
Exit - 98 - *Kings Dominion*

ANIMALS & FARMS

Exit - 152 - *Old Mine Ranch*
Exit - 84 - *Meadow Farm Museum*
Exit - 78 - *Maymont*

HISTORY

Exit - 177 - *Freedom House Museum*
Exit - 177 - *Christ Church*
Exit - 177 - *Friendship Firehouse Museum*
Exit - 177 - *Gadsby's Tavern & Museum*
Exit - 177 - *Stabler-Leadbeater Apothecary Museum*
Exit - 177 - *Mount Vernon, George Washington's*
Exit - 170 / I-395 Exit 4 - *Fort Ward Museum & Historic Site*
Exit - 161 - *Gunston Hall*
Exit - 148 - *National Museum Of The Marine Corps*
Exit - 133 - *George Washington's Ferry Farm*
Exit - 133 - *White Oak Museum*
Exit - 130 - *Fredericksburg Area Museum*
Exit - 130 - *Fredericksburg And Spotsylvania Civil War Battlefields*
Exit - 130 - *Historic Kenmore*
Exit - 130 - *Hugh Mercer Apothecary*
Exit - 130 - *Mary Washington House*
Exit - 130 - *Rising Sun Tavern*
Exit - 126 - *Civil War Life - The Soldier's Museum*
Exit - 78 - *Virginia Historical Society*
Exit - 76 - *Maggie L. Walker National Historic Site*
Exit - 74C - *Museum Of The Confederacy*

HISTORY *(cont.)*

Exit - 74B - *Virginia State Capitol*
Exit - 74B - *St. John's Church*
Exit - 74A - *Richmond National Battlefield Park*
Exit - 74 - *Virginia Aviation Museum*
Exit - 61A - *Henricus Historical Park*
Exit - 61A - *City Point Open Air Museum Walking Tour*
Exit - 61A - *Weston Manor*
Exit - 52 - *Petersburg National Battlefield*
Exit - 52 - *Quartermaster Museum*
Exit - 51 - *Pamplin Historical Park & The National Museum Of The Civil War Soldier*

MUSEUMS

Exit - 177 - *Alexandria Archaeology Museum*
Exit - 177 - *United States Patent And Trademark Office Museum*
Exit - 78 - *Children's Museum Of Richmond*
Exit - 74A - *Federal Reserve Money Museum*

OUTDOOR EXPLORING

Exit - 163 - *Mason Neck State Park*
Exit - 156 - *Leesylvania State Park*
Exit - 80 or 83B - *Lewis Ginter Botanical Garden*
Exit - 74A - *Canal Walk, Richmond*
Exit - 61 - *Pocahontas State Park*

SCIENCE

Exit - 78 - *Science Museum Of Virginia*

SUGGESTED LODGING & DINING

Exit - 177 - *Bugsy's Pizza*
Exit - 177 - *King Street Blues Restaurant*
Exit - 177 - *Hampton Inn Alexandria-Old Town / King Street Metro*
Exit - 176B - *Embassy Suites Old Town*
Exit - 79 - *Embassy Suites Richmond*

ACTIVITIES AT A GLANCE

THE ARTS

Exit - 177 - *Torpedo Factory Art Center*
Exit - 133 - *Riverside Center Dinner Theatre*

TOURS

Exit - 177 - *Potomac Riverboat Company*
Exit - 177 - *Alexandria Walking Tours*
Exit - 177 - *Old Town Scavenger Hunt*
Exit - 177 - *Arlington National Cemetery*
Exit - 130 - *Fredericksburg Trolley Tours*

WELCOME CENTERS

Exit - 131 Mile - Southbound Only
- *Virginia Welcome Center @ Fredericksburg*
Exit - 1 Mile Northbound - (At Virginia/ North Carolina State Line)

GENERAL INFORMATION

Contact the services of interest. Request to be added to their mailing lists.

- [ ] Virginia Tourism Corporation. (804) VISIT-VA or www.virginia.org
- [ ] Virginia Historical Society. www.vahistorical.org
- [ ] Virginia Time Travelers. A program which encourages students to visit historic sites in Virginia. www.timetravelers.org
- [ ] Virginia Civil War Trails. (888) CIVIL WAR or www.civilwar-va.com
- [ ] Virginia State Parks – Richmond. (800) 933-PARK or www.dcr.virginia.gov
- [ ] Virginia Campground Directory. www.virginiacampgrounds.org
- [ ] Virginia Game and Inland Fisheries. (804) 367-1000 or www.dgif.virginia.gov
- [ ] Virginia Marine Resources Commission. (757) 247-2200 or www.mrc.state.va.us
- [ ] Virginia Trails Association. (804) 798-4160 or www.waba.org
- [ ] U.S. – Camping – KOA Campgrounds, www.koa.com
- [ ] Alexandria Tourism. www.visitalexandriava.com
- [ ] Arlington Tourism. www.stayarlington.com
- [ ] Fredericksburg Tourism. www.visitfred.com
- [ ] Richmond Tourism. www.visitrichmondva.com

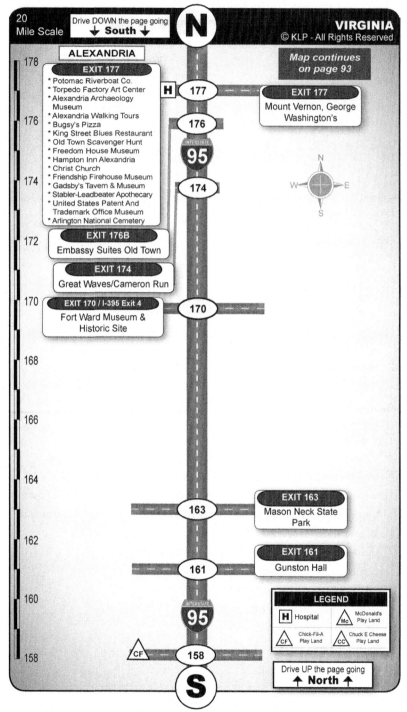

20 Mile Scale

Drive DOWN the page going ↓ **South** ↓

N

VIRGINIA
© KLP - All Rights Reserved

ALEXANDRIA

Map continues on page 93

178

EXIT 177
* Potomac Riverboat Co.
* Torpedo Factory Art Center
* Alexandria Archaeology Museum
* Alexandria Walking Tours
* Bugsy's Pizza
* King Street Blues Restaurant
* Old Town Scavenger Hunt
* Freedom House Museum
* Hampton Inn Alexandria
* Christ Church
* Friendship Firehouse Museum
* Gadsby's Tavern & Museum
* Stabler-Leadbeater Apothecary
* United States Patent And Trademark Office Museum
* Arlington National Cemetery

H 177

EXIT 177
Mount Vernon, George Washington's

176 176

INTERSTATE **95**

174 174

172

EXIT 176B
Embassy Suites Old Town

174

EXIT 174
Great Waves/Cameron Run

170

EXIT 170 / I-395 Exit 4
Fort Ward Museum & Historic Site

170

168

166

164

EXIT 163
Mason Neck State Park

163

162

EXIT 161
Gunston Hall

161

160

INTERSTATE **95**

LEGEND

H Hospital | **Mc** McDonald's Play Land

CF Chick-Fil-A Play Land | **CC** Chuck E Cheese Play Land

158 CF 158

S

Drive UP the page going ↑ **North** ↑

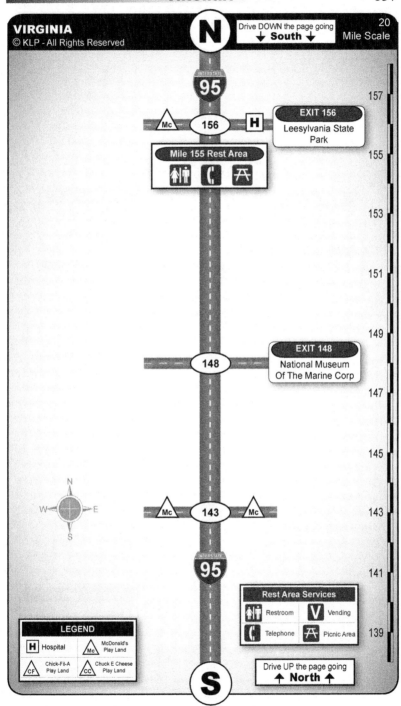

VIRGINIA

N

Drive DOWN the page going
↓ **South** ↓

20
Mile Scale

INTERSTATE
95

157

Mc **156** H

EXIT 156
Leesylvania State Park

155

Mile 155 Rest Area

153

151

149

148

EXIT 148
National Museum Of The Marine Corp

147

145

Mc **143** Mc

143

INTERSTATE
95

141

Rest Area Services

| 👫 Restroom | V Vending |
| 📞 Telephone | 🏕 Picnic Area |

139

LEGEND

| H Hospital | Mc McDonald's Play Land |
| CF Chick-Fil-A Play Land | CC Chuck E Cheese Play Land |

Drive UP the page going
↑ **North** ↑

S

VIRGINIA

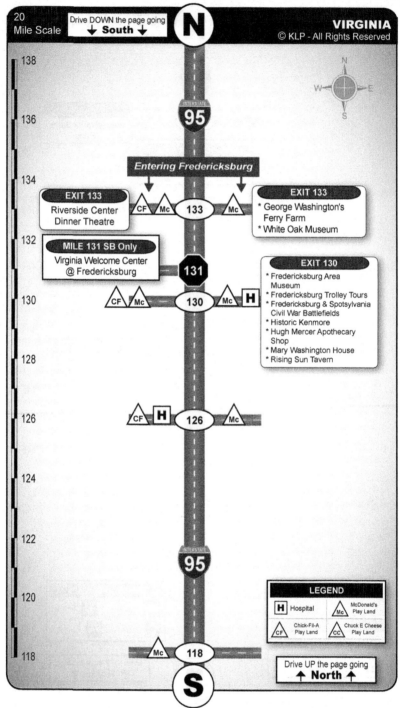

20 Mile Scale

Drive DOWN the page going
↓ **South** ↓

N

VIRGINIA

INTERSTATE **95**

Entering Fredericksburg

EXIT 133
Riverside Center
Dinner Theatre

CF Mc 133 Mc

EXIT 133
* George Washington's Ferry Farm
* White Oak Museum

MILE 131 SB Only
Virginia Welcome Center @ Fredericksburg

131

CF Mc 130 Mc H

EXIT 130
* Fredericksburg Area Museum
* Fredericksburg Trolley Tours
* Fredericksburg & Spotsylvania Civil War Battlefields
* Historic Kenmore
* Hugh Mercer Apothecary Shop
* Mary Washington House
* Rising Sun Tavern

CF H 126 Mc

INTERSTATE **95**

LEGEND

| H Hospital | Mc McDonald's Play Land |
| CF Chick-Fil-A Play Land | CC Chuck E Cheese Play Land |

Mc 118

Drive UP the page going
↑ **North** ↑

S

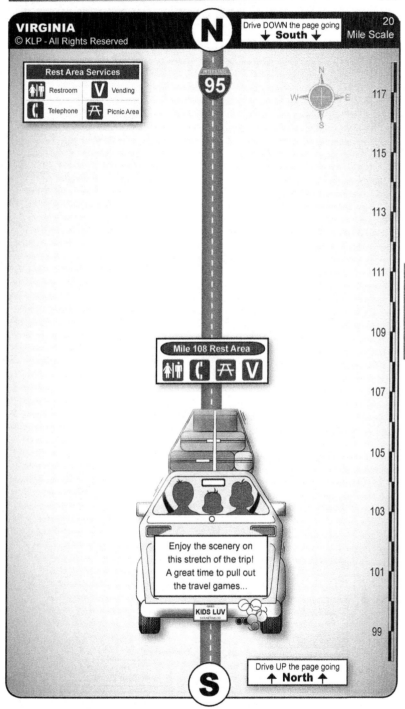

N

Drive DOWN the page going
↓ **South** ↓

20
Mile Scale

INTERSTATE
95

Rest Area Services

🚹 Restroom   V Vending
📞 Telephone   ⛱ Picnic Area

117

115

113

111

109

Mile 108 Rest Area
🚹 📞 ⛱ V

107

105

103

Enjoy the scenery on
this stretch of the trip!
A great time to pull out
the travel games...

101

KIDS LUV

99

Drive UP the page going
↑ **North** ↑

S

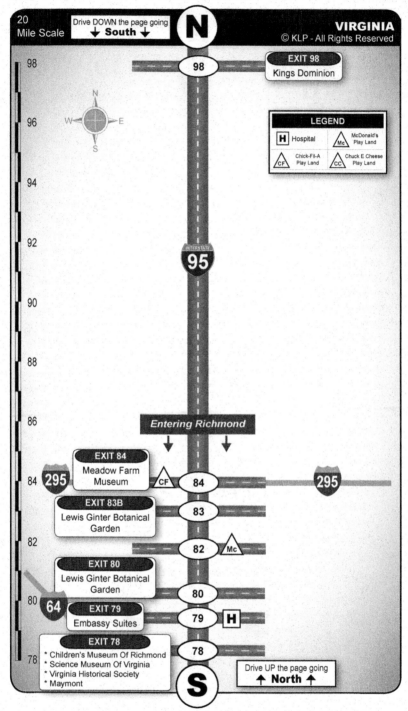

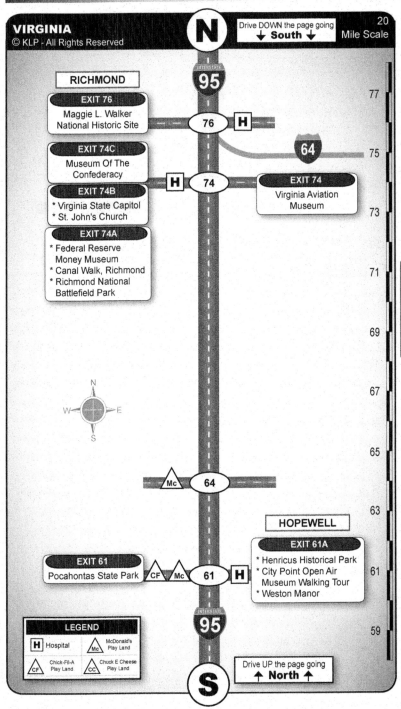

N

Drive DOWN the page going
↓ **South** ↓

20 Mile Scale

RICHMOND

95

77

EXIT 76
Maggie L. Walker
National Historic Site

76 **H**

75

64

EXIT 74C
Museum Of The
Confederacy

H 74

EXIT 74
Virginia Aviation
Museum

73

EXIT 74B
* Virginia State Capitol
* St. John's Church

EXIT 74A
* Federal Reserve
  Money Museum
* Canal Walk, Richmond
* Richmond National
  Battlefield Park

71

69

67

N
W—E
S

65

Mc 64

63

HOPEWELL

EXIT 61A
* Henricus Historical Park
* City Point Open Air
  Museum Walking Tour
* Weston Manor

61

EXIT 61
Pocahontas State Park

CF Mc 61 **H**

95

59

LEGEND

H Hospital

Mc McDonald's Play Land

CF Chick-Fil-A Play Land

CC Chuck E Cheese Play Land

Drive UP the page going
↑ **North** ↑

S

VIRGINIA

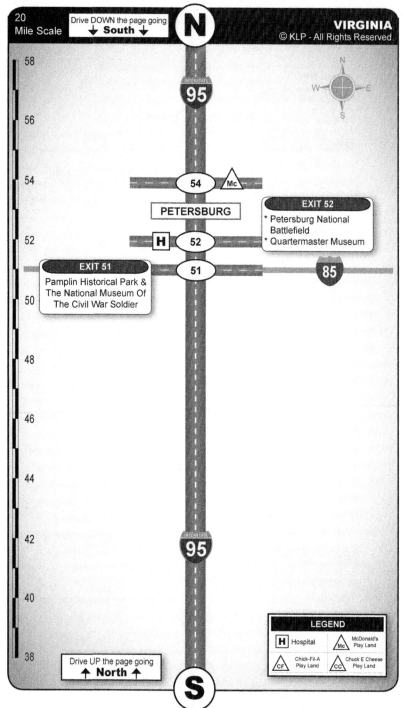

VIRGINIA

20 Mile Scale

Drive DOWN the page going
↓ **South** ↓

PETERSBURG

EXIT 52
* Petersburg National Battlefield
* Quartermaster Museum

EXIT 51
Pamplin Historical Park & The National Museum Of The Civil War Soldier

Drive UP the page going
↑ **North** ↑

LEGEND

| H Hospital | Mc McDonald's Play Land |
| CF Chick-Fil-A Play Land | CC Chuck E Cheese Play Land |

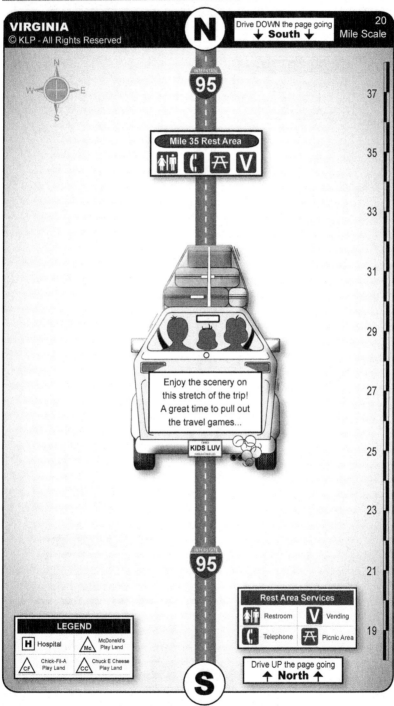

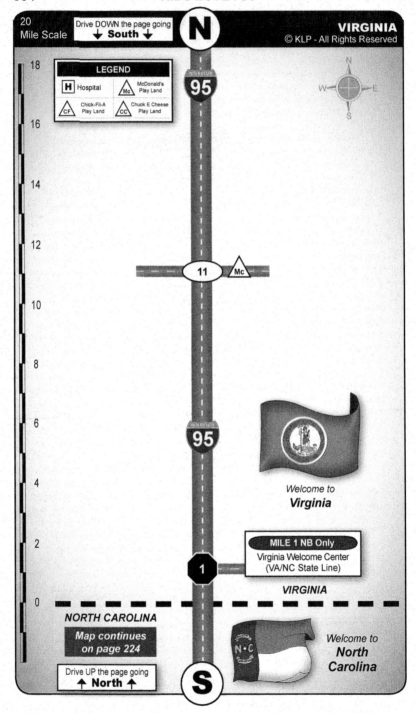

Sites and attractions are listed in order by Exit Number (North to South) and distance from the exit (closest are listed first). Symbols indicated represent:

 Restaurants   Lodging

Exit - 177 (west of I-95)

POTOMAC RIVERBOAT COMPANY

Alexandria - *Union & Cameron Streets (head north on Rte. 1. Then east on King street to City Marina) 22301. www.potomacriverboatco.com. Phone: (703) 684-0580 or (877) 511-2628. Admission: $10.00-$30.00 adult, $8.00-$28.00 senior, $5.00-$17.00 child (2-12). Online coupons. Tours: 5 times daily (each way) - Tuesday-Sunday, 11:30am-9:00pm (May-September). Plus Monday Holidays and Weekends (April & October)*

Some of the tours offered include:

☐ SEAPORT - 50 minute, narrated sightseeing cruise of Alexandria's historic waterfront.

☐ MOUNT VERNON - cruise from "old town" to the Mount Vernon Estate. 50 minutes each way. (Mt. Vernon admission included in ticket price)

☐ MONUMENTS - round trip, 60 minute cruise (each way) past Washington's majestic landmarks. Can get off in Georgetown for a spell and catch a later boat.

☐ PIRATES on the Potomac Cruise - During this 40-minute cruise, children of all ages will be entertained with music and tales of piracy on the Potomac River. This cruise features Alexandria's historic seaport and its landmarks. May through September, Friday, Saturday, and Sunday.

Canine Cruise?

Yes. All are invited, with or without a four legged friend. A howling experience for all! The dog rides free, but the human must pay for their ride.

All tours are narrated with fun facts, history and legends. Sailing schedule is subject to weather and river conditions. Contact by website, brochure or telephone is suggested to obtain current sailing schedule. Some younger children may prefer this method of touring.

Exit - 177 (west of I-95)

TORPEDO FACTORY ART CENTER

Alexandria - *105 North Union Street (on Potomac River @ the corner of King & Union Sts) 22314. Phone: (703) 838-4565. www.torpedofactory.org. Hours: Daily 10:00am-6:00pm. (Thursday until 9:0pm). Closed on Easter, July 4th, Thanksgiving, Christmas, and New Year's Day. Admission: FREE. Note: Art Camps.*

Constructed in 1918 for the manufacturing of torpedoes, the factory now serves as working studios for 82 professional artists. Visitors can purchase wares onsite or simply watch the creative process in action. Gaze at the dozens of studios and ask a question or two of the artists working on something unusual. Watch anything from sculpture, to painting, jewelry, stained glass, weaving, printmaking, ceramics, to photography being created. Some artists work mostly with their hands, others use dozens of tools hanging near their workbenches.

Learn from watching professional artists at work....

ALEXANDRIA ARCHAEOLOGY MUSEUM

Alexandria - *105 North Union Street, #327 (on Potomac River @ the corner of King & Union Sts.- Torpedo Factory Art Center, 3rd Floor) 22314. Phone: (703) 838-4399. www.AlexandriaArchaeology.org. Hours: Tuesday-Friday 10:00am-3:00pm, Saturday 10:00am-5:00pm, Sunday 1:00-5:00pm. Closed most holidays. Admission: FREE. Educators: Lesson plans downloadable on ACTIVITIES & EDUCATION icon.*

Want to go on an archaeology dig? Learn from the experts at an authentic site! Interact with the City archaeologists and volunteers working in the public laboratory (and occasional public dig days). This small space inside the Torpedo Art Factory may appear plain at the window but take a few moments to walk inside and explore a few minutes. You might first notice a small dinosaur skeleton - but is it really a dino? - not! Hone your archeology skills doing the Plate Puzzle: try to put the broken plate back together from

pieces similar to what one might find on a dig. Younger kids have a coloring station nearby to amuse themselves while the other family members try to put a plate together first.

The Alexandria Archaeology Museum offers Family Dig Days, where everyone can participate and learn secrets from the experts. Experience

Trying to reassemble a broken plate...

Alexandria using maps, oral history, heritage through exhibits, self-guided tours, and hands-on discovery kits. View the latest finds from current excavations where archaeologists reconstruct history.

ALEXANDRIA WALKING TOURS

Alexandria - *221 King Street (Ramsay House Visitors Center) 22314. Phone: (703) 838-4200. http://visitalexandriava.com/things_to_do/tours/walking. Admission: $10.00 adult. Parking: Obtain a FREE pass at the Visitor's Center. Note: Prior to receiving your pass, you should find a space and feed the meter to cover the time between parking the car and returning from the Visitors Center with the pass. You'll need to show an ID and give them your license plate number. Tours: Daily tour departs Monday-Saturday at 10:30am and Sunday at 2:00pm from the garden. (March-November) weather permitting. Miscellaneous: While at the Ramsay House, check out all the fun Alex the Unofficial Mascot items - stuffed toys, ornaments and illustrated book. KING STREET TROLLEY: Running 11:30am-10:00pm daily, this FREE trolley runs between N. Union Street and the King Street Metro station, making lots of stops for hopping on and off to check out all the shops, restaurants and attractions found along Old Town's main thoroughfare.*

A 90-minute tour walking by many of Old Town's significant landmarks, as well as little known sites. Learn history beginning from the French / Indian War through current events. Questions will be answered about: Why are there "snowbirds" on roofs? Why are some of the drainpipes marked, Alexandria, DC instead of Virginia? During the Civil War, how was Alexandria used by Union troops? Why is Christ Church considered "in the woods" even though it is located right in town? Where did the first Union soldier die in the Civil War?

Ever heard of an ice well? Where did Washington stay when he was in town? Where did he hold birthday parties? Be sure to look for a "busybody" and the sign of the "pineapple story". As you can tell, the facts and history about Alexandria during the tour will be extensive. Learn about the early history of Alexandria and walk where George Washington and other Virginia patriots walked. It is presented in a fun way to hold your attention by some very enthusiastic and energetic tour guides! Note: The 1½ hour tour is delightful for about 4th graders and up (who have studied American History). Younger children (particularly without strollers) will tire quickly.

Exit - 177 (west of I-95)

BUGSY'S PIZZA

Alexandria - *111 King Street (US 1 north exit to King Street) 22314. Phone: (703) 683-0313. www.bugsyspizza.com.*

Just down the street from the Visitors Center is with original beams in the building made from tobacco boats. All you can eat pizza and salad lunch buffet. Just $6.95. Many pizzas are unique combos to try (especially at the pizza buffet). Across the street is another hometown favorite - The Scoop Ice Cream. If there's a nip in the air and you don't have a fancy for ice cream, have a helping of homemade cobbler (blueberry, apple, cherry or peach) from the pie case on the counter. Ice cream flavors run the spectrum: cherry blossom, lemon custard, peanut butter, maple nut, and new batches are made fresh every day. After all that food, walk just one block to the riverfront.

KING STREET BLUES RESTAURANT

Alexandria - *112 N. St.Asaph St. (just north off King) (Rte 1 north. follow signs to King Street, Old Town) 22314. Phone: (703) 836-8800. www.kingstreetblues.com. Hours: Serving lunch and dinner daily.*

Catching dinner in Old Town Alexandria? Try any place on or near King Street. We liked King Street Blues, a quirky, fun and artsy motif (lots of cutesy pigs) serving Comfort Food with a Southern Accent. Try ribs, smoked pork or chicken, po'boys or something from the KIDS MENU: $4.75 for beverage (in souvenir kids cup) plus one entree like hot dog, mac n cheese or mini burgers or pulled BBQ sandwiches. We especially liked their Crab & Artichoke Dip for an afternoon snack to share. Fun and affordable with a break from "history lessons" of old town.

OLD TOWN SCAVENGER HUNT

Alexandria - *(pick up hunt page at the Christmas Attic at 125 S. Union Street) 22314. Retail store: (703) 548-2829.   www.alexcolonialtours.com/familyfun.html. Tours: You can purchase your Scavenger Hunt at the Christmas Attic (corner of Union and Prince Streets, just two blocks from the Ramsay House Visitor Center). The cost is $4.00 per Hunt map. Open daily. Group Pirate's Treasure tours are scheduled in advance. Cost $12.00 per child. Educators: The hunt is geared towards ages 8-11 who are studying early American history.*

Young Adventurers, you will hunt through the brick-lined streets of historic Old Town Alexandria. Discover clues and facts about George Washington and his seaport hometown. The Hunt is a self-guided walk. On the Hunt you will search for historic places and literally walk in our first President's footsteps. Each hunt takes about 45 minutes. The Hunt is fun for families to take together - split into teams and see who wins!

FREEDOM HOUSE MUSEUM

Alexandria - *1315 Duke Street (old town, near outskirts. King Street Metro is 3 blocks away) 22314. Phone: (703) 836-2858.   www.FreedomHouseMuseum.org. Hours: Monday-Friday 10:00am-4:00pm. Self-guided tours. Guided tours by appt. Admission: FREE.*

Once headquarters for the slave-trade operations in this area, the historic building now houses the Northern Virginia Urban League's newly opened museum. Franklin, Armfield & Co. were the largest domestic slave trading company in the country. Thousands of men, women, and children passed through these doors on the horrific journey to lives of bondage and hard labor in the deep south. Black wire mannequins stage the sad state slaves were reduced to. Cotton was king. Learn why they needed so many slaves. As stewards of property, the Urban League tends to a building that once held slaves captive but now serves to emancipate, educate, and enlighten their descendants!

Exit - 177 (west of I-95)

HAMPTON INN ALEXANDRIA-OLD TOWN / KING STREET METRO

Alexandria - *1616 King Street (US 1 north exit to right onto King Street) 22314. www.hamptoninn.com/en/hp/hotels/index.jhtml?ctyhocn=WASALHX. Phone: (703) 299-9900.*

A nice choice for D.C./Alexandria area lodging. They offer On the House™ hot breakfast buffet served from 6:00-10:00am each morning featuring rotating hot entrees, premium coffees and teas, fresh fruits, cereals, and freshly baked breakfast pastries and are a quick 1 block walk to the Metro or an even quicker step out the door to Old Town historic attractions. There's an outdoor pool, too. Packages and weekend rates around $119.00.

CHRIST CHURCH

Alexandria - *118 North Washington Street (Olde Town, Rte. 1 north one mile. Right on King to Washington) 22314. www.historicchristchurch.org. Phone: (703) 549-1450. Hours: Tuesday-Saturday 10:00am-4:00pm. Visitors are welcome to attend services Sunday mornings. (Visitors can actually sit in the Washington family pew - first come, first served). Admission: FREE, donations accepted.*

Men and women from the parish serve as docents and welcome visitors to Christ Church throughout the year. The docents point out the church's most interesting architectural features and history. Built in 1773, George Washington attended church here (pew #60) when in town and Robert E. Lee was also confirmed here. In the early days, rent was charged for a family pew in lieu of tithes (and if you didn't show up for church...everyone knew!). The Union army took over this church during the Civil War. Although the structure suffered no serious damage, the grave markers were removed and stacked to make room for the camps. No records exist of where the markers were...so it's anybody's guess if the graves are now correctly marked. Find the grave that shows a woman living to be 156 years old...what's up with that?

> Notice the wine goblet shaped pulpit with a sounding board overhead. No microphone was used - then or today.

FRIENDSHIP FIREHOUSE MUSEUM

Alexandria - *107 South Alfred Street, Old Town (US 1 exit north about one mile. Right on Prince, left on S. Alfred) 22314. http://oha.alexandriava.gov/friendship/. Phone: (703) 838-3891. Hours: Saturday and Sunday 1:00-4:00pm. Closed New Years and Christmas. Admission: $2.00*

The Friendship Fire Company was established in 1774, and was the first volunteer fire company in Alexandria. The current firehouse was built in 1855, remodeled in 1871 and renovated in 1992. The Engine Room on the first floor houses hand-drawn fire engines, leather water buckets, axes, sections of early rubber hose and other historic fire-fighting equipment. Fun to look at for a quick trip inside, out of the hot sun.

GADSBY'S TAVERN & MUSEUM

Alexandria - *134 North Royal Street (Olde Town, Rte. 1 north one mile. Right on King. Left onto North Royal) 22314. Phone: (703) 838-4242, Restaurant: (703) 548-1288. www.gadsbystavern.org. Hours: Museum: Tuesday-Saturday 10:00am-5:00pm, Sunday and Monday 1:00-5:00pm. (April-October). Wednesday-Saturday 11:00am-4:00pm, Sunday 1-4:00pm (November-March)   Restaurant: 7 days for lunch/dinner. Colonial entertainment in the evenings. Admission: Museum: $5.00 adult, $3.00 child (5-12). Coupon online. Restaurant prices: Lunch $8.00-$15.00. Child's menu $5-10.00 all day. Dinner prices: Average $25.00. Tours: offered most days right before/after lunch through afternoon. Tours start at a quarter after the hour and a quarter before the hour, lasting approximately 30 minutes. One Sunday each month at 3:00pm Tea with Martha Washington. Tavern Toddlers on Monday mornings. On summer Friday nights they offer tours by lantern for the family. Note: Great combo for lunchtime with families. A free 24-hour parking pass, valid at meters, is available to out-of-town visitors at Ramsay House Visitors Center. Stairs on tour. Educators: Rent Outreach Trunks or schedule themed field trips.*

Take a moment to journey back to the 18th-century tavern and hotel where famous historical figures and everyday people dined and slept. "General Washington's steward had recommended me an inn kept by Mr. Gadsby..." This is the place if you're in the mood for authentic colonial dining (fresh fish, crabcakes, Virginia ham and pyes - potpie puff pastry) that is served by a

A great meal - where Presidents ate!

costumed wait staff who speak old English. The museum is in the 1770 City Tavern and City Hotel where many political and social events occurred (even Washington's birthday parties). Notice the ice well where they kept ice all year long and could serve cold beverages in the heat of summer (something very few establishments could do). Notable guests and stories of visits included on tour are George Washington, Thomas Jefferson, Robert E. Lee, and their wives.

Exit - 177 (west of I-95)

STABLER-LEADBEATER APOTHECARY MUSEUM

Alexandria - *105-107 South Fairfax Street, Old Town (US 1 north exit. First right onto Franklin for 7 blocks. Left onto S Fairfax) 22314. Phone: (703) 838-3852. http://oha.alexandriava.gov/apothecary/ap-mission.html. Hours: Tuesday-Saturday 10:00am-5:00pm, Sunday & Monday 1:00-5:00pm (April-October). Shortened hours and closed Monday and Tuesday (November-March). Closed: New Year's Day, Thanksgiving, Christmas. Admission: $5.00 adult, $3.00 youth (5-12). Children under 5: FREE.*

When the Apothecary closed during the Depression, in 1933, the doors were simply locked, preserving the contents for history. The building re-opened as a museum in 1939. Over 8,000 objects, including pill rollers, mortars and pestles, drug mills, and hand-blown medicine bottles with gold-leaf labels, were left in place. Medicinal herbs and paper labels remain in their wooden drawers. Large show-globes from the mid-19th century remain in the windows. Original apothecaries created their medicine onsite using herbs and other ingredients. The names of famous customers appear in several original documents, including Martha Washington, James Monroe, and Robert E. Lee. According to an 1802 letter from Mount Vernon, "Mrs. Washington desires Mr. Stabler to send by the bearer a quart bottle of his best Castor Oil and the bill for it." Tours of the museum show how the apothecaries plied their trade and give a glimpse into the "drug stores" of early America. Funny how remedies of the past are now creeping back into modern herbal remedies…

UNITED STATES PATENT AND TRADEMARK OFFICE MUSEUM

Alexandria - *600 Dulany Street (in the atrium of the Madison Building, take King St. & Eisenhower Metro stop) 22314. www.uspto.gov/web/offices/ac/ahrpa/opa/museum/. Phone: (571) 272-0095. Hours: Monday-Friday 9:00am-5:00pm, Saturday Noon-5:00pm. Admission: FREE. Note: Now Home to the National Inventors Hall of*

Fame. Educators: several great books are available for purchase at the site: ex. Kids and Inventing. Online, you can access their goKids link or video link for some wonderful motivation.

Looking at the exhibits, you will realize how you take advantage of inventions and rely on trademarks every day of your life. Intellectual property is found in the routines you follow at the beginning of the day, in methods you use for travel, in medical innovations you rely upon for good health, and in the different ways you relax and play. Look over videos, interactives, artifacts and touch-screen technology—featuring patents, trademarks, inventors and inventions. Every season, they change displays of famous patents - like Michael Jackson's anti-gravity boots or Edison's first record. The Talking Gallery of famous inventors is interesting and whimsical but kids really get inspired by the 7-minute movie shown about modern inventors of extreme sports equipment!

ARLINGTON NATIONAL CEMETERY

Arlington - *(Ample paid parking is available to visitors, accessible from Memorial Drive) 22211. www.arlingtoncemetery.org/. Phone: (703) 697-2131, (202) 554-5100 or (888) 868-7707. Hours: The Cemetery opens to the public at 8:00am every day, closing between 5:00-7:00pm. Tours Daily 8:30am-4:30pm (April-September), 9:30-4:30pm (rest of year). Admission: Walking tour is FREE. Tourmobiles fare is $9.00 adult, $4.75 child (3-11) (Arlington Tour). See separate Tourmobile listing for D.C. & Arlington fares. We suggest parking at Arlington and then Tourmobiling around DC. Parking: the cost is $1.75/hour for the first three hours, and $2.00/ hour thereafter. Tours: Begin at Visitor Center on Memorial Drive starting one half hour after cemetery opens until one half hour before cemetery closes. Last tour begins 30 minutes before closing. Closed on Christmas. Miscellaneous: The tourmobile is suggested for kids because the walking tour is too long. The on/ off all day service is perfect for families touring the many sites in the DC area. Please note that the cemetery does not provide wheelchairs or strollers and if you require this service you will need to bring your own.*

John F. Kennedy's gravesite burns an "Eternal Flame"

This is the best spot to visit (especially by tourmobile), to get to the heart of Arlington. Many sites are on, or near the grounds, and some can be toured individually or as part of the tourmobile tour. Why are some of the headstones smaller and empty? The tour includes the Kennedy gravesites; the Tomb of the Unknowns for the Changing of the

Guard ceremony (24/7 - Look how still the guards are!); the Arlington House, The Robert E. Lee Memorial [where Lee lived for 30 years, where he chose to resign his commission in the US Army to defend Virginia in the Civil War, and where Union troops occupied it during the Civil War - Open daily, 9:30am-4:30pm, Free, (703) 557-0613]. Narrators on the tourmobile relate accounts of personal sacrifice and heroism as you ride past the important sites. Lots of little known facts and anecdotes. Check out the newer "Women in Military Service for America Memorial" were you'll see an emotional, patriotic film and learn many little known stories of women who served as water bearers, nurses, and POW's (the building is entirely covered in a "glass ceiling").

Exit - 177 (east of I-95)

MOUNT VERNON, GEORGE WASHINGTON'S

Alexandria (Mount Vernon) - *3200 Mount Vernon Memorial Hwy (end of George Washington Memorial Parkway, due south of exit) 22121. Phone: (703) 780-2000. www.mountvernon.org. Hours: Daily 8:00am-5:00pm (April - August), 9:00am-5:00pm (March, September, October), 9:00am-4:00pm (rest of the year). Admission: $17.00 adult, $16.00 seniors (62+), $8.00 Child (6-11). Food Court Pavilion and expanded Shops at Mount Vernon. Pathways in the historic area consist of gravel, dirt, and bricks, but are stroller accessible. They are not allowed in the Mansion. Nearby is a Working 18th-century mill at George Washington's Gristmill. George Washington's Gristmill is 3 miles away and features guides leading historic tours. Meet a miller and watch the water-wheel operate the stones grinding grain into flour. Learn about the slaves and millers who ground grain 200 years ago. (small additional fee). Mount Vernon welcomes visitors to bring dogs on leashes during daytime visitation hours. The gate attendants provide a bowl of water for your special family friend. Educators: everything you could ever want to study about G.W. is on the Educator/Teachers Resources pages including Biography, Lesson Plans and kids games & quizzes.*

Be sure your children receive the Adventure Map which has puzzles to solve...the kids love it because the map looks like a treasure map!

Explore history and get to know the "real" George Washington. For one reasonable ticket price, this attraction can be explored many ways. If you come during a festival weekend, concentrate on the festival green first. If this is your first family tour, we would suggest you start, depending on the weather, touring the outbuildings, farm and home. Now you have a "feel" for life at Mt. Vernon. Next, apply those heightened senses walking through the Education Center which really uncovers EVERY aspect of our beloved George Washington's character and lifestyle. Now, here's the skinny on all there is to do:

* <u>EDUCATION CENTER:</u> Located just inside the main entrance to Mount Vernon, the Reynolds Museum & Ford Orientation Center introduces visitors to the personality and character of George Washington as his contemporaries knew him with a dramatic 15-minute film. The large-format, Hollywood-style film provides action-oriented insight into the story of Washington's life and enable visitors to "meet" the real George Washington. When the cannons roar, the seats rumble. When you're crossing the Delaware River, the snow falls on you. Another new attraction is the "Mount Vernon in Miniature," an authentic, one-twelfth scale version of the Mansion. Tons of colorful dioramas take you on a personal tour of Washington's life. What I also liked about the Education Wing was how it draws

He's watching you...

kids in: start with Washington's eyes following you to CSI-style forensics on how they "reconstructed" George's face from childhood through old age. Youth, love stories, war drama, touching, smelling, even spying? And, the Revolutionary War Theater – rumbling battles and winters real snow engage you!

* <u>HANDS ON HISTORY ROOM</u> Children can learn the same themes and ideas presented in the Education Center galleries by dressing in 18th-century clothing, putting on stage plays, reading books, exploring activity boxes and games, and learning about Washington's farm animals. There's even a huge Mt. Vernon dollhouse you can play with, girls! Learn how to bridle and sit on a mule; and The Root Cellar - What archeological items could be found in a cellar? (answer: bottles, keys, bones from cooked food).

Now there's a fun-loving First Family for sure...

* <u>PIONEER FARMER</u> - Ever see a round barn? How about a barn where horses walk the 2nd floor? Crack corn, thresh wheat or taste a hoecake. Visit with livestock authentic to George Washington's times (some are heirloom varieties like Hogg Island sheep). A reconstructed slave cabin on the site reflects the living conditions of slaves on the Mount Vernon plantation. The cabin is a major enhancement of the interpretation of slave life at Mount Vernon. (Site open April-October)

* <u>OUTBUILDINGS</u> - Dung Depository (Washington was one of the first composters), coach house and stable, laundry yard, smokehouse, clerk's office and kitchen.

• GEORGE WASHINGTON'S TOMB - See the original site and see the actual vault where George Washington's body now lies.

Of course, the true highlight of this visit will be your HOUSE TOUR. During peak season, be prepared for a 30-90 minute wait to enter. Once inside, you'll learn the history of this very famous house. See mostly authentic

furnishings, Washington's unique color choices for rooms (many are bright and cheerful like the giant green room where he and Martha loved to dance!) Look for the letter press (a carbon copy like machine) that General Washington used to make copies of all letters that were sent. (He wrote so many...and at that time they took so long to get

We tried to imagine George & Martha Washington spending time at "home"...

delivered that sometimes you could forget what you wrote if you didn't keep a copy!). You'll also see a giant globe in his office that strangely is missing one entire continent (could it be that it wasn't discovered yet?). Near the end of the tour, you'll see Washington's private family chambers and the bed in which he died. .

Exit - 176B (west of I-95)

The Metro was a great way get in and out of D.C.

EMBASSY SUITES OLD TOWN

Alexandria - 1900 Diagonal Road (Follow signs to Downtown Alexandria (Duke Street) Follow to Diagonal Road and left. Hotel will be on your right) 22314. Phone: (703) 684-5900. www.embassysuites. com.

Family Fun Packages all year. Your kids get a "kid-tested" pack of goodies, an indoor pool, soft play area for toddlers, and the whole family gets a wonderful cooked to order full breakfast and snacks before dinner. All rooms are suites with separate bedroom, microwave, and refrigerator from around $150.00/night. Overnight parking is $24.00/day. Hotel is directly across the street from the King Street Metro Station (Blue/ Yellow Line/Amtrak/Virginia Rail Express) - the option we suggest for touring D.C.

Exit - 174 (west of I-95)

GREAT WAVES AT CAMERON RUN REGIONAL PARK

Alexandria - 4001 Eisenhower Avenue (I-95/495 exit 174 head north and then east on Eisenhower) 22304. www.nvrpa.org/parks/cameronrun/. Phone: (703) 960-0767. Hours: Pool: (Memorial Day weekend - Labor Day). Batting cage and Mini golf: (mid-March - October). Hours vary. Peak season hours generally between 11:00am-7:00pm. Admission: Pool is $11.00-$15.00. Batting and Mini Golf are $1.00-$6.00 added to pool price. Note: Concessions and picnic areas.

This park offers something for everyone - waterslides, wave pool, lap pool, Play Pool (climb on snakes or alligators in shallow waters), Tad Pool, batting cages and miniature golf.

Exit - 170 (west of I-95) / I-395 Exit 4

FORT WARD MUSEUM & HISTORIC SITE

Alexandria - 4301 West Braddock Road (I-395north, Seminary Road exit) 22304. Phone: (703) 838-4848 or (703) 838-4831(park). www.fortward.org. Hours: Museum: Tuesday-Saturday 10:00am-5:00pm, Sunday Noon-5:00pm. Park: Daily, 9:00am-Sunset. Admission: FREE. Online gift shop coupon. Note: Occasional informal encampments are held on the grounds.

The museum, patterned after a Union headquarters building, houses a Civil War collection and exhibits. When in the Museum, be sure to stop at the three-dimensional model of Fort Ward to see a small scale version of how the site looked during the Civil War. Also see the large map which outlines the extensive ring of forts comprising the Defenses of Washington, called "Mr. Lincoln's Forts." An orientation video provides an excellent overview of the history of Fort Ward, the best preserved of all the Civil War forts around Washington, and the wartime defense of the Union capital. The Fort's Northwest Bastion has been completely restored and the grounds also feature a reconstructed ceremonial gate (decorated with cannonballs) and Officer's Hut. Climb the stockade into the fort and check out the cannon as you pretend to live the everyday life of Civil War soldiers and civilians. After duty in the Defenses of Washington, many were sent to serve in southern campaigns where the conditions of army life were considerably harsher than in the forts and camps around Washington.

Exit - 163 (east of I-95)

MASON NECK STATE PARK

Mason Neck (Lorton) - *7301 High Point Road (exit east on 642 to US 1, then east to SR 242) 22079. Phone: (703) 339-2385 or (703) 339-2380 (visitor center). www.dcr.virginia.gov/state_parks/mas.shtml.   Admission: $4.00-5.00 per car. Miscellaneous: Hiking trails, picnicking and Visitors Center.*

The peninsula is the site of an active heron rookery. The park also attracts several other migrating and non-migrating species of birds, including whistling swans and assorted species of duck. Bald eagles also inhabit the area. The park boasts several hundred acres of hardwood forests consisting of oaks, holly, hickory and other species of trees. In addition, several wetland areas are also found along with birdwatching and guided canoe trips on the Potomac River. More than three miles of hiking trails wind through the park providing a glimpse of nature by the bay. Elevated walkways allow visitors to explore some of the marsh areas in the park. Ten bicycles are available for rent by the hour.

Exit - 161 (east of I-95)

GUNSTON HALL

Alexandria (Mason Neck) - *10709 Gunston Road (I-95 onto US Rte. 1 to SR 242 east) 22079. Phone: (703) 550-9220 or (800) 811-6966. www.gunstonhall.org. Hours: Daily 9:30am-4:30pm. Closed New Years, Thanksgiving, and Christmas. Admission: $10.00 adult, $8.00 senior, $5.00 student (6-18). Online coupon. Tours: Guided house tours are offered every half hour. These tours focus on the life of George Mason and his family; they tell of the slaves, servants, and the others who worked for the Mason family; and point out the architectural features of the house. The house tour takes approximately 45 minutes. Educators: Grade appropriate Curriculum guides and videos can be reserved online.*

See the colonial plantation home of George Mason, author of the Virginia Declaration of Rights and a framer of the United States Constitution. A visit to Gunston Hall begins with the introductory film, George Mason and the

Bill of Rights (11 minutes). Visitors then can view the center's exhibits which highlight details of George Mason's civic career and the lasting influences of his most famous document, The Virginia Declaration of Rights. Exhibits also focus on facets of his personal life as well as aspects of 18th-century plantation culture such as hospitality, building practices, and horticulture. The house has elaborately carved woodwork. Reconstructed outbuildings help to illustrate the work of domestic servants and slaves. There's a nature trail for the kiddies to burn off energy but Special events make this even more interesting. "That all men are born equally free and independent, and have certain inherent natural Rights... among which are the Enjoyment of Life and Liberty, with the Means of acquiring and possessing Property, and pursuing and obtaining Happiness and Safety." -- George Mason. Virginia Declaration of Rights, May, 1776. Sounds familiar-yes?

Exit - 156 (east of I-95)

LEESYLVANIA STATE PARK

Woodbridge - *2001 Daniel Ludwig Drive (go east on Dale Blvd. to right onto US 1. Jefferson Davis Hwy. turn left onto Neabsco Rd. (Route 610) east for about 2 miles) 22191. Phone: (703) 670-0372. www.dcr.virginia.gov/state_parks/lee. shtml. Admission: $4.00-$5.00 per vehicle.*

Located on the Potomac River, this park offers many land and water related activities including biking, picnicking, fishing and boating. Newer boat launching facilities, concessions area, a new visitor center and an environmental education center are available. The park offers four hiking trails for the exploration of the rich natural and historical features of the Potomac. The park boasts many scenic overlooks of the Potomac River including one on the remains of a Civil War Confederate gun battery at Freestone Point. Leesylvania was a home of Virginia's legendary Lee Family. Once a year (in June), there is a Civil War Weekend at Leesylvania. Explore the park's rich Civil War history, tour Freestone Point Battery and Fairfax House, and view a re-enactment of historical happenings. See Civil War era weapons fired where similar guns once blazed.

Exit - 148 (east of I-95)

NATIONAL MUSEUM OF THE MARINE CORPS

Quantico - *(I-95 exit next to the U.S. Marine Corps Base, follow signs) 22134. Phone: (212) 358-0800 or (800) 397-7585. www.usmcmuseum.org. Hours: Daily 9:00am-5:00pm except Christmas Day. Admission: FREE. Miscellaneous: It includes a gift shop, the eateries: Tun Tavern and the Devil Dog Diner, memorial park and artifact restoration. Family Days or Storytimes every weekend. Visitors bringing young children to the National Museum of the Marine Corps are encouraged to speak with a Museum Docent at the Information Desk if they are concerned that the Museum's exhibits may not be age-appropriate for their children. Educators: Gallery Recon scavenger hunts. Education page has Gallery Guides and Worksheets.*

Half an hour's drive from the nation's capital, the National Museum of the Marine Corps explores Marine aviation from the dawn of flight through both world wars and Korea as well as a gallery devoted to the War on Terror. Before entering major galleries, visitors pass through an orientation theater featuring a short, introductory film about the Corps and its history. As they exit the theater, visitors will find themselves in a replica of a recruiting station, from which they will move aboard a bus, the windows of which are television screens transmitting oral histories of Marines recounting their feelings on the verge of boot camp. If you make it through Boot Camp, immerse in realistic exhibits, examine weapons and equipment and use interactive devices to better understand how this small, elite fighting force came to make a large influence on American history. It's a clever way to immerse the kids in military history. Located adjacent to Quantico Marine Corps Base, the museum's 210-foot tilted steel mast and glass atrium with suspended aircraft features is hard to miss seeing.

Exit - 133 (west of I-95)

RIVERSIDE CENTER DINNER THEATRE

Fredericksburg - *95 Riverside Parkway (take Warrenton Rd west. First major street Left onto Stanford. Left onto Riverside) 22406. Phone: (540) 370-4300 or (888) 999-8527. www.rsdinnertheater.com.*

Watch favorite American tales come to life on stage. This professionally performed musical is geared especially for children of all ages. You will be charmed by the cast as they serve a fabulous lunch to your table. Children's Selections include something like Spaghetti with Meatballs. Productions like: Jack and the Giant or Willy Wonka. Most shows (Wednesday thru Sunday) are $40-$50.00. Saturday Matinees and selected weekday matinees, year-round. Lunch and show is $18.00 per person for children's Theater.

Exit - 133 (east of I-95)

GEORGE WASHINGTON'S FERRY FARM

Fredericksburg - *268 Kings Highway (Route 17 east to SR 3 east, along the Rappahannock River) 22407. Phone: (540) 370-0732. www.ferryfarm.org. Hours: Daily 10:00am-4:00pm. Closed January and February except George Washington's Birthday in February. Closed major winter holidays. Admission: $8.00 adult, $4.00 student (ages 6-17 and anyone with a student ID). Discovery Workshops may be slightly more but include activity. Discounted Combo tickets to Ferry Farm & Kenmore. Educators: Educational Trunks and Colonial Games bring history into the classroom. Pick up a trunk of educational tools at Ferry Farm and return it when you have completed your unit. Lesson plans included. FREEBIES: Kid stuff page has puzzles, coloring and games.*

Located 38 miles south of Mount Vernon on the banks of the Rappahannock River, this is the boyhood home of the father of our country...not to mention, the reported place where the famous "cherry tree" incident (and legend) occurred. This was his father's 600 acre plantation where he grew up and later learned how to survey. The current property is under archeological excavations that are ongoing. After taking a look at the exhibits in the Visitors Center, folks can take a self-guided tour of the farm Washington inherited at age 11 and where he lived between the ages of 6 and 20. Only facades of one home are viewed, but new artifacts turn up all the time. We suggest Discovery Workshops for the kids in the summer. Each workshop teaches hands-on activities about Colonial life at Ferry Farm and the Fredericksburg area. Other programs highlight investigating trees, 18th century gardening and games, surveying and wartime camp life. Best of all, the staff here are creative and energetic about the site and interpretation.

WHITE OAK MUSEUM

Fredericksburg (Falmouth) - *985 White Oak Road (US 17 east turns into SR 218, six miles east of Fredericksburg) 22405. www.WhiteOakMuseum.com. Phone: (540) 371-4234. Hours: Wednesday-Sunday 10:00am-5:00pm. Admission: $1.00-$4.00 (age 7+).*

White Oak Museum houses one of the nation's most extensive collections of Civil War artifacts, representing both Union and Confederate troops. Most items were discarded or lost by troops camping in Stafford before and after the Battles in Fredericksburg and Spotsylvania in 1862-1863. One display contains 60,000 bullets collected from soldiers discards or practice shots. A giant cannon ball shot attracts interest, as does the organized display of different types of bottles recovered from camp areas. Life-size replicas of soldiers huts give you an idea of how primitive and sparse shelter was throughout even the winter months. Many Civil War soldiers died of wounds and disease. The museum's newest exhibit is a recently–discovered section of a "corduroy road."

Exit - 131 Mile (SB Only)

VIRGINIA WELCOME CENTER @ FREDERICKSBURG

Fredericksburg - *22404. Phone: (540) 786-8344.*

The new Virginia Welcome Center at Fredericksburg is open and ready for Virginia travelers. Inside you'll find a large Virginia Welcome Center with a dedicated travel research area, more rest room facilities (including family friendly stalls), and enhanced vending. Outside, visitors will find: additional car, truck and bus parking, new landscaping, well-lit secure walking paths, new picnic shelters and tables.

Exit - 130 (east of I-95)

FREDERICKSBURG AREA MUSEUM

Fredericksburg - *1001 Princess Anne Street (Rte. 3 east to corner of Princess Anne and William Streets) 22401. Phone: (540) 371-3037. www.famcc.org. Hours: Monday-Saturday 10am-5:00pm, Sunday Noon-5:00pm. Admission: $7.00 adult, $2.00 student (7-18). Educators: Trail to Freedom Tool Kit under Teachers Resources.*

Housed in the old 1816 Town Hall / Market House, the Federal building survived the destruction of the Civil War. This museum displays artifacts of the town starting with the formation of North America and proceeding to the present. Children enjoy the dinosaur footprints that were found in the area, as well as an Indian hut and Colonial fort, and period weapons used in the Revolutionary and Civil Wars. Look for the actual newspaper from 1767!

For updates & travel games visit: **www.KidsLoveTravel.com**

FREDERICKSBURG TROLLEY TOURS

Fredericksburg - *706 Caroline Street 22401. www.fredericksburgtrolley.com. Phone: (800) 979-3370. Admission: $17.00 adult, $8.00 child (5-12) Tours: Start at the Fredericksburg Visitor Center 600 Caroline St. 75 minute tours depart 3-4 times daily (every couple hours or so).*

Fredericksburg Virginia is America's most historic city. Enjoy an entertaining and informative tour of Fredericksburg aboard the trolley. Your tour will take you back through time. From the days when the Native Americans hunted and farmed the area through the arrival of settlers from Jamestown, Yorktown and other far away lands in the 1600s, and on through the birth of our Nation and its growing pains during the time of the Civil War. Pass and hear information about Chatham House and 50 of the 100 historic homes (even the oldest one). The tavern wench (not a bad name in those times), the Apothecary assistant and "Mary Washington (George's mom)" will come out and wave as you pass by. See the original stonewall of the battlefield. Funny tidbits: Old Stone Warehouse - why is only the 3rd floor showing? Why were some homes built in layers? What happened if you didn't go to church at least twice a month in the Anglican Church? Why did they build narrow homes? What did the two numbers on the unknown soldiers graves mean? A great way to hear the Revolutionary and Civil War history of Fredericksburg with fun tidbits (also a great overview of the museums and restaurants in town). Afterwards, you'll know which spots you want to personally visit.

FREDERICKSBURG AND SPOTSYLVANIA CIVIL WAR BATTLEFIELDS

Fredericksburg - *(I-95 south to Rte. 3 exit east. At intersection of Rte. 3 & Bus Rte. 1) 22407. Phone: (540) 373-6122. www.nps.gov/frsp/index.htm. Hours: Parks open daily dawn to dusk. Visitors Centers open 9:00am-5:00pm daily except Thanksgiving, Christmas and New Years. Admission: $1.00-$2.00 per person (age 10+) for viewing each of the 22-minute movies at 2 battlefields. Visitors Center. Tours: The popular History at Sunset Friday evening walking tours are from June 6-August 15.*

The Civil War was one of America's greatest tragedies and no region suffered more than the Fredericksburg area. Four major battles were fought

Stonewall Jackson died in an outbuilding on the Chandler Plantation at Guinea Station on May 10, 1863. Guinea Station was the busy Confederate supply station during the Chancellorsville Campaign.

here. Eventually, the cost of these battles would be too much for the South to bear. Today, the National Park Service maintains 18 miles of land in the Fredericksburg and Spotsylvania National Military Park. Two visitors centers help interpret four battlefields. A self-guided tour of the battlefields begins at the Fredericksburg Battlefield and continues into Spotsylvania County. In the battlefield parks, wayside exhibits, exhibit shelters, interpretive trails and many historic buildings help tell the story of the Civil War battles. Highlights on the map or audio (rental tape ~$3.00) tour are:

- **WILDERNESS BATTLEFIELD** - May 5-6, 1864. This conflict introduced Union General Grant to Lee in battle. Even though the battle ended in stalemate, Grant pressed southward , "On to Richmond". (Orange, 540-373-4461, Rte. 20, one mile west of Rte. 3)

- **SPOTSYLVANIA BATTLEFIELD** - May 8-21, 1864. On the most direct route to Richmond, warring troops engaged for 2 weeks including 20 hours on May 12 in the most intense hand-to-hand fighting of the war at the "Bloody Angle".

- **CHANCELLORSVILLE BATTLEFIELD** - April 27-May 6, 1863. Action included a spectacular military maneuver by Lee and his most trusted subordinate, "Stonewall Jackson", but the day ended in calamity when Jackson was fatally wounded by his own troops. (I-95, Rte. 3 west)

- **FREDERICKSBURG BATTLEFIELD** - December 11-15, 1862. Called "Lee's most one-sided victory", the battle focused on Sunken Road and the Stone Wall at Marye's Heights.

- **CHATHAM** - across the Rappahannock River off SR218; mansion served as a Union headquarters and field hospital during the Civil War. Clara Burton and Walt Whitman provided care here to wounded soldiers. Visitors can see a new exhibit containing a replica pontoon boat, modeled after those used to cross the Rappahannock River in the Battle of Fredericksburg. A free movie depicts the impact of the Civil War on area residents. Daily 9:00am-5:00pm. FREE. (540) 371-0802.

Exit - 130 (east of I-95)

HISTORIC KENMORE

Fredericksburg - 1201 Washington Avenue (Rte. 3 into town to Rte. 3 Business. Follow William St. Left on Washington) 22401. www.kenmore.org. Phone: (540) 373-3381. Hours: Daily 10:00am-5:00pm (March-December). Closes earlier in November & December. Closed major winter holidays. Admission: $10.00 adult, $5.00 student (ages 6-17 or with student ID). Miscellaneous: Summer Discovery Workshops and Colonial theatre. Kids - be sure to check out their new section on Travels With George Washington!

Kenmore, one of the most elegant Colonial mansions in America, lies in the heart of historic Fredericksburg. Built in 1775 by Fielding Lewis for his wife Betty, the sister of George Washington, the house is currently undergoing a major restoration. Tours focus on the building of the house and the craftsmen and artisans who worked on it. What did colonists use to start fires, make brushes, and protect toddlers from injury? How did the "stucco man" create the beautiful ceilings at Kenmore? What two-century-old clues are hidden behind plaster and paneling? Why are there decorative brick arches in the cellar? Does the house have a secret passage? What unusual object has been stored in the attic for over 100 years? The best time to visit is during Family Tours or special events: Parents and children (age 4 and above) learn about the lives of 18th century Virginians in family tours designed with hands-on activities. No reservations needed. Usually summer weekday mornings or year-round weekend re-enactments.

HUGH MERCER APOTHECARY SHOP

Fredericksburg - 1020 Caroline Street (Old Town) 22401. Phone: (540) 373-3362. www.washingtonheritagemuseums.org/#!hughmercer-apothecary-shop/cie8. Hours: Monday-Saturday 9:00am-4:00pm. Sunday Noon-4:00pm (March-October). Reduced hours (November-December). Closed winter holidays. Admission: $5.00 adult, $2.00 student (6-18). Half price admission on President's Day. Miscellaneous: Living Legacies annual September event features exhibits and demonstrations honoring the crafts of the 18th and 19th centuries.

Dr. Mercer practiced medicine for fifteen years in Fredericksburg. His patients included Mary Washington. Anyone could enjoy walking into this 18th century doctor's office and learning about all the interesting things that were used for medicines back then. While smelling the entertaining scents from unusual (mostly herbal) medicines, visitors may (or may not!) want to view utensils formerly used for draining blood, amputating, pulling teeth and performing operations. You will even see a saw that looks like it belongs in a tool box! On the way out, stop by the garden to view herbs and plants used for medicinal purposes (during those times and even popular now). They've got real leeches in here! Does mom ever say – "You're driving me crazy..."? They've got the perfect medicinal cure here.

MARY WASHINGTON HOUSE

Fredericksburg - 1200 Charles Street (downtown) 22401. Phone: (540) 373-1569. www.washingtonheritagemuseums.org. Hours: Monday-Saturday 11:00am-5:00pm, Sunday Noon-4:00pm. (March-October). Monday-Saturday, 11:00am-4:00pm, Sunday Noon-4:00pm (November-December). Closed January 1,

Thanksgiving, December 24, 25, 31. Admission: $5.00 adult, $2.00 child (6-18). Half price admission on President's Day. Note: Living Legacies annual September event features exhibits and demonstrations honoring the crafts of the 18th and 19th centuries.

Mary Ball Washington spent the last 17 years of her life in this home bought for her by her son, George Washington, in 1772. The white frame house sits on the corner of Charles and Lewis Streets and was in walking distance to Kenmore, home of Mary's daughter Betty Fielding Lewis. Some of Mary's original personal possessions, including her "best dressing glass" and the boxwood bushes she planted years ago are present. The most interesting room is the old kitchen quarters.

Exit - 130 (east of I-95)

RISING SUN TAVERN

Fredericksburg - *1304 Caroline Street, Old Town (follow signs into old town 22401. Phone: (540) 371-1494. www.washingtonheritagemuseums.org. Hours: Monday-Saturday 10:00am-5:00pm, Sunday Noon-4:00pm (March-October). Opens one hour later and closes earlier (November-December). Admission: $5.00 adult, $2.00 student (6-18). Half price admission on President's Day. Miscellaneous: Living Legacies annual September event features exhibits and demonstrations honoring the crafts of the 18th and 19th centuries.*

Built by Charles Washington in 1760 as his home, this building was later operated as a tavern, the only "proper" tavern in the bustling port city of Fredericksburg. Discover popular pub phrases and terms, while learning about the life of a "tavern wench". She'll show you an early cash register, an 18th century mousetrap, and the confined sleeping quarters used then. Visitors can learn about subjects as serious as the separation of educated men from common men. There are silly things, too, like the bathing rituals of those times (they bathed completely only twice a year!). The Rising Sun was a "proper" tavern (as defined in those times)…never more than 5 to a bed!

Exit - 98 (east of I-95)

KINGS DOMINION

Richmond (Doswell) - *1600 Theme Park Way (I-95 EXIT 98) 23047. Phone: (804) 876-5000. www.kingsdominion.com. Hours: Weekends (April-Memorial Day), Daily (Memorial Day-Labor Day), and Weekends (Labor Day - first few weekends in October). Generally opens at 10:00 or 10:30am and closes around 8:00-10:00pm.*

Admission: One-Day General Admission: $41.00-$54.00. Twilight discounts (admission after 4:00pm). Tips: The Eiffel Tower makes a great meeting place and is easy to find from anywhere in the park. Additionally, they provide strollers and wheelchairs for a small rental fee.

During the spring and summer months, you won't want to miss Kings Dominion in nearby Doswell north of Richmond, a 400-acre theme and water park and world-class roller coasters. Kings Dominion soared to new heights with the introduction of its 14th roller coaster, Dominator. This innovative 4,210-foot steel coaster is the longest floorless coaster in the world and has the largest roller coaster loop. Kings Dominion brings the best of Hollywood entertainment to the Mid-Atlantic with one of the largest coaster collections on the East Coast; two children's areas; and WaterWorks, a 19-acre water park included with admission. Try the new Stunt Coaster. WaterWorks features 4-8 awesome slides, Tidal Wave Bay wave pool, Tornado, Zoom Flume raft adventure, Surf City Splash Playhouse, Kiddie Kove, Lil' Barefoot Beach and Lazy Rider. Adults may be supervising, but, kids are in charge at:

- PLANET SNOOPY/FAMILY RIDES: fun theme rides like Boulder Bumpers, Raceway, Scrambler, Flying Ace, Americana, Boo Blasters, Carousel, mini Coasters, Cars, Planes, Trains.

Many shows throughout the day vary from Country, to Today's Hits, to Yesterday's Favorites, to hot Latin Beats, or maybe Nicktoons Summer Jam songs from favorite Nick shows.

Exit - 84 (west of I-95)

MEADOW FARM MUSEUM

Richmond (Glen Allen) - *3400 Mountain Road (I-95 exit 84 to I-295 west to Woodman Road South exit to Mountain Road) 23060. Phone: (804) 501-2130. www.co.henrico.va.us/departments/rec/recreation-centers---facilities/meadowfarm/. Hours: Tuesday-Sunday Noon-4:00pm (early March-November). Weekends only (December, mid-January to early March). Closed many holidays. Admission: FREE. Small fee for some events. If you want to "visit" with living history farm hands, come on theme weekends.*

Step back in time at Meadow Farm Museum with its 19th-century farmhouse, gardens and more than 150 acres of woodlands. Costumed interpreters perform domestic and agricultural tasks throughout the year. Start your visit at the orientation center with everything from old wooden farm tools to hand-make paper dolls. Many of the displays are at a child's eye-level and short storyboards help to explain customs and traditions of the time. The story of the Sheppard family thru the seasons is a great video to watch at least once. Walk around the farm and see the cows, horses, sheep, pigs and fowl that are typical of the nineteenth century. Watch farmhands planting the crops every spring and many other chores including pickling, harvesting, or Dr. Sheppard preparing homemade medicine for his patients. Also outside on the farm, you'll find a barn, smokehouse, doctor's office and blacksmith. You might see the women churning butter and learn how you can make your own at home using one cup of heavy whipping cream-along with a marble-in a jar with tight fitting lid. Shake it hard for a while, pour off liquid and the solid part is sweet, creamy butter. Spread it on fresh bread for an authentic 19th century lunch!

Exit - 80 or 83B (west of I-95)

LEWIS GINTER BOTANICAL GARDEN

Richmond - 1800 Lakeside Avenue (I-95 North take Exit 80. I-95 South take exit 83B - follow signs) 23228. Phone: (804) 262-9887. www.lewisginter.org. Hours: Daily 9:00am-5:00pm. Closed Thanksgiving, Christmas, and New Years. Admission: $11.00 adult, $10.00 senior (55+), $7.00 child (3-12) Note: Gift shop and café (lunch). Children's Discovery Programs and Family Fun Calendar with seasonal events.

Lewis Ginter Botanical Garden brings you new horticultural displays each season. The more than 25 acres of gardens includes the Conservatory glass-domed showcase with exotic and tropical displays; an elegant Victorian-style garden; Asian Valley; the Island Garden, a wetland environment with a stunning display of pitcher plants, water irises and lotuses; a Children's Garden with colorful and interesting plants to attract butterflies and birds, a TreeHouse, international village, Farm and Sand & Waterplay areas. Good to take a stroller along the winding paved paths.

Exit - 79 (west of I-95)

EMBASSY SUITES RICHMOND

Richmond - 2925 Emerywood Pkwy (I-64 west to exit 183C) 23294. Phone: (804) 672-8585. www.embassysuites.com.

Each suite lets the family spread out with a separate living room with sofa bed, galley kitchen with wet bar, microwave, refrigerator and coffeemaker, two phones and two TVs. Your stay includes a complimentary full breakfast (cold and hot, made-to-order foods) plus an evening snack/beverage reception. The hotel also has a tropical atrium indoor pool and whirlpool. So how does a Jacuzzi®, feather pillows, and a warm bathrobe sound? Weekend rates cheaper starting at about $129.00 per night.

Exit - 78 (west of I-95)

CHILDREN'S MUSEUM OF RICHMOND

Richmond - 2626 West Broad Street (I-95/I-64 exit #78 south, adjacent to the Science Museum) 23220. www.c-mor.org. Phone: (804) 474-CMOR or (877) 295-CMOR. Hours: Daily 9:30am-5:00pm. Admission: $8.00 general (age 1+). Seniors pay $1.00 less. Daily science and nature craft times to hands-on make a craft experiments to take home.

Kids from 6 months to 12 years old will ask to go here often. It's a museum where you can touch everything! Kids learn through interactive play - they can catch rain shadows in their hands, tinker with tools working on a child-size car, be a star at the CMOR Playhouse, dig for fossils in the Dino Zone, or

build sand castles in the Backyard exhibit. Here's the highlights of what they like best: Treehouse - climb to treetops to look in an eagle's nest, explore a limestone cave, or float on the James River. Town Square, become a paramedic or shop at the market. Little Farm - a special area dedicated for creeping, crawling, tumbling - Preschoolers only. See the new Splash area, too where young engineers can jump waterfalls and hop in water jets. The noticeable focus here is the crawling and climbing aspects - an educational playplace!

Exit - 78 (west of I-95)

SCIENCE MUSEUM OF VIRGINIA

Richmond - 2500 West Broad Street (off I-95 / I-64, exit #78 south towards Broad Street) 23220. Phone: (804) 367-6552 or (800) 659-1727. www.smv.org. Hours: Monday-Saturday 9:30am-5:00pm, Sunday 11:30am-5:00pm. Closed Thanksgiving and Christmas. Admission: $11.00 adult, $10.00 senior (60+) and child (4-12).

IMAX films $5.00 extra. Note: Café. Shop4Science gift shop. Winter Skating rink. Call For Science - Museum gallery cell phone audio tour. It's free and it's fun! Educators: Teacher Guides - www.smv.org/teachers/teachers-guides.

In a former 1919 train station, the museum offers 250 + hands-on exhibits and demonstrations plus major touring exhibits. Subjects covered include aerospace, astronomy, electricity, physical sciences, computers, crystals, biology, telecommunications, and an IMAX Dome. See rats play basketball. Ride on a Segway®. Find out how it feels to walk on the moon. Play laser pool. Watch a giant-screen film in the museum's IMAX®DOME & Planetarium. The five-story theater with its tilted-dome screen and digital sound system puts you in the middle of the action. In Body Human, start at the "Very Small Gallery" (microscopic cells and DNA) to "my size" systems of the human body. Look at dozens of cells, then start "Seeing Things". At Question Power jump on a stationary bike to see if you can generate as much electricity as the wind does turning a windmill. Check out a small house that's different from yours. Instead of consuming electricity, it gives energy back to the power grid. Explore Newton's laws, gravity, momentum, potential and kinetic energy in whole-body experiences! The Out of this World lets you experience near weightlessness

as well as walk in a life-sized cross-section of a space station lab. Float on air. Look for the Tabletop Science Sites and Demonstration Stations (different each day). Outside see restored trains, take a ride on a working streetcar, and gaze at the giant Aluminaut Submarine (why aluminum?). Note: to take advantage of the many demonstrations and theatre science presentations, check the announcement board as you enter.

The Aluminaut - a retired, famous submarine that could dive 15,000 feet !!

VIRGINIA HISTORICAL SOCIETY

Richmond - *428 North Boulevard (I-95/I-64 East to Exit 78 (Boulevard). right onto Boulevard (heading south) to the corner of Kensington) 23220. Phone: (804) 358-4901. www.vahistorical.org. Hours: Tuesday-Saturday 10:00am-5:00pm, Sunday 1:00-5:00pm. Closed major holidays. Admission: $5.00 adult, $4.00 senior (54+) or $2.00 on Tuesdays, $3.00 child & student. Tours: Gallery Walks take place in the galleries of the Virginia Historical Society. All walks begin at noon unless otherwise indicated. Walks are free with admission and free to members. Reservations are not* required. Educators: The Story of Virginia themes are separated online, each with a teachers guide accompaniment. Note: Museum Shop full of Virginia history items and crafts.

Any Virginian or anyone who wants an overview of the state's historical highlights needs to visit here (and more than once to get it all). Discover the entire "Story of Virginia" at the Virginia Historical Society through videos, storyphones, computer games and other interactive devises that make learning fun for the whole family. You'll start at the orientation theatre. The film shown is an "easy to follow" path of state history. Now, move on to the first inhabitants (Powatan Indians) including a dugout canoe, a wooden musket, and Pocahontas portraits (even a piece of her hat). Move on from the settlers to the Conestoga Wagon display and the move out west (most Virginians who left went towards Ohio). As you progress past the early 1800's (see Revolutionary War stuff along the way), move to the Civil War gallery, and then it's on to the 1900's. Here you'll see an actual streetcar theatre and famous native Virginians (especially sports figures). Visitor and child-friendly, interactive features include a brief orientation film, a cartoon-based computer game on Virginia history, hand-held story phones with additional exhibition information, and question-and-answer games throughout.

Exit - 78 (west of I-95)

MAYMONT

Richmond - *2201 Shields Lake Drive (south on Boulevard, Rte 161 for 2 miles. Continue to follow Rte.161 as it turns. follow signs) 23220. Phone: (804) 358-7166. www.maymont.org. Hours: Exhibits: (Maymont House, Children's Farm Barn & Maymont Shop): Tuesday-Sunday, 12:00-5:00pm. Grounds, Gardens & Visitor Center: Daily, 10:00am-5:00pm. Admission: $2.00-$5.00 at Nature Center, Children's Farm & Maymont House. Miscellaneous: Café. Tram, Carriage Rides (Sundays, Noon-5:00pm) and Hayrides (weekends in summer, 1:00-4:00pm) are $2.00-$5.00 fee per person per ride.*

The otters are always so much fun to watch...

A first visit to Maymont is best started at the Robins Nature & Visitor Center - Maymont's front door-but a history lover will soon find a path to the 1893 Maymont House Museum. A plant lover will find the elaborate Japanese and Italian gardens. For animal lovers there are the Nature Center, Wildlife Exhibits and the Children's Farm. In the Nature Center, thirteen linked aquariums are home to playful river otters, many species of fish, turtles and other creatures. Interactive galleries include a replica of Richmond's flood wall, a weather station and a fish ladder. The Children's Farm introduces little ones to all sorts of barnyard animals. Children are welcome to feed and pet many animals on display. Be sure to bring quarters for the feed dispensers. The Farm is home to a variety of goats, sheep, pigs, chickens, donkeys, rabbits, peafowl (peacocks and peahens), turkeys, cattle, horses, geese and ducks. Rare breeds include Scotch Highland and Dutch Belted cows, the Barbados Blackbelly sheep and others. The envy of zoologists across the nation, Maymont's bear habitat alone is worth a visit. The large terrain includes a rock scramble, a pond (formerly a quarry pit), and multiple areas for climbing, sleeping, hiding and eating. There are also exhibit areas to view bison, red fox, and hundreds of other animals. Also, explore the opulent Victorian mansion, gardens, and other wildlife exhibits.

Exit - 76 (west of I-95)

MAGGIE L. WALKER NATIONAL HISTORIC SITE

Richmond - 600 North 2nd Street (chamberlayne Pkwy south. Left onto West Leigh St. Go 3 blocks) 23219. Phone: (804) 771-2017. www.nps.gov/malw. Hours: Tuesday-Saturday 9:00am-4:30pm. Open one half hour later in summer. Closed major winter holidays and Sundays. Admission: FREE. Tours: offered every half-hour. Educators: Curriculum guides online "For Teachers". Note: The visitor's center has a short film presentation to begin your tour. The film talks from Maggie's point of view talking to children.

The site honors Maggie Walker, a prominent businesswoman, who overcame social obstacles of her time - being physically impaired, black and a woman. She founded the St. Luke Penny Savings Bank, the first chartered bank in the country started by a woman, and became a success in the world of business and finance. Her home, next to the visitor center, has been completely restored to the 1930's appearance with many Walker family furnishings to view. The house has 28 rooms - rather large and ornate. She showed her wealth with a chauffeured limousine, diamond rings and many gold-leafed furnishings. She also was very generous and gave most extra money away. Learn how she helped fellow African-Americans "turn nickels into dollars". The main interpretive exhibits feature the story of her life. The exhibits include many historical photographs, a recreation of the St. Luke Penny Savings Bank teller window, displays of museum artifacts such as Mrs. Walker's dress and St. Luke regalia, and a child's personal St. Luke savings bank (like the ones she gave children in the area). The opening of the new exhibits changes the way visitors view Mrs. Walker's home. Previously, tours left the visitor center and angled across the courtyard entering the home from the rear porch. Now visitors will view the exhibits, then exit onto Leigh Street and enter Mrs. Walker's home from the front door just as invited guests would have arrived during her lifetime.

Exit - 74C (west of I-95)

MUSEUM OF THE CONFEDERACY

Richmond - *1201 East Clay Street (downtown, 2 blocks north of Broad Street @ 12th St.) 23219. Phone: (804) 649-1861. www.moc.org. Hours: Daily 10:00am-5:00pm. Closed Major winter holidays. Admission (separate for each museum) $10.00 adult, $8.00 (62+ and military ID), $6.00 child (7-13). Combo tickets help you save $2-5.00 on admission to both museums. Tours: Guided of the White House start in the basement and cover the first and second floors are daily and last about 40 minutes. Educators: Lesson plans are available for a small fee or download loan online (Education/Tools for Teaching).*

Explore the nations most comprehensive collection of military, political and domestic artifacts and art from the Confederacy, then take a guided tour of the White House, the Civil War residence of Confederate President Jefferson Davis. The home has been restored to its wartime elegance. Museum: 500 wartime flags, 250 uniform pieces and the personal belongings of many Confederate generals like Jefferson Davis, Robert E. Lee, J.E.B. Stuart and Stonewall Jackson. Displays on the lives of free and enslaved African Americans and the giant, 15 foot painting of "The Last Meeting of Lee and Jackson" are here also. White House: The executive mansion of President Jefferson Davis and his family during the Civil War. Children's Activities Days (hands-on activities, games with guide), Civil War encounters (costumed living historian will portray an "eyewitness" to various events), and day camps for kids, too.

Exit - 74B (west of I-95)

VIRGINIA STATE CAPITOL

Richmond - *Capitol Square (take Franklin St. until it becomes Bank St. Capitol entrance is on Bank St) 23219. Phone: (804) 698-1788. www.virginiacapitol.gov. Hours: Monday-Saturday 8:00am-5:00pm, Sunday 1:00-4:00pm. Admission:*

FREE. Tours: One hour long. Last tour leaves at 4:00pm. Gallery seating is also available on a first come, first serve basis. Note: Capitol Café & Gift Shop.

The Capitol was designed by Thomas Jefferson and houses the second oldest legislative body in the western hemisphere. Highlights are: the Houdin statue of George Washington, the hidden interior dome, seen only from inside the building, and busts of the eight Virginia born presidents; the Old Senate Hall and the Old Hall of the House of Delegates, where Aaron Burr was tried for treason in 1807, Robert E. Lee received his commission as commander of the VA troops and the Confederate Congress met during the Civil War. If you have time, guided tours offer more insight into the state's governmental historical figures and stories. Look for the doorknobs throughout the building with the State Seal on them - how many can you count? The Governor's Mansion is the oldest continuously occupied governor's home (1814) in the country. You can view the Capitol grounds from the upstairs window. These tours are probably a little long for the young ones.

> **Can you find the hidden dome?**
> Hint: It's not visible from the outside...

Exit - 74B (east of I-95)

ST. JOHN'S CHURCH

Richmond - *2401 East Broad Street (right onto Franklin. Right at 14th St. Right onto Broad St. 23223. www.historicstjohnschurch.org. Phone: (804) 648-5015. Admission: $9.00 adult, $6.00 senior (62+), $5.00 child (7-18). Tours are conducted Monday through Saturday from 10:00am until 4:00pm. Sunday hours are 1:00pm until 4:00pm. During the summer, open daily until 4:30pm. Tours are on the hour and half-hour and last approximately 20 minutes. Last tour leaves one half hour before closing. Closed New Years, Easter, Thanksgiving and Christmastime. Tours are also subject to close for weddings, funerals, or other church functions. Educators: Wonderful and easy .PDF downloadable activities on their online Education pages. It is best to visit here after the children have studied the Revolutionary War. Then, they are very impressed.*

You can experience the historic significance of St. John's Church by taking a tour led by one of their expert guides. The tour includes a history of the buildings on the grounds of St. John's, highlights of the graveyard, where numerous individuals prominent in Richmond and Virginia history are buried, a tour of the inside of the Church, and a description of the vigorous debate of the Second Virginia Convention, during which Mr. Patrick Henry delivered his famous speech, which has lived on as the most famous cry for freedom in the world - "Give me liberty or give me death." Reenactments of the Second Virginia Convention of 1775 are held Sundays at 2:00pm during the summer. The costumed guide gives excerpts of the speech as it applies to the times.

Exit - 74A *(west of I-95)*

FEDERAL RESERVE MONEY MUSEUM

Richmond - 701 East Byrd Street (Federal Reserve Bank, take SR 195 northwest a few blocks) 23219. www.thefedexperience.org. Phone: (804) 697-8110. Hours: Monday-Friday 9:30am-3:30pm beginning June 2010. Admission: FREE. Educators: Online lesson plans at www.federalreserveeducation.org. FREEBIES: tons of online games from puzzles to treasure hunts to pretending you're the Fed Chairman Game.

A self-guided tour exhibits forms of currency, rare bills (even $100,000 bills!) and gold and silver bars (a favorite of the kids). A great virtual tour of the

museum with a view of the gold bar is available on the website. 500 items depict the history of currency including such items as compressed tea bricks which could be spent or brewed or an actual coin of the Kingdom of Lydia, the birthplace of coinage.

CANAL WALK, RICHMOND

Richmond - Visitor Center at Hillcrest & Riverside Drive (Tredegar Iron Works to 12th St. and James River) 23219. www.venturerichmond.com/experiences/. Phone: (804) 648-6549. Hours: Daily sunrise to sunset. Admission: FREE. Charge for boat rentals or guided tours by boat. Boat Tours: Historic tours leave every hour on the hour and run on the seasonal schedule. Fares are $4.00-$5.00 per person ages 5 and up.

Enjoy a leisurely walk along the restored Kanawha and Haxall canals, with History Medallions pointing out the rich history of Richmond's waterfront. Start your authentic Richmond experience in the River District with an Historic Canal Cruise (April-October) on the restored Kanawha Canal, originally designed by George Washington. When your cruise is over, there's still more to do! A 1¼ mile Canal Walk winds through downtown along the banks of the Haxall Canal, the river and the Kanawha Canal. You can walk to the American Civil War Center at Tredegar Iron Works, explore scenic Brown's Island and Belle Isle, and climb the Flood Wall for more incredible city views.

> The city of Richmond got its name from the bend in the river that's similar to that of the Thames in Richmond, England.

By linking the James River with the Kanawha River in western Virginia, which in turn flowed into Ohio, he hoped to improve transportation and trade with the west. The first section of the canal system circumvented the seven-mile falls near Richmond (the scene of rapids rafting today). First envisioned in 1774, these canals were to be part of a continuous transportation route from the Atlantic Ocean to the Mississippi River. Did you know that in 1888 Richmond built the first commercially successful electric streetcar system in the world?

Exit - 74A (west of I-95)

RICHMOND NATIONAL BATTLEFIELD PARK

Richmond - *470 Tredegar Street (I-95: take exit 74 west then follow signs to Civil War Visitor Center located at 490 Tredegar Street) 23219. Phone: (804) 771-2145. www.nps.gov/rich. Hours: Park battlefields are open sunrise-sunset. Visitor centers at Tredegar Iron Works, Chimborazo and Cold Harbor are open daily 9:00am-5:00pm. Visitor centers at Glendale and Fort Harrison are open daily June through August, 9:00am-5:00pm. Admission: FREE for most sites. Civil War Center: parking fee. Educators: Followup activities available when you book a themed tour.*

Richmond's story is not just the tale of one large Civil War battle, nor even one important campaign. Instead, the park's resources include a naval battle, a key industrial complex, the Confederacy's largest hospital, and dozens of miles of elaborate original fortifications.

- **CHIMBORAZO MEDICAL MUSEUM**: The museum stands on the eastern end of downtown Richmond, at the site of the Civil War's famous Chimborazo Hospital. Between 1861 and 1865 more than 75,000 Confederate soldiers received treatment at this spacious facility. The medical museum tells the story of those patients and the hospital and physicians that cared for them. Using artifacts, uniforms and documents the exhibits describe the state of medicine in 1860 and the care of wounded and sick soldiers on the battlefields and in the many large centralized Richmond hospitals like Chimborazo. A short film supplements the exhibits.

- **AMERICAN CIVIL WAR VISITOR CENTER AT TREDEGAR IRON WORKS**: serves as the gift shop and information center for the War aspects of the James River. The Center's mission is to tell the whole story of the conflict that still shapes our nation. The main exhibit space titled: In the Cause of Liberty, explores the war's causes, course, and legacies through artifacts, media, and programs looking at three essential perspectives—Union, Confederate, and African American. Three floors of exhibits and artifacts are on display. Orientation film is shown every half hour. www.tredegar.org.

Exit - 74A (east of I-95)

VIRGINIA AVIATION MUSEUM

Richmond (Sandston) - 5701 Huntsman Road (Richmond International Airport) 23250. Phone: (804) 236-3622. www.vam.smv.org. Hours: Monday-Saturday 9:30am-5:00pm, Sunday, Noon-5:00pm. Closed Thanksgiving and Christmastime. Admission: $6.50 adult, $5.50 senior (60+), $4.00 child (4-12). Ask for scavenger hunt.

The Virginia Aviation Museum in Sandston has more than 25 vintage aircraft plus the SR-71 Blackbird, a cool supersonic spy plane. See replicas of the three Wright Brothers' gliders, World War II dioramas, antique automobiles and more. You'll see Capt. Dick Merrill's 1930s open cockpit mail plane and a special exhibit on Virginia's legendary Adm. Byrd and his Stars and Stripes (the first American scientific research aircraft to fly in Antarctica). Learn which planes earned the nicknames: Rolls Royce, Cadillac and Flying Bathtub. Enjoy aviation films in the Benn Theater or stroll through the Virginia Aviation Hall of Fame. This shrine to the "Golden Age of Aviation" enhances the Science Museum's aerospace exhibits with its extensive collection of vintage flying machines.

Exit - 61A (east of I-95)

HENRICUS HISTORICAL PARK

Richmond (Chester) - 251 Henricus Park Road (follow Rte. 10 east to first light. Left onto Rte 732, 2 miles. Right onto Rte 615 1 mile. Right on Henricus Park Rd) 23836. Phone: (804) 706-1340. www.henricus.org. Hours: Tuesday-Sunday 10:00am-5:00pm (Feb-December) Admission: $8.00 adult, $6.00 child (3-12). Miscellaneous: Visitors Center and Museum Store.

Henricus was home to Pocahontas, the beginnings of the early plantations and the first English hospital in America. It was built along the James River on land inhabited by the Appomattocks tribe, where Pocahontas grew up. Harsh battles were fought when the English first arrived in America. Henricus Historical Park is where Pocahontas lived and was courted by John Rolfe! It was the marriage between Pocahontas and John Rolfe that helped bring a peaceful coexistence between the two warring factions. Children learn history as costumed interpreters work in the 1611 Citie of Henricus, Virginia's second successful English settlement after Jamestown. Every month carries out a different theme, for example: Harvest, Holidays, Native Americans, Government, Environment, Militia, Archaeology and Colonial. Enjoy nature hikes, birding and fishing at the Dutch Gap Conservation Area.

Exit - 61A (east of I-95)

CITY POINT OPEN AIR MUSEUM WALKING TOUR

Hopewell - *City Point (Hopewell) Historic District (begins on Cedar Lane at St. John's Church, follow signs) 23860. Phone: (800) 541-2461 or (800) 863-8687. www.historichopewell.org/museum.html. Hours: Most buildings that you can tour are at the beginning of the tour and close by 4:30pm. Most open at 10:00am (April-October). Admission: Tour is FREE. Small admission for inside tours of some buildings, if desired. Note: Union fort breastworks and Weston Manor are nearby, as is Sears Mail Order Houses. Hopewell offers a selection of Sears, Roebuck & Company MAIL-ORDER homes in its Crescent Hills neighborhood. Visitors can drive through this area and view homes built from 1926-1937.*

This self-guided tour (brochures available at the Visitors Info Center, exit 9 off I-295) captures the people and events of City Point during the Civil War. Walk down the same streets that Union Generals Grant, Sheridan, and Sherman or President Lincoln did and stop to read insights at 25 wayside exhibits. Of interest to kids along the tour are the St. John's Episcopal Church (505 Cedar Lane, where black and whites were baptized prior to the Civil War and the Union army used the church temporarily as a signal station, a Union stockade, and a place of worship - open to view most weekday mornings; Appomattox Manor (currently being renovated by NPS); City Point Early History Museum at St. Dennis Chapel (exhibits show visitors the 10,000 plus year history of old City Point). At certain sites, children can explore the interior of a Civil War hospital tent, or have photos taken with life size figures of a wounded soldier, President Lincoln, or an Appomattox Indian. Products as diverse as the first automatic dishwasher, the first Kraft paper and cardboard boxes, china and artificial silk have been manufactured in Hopewell. Without a visit to some buildings, the kids might find the tour a little boring.

WESTON MANOR

Hopewell - *(Weston Lane & 21st Avenue, Exit 61A off I-95 head Rt. 10 East) 23860. Phone: (804) 458-4682. www.historichopewell.org. Hours: Monday-Saturday 10:00am-4:30pm, Sunday 1:00-4:30pm (April-October). Admission: $5.00 adult, FREE child under 12.*

Weston was owned by the Eppes family of City Point, originally presented as a wedding gift. Heirs linage includes ties to the Appomattox Plantation and Pocahontas. During the Civil War, Weston was the residence of 12 year old Emma Wood and her family. Later, she wrote a journal of her wartime experiences. Be sure to listen for stories about little Emma's adventures, occupation by Union Troops, and post-war tall tales.

Exit - 61 (west of I-95)

POCAHONTAS STATE PARK

Richmond (Chesterfield) - *10301 State Park Road (Take exit 61 onto Route 10 west, then left onto Route 655 (Beach Road). Go about four miles to State Park) 23832. Phone: (804) 796-4255. www.dcr.virginia.gov/parks/pocahont.htm. Admission: $4.00-5.00 per vehicle.*

Located 20 miles from downtown Richmond, this park has pool swimming, boating, bicycling, camping and group cabins. The Civilian Conservation Corps Museum is dedicated to the Depression-era volunteers who helped to build the state's park system. Algonquin Ecology Camp is available for overnight group camps as is the Heritage Center and the new amphitheater on a sloping hillside. Pocahontas State Park offers five miles of hiking trails around Beaver Lake, a five mile bicycle trail and a trail accessible for persons with disabilities. In addition, numerous trails accessible to hikers and bicyclists wind through the surrounding woodlands. There are also approximately nine miles of bridle trails.

Exit - 52 (east of I-95)

PETERSBURG NATIONAL BATTLEFIELD

Petersburg - *1539 Hickory Hill Road (go thru town to Rte. 36 and follow signs) 23803. www.nps.gov/pete/. Phone: (804) 732-3531 & (804) 458-9504 & (804) 265-8244. Hours: Grounds open from 8:00am-dusk. Grant's Hdqts. (City Point) / Appomattox Manor/ Eastern Front/ Five Forks Battlefield open and staffed year-round 9:00am - 5:00pm. Poplar Grove Cemetery staffed on weekends June-August from 9:00am-5:00pm. Notice: Petersburg National Battlefield is closed on Thanksgiving Day, Christmas Day and New Year's Day. Admission: Eastern Front Visitor Center - September-May: $3.00/adult with a $5.00/car maximum. Educators: Petersburg National Battlefield has developed lessons to explore the state of the country prior to the Civil War including the experiences of southerners and northerners, the causes of the Civil War, the people who participated and fought in the siege of Petersburg, and people's perceptions of this period as reflected in the poetry, music, and literature. Kids can prepare for their visit by going on the "For Kids" Park Fun pages to see ABC Pictionary views of a Soldier's Life. Note: Biking, hiking, auto tour and horseback riding.*

Can you imagine spending almost ten months of the Civil War fighting in one area? Why were the soldiers here for so long? How did they pass their days? What was it like living in the trenches around Petersburg? Learn why Petersburg, Virginia, became the setting for the longest siege in American history when General Ulysses S. Grant failed to capture Richmond in the spring of 1864. Grant settled in to subdue the Confederacy by surrounding Petersburg and cutting off General Robert E. Lee's supply lines into Petersburg and Richmond. On April 2, 1865, nine-and-one-half months after the siege began, Lee evacuated Petersburg. Begin your tour at the park entrance Visitor Center viewing exhibits about the Petersburg campaign, an audiovisual map presentation, battlefield relics, maps, etc. The 4-mile self-guided Tour begins at this point, with some areas reserved for "walk-on" sites only. The Siege Line Tour picks up where the initial tour ends and leads to park areas south and west of Petersburg. An audiotape of the 35+ mile driving tour is available. Summertime is especially fun because costumed interpreters depict army life during the siege.

Exit - 52 (east of I-95)

QUARTERMASTER MUSEUM

Petersburg (Fort Lee) - *(go thru town to Rte. 36 and follow signs. just inside main gate of Fort Lee) 23801. www.qmmuseum.lee.army.mil. Phone: (804) 734-4203. Hours: Tuesday-Friday 10:00am-5:00pm, Saturday and Sunday 11:00am-5:00pm. Closed Monday, Thanksgiving, Christmas and New Years Day. Admission: FREE.*

This supply center was founded only two days after the Army itself in 1775. The Quartermaster is responsible for almost every service function in the Army: food, clothing, transportation, aerial supply, petroleum supply and mortuary services. See the wagon supply vehicle used from the 1890s to WWII. When autos replaced horse-drawn vehicles, the Quartermaster Corps developed the jeep, which became one of the most famous of all military vehicles. They have a jeep used by General George S. Patton, Jr. in WWII. You'll also see a kitchen which could be pulled directly onto the battlefield providing hot meals to soldiers in WWI.

Exit - 51 (west of I-95)

PAMPLIN HISTORICAL PARK & THE NATIONAL MUSEUM OF THE CIVIL WAR SOLDIER

© Photo courtesy of Pamplin Historical Park

Petersburg - 6125 Boydton Plank Road (go on I-85 to exit 63A, follow signs) 23803. Phone: (804) 861-2408 or (877) PAMPLIN. www.pamplinpark. org. Hours: Tuesday-Sunday 9:00am-5:00pm (March-November). Friday-Sunday only (December-February) Summer hours extended until 6:00pm. Admission: $10.00 adult, $5.00 child (6-12). Tours: The cutting edge technology found in Pamplin Historical Park's museums and historic homes now finds its way outdoors. New self-guided tours presented on MP3 technology tell the stories of Tudor Hall Plantation, the Military Fortifications Exhibit and the Breakthrough Battlefield. MP3 players are available at the park and visitors can download audio tours from the website in advance for their personal players. Educators: Classroom activities pre-and-post visit are online. History & Civil War Day Camps.

Pamplin Historical Park delivers a fresh approach to historical museums by combining a blend of new technology and old-fashioned storytelling that immerses visitors in the war and the day-to-day lives of very common soldiers. THE NATIONAL MUSEUM OF THE CIVIL WAR SOLDIER is where visitors can wear a personal audio device and become intimately acquainted with their own comrade,

Help pack your soldier's knapsack...
© Photo courtesy of Pamplin Historical Park

such as Delevan Miller, a 13-year-old drummer boy, throughout the tour. Your soldier/guide (by MP3) takes you to "A soldier's Life" which is the room packed full of artifacts and models and soldiers in army regimen. "Pack Your Knapsack" is where a sergeant tells you how to pick items essential to carry but not weighing more than 16 pounds - it's hard to discard a pot and pan and just bring "light-weight" tin cups, blankets, etc. The "Trial by Fire" display reveals sounds of the war: martial music, marching feet tramping, cannon fire, ground trembling, and PRAY that you don't get shot - Mommy did with a powerful puff of air to the chest! Ending at "A test Of Faith", where names of those who survived or were discharged or POW's is revealed - what was the fate of your chosen "soldier comrade"? This museum is fantastic!

Now, venture outdoors for some more "life-like" experiences. TUDOR HALL PLANTATION - take a short path to the 1812 house that reflects both civilian and military history. One side of the house is furnished as a family would have known it. The other side is outfitted to suit the needs of a Confederate general and his staff. MILITARY ENCAMPMENT AND FORTIFICATIONS EXHIBIT is a scale, authentic-looking scene of daily costumed programs where visitors mingle with soldiers as they spend a typical day in camp, cooking, cleaning equipment or mending clothes and playing games. Listen for the cannon blast every now and then…or learn soldier lingo. What artillery do you use as the enemy gets closer? At The BATTLEFIELD CENTER, kids can enter "The Discovery Tent" and sample Civil War uniforms and period clothing that is just their size. They can also try their hand at interactive computer kiosks that feature fun learning games and quizzes based on what they have seen at the Park. The BREAKTHROUGH THEATER is a multi-media show on the breakthrough battle presented in surround sound with bullets whizzing past and the ground shaking from artillery fire. BREAKTHROUGH TRAIL winds through the battlefield of April 2nd, 1865 where General Grant's Union army broke thru the Confederate lines, ending the 10 month Petersburg Campaign and setting in motion the events leading to Lee's surrender at Appomattox one week later. Audio waysides tell of the fighting and personalities involved.

Plan on a 3-4 hour minimum stay to fully immerse your family in the battlefield experience. This place helps the kids really feel like a Civil War soldier! Our family's favorite Civil War museum, by far!

Exit - 1 Mile NB Only

VIRGINIA WELCOME CENTER (AT VIRGINIA / NORTH CAROLINA STATE LINE)

Skippers - *VIRGINIA WELCOME CENTER @ SKIPPERS 23879. Phone: (434) 634-4113.*

Find brochures, maps and other information. You can even make hotel reservations at this Welcome Center. Of course, plenty of restrooms inside and areas to relax outside.

Travel Journal & Notes:

INTERSTATE 95

Chapter 5
NORTH CAROLINA

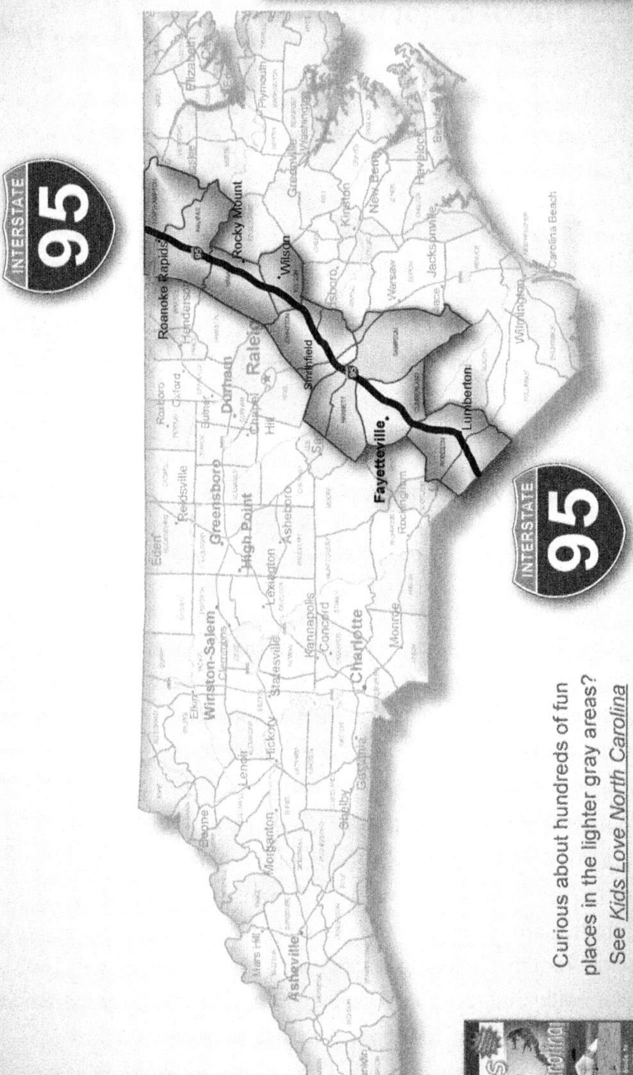

INTERSTATE 95

INTERSTATE 95

NC

Curious about hundreds of fun places in the lighter gray areas? See *Kids Love North Carolina*

DEAR NORTH CAROLINA
TRAVELER

In North Carolina, I-95 runs diagonally across the eastern third of the state, from Roanoke Rapids in the northeast to Rowland in the southwest. North Carolina has a wide range of elevations however, Interstate 95 runs in between the coastal plains and the piedmont and, for the most part, the landscape is flat.

North Carolina was one of the original Thirteen Colonies (visit where it happened at **Historic Halifax**), originally known as Province of Carolina. An English colony was established at Roanoke Island in the island kingdom's first attempt to found a settlement in the Americas. On May 20, 1861, North Carolina was one of the last of the Confederate states to declare secession from the Union, to which it was restored on July 4, 1868. One Civil War battle that took place outside of a family home is the **Bentonville Battlefield Historic Site** in the Goldsboro area.

Kids might not be thrilled about going to the doctor for a check up but wait until they've seen the **Country Doctor Museum** in Bailey – they'll realize how good they have it now – compared to then. Print off the Scavenger Hunt sheet (online) to use as your trick to keep the kids attentive for "little" things.

As you read your guidebook, pay attention to the wealth of **Children's Museums** listed. Several of them are right off the highway, full of hands-on activities and modestly priced to fit any "road trip" budget.

Spend an afternoon in Fayetteville at the **Airborne & Special Operations Museum**, which honors the shared history of airborne and special operations soldiers at Fort Bragg. Parachutes dropping out of the sky, soldiers in bunkers, motion theatre and simulators make the drama of military action very real.

Travel Journal & Notes:

NC

ACTIVITIES AT A GLANCE

HISTORY

Exit - 168 - *Historic Halifax State Historic Site*

Exit - 121 - *Country Doctor Museum*

Exit - 107 - *Charles B. Aycock Birthplace*

Exit - 90 - *Bentonville Battlefield State Historic Site*

MUSEUMS

Exit - 52 - *Airborne And Special Operations Museum*

Exit - 52 - *Fascinate-U Children's Museum*

Exit - 22 - *Exploration Station*

Exit - 14 - *Museum Of The Native American Resource Center*

OUTDOOR EXPLORING

Exit - 173 - *Roanoke River Museum & Canal Trail*

Exit - 173 - *Lake Gaston*

Exit - 160 - *Medoc Mountain State Park*

Exit - 97 - *Clemmons Educational State Forest*

Exit - 52 - *Cape Fear Botanical Garden*

SCIENCE

Exit - 138 - *Rocky Mount Children's Museum & Science Center*

Exit - 119 - *Imagination Station*

SPORTS

Exit - 46 - *Fayetteville Motor Sports Park*

THE ARTS

Exit - 107 - *Whirligigs*

WELCOME CENTERS

Exit - 180 Mile Southbound - *North Carolina Welcome Center*

Exit - 005 Mile Northbound Only - *North Carolina Welcome Center*

GENERAL INFORMATION

Contact the services of interest. Request to be added to their mailing lists.

☐ NC Association of Agricultural Fairs. www.ncagfairs.org.

☐ NC Department of Transportation Ferry Division. Morehead City. (252) 726-6446 or (800) 293-3779 or www.ncdot.gov/ferry.

☐ NC Division of Forest Resources. Raleigh. (919) 733-2162 or www.dfr.state.nc.us.

☐ NC Division of Marine Fisheries. Morehead City. (800) 682-2632 or www.ncfisheries.net.

☐ NC Division of Tourism, Film and Sports Development. Raleigh. (919) 733-8372 or (800) 847-4862 or www.visitnc.com.

☐ NC Historic Sites. Raleigh. (919) 733-7862 or www.ah.dcr.state.nc.us/sections/hs/default.htm.

☐ NC Scenic Byways Program. (877) DOT-4YOU or www.ncdot.org/public/publications.

☐ NC Wildlife Resources Commission. (919) 733-3391 or www.ncwildlife.org.

☐ NC Association of RV Parks & Campgrounds. Garner. www.campinginnorthcarolina.com or (919) 779-5709.

☐ North Carolina Division Of Parks & Recreation, Raleigh. (919) 733-4181 or www.ncparks.gov.

Travel Journal & Notes:

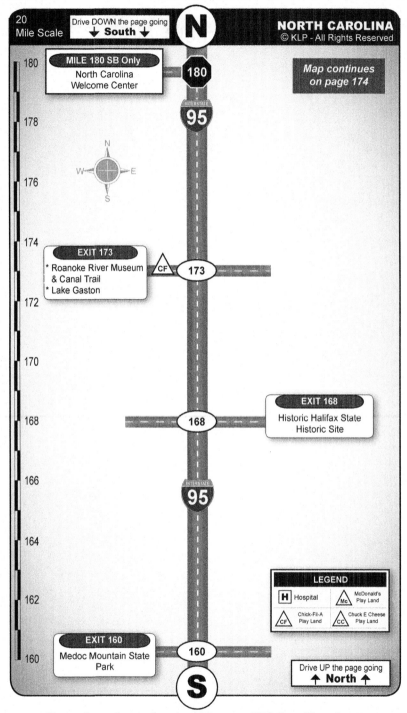

20 Mile Scale

Drive DOWN the page going
↓ **South** ↓

N

NORTH CAROLINA
© KLP - All Rights Reserved

Map continues
on page 174

MILE 180 SB Only
North Carolina
Welcome Center

180

INTERSTATE 95

EXIT 173
* Roanoke River Museum
& Canal Trail
* Lake Gaston

CF 173

EXIT 168
Historic Halifax State
Historic Site

168

INTERSTATE 95

LEGEND

| H | Hospital | Mc | McDonald's Play Land |
| CF | Chick-Fil-A Play Land | CC | Chuck E Cheese Play Land |

EXIT 160
Medoc Mountain State
Park

160

S

Drive UP the page going
↑ **North** ↑

For updates & travel games visit: **www.KidsLoveTravel.com**

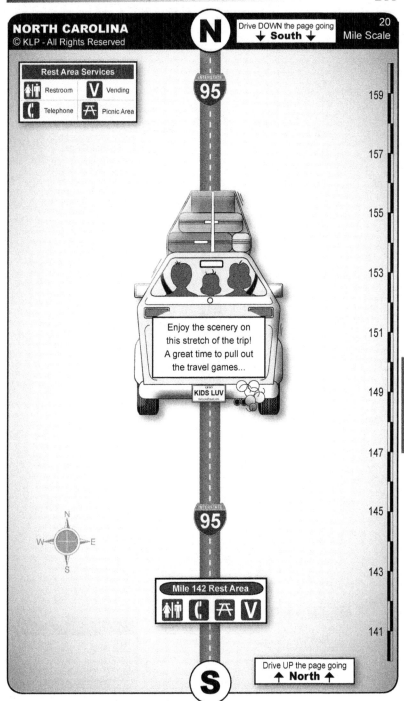

NORTH CAROLINA

Drive DOWN the page going
↓ **South** ↓

20
Mile Scale

Rest Area Services

Restroom V Vending

Telephone Picnic Area

INTERSTATE 95

Enjoy the scenery on
this stretch of the trip!
A great time to pull out
the travel games...

KIDS LUV

INTERSTATE 95

Mile 142 Rest Area

Drive UP the page going
↑ **North** ↑

NC

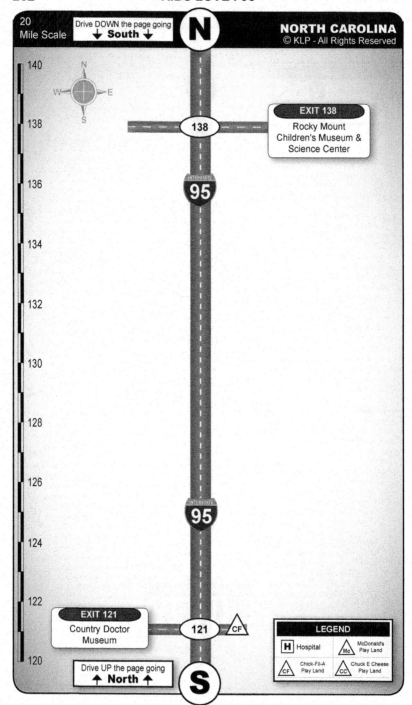

20 Mile Scale

Drive DOWN the page going ↓ **South** ↓

N

NORTH CAROLINA
© KLP - All Rights Reserved

EXIT 138
Rocky Mount
Children's Museum &
Science Center

138

INTERSTATE 95

INTERSTATE 95

EXIT 121
Country Doctor
Museum

121 CF

LEGEND

| **H** Hospital | Mc McDonald's Play Land |
| CF Chick-Fil-A Play Land | CC Chuck E Cheese Play Land |

Drive UP the page going ↑ **North** ↑

S

For updates & travel games visit: **www.KidsLoveTravel.com**

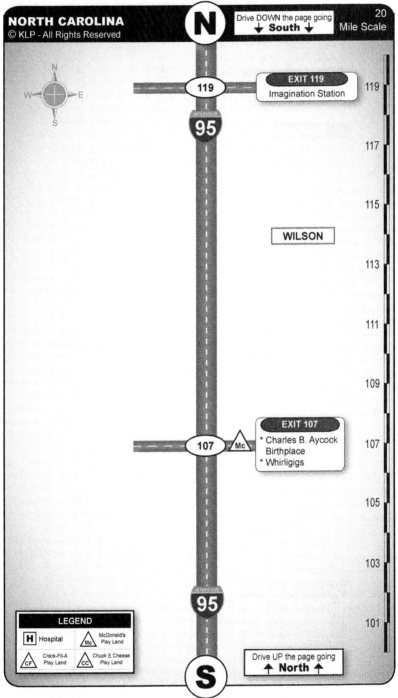

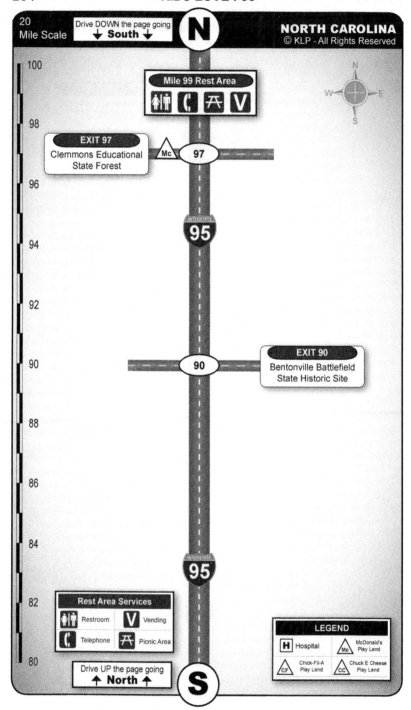

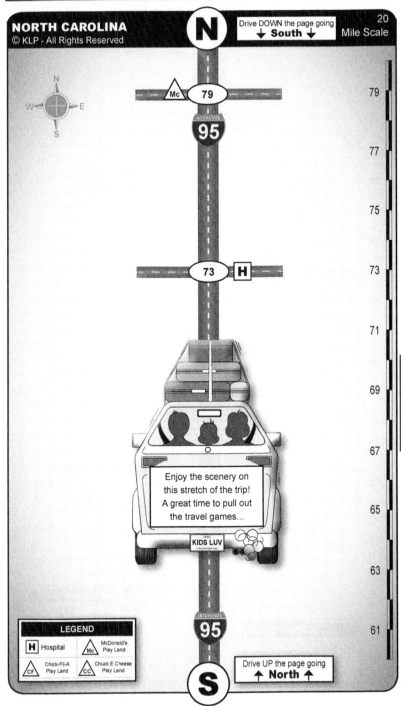

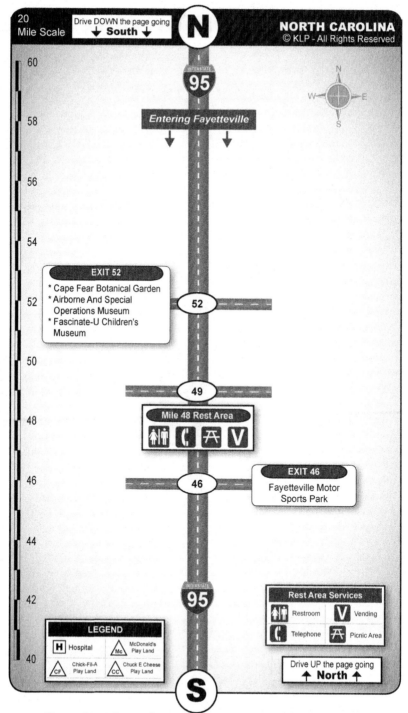

20 Mile Scale

Drive DOWN the page going
↓ **South** ↓

N

95 INTERSTATE

Entering Fayetteville

EXIT 52
* Cape Fear Botanical Garden
* Airborne And Special Operations Museum
* Fascinate-U Children's Museum

52

49

Mile 48 Rest Area

EXIT 46
Fayetteville Motor Sports Park

46

95 INTERSTATE

Rest Area Services

👪 Restroom | V Vending
☎ Telephone | ⛱ Picnic Area

LEGEND

| H | Hospital | Mc | McDonald's Play Land |
| CF | Chick-Fil-A Play Land | CC | Chuck E Cheese Play Land |

Drive UP the page going
↑ **North** ↑

S

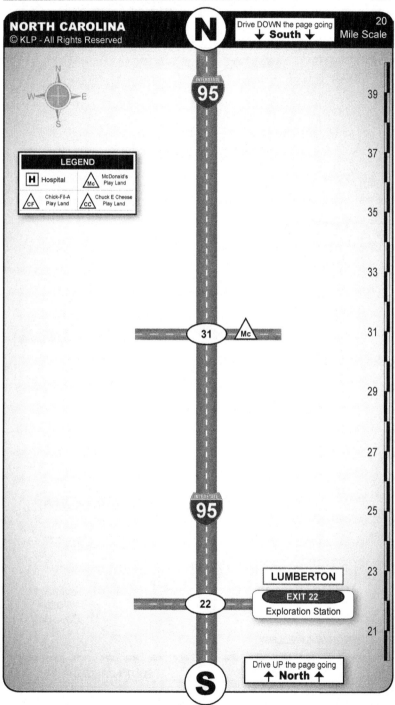

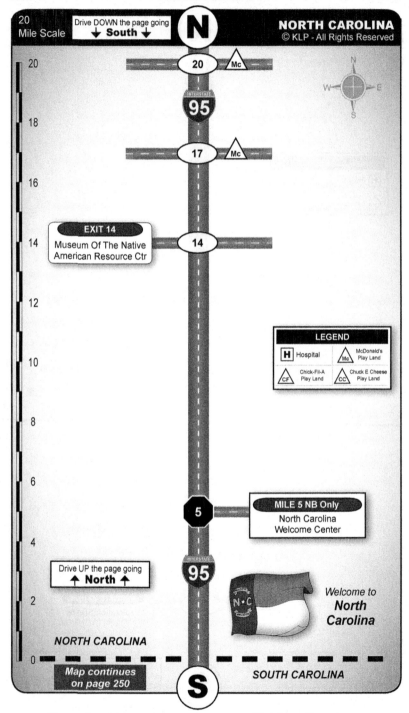

Sites and attractions are listed in order by Exit Number (North to South) and distance from the exit (closest are listed first). Symbols indicated represent:

 Restaurants    Lodging

Mile - 180 SB Only

NORTH CAROLINA WELCOME CENTER

This Welcome Center offers food, fuel, and a traveler information center to motorists. Find brochures, maps and other information. Of course, plenty of restrooms inside and areas to relax outside.

Exit - 173 (west of I-95)

ROANOKE RIVER MUSEUM & CANAL TRAIL

Roanoke Rapids - *Highway 158 27870. www.roanokeriver.com. Phone: (252) 537-2769. Trail open dawn to dusk. Museum Hours: Tuesday-Saturday 10:00am-4:00pm. Admission: $4.00 per person (age 9+).*

□ ROANOKE RIVER FALLS PARK - This safe still water harbor offers easy access to the Roanoke River and the overlook offers an excellent view of the river's picturesque rapids. Canoeing and fishing are among the most popular activities along the river banks. The park has a picnic area with grills and is an entry point to the Roanoke Canal Trail. Located just off Hwy 301 in Weldon.

□ ROANOKE CANAL TRAIL - This trail contains some of the most impressive and best preserved early nineteenth century canal construction in the nation. Begun before 1819, and completed in 1823, the Roanoke Canal was built as the North Carolina segment of the ambitious Roanoke Navigation System. It was designed to connect the Blue Ridge Mountains of Virginia with Norfolk, over a distance of 400 miles. Today you can experience the seven-mile trail along the old Canal in Roanoke Rapids.

□ MUSEUM - The museum tells the fascinating story of transportation and navigation on the Roanoke River and the history of the Roanoke Canal. The storyline weaves together the navigational history of the Roanoke River, the beginning of the railroad, transportation during the Civil War, and the coming of hydro-electric power with the river and the canal as common threads.

Exit - 173 (west of I-95)

LAKE GASTON

Littleton - *2475 Eaton Ferry Road (Visitors Center) (stop in at Visitors Ctr. 1st - then Eaton Ferry bridge by way of U.S. 158, N.C. 903) 27850. Phone: (252) 586-5711. www.lakegastonchamber.com. Admission: FREE.*

Straddling the North Carolina and Virginia border between I-85 and I-95, Lake Gaston has over 20,000 acres of "high quality" water, is 34 miles long, and approximately one and one half miles wide at the lower end of the lake. It has over 350 miles of shoreline offering a wide variety of watersports. Lake Gaston begins at Kerr Dam, a lake built in 1953 for flood control. Lake Gaston is well stocked with game fish which include striped bass or rock fish, large mouth bass, crappie, sunfish and several varieties of catfish. Other species of fish sometimes caught are walleye, yellow perch and chain pickerel. A valid license for either Virginia or North Carolina permits fishing from a boat in either state. No license is required for those under 15.

Exit - 168 (east of I-95)

HISTORIC HALIFAX STATE HISTORIC SITE

Halifax - *St. David & Dobbs Streets (I-95 take exit 168. Follow the signs south on N.C. 903 to the town of Halifax) 27839. Phone: (252) 583-7191 or (800) 522-4282. www.ah.dcr.state.nc.us/sections/hs/halifax/halifax.htm. Hours: Tuesday-Saturday 9:00am-5:00pm. Admission: FREE. Donations accepted. Tours: Guided tours are offered on a rotating schedule. Tour lengths are Owens House, twenty-five minutes; Middle of Town, forty-five minutes; Sally-Billy House, thirty minutes. They ask that groups make reservations in advance. Miscellaneous: Picnic sites and trails that lead to the Roanoke River overlook.*

April 12, 1776, the date commemorated on the North Carolina flag, signifies the Fourth Provincial Congress' adoption of the "Halifax Resolves" during a meeting right here in Halifax. With that action, North Carolina became the first colony to take an official step toward declaring independence from England. The Historic Halifax Visitor's Center offers a thirteen-minute orientation program depicting the history of the first eighty years of Halifax and the surrounding area. A guided walking tour takes you into several authentically restored and furnished buildings. These include the 1760 home of a merchant, the house and law office of a nineteenth-century attorney, and the 1808 home of a wealthy landowner (exhibits and walkways over foundations exposed by the scholar's spade and trowel). The 1833 clerk's office, a jail, Eagle tavern, and a unique archaeological exhibit are also featured on the tour.

Exit - 160 (west of I-95)

MEDOC MOUNTAIN STATE PARK

Hollister - *1541 Medoc State Park Road (west on SR 561 to State Road 1002) 27844. Phone: (252) 445-2280. www.ncparks.gov/Visit/parks/memo/main.php. Hours: Daily 8:00am-dusk. Educators: The Medoc Mountain program introduces students to basic geologic processes and relates them to the Medoc Mountain region. Accompanying the program is a teacher's booklet and workshop, free of charge to educators.*

Medoc Mountain is not really a mountain at all. The "mountain" is a granite outcropping with its highest point reaching 325 feet. It is the remains of the core of an ancient mountain range. Most of the trails are easy or moderate in difficulty, and trail scenery includes an artesian well, granite outcroppings and miniature rapids. Winding along Little Fishing Creek, around the high ridge of Medoc Mountain and through the forests, the trails are the best way to appreciate the beauty and diversity of Medoc Mountain. Picnicking, canoeing, nature study, camping and fishing all await you at this North Carolina State Park.

NC

Exit - 138 (east of I-95)

ROCKY MOUNT CHILDREN'S MUSEUM & SCIENCE CENTER

Rocky Mount - *270 Gay Street (go about 6 miles on US 64 E. Exit 469 for US301 Bus. Follow signs to Imperial Centre for the Arts and Sciences) 27804. Phone: (252) 972-1167. http://museum.imperialcentre.org/. Hours: Tuesday- Saturday 10:00am - 5:00pm, Sunday 1:00-5:00pm. Closed Thanksgiving and Christmas Day.Admission: $6.00 per person (age 2+) includes*

Planetarium. Note: In town (Sunset Avenue on River Drive) is Sunset Park - mini-train, historic carousel, sport courts, and swimming pool (252-972-1151).

The NEW Children's Museum includes 35 interactive learning stations designed to engage "budding scientists" ages 6 months to 6 years. Explore exciting activities like experimenting with music and sounds, opening doors to reveal hidden surprises, and matching characters to their shadows. It is housed in the oldest of the factory buildings which also includes permanent and rotating exhibits, a puppet theater, live animal habitats and a NC coastal "living marsh." An accessible display of permanent and traveling exhibits await you here. For example - Bears, In North Carolina? - N.C. Black Bears are very misunderstood animals. Visit this display and learn the real facts about one of North Carolina's largest land mammals.

The state-of-the-art digital SciDome planetarium features live and recorded sky tours, laser light concert shows and exhibits - Discover the secrets of the stars, moons, and planets in this fascinating astronomical exhibit.

Exit - 121 (west of I-95)

COUNTRY DOCTOR MUSEUM

Bailey - *6642 Peele Road (from Hwy 264, take the Bailey exit south on SR 581. At the first light, turn right on Hwy 264 Alt. At the first left, turn left) 27807. Phone: (252) 235-4165. www.countrydoctormuseum.org. Hours: Tuesday-Saturday 10:00am-4:00pm. Admission: $3.00-$5.00 per person (ages 3+). Educators: Print off the Scavenger Hunt sheet (found under the Tours icon page online) to use as your trick to keep the kids attentive for "little" things.*

Honoring the "old family doctor", this museum consists of the restored offices of two country doctors who practiced from 1857 to 1887. The museum's collections include artifacts relevant to many aspects of health care including nursing, pharmacy, homeopathy, and dentistry. Along with surgical sets and microscopes, the collection now incorporates medicine kits, apothecary equipment, nursing uniforms and memorabilia, and tools that would scare a patient today. You'll read about a lot of home remedies your grandparents may have tried. A medical herb garden located behind the Museum delights visitors throughout the year.

Exit - 119 (east of I-95)

IMAGINATION STATION

Wilson - *224 East Nash Street (Hwy 264 East to Wilson. Take Exit 36B onto Alt 264 East) 27893. Phone: (252) 291-5113. www.imaginescience.org. Hours: Tuesday-Saturday 9:00am-5:00pm, Sunday 1-4pm. Admission: $5.00 (age 4+).*

Located in the historic Wilson Federal Courthouse that was built in 1928, this hands-on science and technology center features over 200 exhibits that are related to the environment, space, and health. All of the exhibits at Imagination Station are hands-on. They want you to push, pull and handle everything. Exotic animals from around the state are a favorite. Especially something they don't get to see in their back yards, like Yoshi, the Imagination Station's favorite iguana. Also included are several boas, pythons, skinks, frogs, turtles, insects, spiders, and even a handful of albino reptiles. The best part is the up-close science experiments and demonstrations. Can you: Generate your own electricity? Look in a mirror and see yourself floating in air? Or, Race against a bat, bear and a cheetah?

Exit - 107 (east of I-95)

CHARLES B. AYCOCK BIRTHPLACE

Fremont - *264 Governor Aycock Road (I-95 to Kenly/Fremont exit. Head southeast on Rte. 222 to south on Rte. 117) 27830. www.nchistoricsites.org/aycock. Phone: (919) 242-5581. Hours: Tuesday-Saturday 9:00am-5:00pm. Admission: FREE. Educators: Teacher Packets are $2.00 each. Purchase at the site or mail a check. Call for dates of regular special events and living history demonstrations.*

The Site features the boyhood home of North Carolina's "Educational Governor". Aycock was elected governor in 1900. His ability to rouse people to support education at the local level stimulated the construction of approximately eleven hundred schools-one for every day he was in office. By the end of his term, citizens had seen enrollment increased, school districts consolidated, and teacher training improved. The farmstead home includes a mid-19th century farm, an 1893 one-room schoolhouse and a modern visitors center. The one-room schoolhouse was moved to the site to represent the grassroots educational revival that became statewide after Governor Aycock's election in 1900.

Exit - 107 (east of I-95)

WHIRLIGIGS

Wilson (Lucama) - *Wiggins Mill Road (I-95 exit 107 north to town. Turn left at light at Clints Korner, go to Wiggins Mill Road. Turn left approximately 4 miles) 27542. Phone: (800) 497-7398. www.wilson-nc.com/Whirligigs.cfm. Hours: Who knows?? Best to stop by the Wilson County Visitors Center just off the freeway for daily schedules. Daylight hours preferred. This is someone's home so respect his privacy and follow any instructions. Admission: FREE.*

Vollis Simpson's Windmill Farm is a remarkable collection of elaborate "whirligigs" produced by local outsider folk artist Vollis Simpson. The works incorporate complex movement and sound as an integral part of the more than 30 GIANT works erected on Simpson's property. Simpson's welded and painted constructions are large in scale and have been exhibited at noted art museums and are featured in downtown Raleigh. Vollis can often be seen at the front of his shop, working non-stop. He's happy to talk to you, but he doesn't ever interrupt his work. Inside, the shop is filled with over a hundred smaller whirlygigs, all completely finished and painted.

Exit - 97 (west of I-95)

CLEMMONS EDUCATIONAL STATE FOREST

Clayton - *2411 Old US 70 West (US 70 west towards Raleigh) 27520. Phone: (919) 553-5651. www.ncesf.org/CESF/home.htm. Hours: Tuesday-Friday 9:00am-5:00pm, Saturday & Sunday 11:00am-5:00pm EST, 11:00am-8:00pm DST (mid-March to mid-November). Admission: FREE. Educators: Go to the link: www.ncesf.org/tg/tg2_main.htm for lots of online curriculum.*

Located between the Piedmont and the Coastal Plain, Clemmons' pine stands and hardwoods are set on rolling terrain highlighted by streams and rock formations. These features are accessible by a series of well-marked trails, accented by exhibits and displays depicting the ecology of the forest. Listen to the "talking" trees and rocks weave tales about the life there; hike the demo trail to see natural resource manager's duties; explore the new exhibit center; picnic, camp or join in on a ranger-conducted environmental education class.

Exit - 90 (east of I-95)

BENTONVILLE BATTLEFIELD STATE HISTORIC SITE

Goldsboro (Four Oaks) - *5466 Harper House Road (U.S. 701 south. Follow signs to State Road 1008) 27524. www.nchistoricsites.org/bentonvi/bentonvi. htm. Phone: (910) 594-0789. Hours: Tuesday-Saturday 9:00am-5:00pm. Closed all major holidays. Admission: FREE. Tours: Guided tours of the Harper House and outbuildings are scheduled on the hour throughout the day. Miscellaneous: Summer Seasonal Living History Program and Artillery Demonstrations. On Saturday, costumed living historians from the 1st /11th NC Troops will conduct weapons demonstrations and hold discussions on the lives of the average Civil War soldier. Highly trained volunteers will also demonstrate the loading and firing of a 3" Ordnance Rifle, a popular Civil War cannon. (one summer Saturday each month)*

The Battle of Bentonville, fought March 19-21, 1865, was the last full-scale

action of the Civil War in which a Confederate army was able to mount a tactical offensive. Walk on the fields where 80,000 Union and Confederate soldiers fought. Tour the nearby Harper House (ca. 1855) furnished as a Civil War field hospital. This is where wounded from both sides were treated in an improvised hospital.

The upstairs rooms of the Harper House feature period domestic furnishings. The Harper children remained at home with their parents when the house was taken over by the Federal XIV Army Corps for use as a field hospital. The site also includes a reconstructed kitchen and slave quarters. The visitor center features a ten-minute audiovisual program explaining the events leading up to the Battle of Bentonville. The center also exhibits artifacts from the battlefield and maps of troop movement during the three days of fighting.

Exit - 52 (west of I-95)

CAPE FEAR BOTANICAL GARDEN

Fayetteville - *536 North Eastern Blvd. (I-95, take Exit 52 (Hwy 24 West). Go approximately 5 miles. Turn right onto Hwy 301N (Eastern Blvd.) Go 1/8 mile. CFBG is on the right) 28302. Phone: (910) 486-0221. www.capefearbg.org. Hours: Daily 10:00am-5:00pm. Admission: $10.00 adult, $9.00 military & senior (65+), $5.00 child (6-12). Note: Treasure Hunt: each month, a new treasure hunt clue worksheet is introduced with different themes. Go out in search of numbered pine cones. Once completed, turn it in for 10% off a gift shop purchase.*

Nestled on 85 acres that overlook Cross Creek and the Cape Fear River, this botanical garden includes numerous species of native plants, wild flowers, and majestic oaks. An authentic 1800s farmhouse and outbuildings are also on site, as well as nature trails, a Heritage Garden, a demonstration garden, and a large gazebo. In the Children's Garden: The Lilliput Labyrinth - based on the tale of Gulliver's Travels. The items Gulliver left behind are giant-sized, which sets the garden's theme of contrasting the immense with the miniature. Must see sculptures are a 15' swing, a 5' pair of eyeglasses, and a 17' chair. The Friendship Garden was established to recognize and appreciate ethnic diversity of the region through the exploration of our shared botanical heritage at a global level. Formed in the shape of a heart, the garden has seven beds, each representing plantings from each continent of the world.

AIRBORNE AND SPECIAL OPERATIONS MUSEUM

Fayetteville - *100 Bragg Boulevard (I-95 exit 52B to NC 24, left on Bragg) 28302. Phone: (910) 483-3003. www.asomf.org. Hours: Tuesday-Saturday 10:00am-5:00pm, Sunday Noon-5:00pm. Closed major winter holidays. Open many Federal holiday Mondays. Admission: FREE. Fee for Simulator (age 8+) is $5.00 each. FREEBIES: Print off scavenger hunts, word searches and crossword puzzles to do on the road. Educators: Curriculum guides (grade appropriate) are on the Education page.*

Have you ever wondered what it was like for that first person to make the decision to jump from a moving airplane in order to serve his country? Well, now you may be able to learn the answer along with some other historically significant facts. The Airborne and Special Operations Museum is the only one of its kind and has newer, state-of-the-art exhibit spaces. The site chronicles the growth of Ft. Bragg and the surrounding area from the inception of Camp Bragg in September of 1918 to modern day construction, with particular attention to the spectacular build-up to World War II. The lobby exhibit features two fully deployed parachutes, a WWII era T-5 round chute and a modern MC-4 square chute. They look very real. Filmed in Vistascope, a high speed 8/35 mm process that presents a huge, stunningly clear image, the movie is designed to put the viewer into the exciting military action and to show military operations in a way never before experienced by the public. Similar to the movie, the Pitch, Roll, and Yaw Vista-Dome Motion Simulator adds another dimension by physically moving a specially designed seating area up to 18 degrees in concert with the film. Suddenly a larger than life film of airborne and special operations becomes almost real. The 24-seat simulator provides visitors with an extreme taste of what the Army's finest are trained to do. The whole museum uses curiosity and visual lighting (or darkness) to get the kids engaged.

Exit - 52 (west of I-95)

FASCINATE-U CHILDREN'S MUSEUM

Fayetteville - *116 Green Street (HWY 24 W, left on Grove to downtown, next to the Markethouse, downtown) 28302. www.fascinate-u.com. Phone: (910) 829-9171. Hours: Tuesday-Friday 9:00am-5:00pm, Saturday 10:00am-5:00pm, Sunday Noon-5:00pm. Open Wednesday evenings until 7:00pm. Admission: $4.00 child, $3.00 adult.*

Fascinate-U began as the brainchild of two young mothers building educational opportunities for the area's children. Housed inside historic City Hall, this magnificent educational forum features a host of innovative role-playing and interactive exhibits that allow children to discover occupations such as banking, grocery, media, government, theater, medicine, and law. Come on in. You can touch and play with everything. In the mini-city everything is kid-sized. Children can go shopping at the Gro-Right Grocery & Deli, put on a judge's robe and pass their sentence-gavel in hand, respond to calls at the 911 Emergency Dispatch Center, and give the weather forecast at the WNUZ center.

Exit - 46 (east of I-95)

FAYETTEVILLE MOTOR SPORTS PARK

Fayetteville - *283 Doc Bennett Road (I-95, take exit 46. Go South on Hwy. 87, turn right at the flashing lights on to Doc Bennett Rd) 28301. Phone: (910) 484-3677. www.fayettevillemotorsportspark.com.*

Professional drag racing that is sanctioned by the International Hot Rod Association is featured at this drag strip and sports park. The Park also features stock car dirt-track racing April through September on Saturday evenings, as well as Streetcar Madness on Friday nights. Sunday Drags: Test N Tune/ Fun & Grudge. Gates Open Noon-5:00pm. Weather permitting. General Admission $10.00. Children 12 and under free.

Exit - 22 (east of I-95)

EXPLORATION STATION

Lumberton - *104 North Chestnut Street (I-95 exit 22 take Fayetteville Rd/Pine St. all the way to 1st St. in town. Take a right and go 2 blocks) 28358. Phone: (910) 738-1114. www.facebook.com/pages/Exploration-Station/116951588345544?sk=info. Hours: Wednesday-Saturday 10:00am-5:00pm, Sunday 1-5pm. Admission: $5.00 per child, adults FREE.*

The Children's Museum contains eleven interactive spaces where kids can play educational make-believe. Dress up and play doctor in the hospital, milk a cow, teach a class in school, shop at the general store or watch ducks cascade down a waterfall. There's a separate play area for infants.

Exit - 14 (west of I-95)

MUSEUM OF THE NATIVE AMERICAN RESOURCE CENTER

Pembroke - *Old Main Building, Univ. of NC at Pembroke (ten miles west of the intersection of U.S. 74 and I- 95) 28372. www.uncp.edu/nativemuseum/. Phone: (910) 521-6282. Hours: Monday-Saturday 8:00am-5:00pm. Admission: FREE.*

A very unique museum and resource center that

contains 19th century artifacts, as well as arts and crafts from Lumbee Indian tribes plus displays contemporary Indian arts and drafts that represent Native Americans all over North America. Favorite family displays include an authentic log canoe and log cabin, Indian dress and music or video presentations. Many other items come from North Carolina Native Americans, with special emphasis on Robeson County Indian people. Particular focus is placed on the largest North Carolina tribe, the Lumbee. Today, the Lumbee number over 50,000, with the majority residing in Robeson and adjoining counties. According to local legends, the Indians of Robeson County are descendants of several tribal groups (three languages families - Eastern Siouan, Iroquoian and Algonquian) and John White's Lost Colony.

Mile - 5 NB Only

NORTH CAROLINA WELCOME CENTER

Phone: (910) 422-8314.

This Welcome Center offers food, fuel, and a traveler information center to motorists. Find brochures, maps and other information. Of course, plenty of restrooms inside and areas to relax outside.

NC

Chapter 6
SOUTH CAROLINA

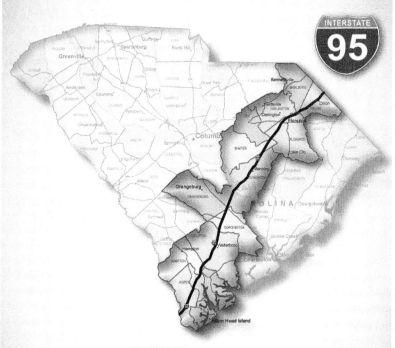

**DEAR
SOUTH CAROLINA
TRAVELER:**

In South Carolina, I-95 runs fairly parallel to the Atlantic Ocean, about 50 miles inland, from Dillon in the northeast to Hardeeville in the south. For the most part, the 198—mile drive is fairly favorable, passing through farmlands, pine forests, blackwater streams and swamps. However, a few notables do exist to break up the monotony.

The entrance into the state is prominently marked by the **South of The Border** amusement complex at the US 301/501 exit. A tourist trap, yes, but who can resist – especially after the myriad of funny billboards drawing you in! Even if you just stop for a bathroom break, a snack and maybe a ride up the Tower – this will be a rest stop the kids will remember forever. (BTW, if you get out of there with just a pit stop – good luck because the kids are mesmerized by this place)

Touring the Pee Dee region, one is quickly reminded of its roots as a commercial center for cotton and tobacco. Florence is a city with history, character, and Southern charm. Chartered in 1871, the original township formed as a railroad terminal. Climb aboard a caboose at the History Museum. The highlights of this town – Redbone, Raceways and Pecans. Within a 10-mile radius, your kids can have their own play area (including a real ice cream truck and treats) at **Redbone Alley**, tour a Hall of Fame and real NASCAR raceway (**Darlington Raceway**) and finish the day with dessert at **Young's Pecans** (don't fill up on the free sample bar)! As you leave the region, jump off some exits to investigate the mysterious **"Swamp Fox" Murals** of the legendary General Francis Marion. A Revolutionary War hero,

Gen. Marion applied guerrilla tactics to torment the British. He usually struck at night and then vanished into the swamps – hence his nickname, "Swamp Fox." Want to see, and walk through a real black swamp? Try **Woods Bay State Natural Area** boardwalk trails OVER the eerie swamp!

Once a predominantly agricultural community, Santee is gateway to many outdoor recreational opportunities in the Santee-Cooper Country. Nestled along I-95 and adjacent to Lake Marion, Santee offers access to some of the best fishing in the Southeast, as well as boating, golfing, camping, wildlife watching and guided nature tours. A flyover on twin high-spans over Lake Marion provides an unexpected scenic break in the center of the highway's length. Fishing poles abound in this area and you can cast your own from shore or by boat – even right outside your cabin at **Santee State Park** or **Santee Indian Mound & Wildlife Refuge**. The mound is fun to climb, too. The view of Lake Marion from the top will beg you to explore every inch of the park. Other notable side trips in this area are a quaint historical museum (with interactives!) at the **Elloree Heritage Museum** and the playful **Swan Lake Iris Garden**. Ok, you may think an iris garden sounds like a ladies garden club hot spot but, really, wait until your kids meet those beautiful, and sometimes noisy, swans! It tickles even the oldest kid's heart to follow these creatures about the wonderful lakeside landscape.

And the food – well, most of it's purely Southern home-cooking (like Grandmas fried chicken or casseroles) but try getting the kids to try some new things by sneaking it in with their favorites. For example, grilled shrimp and GRITS or shredded pork BBQ with GOLDEN BBQ sauce. We've suggested some of the best stops to try new flavors in this chapter.

Heading towards the southernmost part of I-95 in South Carolina, we might suggest stopping at the **Colleton Museum** in Walterboro. The kids can't wait to enter the castle-like structure outside and inside the museum has an ongoing exhibit on "Animals of the ACE," a natural history display featuring wild animals indigenous to the South Carolina Lowcountry. At exit 33, the **Low Country Visitors Center & Museum** is worth stopping at – especially if you plan to venture towards the coast (Hilton Head, Charleston). Our favorite room was the Parlor room and the Gullah items. It's clever how they mix artifacts with items you can purchase and brochures. Kids like the old-fashioned toys and trinkets plus the free samples of fruit cider made in Low Country. Just before you leave SC and cross over the Savannah River bridge, look to your left and notice an elaborate gateway entrance carries the "Welcome to South Carolina" sign.

ACTIVITIES AT A GLANCE

AMUSEMENTS
Exit - 198 - *South Of The Border*

ANIMALS & FARMS
Exit - 164 - *Young Pecan Plantation*
Exit - 164 - *Pee Dee State Farmers Market*
Exit - 153 - *Ovis Hill Farms*
Exit - 135 - *Swan Lake Iris Gardens*

HISTORY
Exit - 160B - *(I-20) Florence Museum Of Art, Science & History*
Exit - 102 - *Santee Indian Mound & Fort Watson Site (Santee National Wildlife Refuge)*
Exit - 98 - *Elloree Heritage Museum & Cultural Center*
Exit - 57 - *Colleton Museum*
Exit - 33 - *Low Country Visitors Center & Museum*

OUTDOOR EXPLORING
Exit - 193 - *Little Pee Dee State Park*
Exit - 141 - *Woods Bay State Natural Area*
Exit - 122 - *Pocotaligo Conservatory Area Park*
Exit - 98 - *Santee State Park*
Exit - 5 - *Savannah River National Wildlife Refuge*

SPORTS
Exit - 164 - *Darlington Raceway & Stock Car Museum*

SUGGESTED LODGING & DINING
Exit - 160B (I-20) - *The Drive-In*
Exit - 160A (I-20) - *Redbone Alley Restaurant*
Exit - 160A - *Hilton Garden Inn - Florence*
Exit - 98 - *Lone Star Barbecue & Mercantile*
Exit - 98 - *Clark's Inn & Restaurant*
Exit - 98 - *Maurice's Barbeque*
Exit - 57 - *Duke's Barbecue*

THE ARTS
Exit - 119 & 132 - *Swamp Fox Murals*

WELCOME CENTERS
Exit - 195 Mile (SB ONLY) - *South Carolina Welcome Center*
Exit - 139 Mile - *Sumter County Welcome Center*
Exit - 100 Mile - *Lake Marion Travel Information Center (SB ONLY) & Santee Rest Stop (NB)*

Contact the services of interest. Request to be added to their mailing lists.

- South Carolina Department of Natural Resources: www.dnr.sc.gov
- South Carolina State Parks: www.SouthCarolinaParks.com
- South Carolina Tourism www.discoverSouthCarolina.com
- Pee Dee Country Tourism: www.peedeetourism.com
- Santee Cooper Country Tourism: www.santeecoopercountry.org
- South Carolina Campgrounds: http://koa.com/where/sc/ or
  http://camping.about.com/od/cgwebpagessc/South_Carolina_Campgrounds_with_Web_pages.htm

Travel Journal & Notes:

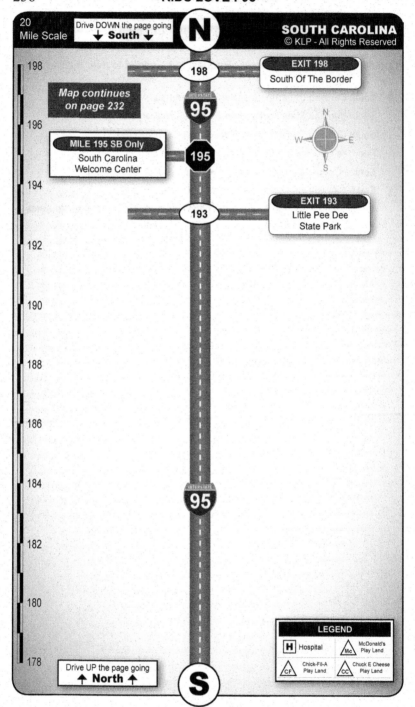

20 Mile Scale

Drive DOWN the page going
↓ **South** ↓

N

198

EXIT 198
South Of The Border

INTERSTATE 95

Map continues
on page 232

196

MILE 195 SB Only
South Carolina
Welcome Center

195

194

EXIT 193
Little Pee Dee
State Park

193

N
W—E
S

192

190

188

186

184

INTERSTATE 95

182

180

LEGEND

H Hospital	McDonald's Play Land
CF Chick-Fil-A Play Land	CC Chuck E Cheese Play Land

178

Drive UP the page going
↑ **North** ↑

S

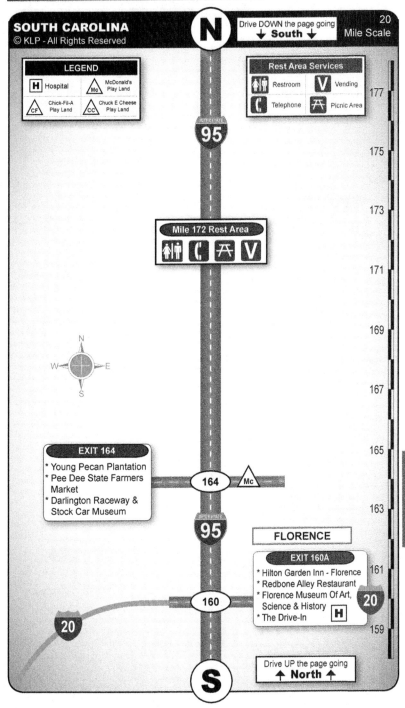

SOUTH CAROLINA

N

Drive DOWN the page going
↓ **South** ↓

20
Mile Scale

LEGEND

| H | Hospital | Mc | McDonald's Play Land |
| CF | Chick-Fil-A Play Land | CC | Chuck E Cheese Play Land |

Rest Area Services

| | Restroom | V | Vending |
| | Telephone | | Picnic Area |

INTERSTATE 95

177

175

173

Mile 172 Rest Area

171

169

167

165

EXIT 164

* Young Pecan Plantation
* Pee Dee State Farmers Market
* Darlington Raceway & Stock Car Museum

164   Mc

163

INTERSTATE 95

FLORENCE

EXIT 160A

* Hilton Garden Inn - Florence
* Redbone Alley Restaurant
* Florence Museum Of Art, Science & History
* The Drive-In   H

161

20

160

20

159

Drive UP the page going
↑ **North** ↑

S

SC

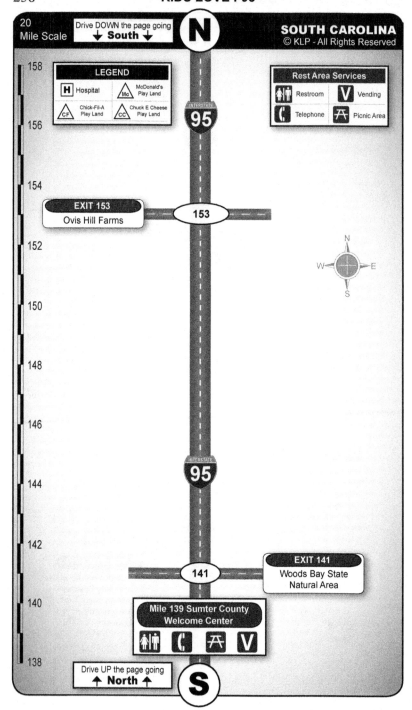

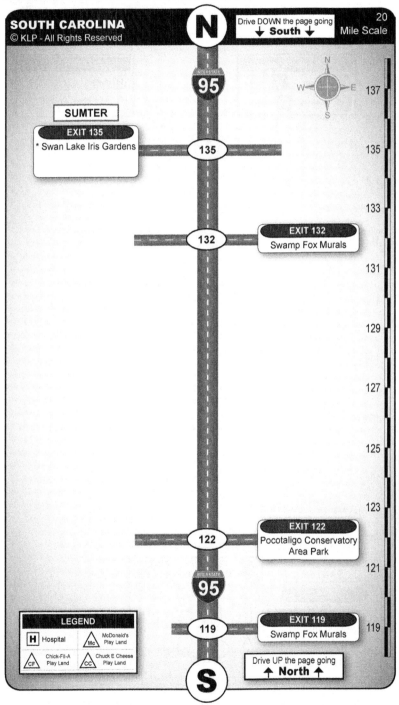

SOUTH CAROLINA

Drive DOWN the page going
↓ **South** ↓

20 Mile Scale

INTERSTATE **95**

SUMTER

EXIT 135
* Swan Lake Iris Gardens

135 — 135

133

EXIT 132
Swamp Fox Murals

132 — 132

131

129

127

125

123

EXIT 122
Pocotaligo Conservatory
Area Park

122 — 122

121

INTERSTATE **95**

119 — 119

EXIT 119
Swamp Fox Murals

LEGEND

| H | Hospital | Mc | McDonald's Play Land |
| CF | Chick-Fil-A Play Land | CC | Chuck E Cheese Play Land |

Drive UP the page going
↑ **North** ↑

S

SC

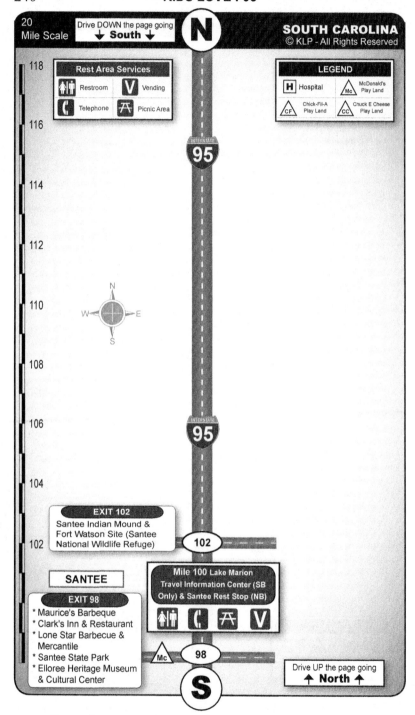

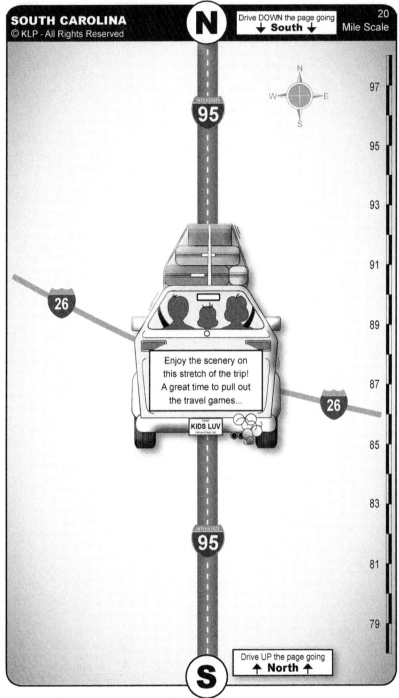

Enjoy the scenery on
this stretch of the trip!
A great time to pull out
the travel games...

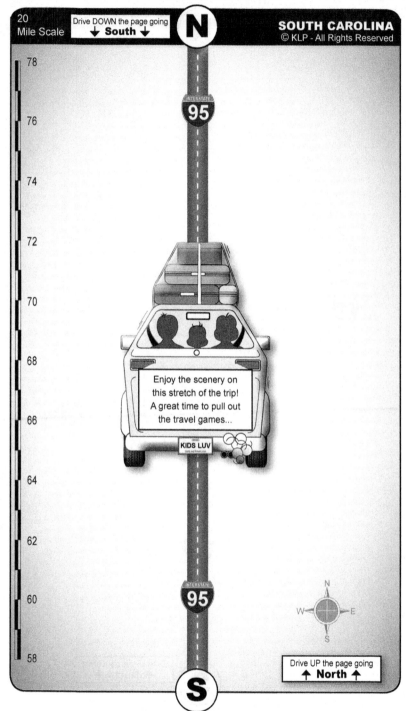

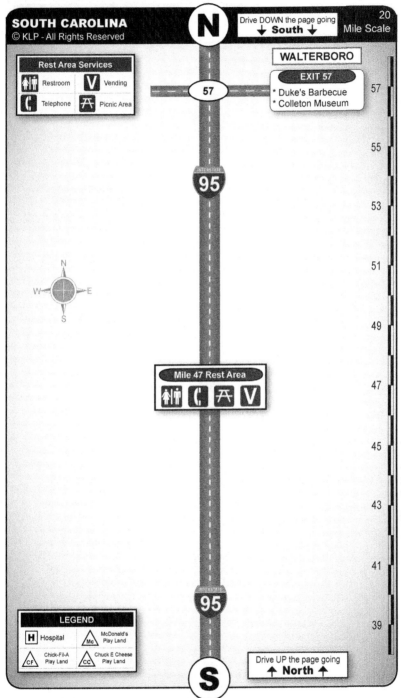

SOUTH CAROLINA

Drive DOWN the page going
↓ **South** ↓

20
Mile Scale

Rest Area Services

Restroom   Vending
Telephone   Picnic Area

WALTERBORO

EXIT 57
* Duke's Barbecue
* Colleton Museum

57

57

55

53

51

49

Mile 47 Rest Area

47

45

43

SC

41

95

LEGEND

H Hospital   Mc McDonald's Play Land
CF Chick-Fil-A Play Land   CC Chuck E Cheese Play Land

39

Drive UP the page going
↑ **North** ↑

S

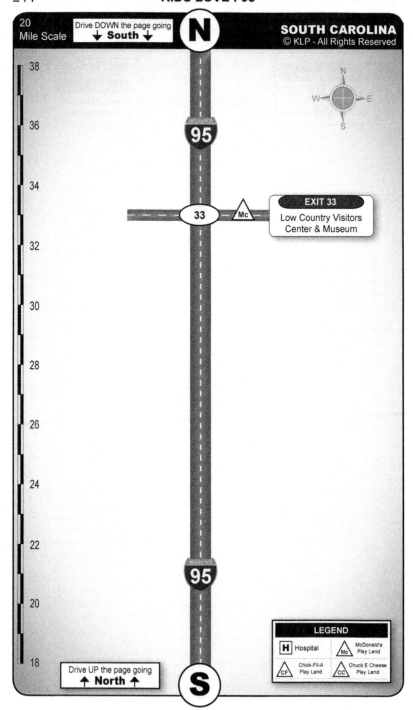

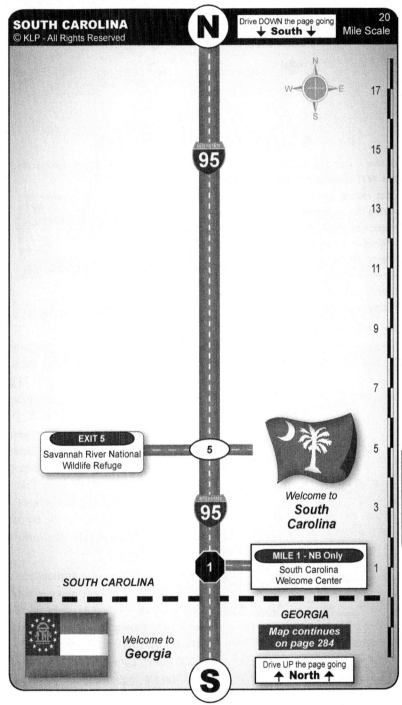

SOUTH CAROLINA
© KLP - All Rights Reserved

Drive DOWN the page going
↓ **South** ↓

20
Mile Scale

N

N
W   E
S

INTERSTATE
95

17

15

13

11

9

7

EXIT 5
Savannah River National
Wildlife Refuge

5

INTERSTATE
95

Welcome to
**South
Carolina**

5

3

SC

MILE 1 - NB Only
South Carolina
Welcome Center

1

1

SOUTH CAROLINA

- -

GEORGIA

**Map continues
on page 284**

Welcome to
Georgia

Drive UP the page going
↑ **North** ↑

S

Sites and attractions are listed in order by Exit Number (North to South) and distance from the exit (closest are listed first). Symbols indicated represent:

  Restaurants   Lodging

Exit - 198 (east of I-95)

SOUTH OF THE BORDER

Dillon - *mm 198, right at NC/SC border off I-95 & US 301 N) 29536. Phone: (843) 774-2411.   www.thesouthoftheborder. com. Hours: Daily, hours for venues varies but generally 7:00am-11:00pm. Note: Pedros Rockey City has oodles of fireworks - big ones, too. Sombrero Room Restaurant serves the best Mexican food in northern South Carolina and three other "faster" food restaurants are on the premises.*

It's so much fun to see how many different ways Pedro tells you to stop by...

The auto trip from the Northeast to the sunny shores of Florida via I-95 takes two good days of driving. Halfway there, a huge alien sombrero nearly 200 feet high suddenly appears in the distance. After enduring an accelerating onslaught of 120 billboards for more than 200 miles, this is what you've waited to see. Drive under Pedro, the attraction's mascot, into a world of Mexico Americana. South of the Border is so named so because it is just "south of the border" – the border between the U.S. states of South Carolina and North Carolina.

Pedro straddles the South of the Border entrance, 97 feet tall, "the largest freestanding sign east of the Mississippi."

This attraction with its Mexican motif offers an amusement park with bumper cars, a Ferris wheel, parachute drop, reptile lagoon, miniature golf and more. South Of The Border has both RV campgrounds and 300 motel rooms spread over its 135 acres. And staying here allows access to

Pedro's Pleasure Dome, with its indoor pool, steam room, and Jacuzzi. Kids will want to use a lot of their spending money at the Mexico Gift Shops as quantity (in bins) is king and the hardest decisions are which of the handfuls of different back scratchers should you get? You may also take a ride in the glass elevator to the top of Pedro's 200-foot tall Sombrero Tower! They say this is an oasis and once you've looked off the top of the tower, you'll see why - nothing, nowhere.

Exit - 195 MILE (SB Only)

SOUTH CAROLINA WELCOME CENTER

Hamer - *(mm 195 near NC/SC border) 29547. Phone: 843/774-4711. Hours: Daily 9:00am-5:00pm.*

Nationally certified travel counselors are ready to assist you with directions and mapping information, and informative brochures to help you discover the treasures of South Carolina. The centers also offer discount coupons for attractions and accommodations and will gladly make reservations for you and your party. Traffic information is readily available as well as weather information for the state. Many of the centers also offer a mail drop for your letters and services such as the AT&T international language line. All of these complimentary services are offered to make your experience in the state relaxing and enjoyable. Bathrooms are also available.

Exit - 193 (east of I-95)

LITTLE PEE DEE STATE PARK

Dillon - *1298 State Park Road (exit 193 onto Hwy9 thru Dillon. Right onto Hwy 57 for several miles. Left onto CR22) 29536. Phone: (843) 774-8872. www. southcarolinaparks.com/park-finder/state-park/881.aspx. Hours: Daily 9:00am-6:00pm (extended to 9:00pm during Daylight Savings Time). Admission: FREE. Note: Pets are allowed in most outdoor areas provided they are kept under physical restraint or on a leash not longer than six feet.*

Named after the blackwater Little Pee Dee River, Little Pee Dee State Park is a subdued setting for those who want to enjoy the park's natural features or fish the still waters of 54-acre Lake Norton. Visitors can explore the park's river swamp, examine features of the Sandhills region and admire an example of the mysterious geological depression unique to the Atlantic Coastal Plain, the Carolina Bay. The Beaver Pond Nature Trail: This 1.3-mile trail to a beaver pond loops back to the original point of entry. Jon boats, canoes and kayaks with life jackets and paddles are available for rent. Private boats are restricted to an electric trolling motor. Guests also enjoy the park's campground, nature trail and picnic area.

Exit - 164 *(west of I-95)*

YOUNG PECAN PLANTATION

Florence - 2005 Babar lane (US 52 west one half mile) 29501. Phone: (843) 66-2452. www.youngplantations.com. Hours: Monday-Friday 9:00am-5:00pm, Saturday 10:00am-4:00pm. Extended Christmas-time hours.

Pecan trees, fresh shelled pecans and candy coated pecans are all available from the retail sales shop at Young Pecan Plantation. These delectable treats are shipped around the world from South Carolina. Our favorite part of the visit is the Sampler Bar - a long counter full of samples of every type of flavored nut including some unique ones: Butter roasted and lightly salted (local fav), Double-Dipped Chocolate, Honey Crisp or Butterscotch. Don't like nuts? Have some ice cream or lunch instead.

The Sampler Bar was great for choosin your favorites...

Once you've chosen your favorite flavors to purchase to take on the road, wander around the store and discover other homemade, and very unusual products. Pick up a few of their homemade ciders…blackberry, peach, strawberry, blueberry, and yes, apple. Wow, the peach is so refreshing!

PEE DEE STATE FARMERS MARKET

Florence - 2513 W. Lucas Street (US Hwy. 52) (just head about one mile west off the exit. Market is on right.) 29501. www.pdfarmersmarket.sc.gov/redbarn.htm. Phone (843) 665-5154. Admission and parking are FREE. Note: Vending machines and restrooms are conveniently located on the premises.

The Pee Dee Farmers Market includes fresh produce for sale plus a 100-year-old barn which houses a pecan kitchen, potter's shop and a café. Elijah Thomas spends a few hours each day at his potter's wheel in his studio at the Red Barn. Visiting with him is a delightful experience for young and old alike.

DARLINGTON RACEWAY & STOCK CAR MUSEUM

Darlington - *1301 Harry Byrd Hwy. (west on Hwy 52, then two miles west of the city of Darlington on highway SC 151) 29540. www.darlingtonraceway.com. Phone: (843) 395-8499. Hours: Monday-Friday 10:00am-5:00pm, Saturday 10:00am-4:00pm, Sunday 11am-4pm. Admission is $5.00 for adults, and FREE for kids under the age of 12. Note: Along with the two major race weekends, there are car shows, driving schools and other activities scheduled.*

When the idea to build a track was conceived, the original landowner, farmer Jack Ramsey, had just one request — don't disturb his fishing pond. Thus, Brasington was forced to change the design from a geometrically correct oval to more of an egg-shape. In doing so, he not only preserved the fishing hole, he made Darlington Raceway one of the most challenging tracks in the country. On Labor Day 1950, Brasington held Darlington Raceway's inaugural race. Over the years, Darlington Raceway has earned a reputation as "the track too tough to tame." Fans can watch the likes of Dale Earnhardt Jr., Jeff Gordon, Bill Elliott, the Wallaces, the Labontes and the Burtons squeeze through the narrow third and fourth turns (remember the pond?). There's always something going on: The Carolina 400 in the spring and the Southern 500 each summer. Here you can view a priceless collection of historic race cars, including the No. 98 Plymouth that won the first race back in 1950. Kids can push buttons near each display and it will play an audio history of each driver. Did you know that the winningest car in the history of stock car racing is a convertible? Occupying

a prominent spot in the back is Darrell Waltrip's 1991 Chevy Lumina, which rolled eight times in one of the most fearsome crashes in stock car history. Waltrip walked away from the incident, and the car stands as an impressive witness to stock car safety. Stop at the museum and gift shop, have lunch in the picnic area, then walk out on the track and just take in the ambiance of the place. If you're a NASCAR fan, it really

The late Dale Earnhardt once said, " ... there's no victory so sweet, so memorable, as whipping Darlington Raceway."

is awesome, even when there isn't a single car running.

Exit - 160A (east of I-95)

HILTON GARDEN INN - FLORENCE

Florence - 2671 Hospitality Blvd. (I-95 Exit 160 A to first light. Turn right on Radio Drive. Turn left at next light onto Hospitality Blvd. Hotel is on the left) 29501. Phone: (843) 432-3001. www.florence.stayhgi.com.

Offers friendly service and a magnificent location with easy access to I-95 and I-20 and Florence's best attractions. Best features include: Fridge, microwave & coffeemaker in every room, Complimentary high-speed Internet, and Evening room service. Work out in the complimentary fitness center, relax in the whirlpool or take a plunge in the indoor heated pool. For your family's comfort and convenience they offer a Children's Menu, high chairs, cribs and playpens. A freshly prepared breakfast is offered daily in the Great American Grill® restaurant, and dinner is also available. All of their chicken dishes are really flavorful. The Pavilion Pantry® convenience mart offers sundries, an assortment of beverages and ready-to-cook meals bound for the in-room microwave oven or refrigerator. Oh, and after traveling all those highway miles, you 'll enjoy their Sleep Deep beds.

REDBONE ALLEY RESTAURANT

Florence - 1903 W Palmetto Street (exit 160A east a few miles on I-20. Left on US 76) 29501. www.redbonealley.com. Hours: Daily lunch & dinner.

Want to visit an outdoor Charleston café - indoors? This restaurant's theme looks very much like a theatrical set. A two-story high space with an open atrium. A back porch with glowing lanterns. An upstairs balcony overlooking the alley. Lowcountry landscape murals painted by Charleston artist David Boatwright. And, a children's area with an ice cream truck smack dab in the middle (stocked with free ice cream treats) of a playspace for toddlers and kids arcades. This space (and the 25c arcade around the corner) are the diversions you've been looking for while you wait for your food. (note: if you're a family with kids, you'll

How cool..getting to play ICE CREAM TRUCK...

most likely get seated in this lively area). The staff start every day early by gathering the day's ingredients -- produce bought directly from local farmers -- honey gathered by South Carolinian beekeepers, Darlington County rice, freshly caught Atlantic seafood and the highest quality aged Western beef flown in daily. The menu really is influenced by French, Mediterranean, African, English and West Indian cooking. Their entrees have a dramatic twist: Low Country Shrimp and Grits or Fried Green Tomatoes & Blackened Shrimp w/ Cajun sauce. How about Cajun fried Quail served over cheese grits? Trust me, this northern girl now loves grits - Redbone grits, that is! If that's too odd for the kids, go with traditional Chicken Planks seasoned with one of 3 different batters. And, there's some form of ham in half the dishes so the flavor is familiar. If you just want traditional Kids menu items, they've got them: eight items - all for just $5. Average lunch $10.00, Average dinner $16.00. Still have room for dessert? How about a grilled pound cake panini "sandwich" made from an heirloom recipe. What an ending to an explosion of new tastes! Named after the owner's daughter's Red Bone coon hound, each restaurant also offers live entertainment and a clothing line featuring the Redbone Alley hound.

FLORENCE MUSEUM OF ART, SCIENCE & HISTORY

Florence - *111 West Cheves Street (downtown 29501. www.florencemuseum.org. Phone: (843) 662-3351. Hours: Tuesday-Saturday 10:00am-5:00pm, Sunday 2:00-5:00pm. Admission: $1.00 general, $3.00 max. per family. Donation box.*

The modern art museum features changing exhibits on one side and some rooms filled with history on the other. Art is either contemporary or Asian, African, ancient Mediterranean or Southwest Pueblo and that's interesting to look at but the kids will also enjoy some of the regional history. Kids focus on the ancient Indian tools and animal skeletons most. The video highlights the history and fame of area people and companies. Did you know ketchup is made here as is the light bulb (or, at least their big corporate offices). It's a nice, quiet stop just blocks away from lunch at the Drive In ...or walk the gardens and picnic in the shade.

Exit - 160A (east of I-95)

THE DRIVE-IN

Florence - *135 E Palmetto Street (I-20 to end, left onto US 76, just a couple blocks past intersection of US 52) 29506. www.thebestdrivein.com. Phone: (843) 669-5141. Hours: Monday-Saturday 10:30am-11:00pm.*

This newly renovated restaurant in downtown Florence has been serving some of the best hot dogs, burgers and shakes since 1957. Though the 50s-style restaurant now flaunts its modern architecture, the outside curb station still exists. Diners will also find other nostalgic items like framed newspaper articles about the restaurant, photos (including images of the original owners) and red and black checkered floors. Co-owner Pauline Kremydas says the articles and pictures "bring back a lot of memories for our customers who used to restaurant hop." The Drive-In is said to have the best fried chicken in the Pee Dee. We think it's very moist but we'll let you be the judge. Stop by and order a chicken snack or dinner and try it for yourself. One thing The Drive-in has now that wasn't around in the 50s is Wi-Fi. Bring your laptop and enjoy a smooth, cool milkshake for lunch. You're in for a good ol' fashion nostalgic treat and a twist. Since the owners are Greek, add a gyro and a piece of baklava (cinnamon-y) to your order.

🍽

Exit - 153 (west of I-95)

OVIS HILL FARMS

Timmonsville - *1501 Weaver St. (exit 153 head west on SR403 just past SR340. Turn left on E. St. Paul. Right on Weaver) 29161. www.ovishillfarm.com. Phone: (843) 346-3646. Hours: Seasonally, Tuesday-Thursday 3:00-6:00pm and Friday and Saturday 10:00am-6:00pm. Other times are available by appointment for group tours. Admission: General Admission: $6.00 per person, Special activities and food extra. Admission for Children 2 and under: FREE.*

Visit a real Farm Store - A veritable "farmers market" with clean and healthy products from a network of local South Carolina farmers: Pasture raised and grass fed Milk and dairy products from Happy cow Creamery, beef, lamb, chicken, organically grown vegetables, hand made products, wool yarns and knit items. But the part kids love best: Animals to pet, feed, milk or watch,

> Pick free sunflowers for someone who brightens your life. Take Highway 52 further east to Effingham.

Border Collie Herding Demonstrations (like the movie "Babe"), Hayrides, Butter making, crafts to make and buy, Food, Sheep Shearing, Wool dying and spinning, and music. Guess how many sheep are on the farm? Answer: 400. Can you count them all?

Exit - 141 (east of I-95)

WOODS BAY STATE PARK

Olanta - *11020 Woods Bay Road (SR 53 east to SR 597 south to SR48 southeast, three miles west of Olanta) 29114. www.southcarolinaparks.com/woodsbay/ introduction.aspx. Phone: (843) 659-4445. Hours: Park is open daily 9:00am-6:00pm. Nature Center is only open sporadically - possibly weekends. Note: Some guest enjoy canoeing & rentals, hiking, fishing, and birding. They have nice shaded picnic spots.*

Woods Bay features a geologic formation known as a Carolina bay. A sand rim is most characteristic with these formations and is most visible along the

southeastern edge. This elliptical depression in its swampy habitat is a mystery. Try to solve the mystery as you study the historical placards along the trail - with Spanish moss drizzling down from above and flecks of on-target bugs in flight skip across the swamp water below. Just stopping to stretch your legs? The park's 500-foot boardwalk and canoeing trail offer a closer view of this rare resource. You actually walk into the Black Swamp! The Mill Pond Nature Trail is an easy 3/4 mile loop.

Exit - 139 MILE

SUMTER COUNTY WELCOME CENTER

Shiloh - *(Shiloh Rest Areas are between exits 135 & 141; both directions) 29080. Phone: (803) 453-5029.*

As you transition from one area (Pee Dee) to another (Santee Cooper), you may want to pick up some brochures and ask staff (if on duty) about specific updates of your trip. We ate our luscious dessert from Redbone Alley on route south at their varied picnic tables. They also had clean rest rooms, vending machines and a pet run.

Exit - 135 (west of I-95)

SWAN LAKE IRIS GARDENS

Sumter - *822 West Liberty Street (US 378/76 west to SR 763 exit straight into town and just past) 29151. Phone: (800) 688-4748. www.sumtersc.gov/swan-lake-iris-*

gardens.aspx. Hours: Gardens daily, 7:30am-dusk. Visitor Center: Monday-Friday 8:30am-5:00pm Admission: FREE. Note: Although the birds are generally friendly, they may exhibit territorial behavior during the mating season and should be approached with reasonable caution.

The black waters of Swan Lake form a setting for Iris Gardens. It's a little enchanting to see many elegant swans (like the Trumpeter Swan or Mute Swan, the swans of fairy tales) to noisy swans like the Whooper Swans. Beside the swans are groupings of Canada geese, mallards, wood ducks, herons and egrets. If you're thinking this is a quiet retreat - think again. Some ducks may be louder than your kid's giggles and squeals as they chase them around in circles. A leisurely 3/4 mile stroll around the lake reveals even more groupings of duck families, and, if you're lucky, some impromptu duck races. More adventure is had along a boardwalk stretching deep into the cypress swamp.

The 150-acre garden also is home to plantings of Japanese iris, which bloom yearly from mid to late May through the beginning of June. Did you know the garden was started by accident? The original owner discarded iris bulbs that had failed and they took root! Southern Living magazine describes the garden as a "lovely mistake" and its been named one of America's "best freebies" by Better Homes & Gardens. Every December, the holiday season blazes into life with the Swan Lake Fantasy of Lights.

Exit - 122 (east of I-95)

POCOTALIGO CONSERVATORY AREA PARK

Manning - *US 301 29102. Phone: (803) 435-4405. Hours: Daily dawn to dusk. Admission: FREE.*

A 1,296-foot boardwalk leads far from the highway into the Pocotaligo Swamp, where wildlife is abundant. Birding is also enjoyed here. Enjoy cypress trees draped with Spanish Moss in this quiet natural area. Boardwalk is handicapped accessible.

Exit - 119 & 132 (east of I-95)

SWAMP FOX MURALS

Manning - *Office: 19 N Brooks St, Clarendon County Chamber of Commerce (historic US 301) 29102. Phone: 803-435-4405. www.clarendonmurals.com. Hours: Daylight hours. Admission: FREE. Note: Victory at Fort Watson Encampment and Reenactment - Late March.*

Did you know?

The number of Revolutionary War engagements in SC is about equal to the combined total of all engagements fought in the other twelve colonies.

Art museums sound boring? Try this alternative, "drive thru" art promoting history with Historic murals (in Manning, Paxville, Summerton & Turbeville): The Swamp Fox, General Francis Marion and his engagements with the British in 1780-81 in St. Mark's Parish, now Clarendon County. Every mural tells a story of the events of the American Revolution in South Carolina. General Marion's forces took part in roughly one-third of the engagements in SC.

See Clarendon County's 22 historic murals in Manning (7 murals), Paxville (1 mural), Summerton (8 murals) and Turbeville (6 murals). Murals depict the Swamp Fox (a favorite - Ox Swamp Mural, corner of Boyce & Boundary,

Manning - Brits gave chase but Marion slips away into Ox Swamp to set an ambush. British gave up the chase and said, "as for the old fox, the devil himself could not catch him." Thus, General Francis Marion became known as the "Swamp Fox", Francis Marion and the Battles of Fort Watson (3 new murals in Summerton), Tearcoat (notice all the different activities going on - this still picture seems to portray action - US 301 in Turbeville, exit 132), Half-Way Swamp, Wyboo Swamp, Patriots, Wagon

Travel, Richbourg Mill, Citizen Soldier, Women in the Backcountry and Burning of Mouzon's (newest for Turbeville) of the American Revolutionary War in South Carolina. Kids gravitate to the action scenes so be sure to view Swamp Fox and Tearcoat murals first.

Exit - 102 (west of I-95)

SANTEE INDIAN MOUND & FORT WATSON SITE (SANTEE NATIONAL WILDLIFE REFUGE)

Summerton - 2125 Fort Watson Road, Santee Nat'l Wildlife Refuge (exit 102 Rte. 301/15. Follow signs to Visitors Center Of Refuge 29148. Phone: (803) 478-2217. www.fws.gov/santee/. Hours: Daily dawn to dusk - refuge. Center: Tuesday - Friday and the First Saturday of each month - 8:00am-4:00pm. Closed federal holidays. Admission: FREE. Note: Fishing on the Refuge: All areas open to boating are

Have fun being the first to climb to the top...

also open to fishing, as well as the Scott's Lake Public Fishing Beach. These areas produce largemouth bass, catfish and bream. See map for fishing areas and boat ramps online.

THE SANTEE INDIAN MOUND is over 3,000 years old and served as a prehistoric ceremonial and subsequent burial for the

Santee Indians. It is the largest ceremonial center found on the coastal plain. Be the first to climb it to the top. Perhaps the mound's greatest notoriety comes from its use as a British fort during the American Revolution. This outpost was built by the British and was at least 30 feet high. Gen. Francis Marion, the Swamp Fox, and Light Horse Harry Lee laid siege to the post April 15-23, 1781, by erecting a tower of logs under the cover of night enabling them to fire into the British stockade. This brought about the surrender of the fort cutting off the main British supply line to Camden, forcing Lord Rawdon to withdraw from that position. The Battle of FORT WATSON is one of the murals featured on the Swamp Fox Murals Trail (see separate listing). From an observation point at the top of Indian mound, visitors can get a panoramic view of Santee Cooper and the countryside.

THE VISITOR'S CENTER has window viewing of wildlife (especially good if weather outside isn't pleasant); an aquarium with fish found in the area's lakes plus some animal dioramas and a "touch table".

THE SANTEE NATIONAL WILDLIFE REFUGE offers notable wildlife tours and exhibits. A walk along the one-mile Wrights Bluff Trail affords families the chance to observe songbirds, wading birds, and several species of waterfowl along swampland and the beautiful lake. Santee just happens to be located in the flyway from Canada to the tropics so birds abound certain times of year.

Exit - 100 MILE

The old I-95 bridge-causeway over Lake Marion is used as a fishing pier now. Lake Marion is famous for trophy quality game fish, especially both small and large mouth bass.

LAKE MARION TRAVEL INFORMATION CENTER (SB ONLY) & SANTEE REST STOP (NB)

Santee - 160 Southrest Lane (I-95 at Santee between exits 98 & 102) 29142.

Phone: (803) 854-2442.

The centers offer discount coupons for attractions and accommodations and will gladly make reservations for you and your party. Traffic information is readily available as well as weather information for the state. Bathrooms are also available plus vending, picnic sites and a pet walk area.

Exit - 98 *(west of I-95)*

MAURICE'S BARBEQUE

Santee - 263 Britain Street (right off the exit, facing the highway) 29142. Phone: (803) 854-3889. www.mauricesbbq.com. Hours: Daily serving early lunch thru 8:00 or 9:00pm.

Barbeque joints that don't appear that nice are typically the best tasting. So is true here. Nothing to look at inside or out but you're greeted by a friendly face who can tell a newbie 100 yards away. They first tell you about their homemade sauce, then offer you a sample of some on some meat to try. This sauce looks different than regular BBQ sauces because it's Golden - made that distinctively different color from a mustard base. We tried all sorts of meats but the brisket with that Golden Regular was the perfect combo. Once you get over how great the odd sauce is, be sure to try something regional as a side - hash over rice. Not the hash you may think - more like a smooth stew over rice - very good. They are cooking every day making fresh hickory pit-cooked ham, pork, chicken, beef and ribs. Like the sauce a lot? Take some of their heirloom recipe home with you...

Exit - 98 *(west of I-95)*

CLARK'S INN & RESTAURANT

Santee - 114 Bradford Blvd. (I-95 exit 98 west on Rte. 6) 29142. Phone: (803) 854-2141. www.clarksinnandrestaurant.com.

In the heart of Santee, South Carolina, this historic Inn & Restaurant first opened in 1946 and is renowned for its warm Southern Hospitality. It's just minutes away from Lakes Marion and Moultrie, famous for its catfish and striped bass. Take an afternoon to relax by the garden pool after a day of fishing, hiking, biking or traveling.

Clark's Restaurant offers delicious Southern meals: Roast Pork, Baked

Chicken, Catfish and Fried Green Tomatoes - Southern Food Heaven. Oh, and try some Million Dollar Bread for an appetizer and save room for dessert - decades old recipe Apple Crisp or Pecan Pie are king here. They have guest rooms, two-room suites with microwaves and refrigerators, as well as luxury suites with full kitchens. There is wireless Internet throughout the property. Our room was spacious with a cute feature - bookshelves lined with an interesting assortment of novels. Most folks I talked to had signed up for one of their golf or fishing vacation packages.

LONE STAR BARBECUE & MERCANTILE

Santee - 2212 State Park Road (west on Hwy 6 less than one mile from Santee) 29142. Phone: (803) 854-2000. www.lonestarbbq.net. Hours: Lunch & Dinner buffets. Only serving Thursday-Sunday.

These 100-year-old authentically restored country stores feature original counters and showcases, old drink boxes, candy jars, vintage displays, old photographs and a wide variety of other antiques that represent a bygone era. Kids won't recognize half the stuff but will have fun trying to figure it out. Look for an old outhouse and a smokehouse out back. A country-style lunch buffet is served, with such evening specials as a Thursday quail & fish fry, Friday barbecue ribs, stewed shrimp and grits on Saturday and a family buffet on Sunday. Basic buffet includes:  Pork barbecue, rice, barbecue hash, fried chicken, cole slaw, macaroni made with plenty of strong cheese and banana pudding. Each day there is a wide variety of fresh country vegetables and salad bar items, prepared from some of the Old South's best recipes. Their food tastes like Grandma used to fix it. Come hungry because at Lone Star, it's always "all you can eat"! Did you know many of the dining tables were made from wood planks of the old schoolhouse nearby?

SANTEE STATE PARK

Santee - *251 State Park Road (1 mi. W. of the town of Santee on Hwy 6) 29142. Phone: (866) 345-PARK. www.southcarolinaparks.com. Hours: Daily 6:00am-10:00pm. Admission: $2.00 adults over age 16. Tours: Fisheagle Lake & Swamp Tours depart from the fishing pier within the park for approximately two hours on Wednesdays, Fridays, Saturdays and Sundays (times may vary). The Fisheagle travels up Lake Marion to one of the cypress swamps that has become a wildlife haven. Tour Prices are: $15.00 adult, $13.00 senior, $10.00 child (ages 3-11). Note: If you head east off the exit and go 8.2 miles to Eutawville, turn left on Redbank Road to INDIAN BLUFF PARK. The park offers a fishing pier, deep-water boat ramp, picnic tables and grills, children's play area, boardwalk, restrooms and bathhouse for your leisure and stretching your legs.*

Rent some bicycles, kayaks or fishing gear to explore this park. Or, take the **FISHEAGLE BOAT TOUR** (800-9-OSPREY or www.fisheagle.net) into the lakes to witness the natural beauty of waterfowl including eagles and osprey. Come face-to-face with alligators or enjoy the lake wildflower gardens. Accommodations include ten pier-based cabins, 20 lakefront vacation cabins, and 158 lakeside campsites on Lake Marion. The pier cabins are octagon shaped and so close to the lake, you literally walk out your door and fish off the pier. Cabins have two bedrooms (sleep 6) with full kitchen, bath and heat or A/C. Outdoorsy folks of all ages enjoy the fishing pier, biking and hiking trails and picnic areas with playgrounds.

Exit - 98 (west of I-95)

ELLOREE HERITAGE MUSEUM & CULTURAL CENTER

See GIANT cotton bales...

Elloree - *2714 Cleveland Street (Rte 6 west right into town, left on Cleveland) 29047. Phone: (803) 897-2225. www.elloreemuseum. org. Hours: Wednesday-Saturday 10:00am-5:00pm Admission: $3.00-$5.00 (ages 6+). Note: the Bluestar Memorial geocache site is now hidden in the town park.*

The town of Elloree is most known for its quaint streets and shops. Rich in history, the

Heritage Museum explores a plantation cotton gin house and how cotton is grown, picked and ginned today. Next, stroll Cleveland Street as it appeared in 1900, with recreated stores, bank and hotel. Further down the exhibit hall is the 18th century Snider cabin and farm yard where you can meet "William J. Snider" and learn the plan for his new town. You can walk into many of the exhibits back here. Try to find the canned peaches or the kitty cat. Look closely

around a corner for the outhouse. This is really one of the cutest small town museums we've seen. Nice way to see what it takes to build a southern town from scratch.

Two blocks away, Joe Miller Park offers picnic tables and playground spaces. Each March the town is the setting for the Elloree Trials Horse Race for thoroughbreds and quarter horses. The town is also home to the bi-annual trash and treasures sales, the annual Winter Lights festival, and the Pork Fest.

"Meet" William J. Snider and learn the plan for his new town...

Exit - 57 *(east of I-95)*

DUKE'S BARBECUE

Walterboro - *949 Robertson Blvd (just follow the signs with big arrows) 29488. Phone: (843) 549-1446. Hours: Duke's is open for lunch and supper only on Thursday, Friday, Saturday and Sunday.*

Duke's is stark. On purpose. Everything about this place is designed to help you concentrate on the hickory-smoked barbecued pork. It is served in big chunks

at a cafeteria line that also includes rice, hash (a stew-like mixture made from pork shoulders), a choice of red sauce that is four-alarm hot or yellow mustard sauce that is sweet and tangy (unique to central South Carolina), and pickles. The drink of choice is sweet tea and each table is outfitted with a few loaves of Sunbeam bread, which is just the right thing for mopping a plate of all its good sauce. Please note the limited hours. In the tradition of the old-time pig-pickin', South Carolinians consider a meal like this a weekend celebration.

COLLETON MUSEUM

Walterboro - *239 N Jefferies Blvd (follow signs off exit into town) 29488. Phone: (843) 549-2303. www.cm-fm.org. Hour: Wednesday-Friday 10:00am-5:00pm, Tuesday Noon-6:00pm, Saturday 10am-2pm. Admission: FREE. Educators: Resource room materials available free of charge.*

Located in the Old Jail (c. 1855), the museum features a permanent collection that explores the county's history from prehistoric times to the early 1900s. The two-story neo-gothic structure resembles a castle so it's hard to miss in town and the kids want to look inside. The museum also has an ongoing exhibit on "Animals of the ACE," a natural history display featuring wild animals indigenous to the South Carolina Lowcountry. The museum also features changing art collections monthly.

Exit - 33 (east of I-95)

LOW COUNTRY VISITORS CENTER & MUSEUM

Yemassee - *1 Lowcountry Lane 29945. www.southcarolinalowcountry.com.*

An Old Century "Shut The Box" Game

Phone: (843) 717-3090. Hours: Daily 9:00am-5:30pm. Admission: FREE.

Housed in the historic Frampton Plantation House, c. 1868, the Lowcountry Visitors Center and Museum features a recreated 1900s plantation parlor, complete with antique furnishings and displays from the region's 10 museums and the SC Artisans Center. Our favorite room was the Parlor room and the Gullah items. It's clever how they mix artifacts with items you can purchase and brochures. Kids like the old-fashioned toys and trinkets plus the free samples of fruit cider made right here in Low Country. Outside, they offer a small walking trail, picnic tables under the huge live oaks, and even a pet walk. Before you leave, be sure to ask if there's a festival going on. They have a festival to celebrate nearly everything: the endangered Gopher Tortoise, watermelons, catfish, rice, harbors and water, shrimp, chilli and even more.

> *Yemassee hosts an annual Shrimp Festival in September, celebrating the abundance of shrimp caught locally each year.*

Exit - 5 (west of I-95)

SAVANNAH RIVER NATIONAL WILDLIFE REFUGE

Hardeeville - *763 Alligator Alley 29927. www.fws.gov/savannah/. Phone: (912) 652-4415. Hours: Daily dawn to dusk. Admission: FREE.*

Established in 1927, the 22,940-acre refuge lies along the Savannah River, protecting numerous kinds of wildlife, from Whitetail deer to alligators. Evidence of the rice industry is found in the refuge with its rice levee remains, foundations of slave quarters, old mill sites and small graveyards. A four-mile driving tour along the refuge levees is open to the public. The tract is known as one of the outstanding refuges along the Atlantic Flyway, which extends from Canada to the Caribbean.

Exit - 1 NB

SOUTH CAROLINA WELCOME CENTER

Hardeeville - *4968 Jasper Hwy (first exit near SC/GA border heading northbound yet south of exit 5) 29927. Phone: (843) 784-3275. Hours: Daily 9:00am-5:00pm.*

Nationally certified travel counselors are ready to assist you with directions and mapping information, and informative brochures to help you discover the treasures of South Carolina. The centers also offer discount coupons for attractions and accommodations and hostesses will gladly make reservations for you and your party. Traffic information is readily available as well as weather information for the state. Many of the centers also offer a mail drop for your letters and services such as the AT&T international language line. All

SC

of these complimentary services are offered to make your experience in the state relaxing and enjoyable. Bathrooms, a pet walk, and picnic areas are also available.

Travel Journal & Notes:

Curious about hundreds of fun
places in the lighter gray areas?
See *Kids Love Georgia*

DEAR GEORGIA TRAVELER:

From Savannah to northern Florida, Interstate 95 is always in close proximity of three features: US 17, marshland and the Atlantic coastline. It begins just past the border of South Carolina at the Savannah River and ends at another river, the St. Marys River, at the Florida state line.

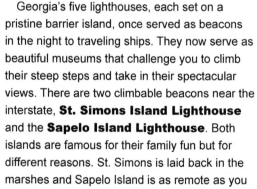

Georgia's five lighthouses, each set on a pristine barrier island, once served as beacons in the night to traveling ships. They now serve as beautiful museums that challenge you to climb their steep steps and take in their spectacular views. There are two climbable beacons near the interstate, **St. Simons Island Lighthouse** and the **Sapelo Island Lighthouse**. Both islands are famous for their family fun but for different reasons. St. Simons is laid back in the marshes and Sapelo Island is as remote as you can get and still be inhabited – by native Geechee no less! Descendents of plantation workers survive on the island and authentic locals give you the grand tour.

On a bluff overlooking what is now the Savannah River, Oglethorpe founded the state and then helped create the nation's first planned city – **Savannah**. Like St. Simons Island, Savannah is best to get an overview of by **Trolley Tour**. On tour, your guide will show you many points of interest but a girl's favorite may just be the **Juliette Gordon Low Birthplace** – the founder of Girl Scouts. Even boys like to hear the stories of how a spunky rich girl liked to be active, artsy and get into mischief.

Like nature? The southern part of I-95 in Georgia is worth getting out and wandering. You can watch dolphins dance on various coastal island **Dolphin Tours**. Rent a bicycle for the day and maybe catch sea turtles on **Jekyll Is.**

AMUSEMENTS

Exit - 29 - *Summer Waves Water Park*
Exit - 3 - *St. Marys Aquatic Center*

ANIMALS & FARMS

Exit - 94 - *Bamboo Farm And Garden*
Exit - 29 - *Georgia Sea Turtle Center*

HISTORY

Exit - 109 - *Old Fort Jackson*
Exit - 102 - *Mighty Eighth Air Force*
Exit - 99 / I-16 East - *Savannah History Museum*
Exit - 99 / I-16 East - *GA Railroad Museum*
Exit - 99/ I-16 East - *Savannah Children's Museum*
Exit - 99 / I-16 East - *Massie Heritage Center*
Exit - 94 - *Wormsloe Historic Site*
Exit - 90 - *Fort McAllister Historic Park*
Exit - 76 - *Seabrook Village*
Exit - 76 - *Fort Morris State Historic Site*
Exit - 49 - *Fort King George Historic Site*
Exit - 42 - *Hofwyl-Broadfield PlantAtion Historic Site*
Exit - 38 - *St. Simons Island Maritime Center*
Exit - 38 - *Fort Frederica / Bloody Marsh Battle Site*
Exit - 29 - *Jekyll Island Museum & Historic District*
Exit - 3 - *St. Marys Submarine Museum*

MUSEUMS

Exit - 99 / I-16 East - *Juliette Gordon Low Birthplace*
Exit - 38 - *St. Simons Island Lighthouse*

OUTDOOR EXPLORING

Exit - 94 - *Savannah Ogeechee Canal Museum And Nature Center*
Exit - 36 - *Mary Ross Waterfront Park*
Exit - 29 - *Tidelands Nature Center*
Exit - 29 - *Jekyll Island Biking*
Exit - 3 - *Cumberland Island National Seashore Museum*
Exit - 3 - *Crooked River State Park*

SPORTS

Exit - 102 - *Oglethorpe Speedway*

SUGGESTED LODGING & DINING

Exit - 109 - *Comfort Suites Savannah Historic District*
Exit - 99 / I-16 East - *Whistle Stop Café*
Exit - 58 - *Blue Heron Bed & Breakfast*
Exit - 38 - *Barbara Jean's Restaurant*
Exit - 38 - *Mullet Bay Restaurant*
Exit - 38 - *Best Western Island Inn*
Exit - 29 - *Villas By The Sea Resort*

TOURS

Exit - 109 - *Savannah Riverboat Co.*
Exit - 99 / I-16 East - *Savannah Trolley Tours, Gray Line*
Exit - 58 - *Sapelo Island Reserve - Geechee Community Tour*
Exit - 38 - *St. Simons Trolley Tour*
Exit - 29 - *Dolphin Tours - Coastal Georgia*
Exit - 3 - *St. Marys Toonerville Trolley & Tram Tours*

WELCOME CENTERS

Exit - 111 Mile Southbound - *Georgia Welcome Center*
Exit - 1 Mile Northbound Only - *Georgia Welcome Center*

Contact the services of interest. Request to be added to their mailing lists.

☐ Georgia State Parks (800) 864-7275 or www.gastateparks.org
☐ Georgia Travel Information (800) VISIT GA or www.exploregeorgia.org
☐ Brunswick And The Golden Isles (St. Simons, Sea Island, Jekyll Island) CVB - (800) 933-Coast or www.bgivb.com
☐ Savannah Area Convention & Visitors Bureau - www.savannahvisit.com.

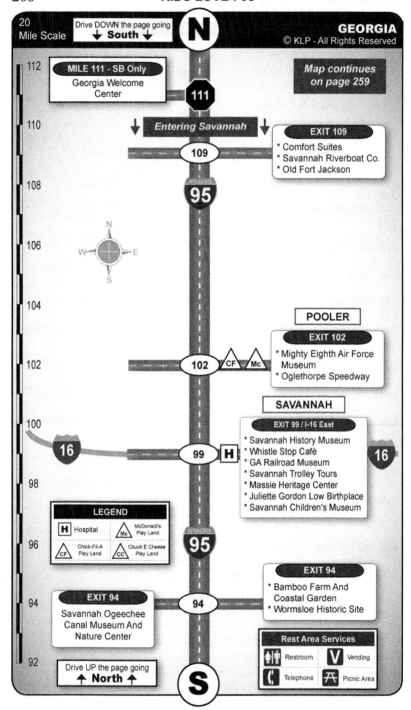

Map continues on page 259

GEORGIA
© KLP - All Rights Reserved

20 Mile Scale

Drive DOWN the page going ↓ **South** ↓

N

112

MILE 111 - SB Only
Georgia Welcome Center

111

110

Entering Savannah ↓

EXIT 109
* Comfort Suites
* Savannah Riverboat Co.
* Old Fort Jackson

109

108

95

106

N
W — E
S

104

POOLER

EXIT 102
* Mighty Eighth Air Force Museum
* Oglethorpe Speedway

102   CF   Mc

SAVANNAH

100

16

EXIT 99 / I-16 East
* Savannah History Museum
* Whistle Stop Café
* GA Railroad Museum
* Savannah Trolley Tours
* Massie Heritage Center
* Juliette Gordon Low Birthplace
* Savannah Children's Museum

99   **H**   **16**

98

LEGEND

| **H** Hospital | McDonald's Play Land (Mc) |
| CF Chick-Fil-A Play Land | CC Chuck E Cheese Play Land |

96

95

EXIT 94
* Bamboo Farm And Coastal Garden
* Wormsloe Historic Site

94

EXIT 94
Savannah Ogeechee Canal Museum And Nature Center

94

Rest Area Services

| Restroom | **V** Vending |
| Telephone | Picnic Area |

92

Drive UP the page going ↑ **North** ↑

S

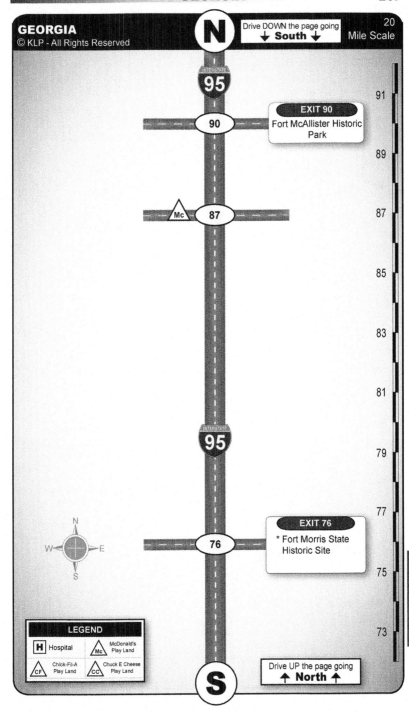

GEORGIA

Drive DOWN the page going
↓ **South** ↓

20 Mile Scale

N

INTERSTATE **95**

91

90

EXIT 90
Fort McAllister Historic Park

89

Mc **87**

87

85

83

81

INTERSTATE **95**

79

77

76

EXIT 76
* Fort Morris State Historic Site

75

73

LEGEND

| H | Hospital | Mc | McDonald's Play Land |
| CF | Chick-Fil-A Play Land | CC | Chuck E Cheese Play Land |

N
W—E
S

Drive UP the page going
↑ **North** ↑

S

GEORGIA

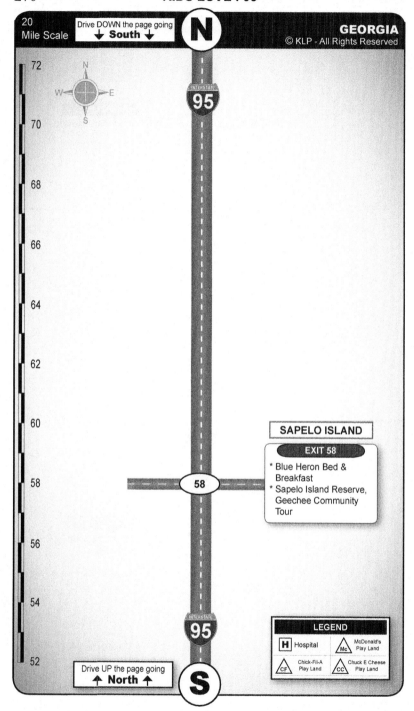

20 Mile Scale

Drive DOWN the page going ↓ **South** ↓

N

GEORGIA

INTERSTATE **95**

72
70
68
66
64
62
60
58
56
54
52

SAPELO ISLAND

EXIT 58

* Blue Heron Bed & Breakfast
* Sapelo Island Reserve, Geechee Community Tour

58

INTERSTATE **95**

Drive UP the page going ↑ **North** ↑

S

LEGEND

| **H** Hospital | Mc McDonald's Play Land |
| CF Chick-Fil-A Play Land | CC Chuck E Cheese Play Land |

For updates & travel games visit: **www.KidsLoveTravel.com**

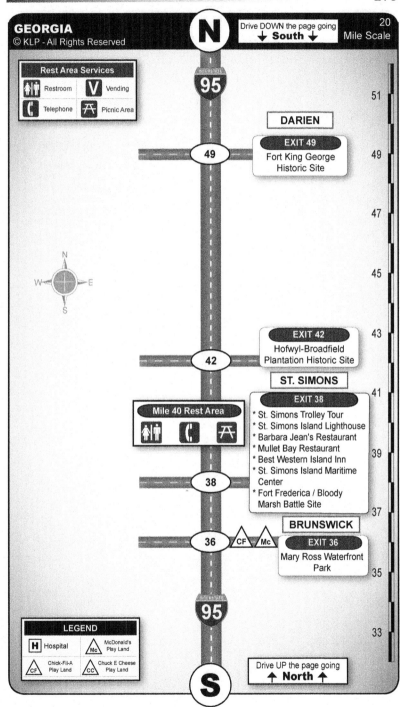

GEORGIA

Drive DOWN the page going
↓ **South** ↓

20
Mile Scale

Rest Area Services

| | Restroom | V | Vending |
| | Telephone | | Picnic Area |

INTERSTATE
95

51

DARIEN

EXIT 49
Fort King George
Historic Site

49

47

45

EXIT 42
Hofwyl-Broadfield
Plantation Historic Site

43

ST. SIMONS

42

41

Mile 40 Rest Area

EXIT 38
* St. Simons Trolley Tour
* St. Simons Island Lighthouse
* Barbara Jean's Restaurant
* Mullet Bay Restaurant
* Best Western Island Inn
* St. Simons Island Maritime
  Center
* Fort Frederica / Bloody
  Marsh Battle Site

39

38

37

BRUNSWICK

36   CF   Mc

EXIT 36
Mary Ross Waterfront
Park

35

INTERSTATE
95

33

LEGEND

| H Hospital | Mc McDonald's Play Land |
| CF Chick-Fil-A Play Land | CC Chuck E Cheese Play Land |

Drive UP the page going
↑ **North** ↑

GEORGIA

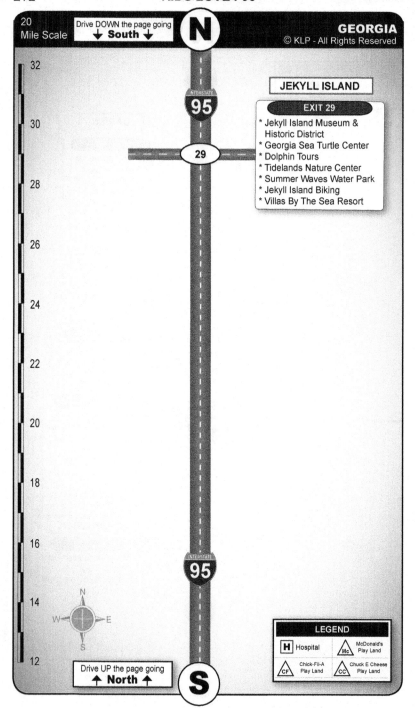

20 Mile Scale

Drive DOWN the page going
↓ South ↓

N

GEORGIA

JEKYLL ISLAND

EXIT 29
* Jekyll Island Museum & Historic District
* Georgia Sea Turtle Center
* Dolphin Tours
* Tidelands Nature Center
* Summer Waves Water Park
* Jekyll Island Biking
* Villas By The Sea Resort

INTERSTATE **95**

29

INTERSTATE **95**

Drive UP the page going
↑ North ↑

S

LEGEND

| H | Hospital | Mc | McDonald's Play Land |
| CF | Chick-Fil-A Play Land | CC | Chuck E Cheese Play Land |

For updates & travel games visit: **www.KidsLoveTravel.com**

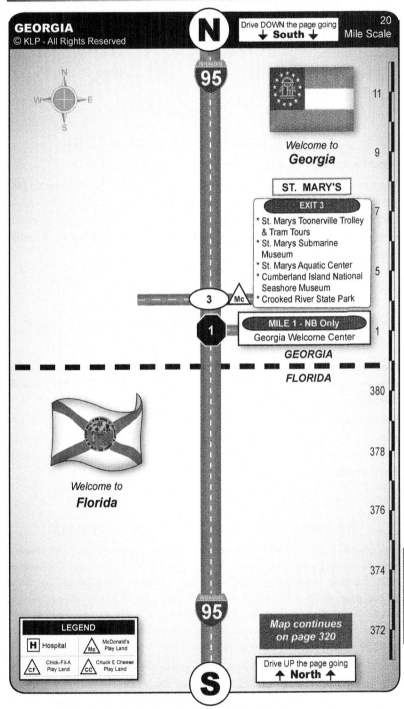

GEORGIA

N

Drive DOWN the page going
↓ **South** ↓

20
Mile Scale

N
W — E
S

INTERSTATE
95

11

9

Welcome to
Georgia

ST. MARY'S

EXIT 3

7

* St. Marys Toonerville Trolley
  & Tram Tours
* St. Marys Submarine
  Museum
* St. Marys Aquatic Center
* Cumberland Island National
  Seashore Museum
* Crooked River State Park

5

3 Mc

MILE 1 - NB Only
Georgia Welcome Center

1

1

GEORGIA

FLORIDA

380

Welcome to
Florida

378

376

374

INTERSTATE
95

GEORGIA

LEGEND

H Hospital

Mc McDonald's
Play Land

CF Chick-Fil-A
Play Land

CC Chuck E Cheese
Play Land

Map continues
on page 320

372

Map continues
on page 320

Drive UP the page going
↑ **North** ↑

S

Sites and attractions are listed in order by Exit Number (North to South) and distance from the exit (closest are listed first). Symbols indicated represent:

 Restaurants   Lodging

Exit - 111 MILE (SB Only)

GEORGIA WELCOME CENTER

(southbound only west of interstate). Phone: (912) 963-2546.

The southbound Welcome Center can be found just after the off-ramp for first southbound truck weighing center, only for both facilities to share an on ramp back to southbound I-95. You'll find a staffed Georgia Visitor Center, clean restrooms, a pet walk, and picnic tables. Visitors Center open business hours, restrooms 24 hours.

Exit - 109 (east of I-95)

COMFORT SUITES SAVANNAH HISTORIC DISTRICT

Savannah - *630 West Bay Street (under bridge) (follow Rte. 21 east into outskirts of historic district. Take Bay Street) 31401. www.comfortsuites.com. Phone: (912) 629-2001.*

Located within walking distance of the historic area including River Street and City Market, each spacious suite has a microwave and frig and full size sofa bed. There is also a heated indoor pool, spa and complimentary deluxe continental breakfast.

SAVANNAH RIVERBOAT COMPANY

Savannah - *9 E River Street (take Rte. 21 to riverfront departing from Savannah's Historic River Street directly behind City Hall) 31412. Phone: (912) 232-6404 or (800) 786-6404. www.savannahriverboat.com. Admission: Sightseeing Tours: $18.95 adult, $9.95 child (12 & under). Luncheon: $19.95-$34.95. Dinner cruises more. Tours: One Hour Sightseeing: Daily once or twice an afternoon (March-November). Winter, weekends only at 2:00pm. Noon Luncheon cruises: Weekends at Noon (1 1/2 hrs.) Miscellaneous: Riverboat Snack Shop onboard.*

Savannah is a river town, so what better way to get an overview of her harbor and port than to cruise. The 600 passenger Savannah River Queen and the

600 passenger Georgia Queen are triple-decker, red, white and blue, vessels that offer a variety of different tours all through the harbor. Relive a bygone era on board one of the replica paddle wheelers for a view of the sites from the water. Hear the Captain's intriguing tales and historic facts as you travel a river once used by industrialists and war maneuvers. Sit back and enjoy the view. Some examples of Holiday Cruises they offer: Thanksgiving, Boat Parade of Lights, Santa Cruise, Easter Cruise and Fantastic Fourth Fireworks Cruise.

OLD FORT JACKSON

Savannah - 1 Fort Jackson Road (Rte 21 east to Bay St. 2 miles east of downtown) 31404. Phone: (912) 232-3945. www.chsgeorgia.org/jackson/home.htm. Hours: Daily 9:00am-5:00pm Admission: $3.75-$4.25 age 6+.

This fort is the oldest remaining brickwork fort. The fort first saw service in the War of 1812 and then again during the Civil War. This fort guards Five Fathom Hole, the 18th century deep-water port in the Savannah River. The fort displays artifacts depicting the history of town and Coastal Georgia. Seasonal demonstrations and exhibits are scheduled for the second weekend of each month.

Exit - 102 (east of I-95)

MIGHTY EIGHTH AIR FORCE MUSEUM

Savannah (Pooler) - 175 Bourne Avenue (I-95 exit 102, just 2 miles south of the Savannah International Airport) 31322. www.mightyeighth.org. Phone: (912) 748-8888. Hours: Daily 9:00am-5:00pm Admission: $10.00 adult, $9.00 senior and $6.00 child (6-12). Educators: pre-visit and post visit materials will be made

available to teachers once the program is booked.

The museum honors the courage, character and patriotism embodied by the men and women of the Eighth Air Force from WWII to the present. You will be moved by the inspiring stories of heroism, courage, and sacrifice as well as remind us of the price that was paid for our freedom.

Fly a bombing mission with a B-17 crew, take a gunner's position aboard a B-17 in defense or view historic aircraft in this modern and well lit indoor museum.

Exit - 102 (east of I-95)

OGLETHORPE SPEEDWAY PARK

Savannah (Pooler) - *200 Jesup Road (I-95, use exit 102 (US Highway 80) and go east three miles) 31322. Phone: (912) 964-RACE. www.ospracing.net.*

This NASCAR sanctioned park entertains thousands every weekend with stock car and go-cart racing. RV campground on site. View website for schedule and fees for each event.

Exit - 99 (east of I-95) / I-16 East

SAVANNAH HISTORY MUSEUM

Savannah - *303 Martin Luther King Jr. (I-16 all the way into town adjacent to the Savannah Info Center) 31401. www.chsgeorgia.org/shm/home.htm. Phone: (912) 238-1779. Hours: Daily 9:00am-5:00pm. Opens at 8:30am weekdays. Admission: $4.00-$7.00 age 2+. Note: nearby (41 ML King Blvd) is the Ships of the Sea collection (miniature ship models) displayed within the Scarbrough House (www. shipsofthesea.org).*

This museum is housed in the old railroad passenger train shed. The Savannah History Museum showcases the city's history from its founding in 1733 to the present day. Inside, you can see exhibits about the Revolutionary War Battle of Savannah, rare dugout canoes from the 1800s, and a changing exhibit of women's fashions from the nineteenth and twentieth centuries. Museum exhibits also include an 1800 cotton gin, Central of Georgia steam locomotive Baldwin #403, Juliette Gordon Low's family carriage, and Forrest Gump's bench (with pictures from the movie and even his little suitcase). An 18-minute video overview of Savannah explains the founding of the city from founding father, Oglethorpe's point of view (excellent start to tour) and a diorama depicts the siege of attacks on the city.

The Forest Gump park bench from the movie "Forest Gump"

WHISTLE STOP CAFÉ

Savannah - *303 Martin Luther King (next to Savannah History Museum & Visitor Center) 31401. Phone: (912) 651-3656.*

At the far end of the Visitors Center station building the cafe serves breakfast and lunch in a railroad car setting. Average menu pricing $4.00-$6.00. Kiddies Caboose Menu has choices of Freightliner Fish, Southbound Spaghetti, Central Georgia Chicken Fingers, or Hobo Beef Stew.

SAVANNAH TROLLEY TOURS, GRAY LINE

Savannah - *Visitors Center pickup (we suggest starting from the Visitors Ctr located on MLK Blvd) 31401. www.trolleytours.com/savannah. Phone: (912) 284-TOUR or (800) 426-2318. Admission: HOP ON/HOP OFF Trolley: $24.95 per adult, $10.95 per child (age 5-11) for fully narrated tour and unlimited on/off privileges at 12 convenient stops until 5:30pm. FREE parking. Tours: Daily 9:00am-4:00pm (leave every 20 minutes). Tour 90-minutes long.*

The official daily tours of the Historic Foundation have more than 20 departures daily through the Historic district and Low Country. You'll see and hear about: The film "Glory" production site in old Revolutionary War ruins; The Mary 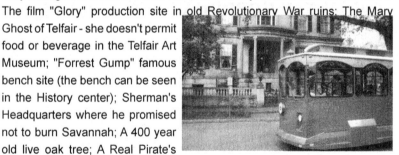 Ghost of Telfair - she doesn't permit food or beverage in the Telfair Art Museum; "Forrest Gump" famous bench site (the bench can be seen in the History center); Sherman's Headquarters where he promised not to burn Savannah; A 400 year old live oak tree; A Real Pirate's House Inn (you might want to avoid this place if you lived in the 1800s - you might have ended up on a pirate boat as a slave); and, pass the founder of the Girl Scouts birthplace. This is absolutely the best way to survey Savannah's numerous historic sites and squares and shops. Start your stay in the city on a tour to decide what places may be of special interest to tour inside.

MASSIE HERITAGE CENTER

Savannah - *207 East Gordon Street (I-16 east all the way into town. Follow signs for Calhoun Square) 31401. Phone: (912) 201-5070. www.massieschool. com. Hours: Monday-Saturday 10:00am-4:00pm, Sunday Noon-4pm. Simply ring the bell to the right of the front doors. Admission: $7.00 adult, $5.00 child*

(5-17). Children under 4 - $2.00. FREEBIE: Massie Heritage Center - A History of Savannah Children's Coloring and Activity History Guide. This is a wonderful print-off activity book to complete as you traverse this famous city and state on your sidetrips on the Georgia coast. Educators: a Kids Page covers more activities - even a cookie recipe and word search.

The old school house provides group participation including the:

- HERITAGE CLASSROOM - You can experience lessons just like those of students a hundred or more years ago... sit up straight and place your folded hands on top of your desk. Lessons include oral recitation and even penmanship using real quill pens. Do your arithmetic and take your spelling test using a slate board.

- SAVANNAH'S CITY PLAN - It is the old city of Savannah as it developed according to James Edward Oglethorpe's plan from 1733 to 1856 when all of the publicly owned land was used up.

- THE DEBATABLE LANDS - Over a span of 12,000 years, Native Americans built villages and forts, burial grounds and playgrounds, and summer and winter camps. When Europeans finally arrived, they built their towns on or near these earlier inhabited sites. The space informs visitors about the history of Chatham County and Coastal Georgia prior to Oglethorpe's arrival in 1733.

Also, displays on the Victorian Era and Classical architecture are covered.

JULIETTE GORDON LOW BIRTHPLACE

Savannah - *10 East Oglethorpe Avenue (I-16 E to town. Do not exit. corner of Bull Street and Oglethorpe Avenue) 31401. www.juliettegordonlowbirthplace.org/. Phone: (912) 233-4501. Hours: Monday-Saturday 10:00am-4:00pm, Sunday 11:00am-4:00pm. Closed winter Wednesday, major holidays. Admission: $9.00 adult, $8.00 student (5-21), $25.00 family. Girl Scout adult chaperone $8.00. Note: Ask for the special visit Girl Scout pin at the Museum shop (about $3.50 to purchase). Guided tours begin every so often.*

Juliette Gordon Low, founder of the Girl Scouts, is one of the most famous women in American history. She was born in Savannah, and her home serves as a Historic Landmark. Begin on a guided tour and hear firsthand about the Gordons, a great American family. From William Washington Gordon I, founder of the Central of Georgia Railroad, to his world famous granddaughter. Enjoy funny stories of the spirited "Nelly" Gordon (loved to slide down the curved staircase) and "Daisy" Low (Juliette, a creative artist - look for

her sculpture and paintings throughout the house). Multi-talented and quirky but severely hearing impaired, Juliette founded the organization of productive fun for young ladies. Come right over! I've got something for the girls of Savannah and all America and all the world and we're going to start it tonight!" - Juliette's famous words that started the Girl Scouts in 1912 to become one of the most significant organizations of the time. She gave the girls of America the career opportunities, outdoor activities and the fun they so desperately wanted.

GEORGIA STATE RAILROAD MUSEUM

Savannah - *655 Louisville Road, 31401 (next to History Museum). Phone: (912) 651-6823. www.chsgeorgia.org/railroad-museum.html. Hours: Daily 9:00am-5:00pm Admission: $10.00 adult, $6.00 child (2-12). Train Rides: Diesel rides 11am, 1pm and 2pm. Steam rides 11am, 1pm, 2pm and 3pm. All Sunday rides at 1pm and 2pm only. Schedule and locomotives subject to change, please call ahead.*

Originally designed to transport valuable Georgia cotton, the 190 miles of rail line between Savannah and Macon formed the longest continuous railroad in the world. As a tribute to the Industrial Revolution, the site includes a massive roundhouse with operational turntable, the oldest portable steam engine int he U.S., and an HO scale model of Savannah. From guided tours of the Museum's office cars and rolling stock to nostalgic train rides, and occasional turntable and blacksmithing demonstrations, there is always something exciting to do and see! Download the Train Ride Schedule for more information about dates and times.

SAVANNAH CHILDREN'S MUSEUM

Savannah - *655 Louisville Road, 31401 (next to GA State Railroad Museum). www.savannahchildrensmuseum.org. Hours: Tuesday-Saturday 10:00am-4:00pm , Sunday 11am-4pm. Admission: $7.50 per person (age 1+).*

Originally designed to transport valuable Georgia cotton, the 190 miles of rail line between Savannah and Macon formed the longest continuous railroad in the world. As a tribute to the Industrial Revolution, the site includes a massive roundhouse with operational turntable, the oldest portable steam engine int he U.S., and an HO scale model of Savannah. From guided tours of the Museum's office cars and rolling stock to nostalgic train rides, and occasional turntable and blacksmithing demonstrations, there is always something exciting to do and see! Download the Train Ride Schedule for more information about dates and times.

Exit - 94 (west of I-95)

SAVANNAH OGEECHEE CANAL MUSEUM AND NATURE CENTER

Savannah - *681 Fort Argyle Road (located off GA 204, only 2.3 miles west of I-95 at exit 94) 31419. Phone: (912) 748-8068. www.savannahogeecheecanal.society. org. Hours: Monday-Friday 10am-4pm, Saturday 9am-5pm, Sunday 1-5pm. Admission: $1.00-$3.00 per person.*

Discover the history of the Savannah Ogeechee Canal at this Museum. Visitors are able to view the remnants of Canal Locks 5 and 6 and see a replica gate and lock model. The Nature Center consists of 184 acres of river swamp, pine flatwoods, and sandhill habitat with low-impact walking trails (something we look for when hiking miles at a time) throughout the area. The Nature Center supports a diverse group of stationary and migratory birds as well as reptiles and other animal life. Kids especially love the gopher tortoise habitat. Studying State History? The Museum and Nature Center is home to Georgia's state tree, the live oak; Georgia's state flower, the Cherokee rose; Georgia's state wildflower, the wild azalea; and Georgia's state reptile, the gopher tortoise. The state bird, the brown thrasher, can also be seen around the Nature Center. A nice, inexpensive visit a little ways from the hub-bub of historic Savannah.

COASTAL GEORGIA BOTANICAL GARDEN

Savannah - *2 Canebrake Road (I-95 exit 94. Go east on GA 204 to Hwy 17 south exit. Travel for one mile) 31419. Phone: (912) 921-5460. www.coastalgeorgiabg.org. Hours: Monday-Friday 8:00am-5:00pm, Saturday 10:00am-5:00pm. Admission: FREE (donations accepted).*

The Bamboo Farm serves as a research and education center that houses a number of plant collections and gardens & research plots that are maintained by UGA staff. The Bamboo Farm is perhaps best known for its collection of more than 140 varieties of shade- and sun-loving bamboos. The oldest grove of bamboo on the property, the Giant Japanese Bamboo, was planted more than 100 years ago. The farm is the largest collection of bamboo available for public viewing in the U.S. Two display gardens, the Cottage Garden and the Xeriscape Garden, are housed at the Bamboo Farm. The Cottage Garden serves as a trial garden where old and new varieties of perennials, annuals and bulbs can be evaluated for their adaptability to the southeastern coastal climate and soil. The Xeriscape Garden demonstrates the seven principles of water-wise landscaping and is used to teach water conservation practices to local gardeners and landscapers. Doesn't this sound like a nice walk to stretch your legs after driving for hours?

Exit - 94 (east of I-95)

WORMSLOE HISTORIC SITE

Savannah - 7601 Skidaway Road (head east on Rte.204.10 miles southeast of Savannah's historic district) 31406. http://gastateparks.org/info/wormsloe/. Phone: (912) 353-3023. Hours: Tuesday-Sunday 9:00am-5:00pm. Closed Mondays except holidays. Admission: $4.50-$10.00 per person. Educators: click on the fact sheet details online.

An avenue lined with live oaks leads to the tabby ruins of Wormsloe, the colonial estate constructed by Noble Jones, one of Georgia's first settlers. Jones was an English physician and carpenter who carved out an even wider career in the colonial wilderness. He came to Savannah with James Oglethorpe in 1733 and commanded a company of Marines, served as constable, Indian agent, surveyor and a member of the Royal Council. He was also one of the few original settlers to survive hunger, Indians and Spaniards in this new

wilderness. Today, visitors can view artifacts excavated at the site and watch a film about the founding of the 13th colony. A scenic nature trail leads to the living history area where, during special programs, costumed staff show skills and crafts necessary to early settlers. The living history programs are the best time to visit as a family.

Exit - 90 (east of I-95)

FORT MCALLISTER HISTORIC PARK

Richmond Hill - 3894 Fort McAllister Road (10 miles east of I-95 on GA Spur 144, exit 90) 31324. Phone: (912) 727-2339. http://gastateparks.org/FortMcAllister/. Hours: Daily 8:00am-5:00pm (museum). Park open 7:00am-10:00pm. Admission: $3.50-$5.00 per person. Educators: link to detailed information about the fort and the short battle that ended Sherman's March to the Sea.

The sand and mud earthworks were attacked seven times by Union ironclads, but did not fall until captured in 1864 by General Sherman during his infamous "March to the Sea". The museum interprets the best-preserved earthwork fortification of the Civil War using numerous themed displays. The interior design of the museum resembles a bombproof shelter and also contains a gift shop and shows a video on the history of the site regularly. This park is a quiet location for camping, hiking, fishing and picnicking. There are 4.3 miles of hiking and biking trails.

Exit - 76 (east of I-95)

FORT MORRIS STATE HISTORIC SITE

Midway - *2559 Fort Morris Road (I-95 exit 76 via Islands Highway and Fort Morris Road) 31320. Phone: (912) 884-5999. http://gastateparks.org/FortMorris/. Hours: Thursday-Saturday 9:00am-5:00pm. Admission: $2.75-$4.00.*

When the Continental Congress convened in 1776, the delegates recognized the importance of a fort to protect their growing seaport from the British. When the British demanded the fort's surrender in 1778, the defiant Col. John McIntosh replied, "Come and take it!" The British refused and withdrew back to Florida. This Revolutionary War fort was eventually captured by the British in 1779, then used again by Americans during the war of 1812. Today, visitors can stand within the earthwork remains and view scenic Saint Catherine's Sound. A museum and film describe the colonial port of Sunbury and the site's history. There is a one mile nature trail on the premises. Reenactments occur seasonally.

Exit - 58 (east of I-95)

BLUE HERON BED & BREAKFAST

Darien - *1346 Blue Heron Lane SE (I-95 exit 58, GA 99 southeast towards Sapelo Island ferry, 1 1/2 mile before ferry, left on Sea Breeze Drive) 31305. Phone: (912) 437-4304. www.blueheroninngacoast.com.*

Wanna spend the overnight on a real marsh (teaming with shrimp, blue crab, blue heron, egrets and maybe an alligator or snake)? Most all the rooms are facing the marsh, with private balconies. A luscious freshly prepared gourmet breakfast (their signature lime French toast - or plain for the kids) is part of your stay. Bill and Jan are gracious hosts and the modern home is minutes away from the ferry over to Sapelo Island where you can tour the remote island (see separate listing). Have a boat? The owners say families can stay for days if they bring water transportation. Nice combo for adventuresome families. Great comfy hospitality inside, yet wildlife galore outside. Rates around $100-150.00/night.

SAPELO ISLAND RESERVE - GEECHEE COMMUNITY TOUR

Darien (Sapelo Island) - *Sapelo Island Visitors Center, 1766 Landing Road, SE (go east on GA 99 to Meridian, follow signs to ferry and Reserve) 31305. Phone: (912) 437-3224. http://gastateparks.org/info/sapelo/ or www.sapelonerr.org. Hours: Mainland Visitors Center: Tuesday-Friday 7:30am-5:30pm, Saturday 8:00am-5:30pm, Sunday 1:30-5:00pm. Admission: 1/2 day tours: $10.00 adult, $6.00 child (6-12). Tours: Half- and full-day tours Wednesday 8:30am-12:30pm (mansion and Island) and Saturday 9:00am-1:00pm (lighthouse and island). An additional tour is offered Friday 8:30am-12:30pm (lighthouse and island) - summer only Extended tour offered the last Tuesday of the Month (March-October), 8:30am-3:00pm (lighthouse, mansion and island). Reservations are required. Note: Check in at the Visitors Center where you can orient to the area via displays on the history and culture of this remote island. Pack a backpack with snacks and water or purchase food at the small café on the island (a stop on the tour).*

This unique, undeveloped barrier island is one of the last places where the Geechee culture is lovingly maintained by residents, many of whom are the descendants of slaves. The similarities that link the cultures of Georgia's sea islands and the Windward Rice Coast of West Africa are generally referred to as the "Gullah Connection." Geechee distinguishes the language and slaves of Coastal Georgia. Gullah dialects, which combine English with the languages of African tribes, is still somewhat spoken here. During the guided tour of the island you will visit the antebellum mansion or the restored lighthouse, depending on the day that you visit. You'll see virtually every facet of a barrier island's natural community, from the forested uplands, to the vast

Jenny tries her hand at "cast-net" fishing and seems like a natural...

salt marsh, and the complex beach and dunes systems. We learned and saw: ruins of a sugar mill; sampling leaves from a Toothache Tree (Prickly Ash) - we bit them and then rubbed it on our tongue or gums - it numbs it!; talked with natives, especially chatting with Geechee woman, Cornelia for a story or two; casting a net and examining your catch; stop at the Post Office and mail yourself a postcard from  the Island; exploring the Reynolds Mansion (highlights were the solarium, gameroom and circus ballroom - want to spend a couple of nights? You can – group rates are available!); climbing the winding stairs of the lighthouse; and finally, exploring the beach or wading in the water. Like sand dollars and starfish? You can collect gobs of them as a souvenirs!

Exit - 49 (east of I-95)

FORT KING GEORGE HISTORIC SITE

Darien - *320 McIntosh Rd SE (I-95 exit 49 east) 31305. Phone: (912) 437-4770. http://gastateparks.org/info/ftkinggeorge/. Hours: Tuesday-Sunday 9:00am-5:00pm. Closed Mondays (except holidays), Closed Tuesdays when open on Monday, and winter holidays. Admission: $4.50-$7.00. Educators: There's a link to Teacher's Curriculum on the home page and it has some thorough lesson plans for teachers and worksheets for students.*

From 1721 until 1736, Fort King George was the southern outpost of the British Empire in North America. His Majesty's Independent Company garrisoned the fort. They endured incredible hardships from disease, threats from the Spanish and Indian nations, and the harsh, unfamiliar coastal environment. After  the fort was abandoned, General James Oglethorpe brought Scottish Highlanders to the site in 1736. The settlement eventually became the town of Darien and saw milling became a major industry. A museum and film cover the Guale Indians, the Santo Domingo de Talaje mission, Fort King George, the Scots of Darien and 19th century sawmilling when Darien became a major seaport. Walk around a fort replica as well as remains of three sawmills and tabby ruins.

Exit - 42 (east of I-95)

HOFWYL-BROADFIELD PLANTATION HISTORIC SITE

Brunswick - *US Hwy 17 North (I-95 exit 42 east on US 17) 31525. Phone: (912) 264-7333. http://gastateparks.org/info/hofwyl/. Hours: Thursday-Saturday 9:00am-5:00pm. Last main house tour 45 minutes before closing. Closed Thanksgiving, Christmas Day and New Year's Day. Admission: $4.50-$7.50.*

Around 1807, what was once a vast cypress swamp gave way to a man named Brailsford who carved from the terrain a rice plantation along the banks of the Altamaha River. Some 350 slaves worked the highly productive venture until war, hurricanes and the abolition of slavery caused its decline. Visitors today can see a model of a busy rice plantation, furnishings, and a brief film on the plantation's history before walking a short trail to the antebellum home. The site also includes a nature trail that leads back to the Visitor Center along the edge of the marsh where rice once flourished.

Exit - 38 (east of I-95)

ST. SIMONS TROLLEY TOUR

St. Simons Island - *117 Mallery Street (Rte. 25 south to Causeway to The Village/Pier area, between Lighthouse and Visitors Center) 31522. Phone: (912) 638-8954. www.stsimonstours.com. Admission: $23.00 adult, $10.00 child (4-12). Tours: 11:00am ONLY. Reservations or tickets in advance are not required, but arrive early for scheduled departures. Tours are 1.5 hours long.*

Tour historic St. Simons Island on an antique trolley. Start with this tour to orient the family and give clues to sites you'll want to visit during your stay. The humorous and delightful drive-by tour includes the lighthouse, Bloody Marsh, Fort Frederica, Retreat Plantation (where relics from slavery days still exist), and a walking tour of Christ Church (what famous Presidents have attended church here?). Hear stories about the slave family that owns the best property on the Island (Neptune). What is tabby? Do you hear footsteps from Frederic the Friendly ghost when walking up the

See one of the largest live oak trees in the area...

lighthouse stairs? What is the #1 food produced by the marshes? Why is Spanish moss not Spanish? Nor, is it something you would want to bag up and take home. It's possible, when looking closely at certain of the oak trees that cover the island, to find one actually looking back at you. These are the Tree Spirits-lovingly carved faces emerging from the trees. Your tour guide will point some out to you. The images portray the sailors who lost their lives at sea aboard the sailing ships that were once made from St. Simons Island oak. Their sad, sorrowful expressions seem to reflect the grieving appearance of the trees themselves with their drooping branches and moss.

> The last time it snowed on St. Simons Island was in 1989.

ST. SIMONS ISLAND LIGHTHOUSE

St. Simons Island - *101 12th Street (SR 25 south to Causeway to St. Simons - Beachview Drive, oceanfront) 31522. www.saintsimonslighthouse.org. Phone: (912) 638-4666. Hours: Monday-Saturday 10:00am-5:00pm, Sunday 1:30-5:00pm. Last climb to top is at 4:30pm. Admission: $12.00 adult, $5.00 child (age 6-12). Includes admission to Maritime Center.*

This lighthouse is the oldest brick structure in the area and is still maintained as an operational light by the US Coast Guard. The 104-foot-tall lighthouse has 129 interior steps. It sits behind the lightkeeper's dwelling which now houses the Museum. The second floor of the lightkeepers building is set up just as it would be in 1800s. The best part of the site for families is the climb up the six flights of stairs to the top of the light for a look around. Great view! Notice that most lighthouses are made of brick but this one is mostly locally made tabby mixture.

BARBARA JEAN'S RESTAURANT

St. Simons Island - *214 Mallery Street (Village) 31522. Phone: (912) 634-6500. www.barbara-jeans.com.*

Famous for "Eastern shore" crab cakes (best ever) and home-style entrees (like meatloaf) with southern style sides (greens, squash casserole). There is little doubt that they are best known for Crab Cakes, but their She Crab Soup, slightly mysterious "Chocolate Stuff" dessert and homemade breads have an aggressive following as well. Open Lunch & Dinner daily. Kids Menu around $5.00.

MULLET BAY RESTAURANT

St. Simons Island - *512 Ocean Boulevard (Village area) (spur 25 to US17S to Causeway over to Island. Restaurant on main thoroughfare) 31522. Phone: (912) 638-0703. www.mulletbayrestaurant.com.*

Seafood, steaks, sandwiches, chicken, burgers, po-boys. They have shrimp on the menu cooked to about any way you can think of. Kids (and parents) can crayon on the table cloth. Kids menu (from $1.95). Casual dining, moderate prices, dining indoors and outdoors. L, D daily.

Exit - 38 (east of I-95)

ISLAND INN

St. Simons Island - *301 Main Street (Plantation Village (follow causeway straight on Demere, left into complex) 31522. . Phone: (912) 638-7805. www. islandinnsanibel.com*

Enjoy the sub-tropical landscaping around the outdoor pool or unwind in the bubbling hot tub beneath the gazebo. This St. Simons hotel is also nestled among the island's legendary folklore tree spirits crafted by sculptor Keith Jennings. Hotel guests will appreciate the nearby Village and Pier offering a variety of specialty shops and dining options. The hotel's proximity to the beach makes it an ideal spot for guests to participate in fishing, kayaking, horseback riding and biking. They have a complimentary deluxe continental breakfast bar and bike rentals on site.

ST. SIMONS ISLAND MARITIME CENTER

St. Simons Island - *4201 1st Street (SR 25 south to Causeway to St. Simons - on East Beach) 31522. www.saintsimonslighthouse.org/maritime.html. Phone: (912) 638-4666. Hours: Monday-Saturday 10:00am-5:00pm, Sunday 1:30-5:00pm. Admission: $12.00 adult, $5.00 child (6-12). Includes Lighthouse Museum.*

Located in the former U.S. Coast Guard Station, the Maritime Center offers an exciting look at coastal Georgia natural assets, while highlighting some of the area's maritime and

Learning Nautical Knots

military history. Visitors are guided through the museum by "Ollie", a fictional character based on journal entries and historical accounts by various Coast Guard personnel stationed at St. Simons Island during World War II. Seven galleries feature a variety of hands-on exhibits and activities (like learning how to tie knots like sailors).

FORT FREDERICA / BLOODY MARSH BATTLE SITE

St. Simons Island - *6515 Frederica Road (Spur 25 to US 17S to Causeway - off Sea Island Road on Rte. 9, Battle site is 5 miles south of Fort) 31522. Phone: (912) 638-3639. www.nps.gov/fofr/. Hours: Daily 9:00am-5:00pm. Closed Christmas Day. Admission: $3.00 per person (age 16+). Note: "Fort Frederica: History Uncovered". The film is shown in the visitor center every 30 minutes. Educators: thorough lesson plans: www.nps.gov/fofr/forteachers/curriculummaterials.htm*

When General James Oglethorpe claimed Georgia territory for England, it was important to build settlements within forts. He found this site on the river bank and named it Frederica. By the 1740s, Frederica was a thriving village of about 500 citizens. When Spanish troops sought to capture St. Simons Island in 1742, Oglethorpe's men won a decisive victory in what is now called The Battle of Bloody Marsh. In July of 1742, an outnumbered force of British troops ambushed and defeated Spanish troops, halting an attack aimed at Fort Frederica. The battle proved to be the turning point in the Spanish invasion of Georgia. By the late 1740s the fort was not needed and disbanded. Today, you can visit the site of Fort Frederica and see the ruins of the fortifications, barracks and homes. A museum, film, dioramas, tours, and demonstrations bring the settlement vividly to life.

Exit - 36 (east of I-95)

MARY ROSS WATERFRONT PARK

Brunswick - *(follow Rte. 341 into town. Brunswick Harbor Market at the end of Gloucester Street) 31520. Hours: Daylight Admission: FREE.*

A scaled-down replica of the WWII workhorse ship, the Liberty Ship is docked here. The park also has outdoor musical playscape (make music on the playground equipment), staged pavilion, farmers market and amphitheater. Brunswick is one of the shrimp capitals of the world. The shrimp fleet may be seen from Bay Street (US 341) between Gloucester and Prince Streets - best late afternoon when the ships come in.

Exit - 29 (east of I-95)

JEKYLL ISLAND MUSEUM & HISTORIC DISTRICT

Jekyll Island - *100 Stable Road (follow US 17 & GA520 into Historic District. west end of island directly across from entrance to Island Club) 31527. Phone: (912) 635-4036. www.jekyllisland.com. Hours: Daily 9:00am-5:00pm, except holidays. Tours: availability and pricing subject to change. For more information on pricing and tour availability or to make reservations, please call Jekyll Island Museum.*

Take a brief walk through the American Indian history, past the Millionaire's era, then up to the present time on the island. Simulate the first intercontinental phone call made using two old-fashioned pay phones. Or, light up the Archeological Mystery boxes and see what glows.

GEORGIA SEA TURTLE CENTER

Jekyll Island - *214 Stable Road (follow US 17 & GA520 into Historic District) 31527. www.georgiaseaturtlecenter.org. Phone: (912) 635-2284 or (912) 635-4036 Center. Hours: Monday 10:00am-2:00pm, Tuesday-Sunday 9:00am-5:00pm. Closed winter Mondays & Holidays. Admission: $5.00-$7.00 age 4+. Tours: 8:30 and 9:30pm (June thru mid-August). Any age is welcome with a parent; children over age 12 can participate unattended with parental permission. Note: Video presentation and exhibits detail the history of the island from the native inhabitants to the present.*

Be especially careful during the turtle "rush hour"...

TURTLE WALKS: Under a cover of darkness, female Loggerhead sea turtles swim ashore, make their way across the sand, dig their nests and lay their eggs. Designated a threatened species by state and federal law, loggerhead sea turtles have found safe haven on Jekyll Island. Their nests, tucked among the dunes of Island beaches are the treasure find of the tours. Following a description of sea turtles and their habitat, local wildlife guides conduct shoreline walks in search of turtle tracks and nesting mothers. From a safe distance, participants view the fascinating pageant of life as 80-100 eggs are deposited in the nest.

<u>CENTER</u>: The old Power Plant is now used as a combination of exhibit space, hospital, classroom, office, and gift shop, all rolled into one. The Georgia Sea Turtle Center has had a wide variety of patients come through its doors since opening in June 2007. Visitors to the Georgia Sea Turtle Center will explore exhibits on sea turtle conservation, rehabilitation, and their amazing journey from egg to adulthood. Daily programs include patient updates and dinnertime feeding.

Each "guest" has a story to tell...

DOLPHIN TOURS - COASTAL GEORGIA

Jekyll Island - *1 Pier Road (follow US 17 & GA520 into Historic District - departs from Historic Jekyll Island Wharf marina) 31527. Phone: (912) 635-3152. www.captainphillip.com. Admission: $24.00 adult, $12.00 child (2-10). Tours: 90 minutes long. Departures Monday-Saturday at 11:00am & 1:30pm. Off season (Labor Day-February) are only Tuesday and Saturday at 11:00am. Leave from St. Simons Marina. See website for additional tours leaving from Jekyll Island Historic site marina/wharf. Note: Boats are fully sun-covered with bathrooms on board.*

See dolphin frolicking in their natural habitat as you explore the marshes, the sound and tidal rivers. Comfortable, shaded tour boats offer plenty of move-about room to get a great view of the dolphins. Cruise the inland waters, so it is never rough. You will also enjoy marvelous views of shrimp boats, local birds and wildlife. Adequate and comfortable seating allows a maximum of 40 passengers. The captain and crew share a relaxed overview of the coastal environment.

TIDELANDS NATURE CENTER

Jekyll Island - *100 S Riverview Drive (next to Summer Waves Water Park - turn right shortly after you bridge over the marsh) 31527. Phone: (912) 635-5032. www.tidelands4h.org. Hours: Monday-Friday 9:00am-4:00pm, Saturday-Sunday 10:00am-2:00pm. Admission: Suggested $4.00 (age 3+). $3.00-$5.00 for guided walks. Boat rentals - $15.00/hour.*

Have you ever touched a live seashell? Now you can. Stop by and visit a young sea turtle, corn snake, fish, alligators and other species native to Georgia's coast. A new shark exhibit opened recently. Aquariums and touch tanks on site specialize in the local ecosystems. Touch a starfish and many crabs - even pet turtles. The touch box room is a stop for kids (near the end so they can apply what they've learned). Our favorite part has to be the hatchling loggerhead turtles that are being raised here. You'll be mesmerized as they watch you and show off their giraffe-like legs, thick "log" neck and pretty yellow, orange and brown color. (Note: if you can't go out looking for turtle nests - they have a great diorama of a mother nesting that shows the instinctive habit they have every summer). There is also a self-guided nature trail. Sign up for nature walks to the beach or marsh. Maybe even go seining - kick off your shoes and learn to use a seine net to capture creatures in the surf.

Exit - 29 (east of I-95)

SUMMER WAVES WATER PARK

Jekyll Island - 210 South Riverview Drive (next to the marsh on Riverview Drive) 31527. Phone: (912) 635-2074. www.jekyllisland.com/summerwaves/. Hours: Vary by season. Daily from Memorial Day to Labor Day and on select weekends in May and September. Monday-Thursday 10:00am-6:00pm, Friday-Saturday 10:00am-8:00pm, Sunday 11:00am-7:00pm. Admission: $16.00-$20.00 (age 4+). $11.00 senior (60+) and Night Splash. Note: Changing areas, restrooms and eateries are available.

More than one million gallons of splashing water fun and 11 acres of rides. Gather your courage for the Pirates Passage, a totally enclosed speed flume that jets riders over three humps in total darkness or the Force 3 inner tube flume. Or, catch a wave in the Frantic Atlantic wave pool and enjoy a lazy inner tube ride on Turtle Creek. For kids under 48" tall, Summer Waves kiddie pool offers carefully supervised water playgrounds complete with slides and waterfalls in just 12 inches of bubbling water. (inner tubes and life vests are provided throughout the park at no charge).

JEKYLL ISLAND BIKING

Jekyll Island - Beachview Drive (follow signs to island, middle of beach side. Route begins at mini golf) 31527. www.jekyllisland.com/activities/ biking.asp. Phone: (912) 635-2648 or (877) 4JEKYLL. Hours: Daily 9:00am to 5:00 to 7:00pm. Admission: Rentals: $5.00-$7.00 per hour or $11.50+ per day per

Want to get the kids exploring more? Try the many geocache sites on the island: www.jekyllisland.com/geocaching/

GEORGIA

bike. Helmets and child seats or baskets available. Georgia law requires children 13 and under to wear bike helmets. FREE is you bring own bikes. Note: Mini-golf ~$6.00 per game. Two courses.

More than 20 miles of paved paths circle the island, providing a scenic ride for both the serious cyclist and pleasure biker. Starting from the rentals by mini-golf, travel two miles along the beach with ocean views and dunes. Continue on the North Loop past canopies of live oaks. To extend the ride, take the path to your right by the gate past Villas by the Sea to meander through the Clam Creek area. You'll be right in the middle of a marsh. Loop around the fishing piers, down more canopies of oaks draped in Spanish Moss towards the Historic District. Once in the Historic District, continue straight toward Jekyll Island Club on road ahead. Pass behind the hotel, by Faith Chapel and Villa Marianna. Continue down Old Plantation Road and stop at the Island Museum. Want more forest environs? Head to South Loop near Tidelands Nature Center. Once through the forest, head out towards the Beach again and see "Glory" Beach, where the movie was filmed.

Over 20 miles of trails...what fun!

VILLAS BY THE SEA RESORT HOTEL

Jekyll Island - *1175 N Beachview Drive (follow US 17 & GA520 to island. Turn left on Beachview) 31527. www.villasbythesearesort.com. Phone: (912) 635-2521 or (800) 841-6262.*

Lovely villas with fully equipped kitchens, private living room/dining areas full baths, separate bedroom(s) and private patio or balcony. 1,2, or 3-bedroom villas nestled among 17 acres of stately oaks with a partially shaded large pool area and 2,000 feet of oceanside beach. Restaurant with early bird specials and a Kids Menu. Other amenities include bicycle rentals for Jekyll's 20 miles of scenic paved trails, playground, volleyball, badminton, and basketball. $100.00-$200.00 per night. Lower rates available for mid-week and weekly stays.

Exit - 3 (east of I-95)

ST. MARYS TOONERVILLE TROLLEY & TRAM TOURS

St. Marys - *406 Osborne Road (Rte 40 east into town) 31558. Phone: (800) 868-8687 OR (866) 386-8729. www.stmaryswelcome.com/toontrolleyV2.html. Note: The tour meets at the flag pole on the waterfront.*

TOONERVILLE TROLLEY - "See You In The Funny Papers!" This saying originated by Roy Crane in his 1935 "Wash Tubbs & Easy" comic strip. The strip featured the many local personalities who used this railcar to commute from St. Marys to Kingsland in the late 1920s. Trolley tours were conducted for two summers, and then the vintage machine was retired to its current place of honor on Osborne Street.

TRAM TOURS: Take a Historic ride through St. Mary's including historic 1800s churches. Call for Tram tours price and reservations.

ST. MARYS SUBMARINE MUSEUM

St. Marys - *102 St. Marys Street West, waterfront (Rte 40 into town) 31558. Phone: (912) 882-ASUB. www.stmaryssubmuseum.com. Hours: Tuesday-Saturday 10:00am-4:00pm, Sunday 1:00-5:00pm. Admission: $3.00-$5.00 (age 6+).*

Get ready to see firsthand a working periscope, models of torpedoes, and many displays made from actual submarines. See a deep-sea diving suit and submarine uniforms, command plaques, photographs and models of submarines, an area for watching movies on submarines, working sonar panels, and a gift shop. Walls and walls of memorabilia track the history of the submarine.

ST. MARYS AQUATIC CENTER

St. Marys - *301 Herb Bauer Drive (Rte. 40 into town, just south off 40, south of the St. Marys Airport) 31558. Phone: (912) 673-8118. www.funatsmac.com. Hours: Monday-Friday 11:00am-6:00pm, Saturday 10:00am-6:00pm, Sunday 1:00-6:00pm (June- mid August). Weekends only (late April, May, late August, September). Admission: $7.00-$10.00 per person. Less for toddlers, juniors and seniors.*

This brand new 7 acre water play area has something for the whole family. Adults can relax in a tube as you float around the park in the endless river or get in some exercise swimming in the lap pool. There is also a two story tall slide full of twists and turns that is sure to be exciting. Kids over four feet tall can ride the big slide, but the big attraction for the little ones is the play pool with dozens of ways to squirt, spray and splatter your friends with gallons of water.

CUMBERLAND ISLAND NATIONAL SEASHORE MUSEUM

St. Marys - Osborne St (Rte. 40) (Visitors Ctr. is located at the Dungeness Dock on the Island. The inland museum is just blocks from the water) 31558. Phone: (912) 882-4335 or (888) 817-3421. www.nps.gov/cuis/siteindex.htm. Hours: Ice House Museum: 8:00am-4:00pm daily. Mainland Museum: 1:00-4:00pm. Generally, two ferry departures per day operating. Admission: Day Use Fee: $4.00 per person/ visit (age 16+). Ferry Price (round trip): $20.00 adult, $18.00 senior (65+), and $14.00 child (12 and under). Note: The ferry does not transport pets, bicycles, kayaks, or cars. Boating, camping, fishing and hiking are activities available on the island. Educators: Ask for Scavenger Hunt or activity sheets at visitors center.

Once home to several of the Carnegie family's splendid estates, Cumberland Island is now home to hundreds of wild horses, a resort inn and some of the most beautiful camping on the East Coast. It is Georgia's largest and southernmost barrier island, with pristine maritime forests, undeveloped beaches and wide marshes. It is well known for its sea turtles, wild turkeys, wild horses, armadillos, abundant shore birds, dune fields, maritime forests, salt marshes, and historic structures. Special Programs conducted by rangers (on the island) are at 4:00pm dockside each afternoon when the ferry is operating. The Mainland Museum is located on Osborne Street, two blocks from the waterfront. The museum houses a collection of artifacts from Cumberland Island to highlight the people of the island. The lives of Native Americans, African Americans, the Carnegie family as well as others who lived on the island in the 19th and 20th centuries are seen in the island environment. This is the first major effort to bring the island story to mainland facilities. Another portion of the total collection is still on display on the island.

CROOKED RIVER STATE PARK

St. Marys - 6222 Charlie Smith St. Highway (8 miles east of I-95 exit 3, LEFT on Charlie Smith hwy) 31558. http://gastateparks.org/CrookedRiver. Phone: (912) 882-5256. Hours: Daily 7:00am-10:00pm. Admission: $5.00 daily vehicle parking fee.

This park offers cozy facilities with views of salt marshes and Spanish moss-draped oaks. Campsites are surrounded by oaks, while cottages overlook the river. Hikers can explore the nature trails (4 miles), which winds through maritime forest and salt marsh. Visitors may venture to the nearby ruins of the tabby "McIntosh Sugar Works" mill, built around 1825 and later used as a starch factory during the Civil War. Just down the road is the ferry to famous Cumberland Island National Seashore known for secluded beaches. The park also has an Olympic-size pool and bathhouse and a miniature golf course.

Exit - 1 MILE (NB Only)

GEORGIA WELCOME CENTER - NORTHBOUND ONLY

St. Marys - *(exit 1 and the Welcome Center run alongside each other)* .

You'll find a staffed Georgia Visitor Center, clean restrooms, a pet walk, and large covered picnic tables. Visitors Center open business hours, restrooms 24 hours.

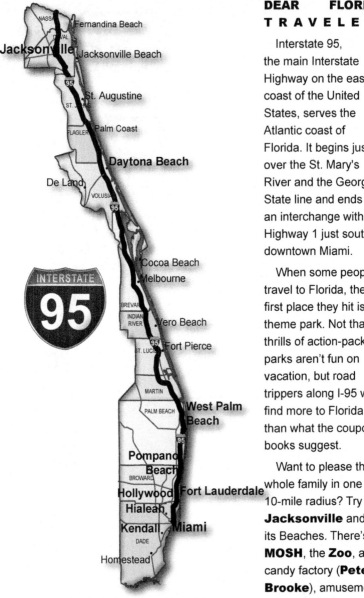

DEAR   FLORIDA
T R A V E L E R :

Interstate 95, the main Interstate Highway on the east coast of the United States, serves the Atlantic coast of Florida. It begins just over the St. Mary's River and the Georgia State line and ends at an interchange with US Highway 1 just south of downtown Miami.

When some people travel to Florida, the first place they hit is a theme park. Not that thrills of action-packed parks aren't fun on vacation, but road trippers along I-95 will find more to Florida than what the coupon books suggest.

Want to please the whole family in one 10-mile radius? Try **Jacksonville** and its Beaches. There's **MOSH**, the **Zoo**, a candy factory (**Peter Brooke**), amusements and a waterpark all within a few miles of the easy-to-manage **Jacksonville Beach**. Play with science, art, watch jaguars swim, feed a live giraffe, and sample chocolate covered popcorn after you finish building sand castles on the beach.

For updates & travel games visit: **www.KidsLoveTravel.com**

For the perfect match of history and exploration, **St. Augustine** is like taking a trip through the pages of history, with its cobbled streets, quaint buildings and living re-enactors. Take a stroll through a village where Ponce deLeon tried to find the **Fountain of Youth**, Spanish conquistadors set up a colony along St. George Street, the **Old Fort (Castillo de San Marcos)** sits on one riverbank, and the rewarding climb to the top of the **St. Augustine Lighthouse** on the other. Although the Old City is a favorite among walkers, we'd suggest parking on the outskirts and touring the sites by boat or trolley. The **Schooner Freedom** is docked just before you cross the bridge and is known for their "interactions" with the guests – whether that be pirates, dolphins, hoisting the sail or enjoying the sunset. **Old Town Trolley Tours** is the mode we used most. After your first roundabout the Old City, try to decide where to step off first. Will it be the **Old Jail**, the **Oldest House or the Oldest Wooden School House** in the USA?

The Ripley's Believe it or Not in St. Augustine gets you in the mood for the next exciting city – **Daytona Beach**! As home to the Daytona 500 at the International Speedway with its track tours and ultra-speed racing amusements: **Daytona 500 Experience**, Daytona Beach, Florida, is a family-friendly area where you can DRIVE ON THE BEACH, surf and participate in other water sports. Just stop at any kiosk near the water and you'll find thrills to your heart's content. Snuck into the quiet city streets is a wonderful chocolate factory store, **Angell & Phelps** and on the southernmost point of the city lie Ponce Inlet and the beautiful landscape and sea life surrounding the **Ponce de Leon Inlet Lighthouse**.

Nature is an essential part of the Florida lifestyle. With an average yearly temperature of around 72 degrees, vibrant wildlife and an array of outdoor activities, who can blame visitors for loving to be outside most of the time?

You won't find many places where nature exists in harmony with technology more than it does in **Cape Canaveral** on Florida's Space Coast. You'll also find pristine beaches, totally family-oriented resorts, and the big attraction – the Space Center.

Visit the **Kennedy Space Center Visitor Complex**, which tells the story of NASA's exploration of space through interactive exhibits, movies and tours that are sure to engage your wonderment. Witness actual components of the International Space Station being readied for their trip into orbit, or enter the full-scale mock-up of the habitation module that space station crews will call home. Other highlights include meeting real astronauts and enjoying tons of virtual space encounters and play areas.

Amazingly, **Merritt Island National Wildlife Refuge** exists on the same land that hosts the Kennedy Space Center. This 220-square-mile refuge is home to more endangered species than any other refuge in the United States, including the southern bald eagle and Atlantic loggerhead turtle. Here, gators soak in the sun at the edge of inland waterways; raccoons, bobcats and armadillos roam the refuge; and gentle manatees (sea cows) swim in the waters of the Indian River.

Now past the middle of I-95 in Florida, you won't want to miss a few "treasures" we nearly missed. If you want the Orlando experience on a more relaxed scale, try an overnight or two at **Disney's Vero Beach Resort**. Still the magic, just not all the fuss of amusements. The fun is going treasure hunting along the coastline. The men in our family became full-throttle treasure hunters after an inexpensive visit to the **McLarty Treasure Museum**. Between the movie and the stories from locals hanging out to chat about the latest finds, you're engaged and ready to find something shiny.

If you weren't excited enough, follow A1A (just a few miles east of I-95) south and create some electricity at the **FPL Energy Encounter** on Hutchinson Island. A pirate parrot mascot leads the way to a cool science scavenger hunt revolving around nuclear power.

The big cities of **Fort Lauderdale** and **Miami** finish our tour de Florida. Fort Lauderdale's beaches are, of course, a popular draw. Stroll, bike, or skate along Atlantic Boulevard and the Beach Promenade, or take part in the many watersports available, such as kite surfing. But if, or when, you tire of the beach, plan a special tropical dinner show at **Mai Kai Polynesian Revue** and learn to hula dance sipping a "coconutty" drink.

Our final destination, the place where Interstate 95 began (or, in our case, ends) is Miami. While there are lots of attractions to choose from, your budget may only permit one or two. To help you decide, take the amusing **South Beach Duck Tours** of Miami Beach and quack along the way as you "waddle" through highlight districts of the city. Some of our favorite spots are much further south of exit 1 (so they're not listed – headed towards the Keys - see _Kids Love Florida_) but one that is easy to reach is the **Miami Seaquarium**. Some areas are grandiose (like their sea creature shows) but some are cute and quiet. Education is stressed as much as showmanship – and you know those whales and dolphins can really show off!

ACTIVITIES AT A GLANCE

AMUSEMENTS

Exit - 348 - *Adventure Landing*
Exit - 261 - *Daytona 500 Experience*

ANIMALS & FARMS

Exit - 358 - *Jacksonville Zoo And Gardens*
Exit - 311 - *St. Augustine Alligator Farm Zoological Park*
Exit - 305 - *Marineland's Dolphin Conservation Center*
Exit - 215 - *Jungle Adventures*
Exit - 191 - *Brevard Zoo*
Exit - 131A - *Manatee Observation And Education Center*
Exit - 83 - *Loggerhead Marinelife Center*
Exit - 68 - *Palm Beach Zoo At Dreher Park*
Exit - 39 - *Butterfly World*
Exit - 24 / I-595 West - *Flamingo Gardens*
Exit - 2D / I-395 East - *Jungle Island*
Exit - 1A - *Miami Seaquarium*

HISTORY

Exit - 362 - *Fort Caroline National Monument*
Exit - 318 - *Old Jail*
Exit - 318 - *Old Florida Museum*
Exit - 318 - *Fountain Of Youth, Ponce De Leon's*
Exit - 318 - *Castillo De San Marcos, The Old Fort*
Exit - 318 - *Oldest Wooden School House In The United States*
Exit - 318 - *Colonial Spanish Quarter*
Exit - 318 - *Old St. Augustine Village*
Exit - 318 - *Oldest House Museum Complex*
Exit - 318 - *Fort Mose*
Exit - 311 - *St. Augustine Lighthouse And Museum*

HISTORY (cont.)

Exit - 305 - *Fort Matanzas National Monument*
Exit - 268 - *Tomoka State Park Mounds And Middens*
Exit - 256 - *Ponce De Leon Inlet Lighthouse*
Exit - 215 - *Valiant Air Command Warbird Museum*
Exit - 138 - *National Navy UDT/Seal (Frogman) Museum*
Exit - 87 - *Jupiter Inlet Lighthouse*
Exit - 57 - *Schoolhouse Children's Museum*
Exit - 27 - *Fort Lauderdale History Center*
Exit - 1A - *Coral Gables' Venetian Pool*
Exit - 1A - *Barnacle Historic State Park*

MUSEUMS

Exit - 318 - *Ripley's Believe It Or Not! Museum*
Exit - 215 - *American Police Hall Of Fame & Museum*
Exit - 156 - *McLarty Treasure Museum*
Exit - 156 - *Mel Fisher's Treasure Museum*
Exit - 27 - *International Swimming Hall Of Fame*
Exit - 23 - *Fishing Hall Of Fame & Museum (IGFA)*
Exit - 2D / I-395 East - *Miami Children's Museum*

OUTDOOR EXPLORING

Exit - 348 - *Jacksonville Beach*
Exit - 311 - *Anastasia State Park & St. Augustine Beach*
Exit - 298 - *Faver-Dykes State Park*
Exit - 298 - *Washington Oaks Gardens State Park*
Exit - 284 - *Gamble Rogers Memorial State Recreation Area At Flagler*

ACTIVITIES AT A GLANCE

OUTDOOR EXPLORING (cont.)

Exit - 261 - *Daytona Beach, The Beach*

Exit - 256 - *Sugar Mill Botantical Gardens*

Exit - 220 - *Merritt Island National Wildlife Refuge*

Exit - 156 - *Environmental Learning Center*

Exit - 156 - *Pelican Island National Wildlife Refuge*

Exit - 129 - *Treasure Coast Beaches*

Exit - 126 - *Oxbow Eco-Center*

Exit - 118 - *Savannas Preserve State Park*

Exit - 101 - *Seabranch Preserve State Park*

Exit - 96 - *Jonathan Dickinson State Park*

Exit - 77 - *John D. MacArthur Beach State Park*

Exit - 52 - *Loxahatchee, Arm National Wildlife Refuge*

Exit - 29 - *Hugh Taylor Birch State Recreation Area*

Exit - 21 - *Anne Kolb Nature Center*

Exit - 1A - *Fairchild Tropical Botanic Garden*

Exit - 1A - *Pinecrest Gardens*

Exit - 1A - *Bill Baggs Cape Florida State Park*

SCIENCE

Exit - 353B - *Tree Hill Nature Center*

Exit - 350 - *Museum Of Science And History (MOSH)*

Exit - 261 - *Museum Of Arts And Sciences*

Exit - 256 - *Marine Science Center*

Exit - 215 - *Kennedy Space Center Visitor Complex*

SCIENCE (cont.)

Exit - 202 - *Brevard Museum Of History & Natural Science*

Exit - 131 - *FPL Energy Encounter*

Exit - 131 - *Smithsonian Marine Station At Fort Pierce*

Exit - 101 - *Florida Oceanographic Coastal Center*

Exit - 68 - *South Florida Science Museum*

Exit - 44 - *Gumbo Limbo Nature Center*

Exit - 27 - *Museum Of Discovery & Science*

Exit - 24 / I-595 West - *Buehler Planetarium & Observatory*

Exit - 1A - *Miami Museum Of Science & Planetarium*

Exit - 1A - *Biscayne Nature Center / Marjory Stoneman Douglas*

SPORTS

Exit - 323 - *World Golf Hall Of Fame & Imax Theater*

SUGGESTED LODGING & DINING

Exit - 348 - *Quality Suites Oceanfront - Jacksonville Beach*

Exit - 318 - *Howard Johnson Inn- Historic St. Augustine*

Exit - 318 - *Barnacle Bill's*

Exit - 318 - *Harry's Seafood Bar & Grille*

Exit - 311 - *The Conch House Restaurant*

Exit - 261 - *Bubba Gump Shrimp Company*

Exit - 261 - *Best Western Aku Tiki*

Exit - 220 - *Dixie Crossroads Seafood Restaurant*

Exit - 205 - *Ron Jon Cape Caribe Resort*

Exit - 156 - *Captain Hiram's Resort*

Exit - 147 - *Ocean Grill*

ACTIVITIES AT A GLANCE

SUGGESTED LODGING
& DINING (cont.)

Exit - 147 - *Disney's Vero Beach Resort*
Exit - 31 - *Mai Kai Polynesian Revue*
Exit - 29 - *Pelican Beach Resort*

THE ARTS

Exit - 351 - *Cummer Museum Of Art*
Exit - 350 - *Museum Of Contemporary Art (MOCA)*

TOURS

Exit - 350B - *Peterbrooke Chocolatier Production Center*
Exit - 318 - *Old Town Trolley Tours Of St. Augustine*
Exit - 311 - *Whetstone Chocolates Factory Tour*
Exit - 311 - *Schooner Freedom*

TOURS (cont.)

Exit - 261 - *Chocolate Factory, Angell & Phelps*
Exit - 261 - *A Tiny Cruise Line*
Exit - 201 - *Island Boat Lines*
Exit - 156 - *River Queen Cruises*
Exit - 27 - *Sea Experience Glassbottom Boat & Snorkeling Tours*
Exit - 27 - *Jungle Queen Riverboat*
Exit - 25 - *Water Bus*
Exit - 2D / I-395 East - *Miami Duck Tours*
Exit - 2D / I-395 East - *Island Queen & Bayside Blaster*

WELCOME CENTER

Exit - 379 Mile SB Only - *Florida Welcome Center*

GENERAL INFORMATION

Contact the services of interest. Request to be added to their mailing lists.

- Florida Bicycle Association: (407) 327-3941 or www.floridabicycle.org
- Bike Florida: (352) 376-6044 or www.bikeflorida.org
- Office of Greenways and Trails: www.floridagreenwaysandtrails.com
- Florida State Parks: (850) 488-9872 or www.floridastateparks.org
- Visit Florida: (888) 7FLA-USA or www.visitflorida.com
- National Camping Information: www.gocampingamerica.com
- Indian River County (Vero Beach): www.indianriverchamber.com
- Greater Miami And Beaches: (800) 955-3646 or www.MiamiandBeaches.com
- St. Lucie County (Fort Pierce, Port St. Lucie, Hutchinson Island): www.visitstluciefla.com or (800) 344-TGIF.
- Fort Lauderdale: www.sunny.org
- Space Coast (Cape Canaveral, Titusville, Cocoa Beach): www.space-coast.com
- Daytona Beach: (800) 544-0415 or www.daytonabeach.org
- St. Augustine, Ponte Vedra & The Beaches: (800) 418-7529 or www.Getaway4Florida.com

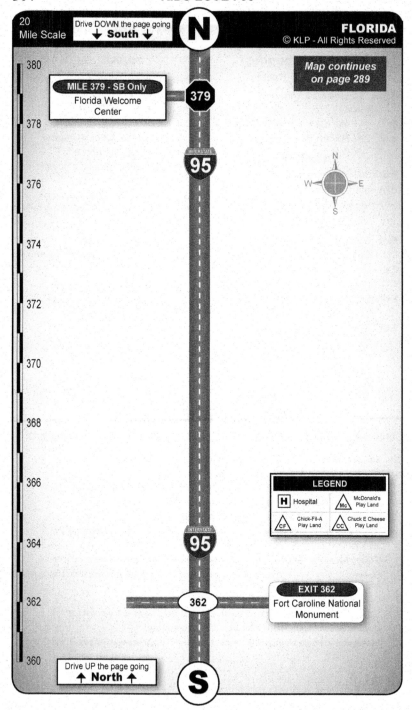

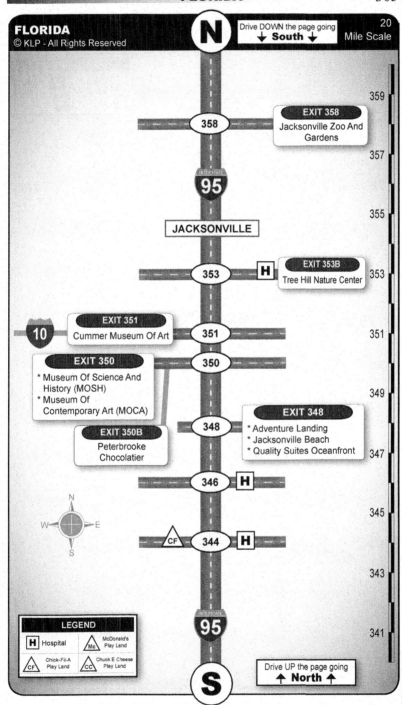

N

Drive DOWN the page going
↓ **South** ↓

20 Mile Scale

359

358 — **EXIT 358** Jacksonville Zoo And Gardens

357

INTERSTATE 95

355

JACKSONVILLE

353 H — **EXIT 353B** Tree Hill Nature Center — 353

10 — **EXIT 351** Cummer Museum Of Art — **351** — 351

EXIT 350 **350**
* Museum Of Science And History (MOSH)
* Museum Of Contemporary Art (MOCA)

349

EXIT 348 **348**
* Adventure Landing
* Jacksonville Beach
* Quality Suites Oceanfront

EXIT 350B Peterbrooke Chocolatier

347

346 H

345

CF **344** H

343

INTERSTATE 95

341

N
W — E
S

LEGEND
| H | Hospital | Mc | McDonald's Play Land |
| CF | Chick-Fil-A Play Land | CC | Chuck E Cheese Play Land |

Drive UP the page going
↑ **North** ↑

S

FLORIDA

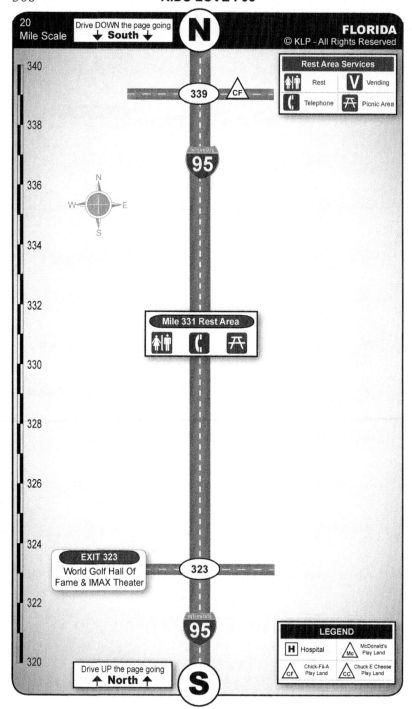

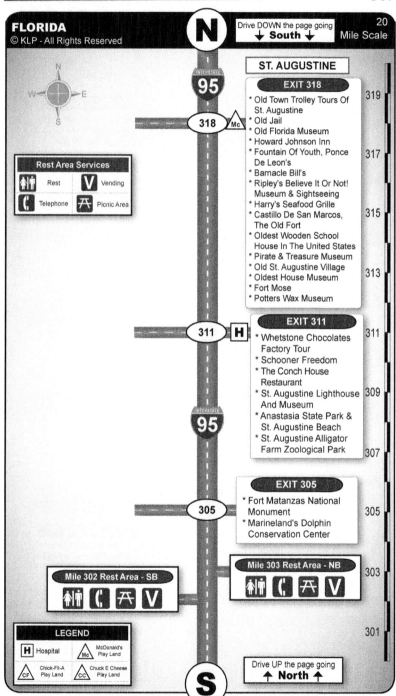

N

Drive DOWN the page going
↓ **South** ↓

20 Mile Scale

INTERSTATE **95**

ST. AUGUSTINE

319

EXIT 318

318 Mc

* Old Town Trolley Tours Of St. Augustine
* Old Jail
* Old Florida Museum
* Howard Johnson Inn
* Fountain Of Youth, Ponce De Leon's
* Barnacle Bill's
* Ripley's Believe It Or Not! Museum & Sightseeing
* Harry's Seafood Grille
* Castillo De San Marcos, The Old Fort
* Oldest Wooden School House In The United States
* Pirate & Treasure Museum
* Old St. Augustine Village
* Oldest House Museum
* Fort Mose
* Potters Wax Museum

317

315

313

Rest Area Services

| 🚻 | Rest | V | Vending |
| ☎ | Telephone | 🏕 | Picnic Area |

311 H

EXIT 311

* Whetstone Chocolates Factory Tour
* Schooner Freedom
* The Conch House Restaurant
* St. Augustine Lighthouse And Museum
* Anastasia State Park & St. Augustine Beach
* St. Augustine Alligator Farm Zoological Park

311

309

307

INTERSTATE **95**

EXIT 305

305

* Fort Matanzas National Monument
* Marineland's Dolphin Conservation Center

305

Mile 303 Rest Area - NB

🚻 ☎ 🏕 V

303

Mile 302 Rest Area - SB

🚻 ☎ 🏕 V

301

LEGEND

| H | Hospital | Mc | McDonald's Play Land |
| CF | Chick-Fil-A Play Land | CC | Chuck E Cheese Play Land |

Drive UP the page going
↑ **North** ↑

S

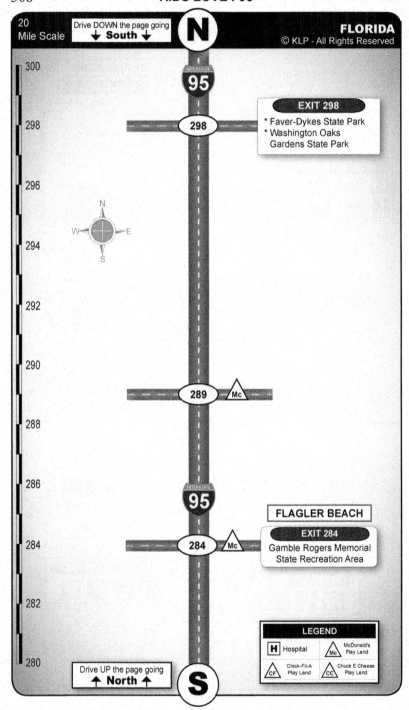

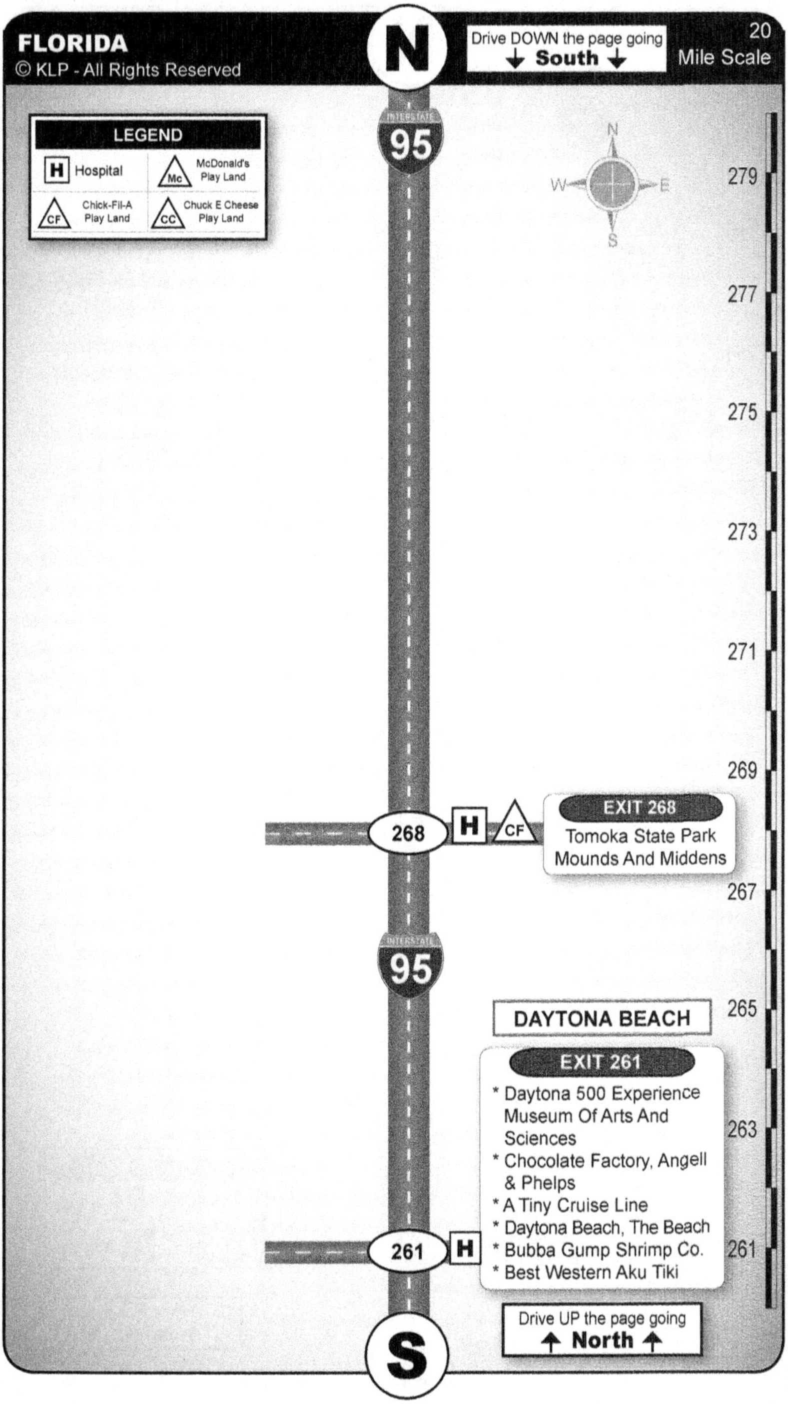

FLORIDA

N

Drive DOWN the page going
↓ **South** ↓

20 Mile Scale

INTERSTATE **95**

LEGEND

| H | Hospital | Mc | McDonald's Play Land |
| CF | Chick-Fil-A Play Land | CC | Chuck E Cheese Play Land |

279

277

275

273

271

269

268 H CF

EXIT 268
Tomoka State Park
Mounds And Middens

267

INTERSTATE **95**

265

DAYTONA BEACH

EXIT 261

* Daytona 500 Experience Museum Of Arts And Sciences
* Chocolate Factory, Angell & Phelps
* A Tiny Cruise Line
* Daytona Beach, The Beach
* Bubba Gump Shrimp Co.
* Best Western Aku Tiki

263

261 H

261

Drive UP the page going
↑ **North** ↑

S

FLORIDA

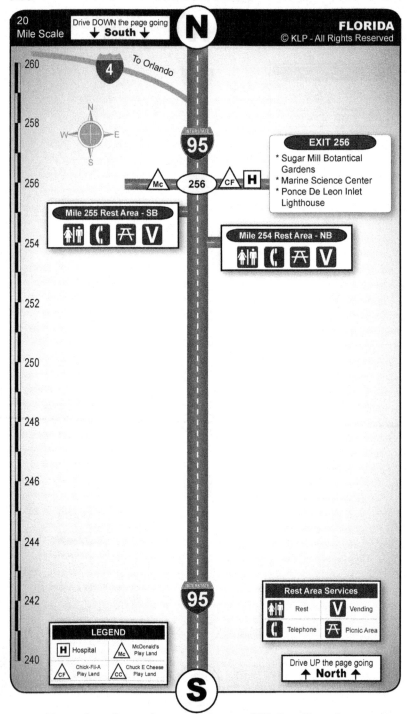

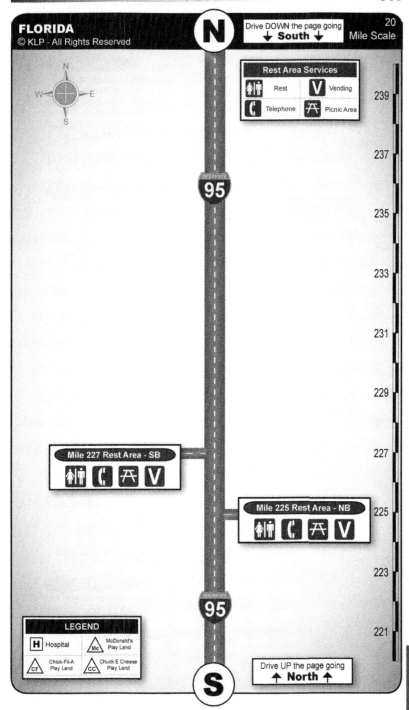

Drive DOWN the page going
↓ **South** ↓

20
Mile Scale

Rest Area Services

Rest
Vending
Telephone
Picnic Area

239
237
235
233
231
229
227

Mile 227 Rest Area - SB

225

Mile 225 Rest Area - NB

223
221

LEGEND

H Hospital
Mc McDonald's Play Land
CF Chick-Fil-A Play Land
CC Chuck E Cheese Play Land

Drive UP the page going
↑ **North** ↑

FLORIDA

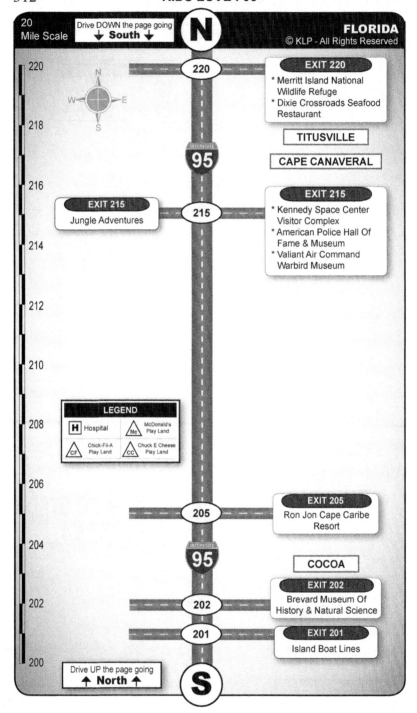

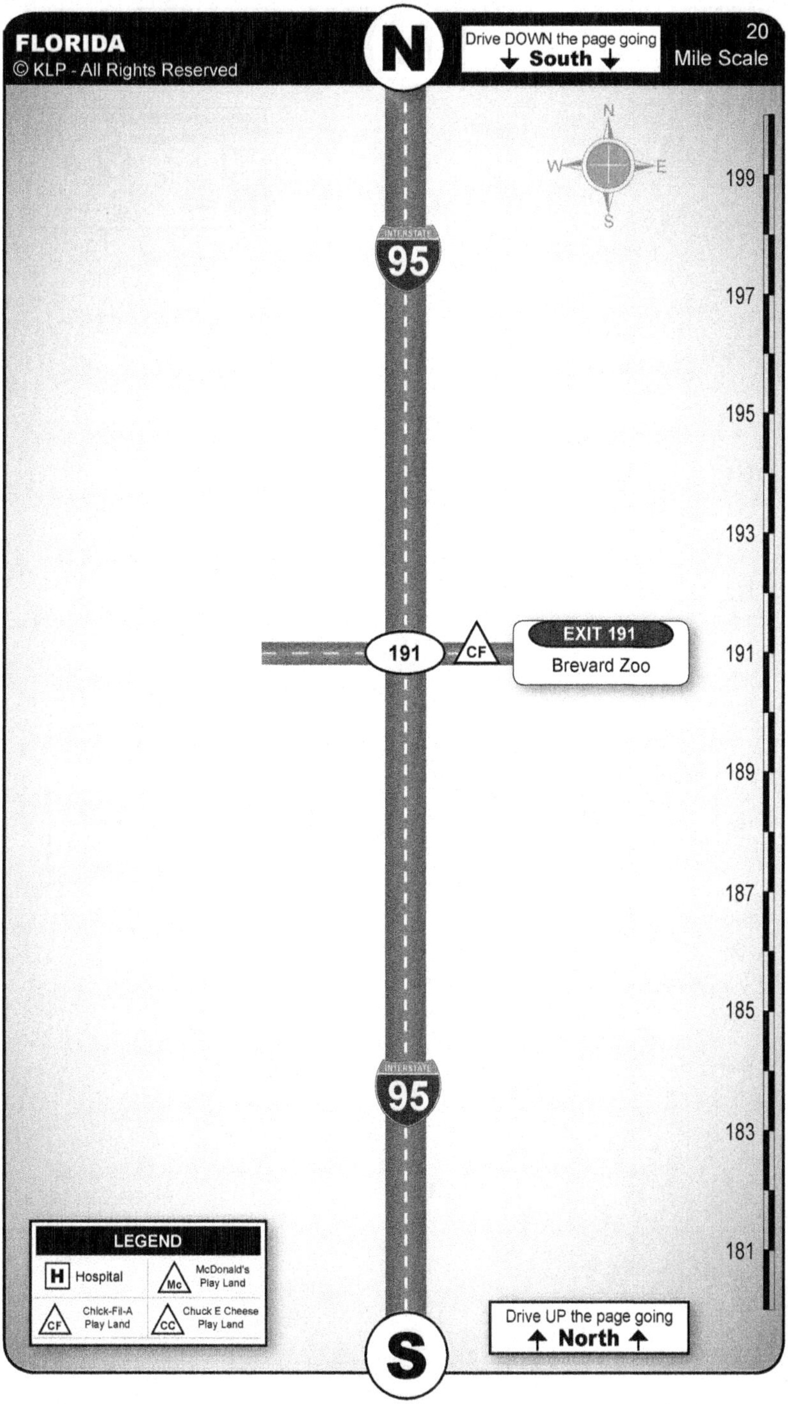

N

Drive DOWN the page going
↓ **South** ↓

20
Mile Scale

N
W ⊕ E
S

199

INTERSTATE
95

197

195

193

191 CF

EXIT 191
Brevard Zoo

191

189

187

185

INTERSTATE
95

183

LEGEND

| H | Hospital | Mc | McDonald's Play Land |
| CF | Chick-Fil-A Play Land | CC | Chuck E Cheese Play Land |

181

Drive UP the page going
↑ **North** ↑

S

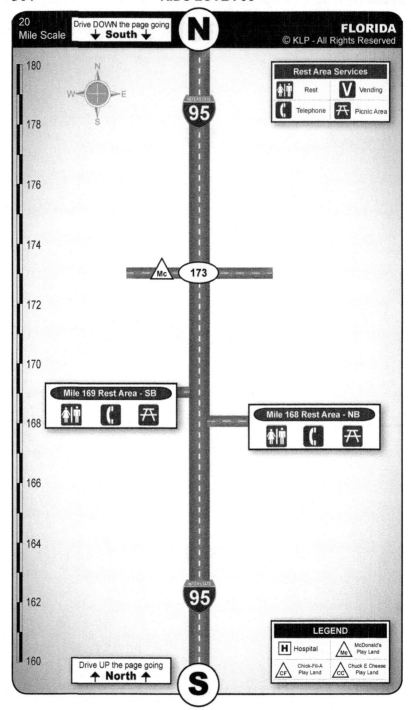

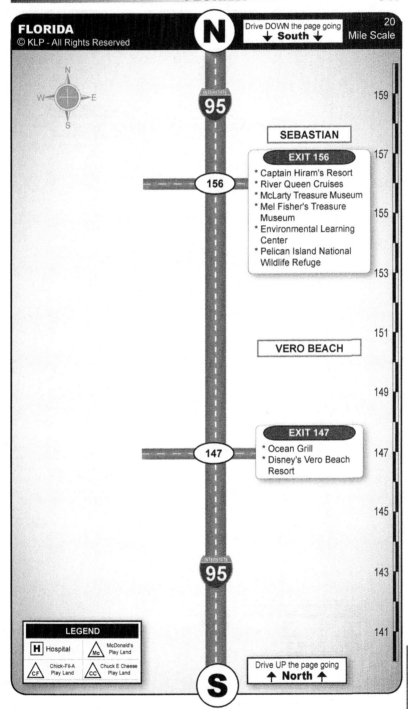

FLORIDA

Drive DOWN the page going
↓ **South** ↓

20
Mile Scale

SEBASTIAN

EXIT 156
* Captain Hiram's Resort
* River Queen Cruises
* McLarty Treasure Museum
* Mel Fisher's Treasure Museum
* Environmental Learning Center
* Pelican Island National Wildlife Refuge

VERO BEACH

EXIT 147
* Ocean Grill
* Disney's Vero Beach Resort

159
157
155
153
151
149
147
145
143
141

LEGEND
| H | Hospital | Mc | McDonald's Play Land |
| CF | Chick-Fil-A Play Land | CC | Chuck E Cheese Play Land |

Drive UP the page going
↑ **North** ↑

FLORIDA

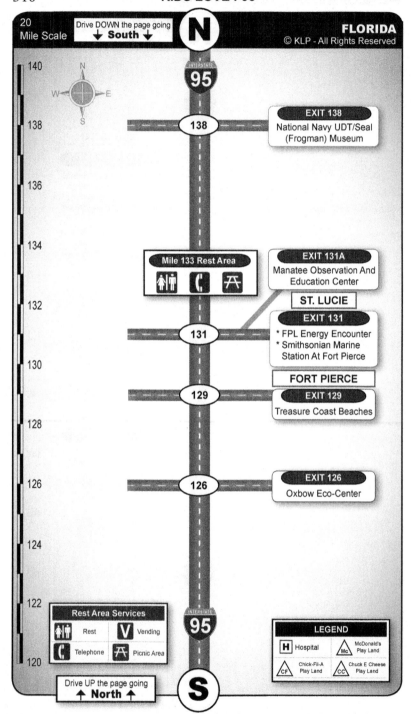

20 Mile Scale

Drive DOWN the page going
↓ **South** ↓

N

FLORIDA
© KLP - All Rights Reserved

INTERSTATE **95**

N W E S

140
138
136
134
132
130
128
126
124
122
120

138
EXIT 138
National Navy UDT/Seal
(Frogman) Museum

Mile 133 Rest Area

EXIT 131A
Manatee Observation And
Education Center

ST. LUCIE

131
EXIT 131
* FPL Energy Encounter
* Smithsonian Marine
  Station At Fort Pierce

FORT PIERCE

129
EXIT 129
Treasure Coast Beaches

126
EXIT 126
Oxbow Eco-Center

INTERSTATE **95**

Rest Area Services
- Rest
- **V** Vending
- Telephone
- Picnic Area

LEGEND
- **H** Hospital
- **Mc** McDonald's Play Land
- **CF** Chick-Fil-A Play Land
- **CC** Chuck E Cheese Play Land

Drive UP the page going
↑ **North** ↑

S

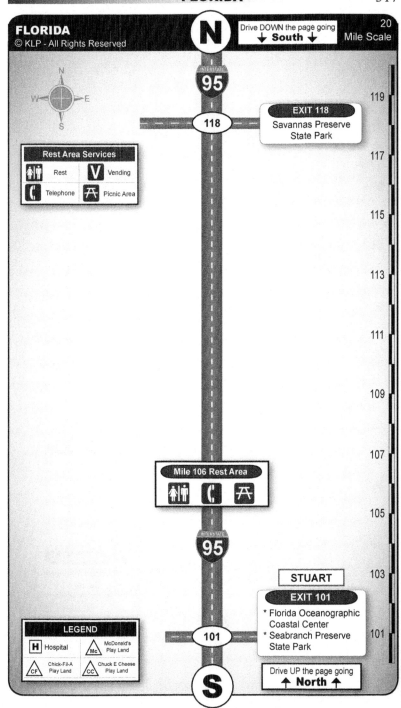

KIDS LOVE I-95

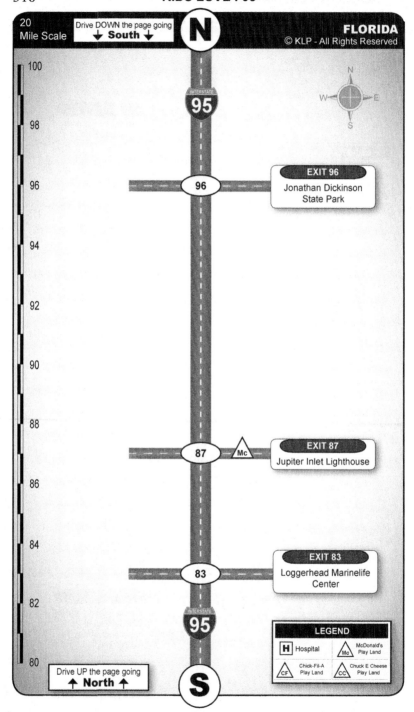

FLORIDA

20 Mile Scale

Drive DOWN the page going ↓ **South** ↓

N

INTERSTATE **95**

EXIT 96
Jonathan Dickinson State Park

EXIT 87
Jupiter Inlet Lighthouse

EXIT 83
Loggerhead Marinelife Center

INTERSTATE **95**

Drive UP the page going ↑ **North** ↑

S

LEGEND

| H | Hospital | Mc | McDonald's Play Land |
| CF | Chick-Fil-A Play Land | CC | Chuck E Cheese Play Land |

For updates & travel games visit: **www.KidsLoveTravel.com**

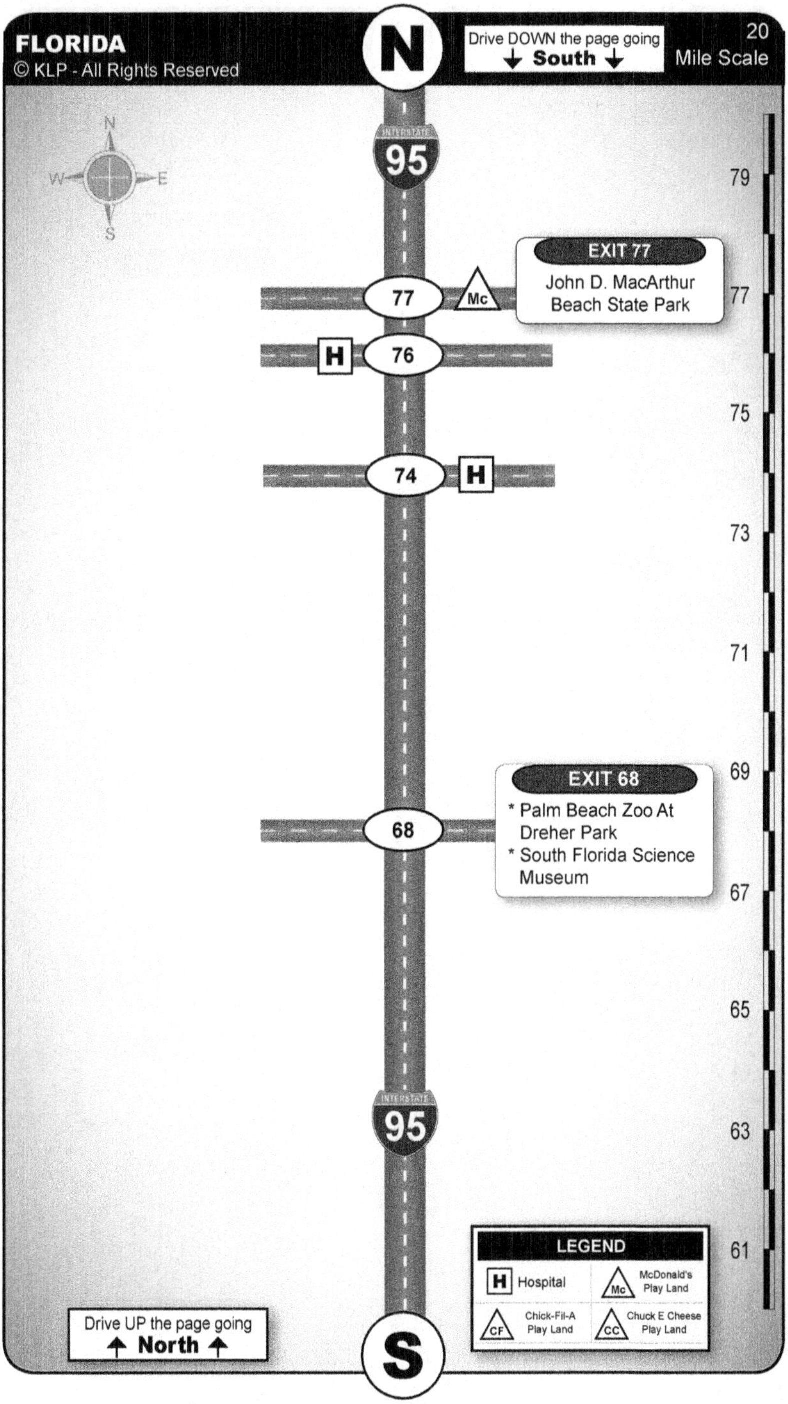

FLORIDA

N

Drive DOWN the page going
↓ **South** ↓

20 Mile Scale

INTERSTATE 95

79

EXIT 77
John D. MacArthur
Beach State Park

77 · Mc

77

H · 76

76

75

74 · **H**

73

71

69

EXIT 68
* Palm Beach Zoo At
  Dreher Park
* South Florida Science
  Museum

68

67

65

INTERSTATE 95

63

LEGEND	
H Hospital	Mc McDonald's Play Land
CF Chick-Fil-A Play Land	CC Chuck E Cheese Play Land

61

Drive UP the page going
↑ **North** ↑

S

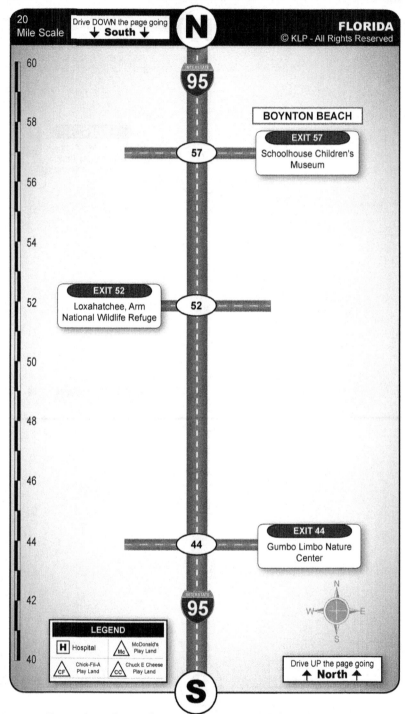

20 Mile Scale

Drive DOWN the page going
↓ **South** ↓

N

INTERSTATE 95

60

58

BOYNTON BEACH

EXIT 57
Schoolhouse Children's Museum

57

56

54

EXIT 52
Loxahatchee, Arm National Wildlife Refuge

52

50

48

46

EXIT 44
Gumbo Limbo Nature Center

44

42

INTERSTATE 95

LEGEND

| H | Hospital | Mc | McDonald's Play Land |
| CF | Chick-Fil-A Play Land | CC | Chuck E Cheese Play Land |

40

Drive UP the page going
↑ **North** ↑

S

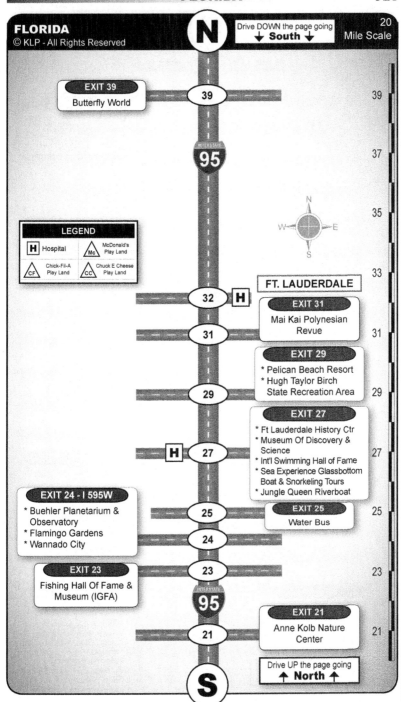

FLORIDA

N

Drive DOWN the page going
↓ **South** ↓

20 Mile Scale

EXIT 39
Butterfly World

39

INTERSTATE **95**

37

35

LEGEND

| **H** Hospital | **Mc** McDonald's Play Land |
| **CF** Chick-Fil-A Play Land | **CC** Chuck E Cheese Play Land |

33

FT. LAUDERDALE

H 32

EXIT 31
Mai Kai Polynesian Revue

31

31

EXIT 29
* Pelican Beach Resort
* Hugh Taylor Birch State Recreation Area

29

29

EXIT 27
* Ft Lauderdale History Ctr
* Museum Of Discovery & Science
* Int'l Swimming Hall of Fame
* Sea Experience Glassbottom Boat & Snorkeling Tours
* Jungle Queen Riverboat

H 27

27

EXIT 24 - I 595W
* Buehler Planetarium & Observatory
* Flamingo Gardens
* Wannado City

25

EXIT 25
Water Bus

25

24

EXIT 23
Fishing Hall Of Fame & Museum (IGFA)

23

INTERSTATE **95**

EXIT 21
Anne Kolb Nature Center

21

21

Drive UP the page going
↑ **North** ↑

S

FLORIDA

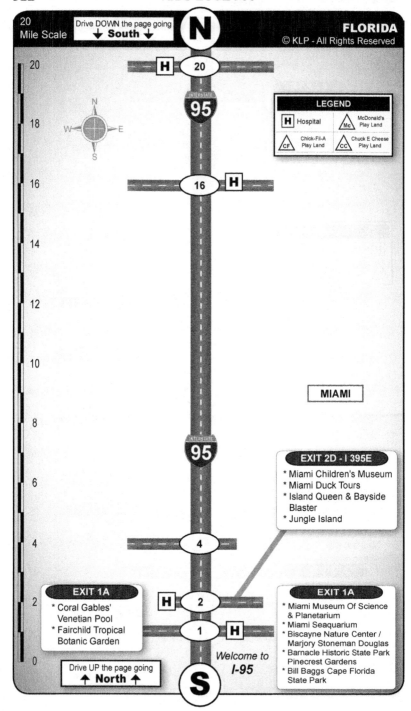

FLORIDA

20 Mile Scale

Drive DOWN the page going
↓ **South** ↓

N

H 20

INTERSTATE 95

LEGEND

H Hospital | Mc McDonald's Play Land
CF Chick-Fil-A Play Land | CC Chuck E Cheese Play Land

16 H

MIAMI

INTERSTATE 95

EXIT 2D - I 395E
* Miami Children's Museum
* Miami Duck Tours
* Island Queen & Bayside Blaster
* Jungle Island

4

EXIT 1A
* Coral Gables' Venetian Pool
* Fairchild Tropical Botanic Garden

H 2

H 1 H

EXIT 1A
* Miami Museum Of Science & Planetarium
* Miami Seaquarium
* Biscayne Nature Center / Marjory Stoneman Douglas
* Barnacle Historic State Park Pinecrest Gardens
* Bill Baggs Cape Florida State Park

Welcome to **I-95**

Drive UP the page going
↑ **North** ↑

S

For updates & travel games visit: **www.KidsLoveTravel.com**

Sites and attractions are listed in order by Exit Number (North to South) and distance from the exit (closest are listed first). Symbols indicated represent:

 Restaurants   Lodging

Exit - 379 (west of I-95) SB Only

FLORIDA WELCOME CENTER

Yulee - *(shortly after exit 380, off to right side of road-southbound only) .*

Since 1949, millions of auto travelers entering Florida along the major thoroughfares have found a warm greeting at the Official Florida Welcome Centers. In addition to the traditional cup of complimentary Florida citrus juice, these visitors have found friendly, informative staff people and a vast assortment of brochures promoting all that the state has to offer.

Each center is staffed by personnel who have undergone rigorous training to receive national Information Specialist certification. Along with in-person information, Welcome Center visitors learn about the state's diverse destinations. Each highway Welcome Center has a designated area for visitors traveling with children. The VISIT FLORIDA Kid's Corner offers a "play" area to educate and entertain the children while the parents get the travel information they need from the Welcome Center staff. The Official Florida Welcome Centers also provide Official Florida Transportation Maps to all visitors. In addition, the Welcome Centers offer clean, well maintained rest room facilities and all are handicapped accessible. Vending machines and pay phones are on-site. Designated areas in each parking lot accommodate large bus, RV and truck parking.

Exit - 362 (east of I-95)

FORT CAROLINE NATIONAL MONUMENT

Jacksonville - *12713 Fort Caroline Road (exit at Florida Route 9A (Exit #362). Route 9A crosses the St. Johns River. Exit at Monument Road, follow the brown signs to the left, and travel to Fort Caroline Rd) 32099. Phone: (904) 641-7155. www.nps.gov/foca/index.htm. Hours: Daily except Christmas 9:00am-5:00pm. Admission: FREE. Educators: wonderful array of pre-and-post activities on the For Teachers/Curriculum Materials page of website.*

Fort Caroline on the banks of the St. Johns River was settled by the French Huguenots in 1564 and is the site of the first Protestant colony in the New World. The 130-acre memorial is located in East Arlington off Fort Caroline Road. It features a replica of the original fort, a museum with French and Indian artifacts and several nature trails which provide excellent hiking. The nearby Roosevelt Area has additional nature trails.

Exit - 358 (east of I-95)

JACKSONVILLE ZOO AND GARDENS

Jacksonville - 8605 Zoo Parkway (Take exit number 358 to Zoo Parkway/ Heckscher Drive East) 32218. Phone: (904) 757-4463. www.jaxzoo.org. Hours: Daily 9:00am-5:00pm. Extended until 6:00pm on weekends and holidays. Admission: $15.95 adult, $13.95 senior (65+), $10.95 child (3-12). Parking FREE. FREEBIES: online games/activities on Jazoos Kids Zone.

Escape to the Jacksonville Zoo and Gardens for the only walking safari in Northeast Florida. Each year, it seems, they're targeted to add something new. Check in at the Main Camp, then it's off to the Bird Aviary (free flight enclosure) and the Plains of East Africa. In the Aviary, we noticed the birds of flight really enjoy winging right over your head! Loved the spoonbills and the funky looking Harpy Eagle (1/2 owl, 1/2 eagle)? Walk along the 1,400 foot boardwalk overlooking the Plains and see the native animals like: Nile Crocodile, the warthog, gazelle, cheetah, the white rhino, or the zebra along the walk. Lions, monkeys and leopard reside here, too. Take a close-up look at Great Apes then back to Wild Florida natives like black bears, otters, bobcats, alligators, and Florida panthers. The alligators are located near the Reptile House and are fed every Saturday at 2:00pm during the warm weather (do we really need to see this?) The Australian Adventure attraction includes beloved kangaroos, wallabies and the koalas. A highlight of this attraction is the lorikeets that can be fed by visitors. Range of the Jaguar focuses on a neotropical rain forest setting and, of course, highlights jaguar. Find out how one jaguar learned to swim. Can you find the black jaguar's spots? Stingray Bay is the place where you can pet and feed stingrays (for a small fee).

Mr. Giraffe asks for food...

The Giraffe Overlook was designed to allow guests to get eye to eye with the tall giraffes. The kids actually got to feed a live giraffe ($2.00 fee) at the overlook area! Finally, kids wild to play? Try the Wildlife Carousel or the Kids Play Park. Climb, jump, and get wet in the Splash Ground and Plaza. Find your way through two mazes and discover and create in the Discovery Bldg. In Forest Play, climb like a squirrel or nest like an eagle. Crawl like a spider or swing like a monkey. Brush AND pet pygmy goats in the Animal Care area or enjoy snacks in the Play Park Cafe. Several cafe areas actually overlook animals roaming their habitats.

Exit - 353B (east of I-95)

TREE HILL NATURE CENTER

Jacksonville - *7152 Lone Star Road (take US 90 east to University Blvd exit north. Right on Lone Star for few blocks) 32211. www.treehill.org. Phone: (904) 724-4646. Hours: Monday-Saturday 8:00am-4:30pm. Admission: $2.00-$4.00 per person (students and above).*

Tree Hill, Jacksonville's Nature Center, is comprised of 53 acres of urban wilderness. Tree Hill's exhibits on energy, natural history and native wildlife species are all located in the pyramid museum. An interactive exhibit on solar energy teaches visitors about electricity and energy conservation. Photovoltaic panels on the buildings exterior convert sunlight to electricity and power the displays. Dioramas depicting life 12,000 years ago in Florida are accompanied by fossils and replicas of ancient animal life. Do Bears Live in Florida? Yes! Florida is home to the Florida Black Bear, which is a subspecies of the American Black Bear. Outside, roam the acres of trails using a self-guided map from the center.

Exit - 351 (west of I-95)

CUMMER MUSEUM OF ART

Jacksonville - *829 Riverside Ave. (head south on US 17 to north bank of the St. Johns River) 32204. Phone: (904) 356-6857. www.cummer.org. Hours: Tuesday-Saturday 10:00am-4:00pm, Sunday Noon-5:00pm. Open some evenings until 9:00pm. Admission: $10.00 adult, $6.00 senior and child (ages 6+). Admission is FREE on Tuesday nights. Educators: a wonderful way to mix art and Florida history is done online under the Education/For Kids link.*

The Cummer is the largest fine art museum in Northeast Florida. Noted for Old Master and American paintings, beautiful formal gardens and renowned collection of Meissen porcelain. National award-winning art education center enhances the cultural experience of more than 150,000 visitors annually. The newly renovated Art Connections contains hands-on, interactive exhibits designed to raise visitors' understanding of the art in the museum's permanent collection. There are exhibits that are high tech and low tech, exhibits that allow for individual exploration and group interaction, and exhibits that encourage physical activity and quiet contemplation. In Art Connections, it is possible to walk through a painting, create patterns through dance, make a collage, listen to a sculpture, or paint with a virtual paintbrush.

Exit - 350B (west of I-95)

PETERBROOKE CHOCOLATIER PRODUCTION CENTER

Jacksonville - *1470 San Marco Blvd (right on Hendricks, left on Cedar, on-street parking on San Marco) 32207. Phone: (904) 398-2489. www.peterbrooke.*

Chocolate covered potato chips?

com. Hours: Monday-Friday 10:00am-5:00pm. Store open weekends and weekday evenings also.

Just over the bridge, follow your nose to a chocolate factory. You can literally smell the chocolate in the air as you approach and park. Peterbrooke has been a fixture in NE Florida since 1983. Its visionary, Phyllis Geiger, named her business after her children Peter and Brooke. Pre-arrange a short group tour (takes about 20 minutes with a video and live demo of chocolate tempering and dipping). Or, anytime they're open, you can watch the ladies through the viewing windows as they coat or drench yummy Oreos, Graham Crackers, Lays Potato Chips or Popcorn - all great by themselves, but better in Chocolate! Be sure to try a sample of their signature item, chocolate-covered popcorn - it will clinch you wanting to buy some to take home.

Did You Know...

Chocolate contains the highest concentration of phenylethylamine (in any food) which is the brain chemical produced when a person is in love!

Exit - 350 (west of I-95)

MUSEUM OF SCIENCE & HISTORY (MOSH)

Jacksonville - 1025 Museum Circle (I-95 Main Street Bridge exit north one block, left on Museum Circle) 32207. Phone: (904) 396-MOSH. www.themosh.org. Hours: Monday-Friday 10:00am-5:00pm, Saturday until 6:00pm, Sunday Noon-5:00pm. Admission: $10.00 adult, $8.00 senior and active military, $6.00 child (3-12).

Don't you love the life-size Right Whale that greats you in the beautiful Atlantic Tails room? Because it's life-size (giant), it's a little intimidating. Dolphins and Manatees are displayed here, too, as you interact with this hands-on exhibit space. In other spaces, kids (and their adults) can find out how much water they use or how much water content is <u>in</u> their body. Next, maybe launch a hot air balloon, test your skills on the gravity table, send a rocket soaring, or make loud music. Check the list of Planetarium and Science Theater shows for cosmic, electrifying and explosive science demonstrations (extra fee). Like live animals? They have plenty, indoors and out. Visit live snakes, birds, spiders, alligators, frogs, lizards and turtles (such cuties) native to Northeast Florida. Tonca, the 120-pound

That's "music" to my ears ...

alligator snapping turtle has a new, improved exhibit house. A scary, intriguing creature. MOSH's oldest resident, the dino Allosaurus skeleton, is here and more history is in Currents of Time: A History of Jacksonville and NE Florida. Journey through 12,000 years of regional history as this exhibit brings colonization, war time, the Great Fire and the 50s.

MUSEUM OF CONTEMPORARY ART (MOCA)

Jacksonville - 333 N. Laura Street (follow US 1 to historic Hemming Plaza next to City Hall) 32202. Phone: (904) 366-6911. www.mocajacksonville.org. Hours: Tuesday-Saturday 11:00am-5:00pm, Sunday Noon-5:00pm. Open until 9:00pm on Thursdays. Admission: $5.00-$8.00 (student plus). Wednesday evenings are FREE for Artwalk.

JMOMA is the largest modern & contemporary art museum in the Southeast. Film series and lectures are offered in the 125-seat theater. Family fun in the fifth floor ArtExplorium Loft. Café Nola is open for lunch, weekdays. Jacksonville Museum of Modern Art's ArtExplorium Loft is a family learning center that offers an alternative to the traditionally hands-off approach of museum visits. The Loft offers hands-on activities inspired by the Museum's collection. This vibrant and colorful space features 16 stimulating learning stations where children and adults alike can learn more about modern and contemporary art.

Exit - 348 (east of I-95)

ADVENTURE LANDING

Jacksonville Beach - *1944 Beach Blvd (U.S. 90) (On Beach Boulevard just east of the Intracoastal Waterway) 32250. www.adventurelanding.com/jaxbeach/. Phone: (904) 246-4386. Hours: Run seasonally so check web for current season. Admission: Waterpark runs $23.00-$28.00 or nitesplash (take about $10 off). Dry play is $7.00-$10.00 per play or a Quest Pass for $16.99. Waterpark passes run around $28.00. Go online for Daily Specials & Military Special.*

The park includes a water park with slides and a riverway, a go-kart track, miniature golf, laser tag arena batting cage and an arcade with a wide variety of games. We choose to go a little each day - doing the waterpark thing during the hottest part of the day. They have a bowl and half pipe and very long-g-g water slides for the tweens and teens plus a special kiddie area and another Shipwreck Island slide and waterplay area for kids. A wavepool, lazy river and plenty of lifeguards gave this a "thumbs up" from the kids and parents who want a small "adventure" waterpark that is clean and manageable. Dry off at their wide offering of "land" activities such as: go-karts, amusement rides, laser tag, miniature golf and batting cages. Every area was so clean.

JACKSONVILLE BEACH

Jacksonville Beach - *Eleven North Third Street (US 90 east about 10 miles to waterfront signs) 32250. Phone: (904) 247-6268. www.jacksonvillebeach.org.*

Discover northeast Florida's best-kept secret, Jacksonville Beach. Tucked away on a barrier island east of Jacksonville on Florida's famous A1A, you'll find miles of uncrowded white sandy beaches. With the Intracoastal Waterway, St. Johns River and the Atlantic Ocean to choose from Jacksonville Beach offers lots of opportunities whether you are a fisherman, a golfer, or a family looking for good clean fun. Play in the ocean, walk or collect seashells along the beach, or stroll along the Sea Walk and watch for porpoise year-round or the northern right-whales that winter off the coast. At the Sea Walk Pavilion, you'll find concerts or festivals nearly every weekend from April through October. In May and June, the SeaWalk area shows classic films on the giant screen (Moonlight Movies - free). The best part - park you vehicle and walk the well-maintained beachfront and splash and play in the water. Our experience was a less crowded, family setting. Occasional foot showers and restrooms available. The small boardwalk area (SeaWalk) is the best place to brush off the sand and grab a bite to eat or do some light shopping.

JACKSONVILLE BEACHFRONT HOTEL

Jacksonville Beach - *11 North 1st Street (Rte. 202 east all the way to A1A, head north a little ways) 32250. www.qualitysuitesjacksonvillebeach.com. Phone: (904) 435-3535.*

A GREAT place for building sandcastles...

Stay at the beach at the very family-friendly, right on the waterfront / boardwalk, lodging of the Quality Suites Oceanfront, an all-suites hotel featuring southern Mediterranean hospitality in a tropical resort setting. Every suite has a bedroom, bathroom and living space with a sofa bed. Better yet, they have a micro/frig and sink kitchenette in between so you can prepare a simple entree or reheat leftovers. The rooms were spacious and clean and after a day on the sand and water, retreat to a light snacks and sodas reception around dinnertime or a dip in the outdoor pool and hot tub. As a guest of Quality Suites Oceanfront in Jacksonville Beach, you'll have a complimentary hot buffet breakfast each morning in the breakfast room. Help yourself to delicious hot and cold items, including bacon, eggs, sausage, biscuits, and a wide selection of beverages, fruit, and pastries. Weekday rates about half of normal $200.00 plus weekend rates.

Exit - 323 (west of I-95)

WORLD GOLF HALL OF FAME & IMAX THEATER

St. Augustine - *1 World Golf Place, World Golf Village (I-95 exit 323) 32092. Phone: (904) 940-4123 or (800) WGVGOLF. www.wgv.com. Hours: Monday-Saturday 10:00am-6:00pm. Sunday Noon-6:00pm. Admission: $19.50 adult, $18.50 senior (55+), $10.00 student, military, $5.00 child (5-12). Your ticket includes all-day admission to the museum and its special exhibits, and a round on the 18-hole natural grass putting course. Tours: Hear stories directly from Hall of Fame members when you add an Audio Tour to your admission. Audio Tours may be purchased at the box office: $3.00/person or two for $5.00. IMAX $5.00 extra.*

The World Golf Hall of Fame presents golf's story in more than 70 separate exhibits that combine historic artifacts with the latest in golf interactive technology. Historical and interactive exhibits enable visitors to experience some of golf's most exciting moments and players. The adjacent IMAX Theater is a larger-than-life adventure where the visitor becomes part of the experience. Great stop if your family really LOVES following/playing golf.

Exit - 318 (east of I-95)

OLD TOWN TROLLEY TOURS OF ST. AUGUSTINE

St. Augustine - *167 San Marco Avenue (I-95 to SR 16, left on US 1, left at Ford Dealership) 32084. Phone: (904) 829-3800 or (800) 868-7482. www.trolleytours.com. Hours: Daily 8:30am-5:00pm. Admission: $25.00 adult, $10.00 child (6-12). Free parking. Save a little if you buy online.*

The tours provide historically accurate information accented by anecdotes and tales of the colorful parts of the city's history. Historical characters of the past whose legacy endures include Ponce de Leon and his Fountain of Youth, and renowned Spanish explorer Pedro Menendez de Aviles, who founded the city more than 435 years ago. Did

Step back in time on St. George Street

you know this town is the oldest, continuously occupied European settlement in the continental United States? Notice several different architectural stylings ranging from simple tabby cottages along brick lanes to more modern structures capped by towers, turrets and red clay roofs. St. Augustine is home to some of the oldest original structures and sites in the U.S., including The Oldest House (1704), The Oldest Wooden Schoolhouse (1804), the Oldest Store Museum (1840) and the Old Jail (1891). The tour covers over 100 sights of interest and has 19 stops where you can hop on or off to sightsee, shop or dine. The tour includes a three-day pass onboard the trolley, free tickets to the St. Augustine History Museum, and a free pass on the St. Augustine Beach Bus. Look for the green and orange trolleys at the Old Jail complex to start at stop one. This is, by far, the best way to learn about the town and not have to find parking (difficult in small historic streets). Go around the tour once, completely, to determine what you want to get off and see on the next round. The trolleys pick up at each stop every 15 minutes so it's easy on and off. Our favorite stops were the Old Jail and St. George Street. Looking for something different for lunch? Try the Columbia Restaurant on St. George for authentically prepared Cuban food.

OLD JAIL

St. Augustine - *167 San Marco Avenue (US 1 just one mile north of the Old Fort and Historic District) 32084. Phone: (904) 829-3800. www.trustedtours.*

com/store/St-Augustine-Old-Jail-C209.aspx. Hours: Daily 8:30am to 4:30pm. Closed Easter, Thanksgiving, Christmas. Admission: $9.50 adult, $5.50 child (ages 6-12).

"You're Goin to Jail" cries the jail keeper. Experience a first person tour as the sheriff and his staff incarcerate your group tour. Completed in 1891, the jail housed prisoners for over 60 years. It is one of the few surviving 19th century jails. Explore the sheriff's quarters where he and his wife lived adjacent to 72 prisoners. The guest "prisoners" are led by costumed wardens from room to room. Do you know where the name "jailbirds" comes from? Try being one in the giant bird cage cell outside. Lady inmates worked all day in the kitchen while

Learn why prisoners were called, "Jailbirds"

men have to work the chain gang. You can almost set your watch by the morning jailbreak at the Old Jail. Seasonally and most weekend mornings, a 1908-era inmate (in their black-white striped attire) tries to flee aboard a trolley filled with passengers. The fact that the escape ends with being re-captured by the sheriff and his deputies doesn't seem to dim the prisoners' enthusiasm for their rollicking run through the parking lot. Try to catch this. Our kids loved this site - especially the actor guides - who, at some points, were so believable, I think the kids really feel like they might have to do some hard time. It's light enough, mixed with humor, that it shouldn't scare kids, though. Before you leave, visit the gift shop and purchase some fun re-enacting clothes and hats to use for dress-up when you get home.

Exit - 318 (east of I-95)

OLD FLORIDA MUSEUM @ FORT MENENDEZ

St. Augustine - *259 San Marco Avenue (I-95 exit 318, go 7 miles, just one block past US 1) 32084. www.oldfloridamuseum.com. Phone: (904) 824-8874 or (800) 813-3208. Hours: Daily 10:00am-4:00pm. Admission: $8.00-$11.00 (age 4+).*

St. Augustine's only hands-on history museum. Games, weapons, foods and tools convey how life changed and how it has remained somewhat the same from Indian to pioneer times. Guests actually get to try their hand at daily chores such as corn grinding, tabby making, or quill pen writing. Everyone can actually touch a silver bar from Spanish treasure. Kids like earning gold, buying and trading items and parents try to wager with villagers.

HOWARD JOHNSON INN - HISTORIC ST. AUGUSTINE

St. Augustine - *137 San Marco Avenue (I-95 exit 318, SR 16 east 5 miles, then right on San Marco for one mile) 32084. www.staugustinehojo.com. Phone: (904) 824-4641.*

The Howard Johnson Express Inn is located in the heart of St. Augustine's beautiful downtown Historic District, directly in front of the world-renowned Ponce De Leons Fountain of Youth. It is the only hotel included on the route of the Old Town Trolleys and the St. Augustine Sightseeing Trains as they cruise through the grounds to view the magnificent Old Senator, a 600 year old Live Oak Tree, which stands as a silent witness to Don Juan Ponce De Leons discovery and naming of the continent La Florida in 1513. Free Continental Breakfast daily and Outdoor Pool with heated Jacuzzi. Each room includes a micro/frig and the average room rate starts at around $65.00 (non-peak). For a little more, you can rent a family suite with a private bedroom (start at $120.00). The hotel is directly in front of the Fountain of Youth and you never know, they may have secretly tapped into the Fountain's water supply. So, when you take your shower or bath - you might lose 10 years - wishful thinking!

FOUNTAIN OF YOUTH, PONCE DE LEON'S

St. Augustine - *11 Magnolia Avenue (follow signs into downtown, right behind the Ho-Jo Hotel or the Old Jail) 32084. Phone: (904) 829-3168 or (800) 356-8222. www.fountainofyouthflorida.com. Hours: Daily 9:00am-5:00pm. Closed Christmas Day. Admission: $12.00 adult, $11.00 senior, $8.00 child (6-12). Online discounts*

Ponce de Leon's Fountain of Youth National Archaeological Park exhibits foundations and artifacts of the first St. Augustine mission and colony. This is the REAL legendary eternal spring! And, at the end of your tour, you are provided the opportunity to sip from the Fountain of Youth! Kids generally can't handle the odor (slight sulfur smell) of the mineralized water but adults drink it up quick (I wonder

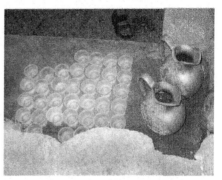

Fountain of Youth samples...try it!

why?). In the Spring Room, you'll also learn about the authentic stone cross found during excavation of the site. Ponce deLeon's personal journey papers were found here - documenting his journey and findings. Other areas include the Explorers Globe and the Navigators' Planetarium. Here, you can visualize the Age of Exploration and discover the clever ways navigators used the stars to find their way to new lands. Outdoors, visitors can go through Christian Indian burial grounds and see the Smithsonian site documented as the first original colony. They have several exhibits with moving, life-sized dioramas depicting the Indian Town and the Historic Landing of Ponce de Leon's fleet and meeting the giant Timucuan Indians. Once you see the life-size Indian chief statue, you'll understand why short Spaniards felt the native's secret was in the water! Really interesting place - a must see in town.

Exit - 318 (east of I-95)

BARNACLE BILL'S

St. Augustine - *14 Castillo Drive (downtown, north of Old City 'town") 32084. Phone: (904) 824-3663. www.barnaclebillsonline.com.*

Restaurant favorites include: Homemade Onion Rings, Fried Shrimp, Clam Chowder, Matanzas Shrimp, Shrimp Menendez Salad, and Banana Delight for dessert (like a banana split pie). Dat'l Do-It is the spicy variation. They have their own sauces that you can purchase if you get hooked. The Kids Menu is mostly seafood (fried) and a burger or chicken fingers (average $7.50 includes 2 veggies). We think their appetizers and combos offer the best variety and average about $12.00 for dinner entrees with all the fixins. Ask them to prepare their fish Matanzas style - so good! We loved the Datil pepper sauce they've concocted, too - sweet hot pepper sauce - actually, all of their sauces and service staff are excellent. Lunch and Dinner daily. Another location is on A1A Beachside.

RIPLEY'S BELIEVE IT OR NOT! MUSEUM

St. Augustine - *19 San Marco Avenue (I-95 exit 318/SR 16, travel east for 5 miles to US 1, turn south one mile to Castillo Drive east) 32084. www.staugustine-ripleys.com. Phone: (904) 824-1606. Hours: Daily 9:00am-7:00pm (Friday & Saturday until 8:00pm). Admission: $12.99 adult, $6.99 child (5-12). Online coupons.*

Explore over 800 exhibits of crazy, unique and very strange oddities. The site is Castle Warden, an Historic Moorish Revival style mansion filled with fun mind benders and exciting action and creepy sounds. Look for a family favorite - the giant erector set (almost three stories) ferris wheel. Every Ripley's is as bizarre as the next…this one happens to be the original. Parking is available but it's very easily accessible by trolley or train tour, too (it's one of their stops).

A scale Ferris Wheel made from an erector set…<u>nearly 3 stories tall</u>

RIPLEY'S SIGHTSEEING TRAINS

St. Augustine - 170 San Marco Avenue (Old Sugar Mill) 32084. Phone: (904) 829-6545. www.sightseeingtrains.com. Hours: Open daily 8:30am-5:00pm. Admission: $20.99 adult, $8.99 child (6-12).

A good way to explore historic St Augustine. The scenic 7-mile tour stops at several of the city's most popular attractions, historic sites, restaurants and shops. The entire tour takes approximately one hour - but you may step on and off the train at any of the 20 stops - and your ticket is good for 3 consecutive days of travel. The trolley and the train stop at nearly the same spots. The first wax museum founded in the U.S. has received acclaim for its authenticity and unique costuming. Holding more than 160 life-size figures, .

HARRY'S SEAFOOD BAR & GRILLE

St. Augustine - 46 Avenida Menendez (head into old city, just off San Marco Ave., on right before St. George St) 32084. www.HookedOnHarrys.com. Phone: (904) 824-7765.

Enjoy seafood, steaks, pasta and authentic New Orleans dishes indoors or out on the multi-level courtyard across from St. Augustine's bayfront. Specialties include New Orleans-style shrimp, shrimp etouffee and pasta chicken Louisianne. Anything with Harry's in the name is super flavorful and the portions (even appetizers) are large. The Kids Menu has puzzles and the varied entrees run around $5.00 and include fries and a souvenir cup soda. Nightly courtyard entertainment. Great Key Lime pie, too. Lunch ~$12.00, Dinner ~$19.00 average.

CASTILLO DE SAN MARCOS, THE OLD FORT

St. Augustine - One S. Castillo Drive (I-95 exit Rte. 16 downtown to US 1, turn right for 2 miles, left on Castillo) 32084. Phone: (904) 829-6506. www.nps.gov/casa. Hours: 8:45am-5:15pm every day of the year except December 25. (The ticket booth closes at 4:45pm). Admission: $7.00 Adults, age 16 and above (7 day pass). Educators: click on For Teachers for activities.

This national monument reflects the prevalent

Spanish heritage and the impenetrable fort is the nation's oldest masonry fortress with Spanish soldier re-enactors firing cannons. Here lies a history of the forces and events which have shaped world history. Be sure to listen in on a costumed soldier's tales and climb the stairs to the roof for great photo ops and

> Burning rapidly when ignited, gun powder expands 600 times its volume creating pressures that can hurl a cannonball up to 3.5 miles!

views. Did you know they recently discovered a secret room in the fort? It's open to crawl into, if you dare. . .

ST. AUGUSTINE PIRATE & TREASURE MUSEUM

St. Augustine - *12 S Castillo Drive (across the street from Old Fort) 32084. Phone: (877) GO PLUNDER. www.thepiratemuseum.com. Hours: Daily 10am-8pm. Admission: $12.99 adult, $6.99 child.*

America's oldest city proves the ideal site for a pirate museum. Numerous treasure fleets actually tucked into its harbor for provisions and crew rest and relaxation before making the perilous run across the Atlantic. Privateer Sir Francis Drake (in 1586) and brigand Robert Searles (in 1668) burned St. Augustine to the ground in their quests for booty, slaves, food, water and anything else that took their fancy. Offering exciting adventures in nine themed areas, it actually houses one of only two Jolly Roger flags in existence, not to mention the only authentic treasure chest in the world; the original journal of Captain Kidd's last voyage; and rare pirate-wanted poster offering a huge sum for the capture of the famous pirates. It's in the Rogues Tavern section of the museum visitors learn about salmagundi - the ingredients in the jaw-dropping kitchen-sink "hodgepodge" concoction of turtle, fish, chicken, pig, cow, pigeon, spiced wine, herbs, palm hearts, garlic, oil, hard-boiled eggs, the odd parrot who knows? ARG...YUK!

Exit - 318 (east of I-95)

POTTER'S WAX MUSEUM

St. Augustine - *17 King Street (just west of the Bridge of Lions) 32084. Phone: (904) 829-9056. www.potterswax.com. Hours: Sunday-Thursday 9am-5pm, Friday-Saturday 9am-9pm. Admission: $7-$10.00 (ages 6+).*

Holding more than 160 life-size figures, view characters from historical, political, royal and motion picture fame. From Beethoven to Sylvester Stallone's "Rambo". You'll catch some poets, composers, authors, artists, explorers, and religious leaders, too. See the world's only working wax studio on display to the public. There are some horror scenes and the characters are more adult-friendly movie and TV stars.

OLDEST WOODEN SCHOOL HOUSE IN THE UNITED STATES

St. Augustine - 14 St. George Street (follow signs into old city, across from Old Fort) 32084. www.oldestwoodenschoolhouse.com. Phone: (904) 824-0192 or (888) 653-7245. Hours: Daily 9:00am-5:00pm. Admission: $2.00-$3.00 (age 6+).

Let your first lesson in history start here. This "1st" school is over 200 years old and made of red cedar and cypress. Sit with the animated schoolmaster and the pupils as they show you what school life was like in the 1700s. Why the dunce cap? Compare your school days with those of the old days. If you pay attention, you can get a diploma as a souvenir of your visit. This is a really cute site and worth a quick visit.

DOW MUSEUM OF HISTORIC HOMES

St. Augustine - 149 Cordova Street (207 into town. south of the plaza, enter on Cordova St. near Bridge St. one block south of King St) 32084. Phone: (904) 823-9722. www.trolleytours.com/st-augustine/old-village.asp. Hours: Monday-Saturday 10:00am-4:30pm, Sunday 11:00am-4:30pm. Admission: $5.00-$7.00 (age 6+).

On just one city block, discover over 400 years of history hidden amongst courtyards of historic houses original to the site. Inside these homes, you'll find exhibits reflecting the town's history. We liked the variety of time periods from Spanish Colonial to American Territorial to a Prince's home and, our favorite, "the crooked house" - the red, leaning Carpenter House. There are no interpreters so this may be boring to children who do not like to read many placards.

OLDEST HOUSE MUSEUM COMPLEX

St. Augustine - 14 St. Francis Street (US 1 to King Street East, right on Avenida Menendez, right on St. Francis) 32084. Phone: (904) 824-2872. www. staugustinehistoricalsociety.org/oldhouse.html. Hours: Daily 9:00am-5:00pm. Admission: $8.00 adult, $7.00 senior, $4.00 child (6+), $18.00 family. Educators: go online under Teachers Resources for time lines and vocabulary materials you can use in the classroom: www.flahum.org/colonial.

The Oldest House Museum Complex features the Gonzalez-Alvarez House, Florida's oldest Spanish Colonial dwelling and the Manucy Museum, and the Museum of Florida's Military. This block was a haven for sea captains, writers, rebels, tourists and travelers. Learn about Seminoles and statehood, food and fashion, bathing and bed bugs. Trace more than 400 years of the city's history, soldiers, gardens and a museum store. Guided tours are every half hour.

FORT MOSE

St. Augustine - Saratoga Blvd. (SR 16 east to US 1. Follow sign for Fort Mose) 32084. Phone: (904) 461-2033. www.floridastateparks.org/fortmose/. Hours: Daily 8:00am-sunset. Visitor Center is open Thursday-Monday from 9:00am-5:00pm. Admission: $2.00 per person museum fee.

The new Fort Mose Visitor Center is a visual, highly interactive introduction to the outdoor original site. The boardwalk provides a fantastic view into a tidal salt marsh and ends at a benched platform with expansive views of the original Fort Mose sites, a bird rookery, and miles of salt marsh. In 1738, the Spanish governor of Florida chartered Fort Mose as a settlement for freed Africans who had fled slavery in the British Carolinas. When Spain ceded Florida to Britain in 1763, the inhabitants of Fort Mose migrated to Cuba. As the first free African American settlement in what is now the United States, Fort Mose represents a story of courage, determination, and perseverance. The stories of Africans fleeing to freedom and of Native American Indians who aided them, as well as tales of the many other people touched by Fort Mose tend to inspire folks.

Exit - 311 (east of I-95)

WHETSTONE CHOCOLATES FACTORY TOUR

St. Augustine - 139 King Street (Business US 1) 32084. Phone: (904) 217-0275. www.whetstonechocolates.com. Admission: $8.00 adult, $5.50 child (5-17). Tours: daily, best by reservation. Includes four tasting stations.

Enjoy the introductory 15-minute video, then walk through the factory to watch chocolates being made. Kids get to activate a robot and see 500-pounds of melting chocolate. Visit the gift shop at the end of the tour.

SCHOONER FREEDOM

St. Augustine - *111 Avenida Menendez (departs from City Marina, next to Bridge of Lions) 32085. Phone: (904) 810-1010. www.schoonerfreedom.com. Admission: $35.00 adult, $25.00 child (2-15). Sunset sail is $10.00 more. Pirate tours even more. Tours: Day, evening and ghost/pirate cruises. Family Sails are cheaper. Most tours are two hours. Most tours include grog (drinks or soda or water).*

Sailing buddies...

The 72-foot Schooner Freedom, St. Augustine's only Tallship, departs daily for cruises. Take a step back in time and experience the romance and adventure on the high seas while sailing the waters adjacent to historic St. Augustine. Dolphins, seabirds, pilot whales (wintering) and manatees are among the creatures encountered on the guided tours. The sunset tour is excellent and the kids get to help raise the sails, heave lines and take the helm. Dolphins often make playful escorts as gentle sea breezes fill the ships sails. The sunset tour offers a beautiful dusk view of the historic city!

THE CONCH HOUSE RESTAURANT

St. Augustine - *57 Comares Avenue (SR 207 east to Anastasia Island. One mile south of the bridge of Lions. Right onto Comares Ave) 32080. Phone: (800) 940-6256. www.conch-house.com.*

Come and visit the Conch House Restaurant and take a little trip to the Caribbean. Sit down under a palm tree on their outside deck or dine in unique grass huts out over the water. If the weather isn't cooperating, the covered patio overlooking beautiful Salt Run is the place to be. They specialize in seafood and Caribbean style cooking, offering fresh seafood, steaks, great chicken dishes, and delightful salads. Try anything Caribbean or their award-winning conch chowder or fritters. Kids Menu ranges from $5.00-$8.00 with fries. Lunch - $9-13.00, Dinner - $22.00 average. The state of the art 200 slip marina is conveniently located on Salt Run just off the Intracoastal waterway.

Exit - 311 (east of I-95)

ST. AUGUSTINE LIGHTHOUSE & MUSEUM

St. Augustine - 81 Lighthouse Avenue (on A1A, one mile south of downtown) 32080. Phone: (904) 829-0745. www.staugustinelighthouse.com. Hours: Daily 9:00am-6:00pm. Admission: $7.95-$9.95. Child under 44" tall FREE (must be 44" to climb). Includes Museum & Audio Tour plus climb to top. Online coupon.

Discover St. Augustine's rich maritime history at the site of Florida's first lighthouse. Climb 219 steps to the top of the 165-foot tower for a breathtaking view of historic downtown and the beaches. An interpreter is waiting for you up top to answer questions and explain the different views. There are exhibits to look at in the restored keepers' house pertaining to the Coast Guard in WWII, shipwrecks, and the lives of the keepers and their families. Hands-on activities include touching a real cannon ball or learning to make knots with real sailor's rope. Want to engage the kids more? Be sure to pick up a pencil and

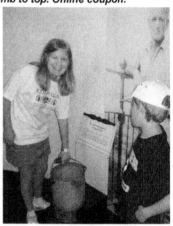

Try your hand at carrying the oil fuel for the lighthouse...

Scavenger Hunt challenge. Do not leave one stone unturned or one display board unnoticed because answers are all around you. Read about the story of the cat who fell from the top of the lighthouse and lived (although he wasn't happy with his master for some time). The lighthouse keepers museum covers a lot of ground without getting too detailed for kids. The museum store carries lots of lighthouse-themed gifts. Honestly, this is probably the best maintained lighthouse facility and safest climbing stairs we have explored.

ANASTASIA STATE PARK & ST. AUGUSTINE BEACH

St. Augustine - 1340 A1A South (Go east on State Road 207. Turn right on State Road 312. Turn left on A1A) 32080. www.floridastateparks.org/anastasia/. Phone: (904) 461-2033. Admission: $8.00 per vehicle. Note: geocaches hidden here.

Located on Anastasia Island, this 1,700-acre bird sanctuary is rich with miles of beach, lagoon waterways, wildlife and sweeping sand dunes. A self-guided nature trail offers an opportunity to walk ancient sand dunes covered by a coastal hammock of live oak, red bay and Southern magnolia trees. Sabal palms and sea oats grow wild on 20-foot-high dunes. The 24-miles of unspoiled, sandy beaches on the island are a surprise for visitors…and you may not pass many visitors at all for a stretch. The park offers seaside facilities for camping, hiking, fishing, picnics, barbecues, nature walks and beach volleyball. Flanked by the Atlantic Ocean on the east, pleasant year-round weather encourages exploration of St. Augustine Beaches, just up the road. Their beaches have some vehicle access areas towards the south end. Public access areas are well marked and the beach sand is piled high and sugary clean on the dunes and full of seashells near the water. If you can tear yourself away from the water and beach, try a friendly game of miniature golf and have an ice cream at Fiesta Falls. This pirate and water-themed mini-golf and picnic facility serves ice cream treats and has a well-maintained course with putting holes that are really unusual and fun to figure out.

ST. AUGUSTINE ALLIGATOR FARM ZOOLOGICAL PARK

St. Augustine - *999 Anastasia Blvd. (South A1A) (head into St. Augustine. Then, 2 miles south after crossing the Bridge of Lions) 32080. Phone: (904) 824-3337. www.alligatorfarm.com. Hours: Daily 9:00am-5:00pm (until 6:00pm summers). Admission: $22.95 adult, $11.95 child (3-11). Crocodile Crossing Zipline $35.00 each course. Educators: print downloads for a Scavenger Hunt located under Your Visit/Teacher Resources. FREEBIES: on that same page, you can print off a coloring page, word search, connect the dots and a maze activity sheet.*

See all 23 species of crocodilians (that's fun to say) from around the world including rare white alligators. Shows every hour include the "Rainforest Review", featuring macaws and cockatoos and Alligator Feedings twice daily. The natural rookery is home to hundreds of egret, ibis, heron and other wading birds and is part of the Florida Birding Trail. The park is home to many exotic and endangered animals, too.

Crocodile Crossing: Across seven-acres on the two challenging courses, you'll experience having live alligators and crocodiles right under your toes, tropical birds at eye level and red-ruffed lemurs nearly at arm's length. More than 50 different obstacles will have you surfing through the sky, swinging like a spider monkey and climbing like a gecko.

Exit - 305 (east of I-95)

FORT MATANZAS NATIONAL MONUMENT

A Fort Matanzas Scavenger Hunt is printable online under: For Teachers

St. Augustine - 8635 A1A South (SR206 east and then south on A1A a couple of miles) 32080. Phone: (904) 471-0118. www.nps.gov/foma. Hours: Daily 9:00am-5:30pm except Christmas day. Admission: FREE. There are no fees to enter the park or to take the ferry to the fort. The 35-passenger ferry operates on a first come basis. Educators: Thorough, age-based lesson plans and tests are online on the For Teachers page.

On this site in 1565, the Spanish in a struggle killed 245 French Huguenots

A tiny, tough fort...but it never saw a battle!

over control of Florida (Matanzas means "place of slaughter"). In 1742, the Spanish built Fort Matanzas here, a small-fortified watchtower that guarded the Southern entrance to St. Augustine. This fort is one of two remaining watchtower forts made from coquina rock. Hardly used, it did play a small part in passage

of Spanish treasure fleets on their way back from the Caribbean to Spain. If you can climb the rooftop ladder, you'll get a great view from the top. The short boat ride (5 minutes long) runs about every hour and there is a good historical interpretation just outside. If you want, explore the boardwalked nature trail (about 1/2 mile) or beaches and fishing in the bay.

MARINELAND'S DOLPHIN CONSERVATION CENTER

St. Augustine - 9600 Oceanshore Blvd. (SR 206 east to right on A1A. located ocean front on A1A) 32080. Phone: (904) 471-1111. www.marineland.net. Hours: Daily 8:30am-4:30pm. Admission: General: $11.95 adult, $6.95 child (under 13). Educators: Teacher Packets and Observation Sheets and FAQ are online under:

Education/For Educators. FREEBIES: Scavenger Hunt online under Education.

The newest focus - more research orientation and a special project with special needs kids. Gone are the days of circus routines and jumping through hoops while loud music and narration set the tone. Now the guests join animals in their habitats and make a physical and emotional connection. Programs such as The Quest, The Immersion and Discover Dolphins lead you into a watery world like none you've ever experienced before. Swim and dive in the water with live dolphins (extra fee around $209 per person). Looking for something less adventurous? Keep your feet on dry land as you meet the dolphins in their Touch and Feed program, or Dolphin Designs for the artistically inclined (again, additional fee). Check their website for current offerings.

Exit - 298 (east of I-95)

FAVER-DYKES STATE PARK

St. Augustine - *1000 Faver Dykes Road (just off I-95, follow signs) 32086. Phone: (904) 794-0997. www.floridastateparks.org/faverdykes/. Hours: Daily 8:00am-sunset. Admission: $5.00 per vehicle for up to 8 people. Camping and canoe rentals.*

Noted for its pristine condition, this tranquil park borders Pellicer Creek as it winds along Florida's east coast highways down to the Matanzas River. Fishing, picnicking, and nature walks are popular activities. Pellicer Creek is a designated state canoe trail and visitors can rent canoes at the park. A full-facility campground is available for overnight stays.

WASHINGTON OAKS GARDENS STATE PARK

St Augustine (Palm Coast) - *6400 N. Oceanshore Blvd. (two miles south of Marineland on State Road A1A) 32173. www.floridastateparks.org/washingtonoaks/. Phone: (386) 446-6780. Hours: Daily 8:00am-sunset. Admission: $5.00 per vehicle.*

The park features formal gardens and a unique shoreline of coquina rock on its Atlantic beach side. A number of short trails provide opportunities for hiking and bicycling. Visitors can learn about the park's natural and cultural resources in the visitor center.

Exit - 284 (east of I-95)

GAMBLE ROGERS MEMORIAL STATE RECREATION AREA AT FLAGLER BEACH

Flagler Beach - *3100 South A1A (I-95 exit 284, south on A1A approx. 3 miles) 32136. Phone: (386) 517-2086. www.floridastateparks.org/gamblerogers/. Hours: Daily 8:00am-sunset. Admission: $5.00 per vehicle. Note: NORTH PENINSULA STATE PARK is just 4 miles south of Flagler Beach (www.floridastateparks.org/ northpeninsula/) and offers more than two miles of beautiful, unspoiled Atlantic beaches.*

A windswept beach named for Florida folk singer Gamble Rogers and railroad baron Henry Flagler. Bordered by the Atlantic Ocean to the east and the Intracoastal Waterway to the west this 144 acre park offers coastal camping, picnicking, swimming, fishing and scenic relaxation. A1A Ocean Shore Scenic Highway spans a seven-mile stretch of Flagler County's beach between quiet Flagler Beach and Beverly Beach. A bicycle/pedestrian path parallels the scenic corridor and provides recreation for the cyclist, jogger and peace-loving stroller. At night during the months of May through early September endangered and threatened Loggerhead, Green and the rare Leatherback sea turtles crawl on the beach to nest and lay their eggs as they have done for thousands of years. A wide variety of bird life can be observed during the fall, winter and spring months.

Exit - 268 (east of I-95)

TOMOKA STATE PARK MOUNDS AND MIDDENS

Ormond Beach - *2099 North Beach Street (3 miles north of Ormond Beach) 32174. Phone: (386) 676-4050. www.floridastateparks.org/tomoka. Hours: Daily 8:00am-sundown. Admission: $5.00 per vehicle. Note: just 2 miles north of the state park lies Dummett Sugar Mill Ruins, these ruins are of what is believed to be the first steam-powered sugar mill in Florida. (free admission)*

This site was once the site of the Timucuan Indian Village of Nocorocco. It later became the Mount Oswald Plantation in 1766. Today, the 1,540-acre park offers camping, fishing, nature trails, picnic areas, a boat launch and canoe rentals for access to Tomoka River. The remains of Fort McCrea (in the area of Tomoka State Park) are known as the ADDISON BLOCKHOUSE. The blockhouse, manned by South Carolina militia men, was made to guard the Carrickfergus plantation. A skirmish occurred in early 1836 and when the militia men barely survived they soon abandoned the fort. The old blockhouse can be visited, but one has to bushwhack through the woods a bit.

Exit - 261 (east of I-95)

DAYTONA 500 EXPERIENCE

Daytona Beach - *1801 W. International Speedway Blvd. (I-95 exit 261 or I-4 exit 129) 32114. Phone: (386) 947-6800 or (386) 253-RACE. www.daytona500experience.com. Hours: Open daily 10:00am-6:00pm. Admission: $16.00 adult, $10.00 child (6-12). Upgraded packages are available. All Access extras tour is best: add $7.00.*

SPEEDWAY: The 2.5 mile super speedway lives up to its billing as the World Center of Racing as it is involved in some type of high-speed activity every day for more than four months of the year - from stock cars (Daytona 500 and Pepsi 500) and sports cars to motorcycles and go-carts. The new infield allows fans to stroll along the FAN ZONE with activities. The TRACK TOUR takes you along the bottom of the track. We wondered why they weren't taking us on the track. Did you know the track is banked 17 to 31 degrees - even at the start line? Imagine 4 story high asphalt walls that only hold cars on track if they're going 95 mph or more! And, get a good look at the lake

...the famous banked curves

right in the middle of the track - stocked with fish. One stop on the tour is Victory Lane for photo ops. Tours run 10am-3pm.

DAYTONA USA: An interactive motorsports attraction designed to entertain and inform race fans about the history of motorsports in the Daytona Beach area. Especially fun for NASCAR fans. Included in the indoor attraction are opportunities for visitors to participate in a NASCAR Nextel Cup Series stock car pit stop; talk to favorite competitors (via video); take a walk through the history of Daytona Beach racing and play radio or television announcer by calling a race. Begin with a piece-by-piece breakdown of a racecar as the body, chassis and tires move apart to reveal all the precision parts - you don't just put in gas and go....The Great Moments video is worth a sit down to see stunning finishes. Racing simulator rides Acceleration Alley and Daytona

Dreams laps are also available along with daily track tours and NASCAR 3D: The IMAX Experience presentation.

See the current winner...straight from Victory Lane!

MUSEUM OF ARTS AND SCIENCES

Daytona Beach - *352 S. Nova Road (I-95 exit 261, Rte. 92 east to Nova Rd south) 32114. Phone: (386) 255-0285. www.moas.org. Hours: Tuesday-Saturday 9:00am-5:00pm, Sunday 11:00am-5:00pm. Admission: $12.95 adult, $10.95 senior, $6.95 child (6-17). Note: There's a planetarium here, too.*

The site features a Center for Florida History that is home to a 13-foot tall, 130,000 year-old Giant Ground Sloth, which was found during a road excavation/expansion project in 1974. The amazingly complete skeleton is considered one of the finest specimens of its kind in North America. You can't miss it as you're wowed turning the corner! The Family Museum has a huge collection of Teddy Bears and Coca-cola artifacts plus other fun displays. See displays on the invention of cola bottling and the first Coke to go to space. The giant teddy bears capture everyone's heart and the rail cars outside are exciting to look through. Children can make their own discoveries in the Children's Wing through interactive exhibits, games and activities in this area. Design a pizza, play with pulleys, dinos, puzzles, and light. Make a new face, make music with lasers or freeze your hand in the Science Corner. The Preserve Discovery Center allows visitors to follow a one mile network of boardwalk trails leading to interactive, outdoor exhibits. The museum is also renown for its multi-cultural exhibitions. The Cuban exhibit features great examples of modern Cuban art and the African Wing contains 165 objects from numerous African ethnic groups. Look for carved commemorative staffs, ritual ornaments, and 130 pieces of Ashante gold highlighting this collection of art.

Exit - 261 (east of I-95)

CHOCOLATE FACTORY, ANGELL & PHELPS

Daytona Beach - *154 S. Beach Street (SR 92 all the way into town on the main street) 32114. Phone: (386) 252-6531. www.angellandphelps.com. Admission: FREE. Tours: 30 minute long tours are offered Monday-Saturday, On the hour, beginning at 10:00am. Last tour at 4:00pm.*

Free guided tours take visitors down a viewing hallway and behind the scenes of how chocolate candies are made from scratch and box shipped to chocolate lovers nationwide. The company was started in the 1920s (before air conditioning) by two women. Learn about their original recipes and see some original equipment. Why do they use copper kettles for cooking? Folks especially are wowed looking at workers around the giant vats of caramel or spinning chocolate. Ever seen a chocolate waterfall?

A TINY CRUISE LINE

Daytona Beach - *501 S. Beach Street (Halifax Harbor Marina) 32114. Phone: (386) 226-2343. www.visitdaytona.com/tinycruise. Admission: Waterway $12.00-$20.00, Riverfront or Rivertown $8.00-$14.00. Tours: Lunchtime Waterway tour. Riverfront and Rivertown are offered in the afternoon.*

Dolphin, jumping fish and wading birds are close by as you quietly glide past islands and estates or delightful 1890s style fantail launch. The River is a treasure trove of timeless stories and beautiful sights, always changing, always entertaining, let them share it with you.

DAYTONA BEACH, THE BEACH

Daytona Beach - *250 N. Atlantic Avenue (Ocean Walk) 32118. Phone: (386) 257-5367.*

The beach is up to 500 feet wide at low tide and is perfect for castle building, cycling, fishing or just relaxing in the sun. While at the beach, watersports abound and rentals are everywhere. The Atlantic Ocean is perfect for swimming especially during spring and summer when temperatures range from 74-80 degrees. Visit the Boardwalk with its arcades, rides, the Clocktower and "Speeding Through Time" exhibit, and concerts at the open-air bandshell. All along Atlantic Avenue (www.volusia.org/parks) are public beachside parks, some with sport courts, fishing docks, spirting fountains, playgrounds and restrooms. On South Atlantic Avenue, there are many vehicle driving beach access points ($5.00 per day per vehicle). It is unbelievable to be driving on

FLORIDA

the sand, just several feet from the ocean! If you and your family can manage to tear yourselves away from the beach, walk over to OceanWalk. The area's newest shopping, dining and entertainment district, Ocean Walk Shoppes are family fun. Enjoy the 10-cinema theater complex and many new fun eateries like Bubba Gumps. Across the street is Daytona Lagoon waterpark and amusement center (be careful with kids if a lot of teens are hanging out here - they may be too rowdy and rough on the rides).

Driving on the beach...that was unique!

BUBBA GUMP SHRIMP COMPANY

Daytona Beach - *Ocean Walk Shoppes, 250 North Atlantic Avenue (head to oceanfront) 32118. Phone: (386) 947-8433. www.BubbaGump.com.*

This restaurant captures the charm that made Paramount Picture's "Forrest Gump" such a smash hit. The restaurant offers quality seafood in a casual, family atmosphere. Steamed shrimp, fried shrimp, coconut shrimp, grilled shrimp...Well, you get the picture. Did you know Americans eat a billion pounds of shrimp a year and is the nation's favorite seafood? Try their Hush Pups and any entrée that mentions spicy - so many flavors blended so well! Other favorites include: Bucket of Boat Trash (much better than it sounds), Shrimp New Orleans and mouthwatering Dixie Style Ribs or Pork BBQ. Kids Menu includes burgers, pizza, fish & chips, mac n cheese, chicken strips and Hubba Bubba Fried Shrimp...all around $5.00. Scrawled "Gumpisms" grace the varnished tabletops and guests can try on plaster casts of Forrest's running shoes at the famed bus bench in front of each restaurant. Trivia: What did Mrs. Gump always tell Forrest life was like - purchase a box in their gift shop. Prices are moderate for most dishes, a little higher for seafood/famous shrimp dishes but well worth the taste and portion size. Try one of their lemonades as a beverage. Yummy, flavorful food and such a fun staff!

Exit - 261 (east of I-95)

BEST WESTERN AKU TIKI

Daytona Beach - *2225 South Atlantic Avenue (US92 east to south (right) on Atlantic Ave.) 32118. www.bwakutiki.com. Phone: (866) 734-7746 or (386) 252-9631.*

Directly on the ocean, overlooking the miles of soft-white sand on the "World's Most Famous Beach", the Best Western Aku Tiki Inn is the affordable, ideally located beach family resort. You will be conveniently located to the Daytona International Speedway and Florida's many attractions. It is on the quiet strip of shops and eateries and many room's patios face the ocean. All rooms have mini-frig and microwaves and some have kitchenettes. Most rooms have two queen beds. Special rates start under $100.00. They have a large outdoor pool, kiddie pool, sport courts and ping-pong table facing the ocean. Just one half mile down the road is vehicle or bicycle beach access - yes, the sand is hard enough to drive on and most certainly bike on (during low tide only, a $5.00 all day vehicle pass is needed for car driving).

Exit - 256 (east of I-95)

SUGAR MILL BOTANICAL GARDENS

Port Orange - *950 Old Sugar Mill Road (follow signs off freeway) 32121. Phone: (386) 767-1735. www.dunlawtonsugarmillgardens.org. Hours: Daily dawn to dusk, basically 8:00am-6:00pm. Admission: FREE.*

Stroll amid 12 acres of dense botanical gardens surrounding the ruins of a19th century English sugar mill. The gardens are also home to 40-year old dinosaur statues erected when the site was known as the Bongoland amusement park. Check out the human sundial - when standing on the sundial, visitors can determine the time of day by their own shadow.

MARINE SCIENCE CENTER

Ponce Inlet - *100 Lighthouse Drive (south on S. Atlantic Ave/CR4075 into Ponce Inlet. Right on Harbour Village, left on S. Peninsula, left on Lighthouse) 32127. Phone: (386) 304-5545. www.marinesciencecenter.com. Hours: Tuesday-Saturday 10:00am-4:00pm, Sunday Noon-4:00pm. Admission: $2.00-$5.00 (age 3+).*

The Center opened to provide an innovative learning experience where visitors can discover, enjoy and appreciate the many wonders of marine science. The Center houses a wet/dry classroom and lab, gift shop, a sea turtle rehab facility, and a 5,000 gallon artificial reef aquarium, as well as interactive displays on mangroves and whales. Look for science drawers and microscopes. Can you find the guitar fish? How about the psychedelic fish and "Dory" Tang fish in the coral reef. Probably the best part - the turtle rehab tanks. Profiles of each rescued turtle help you learn more about their

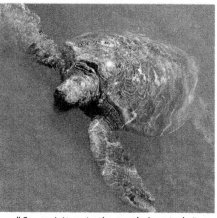

"Come visit us in the turtle hospital..."

problems surviving our modern world. A boardwalk and nature trail system extends throughout the park allowing for wildlife and habitat observation.

PONCE DE LEON INLET LIGHTHOUSE

Ponce Inlet - *4931 S. Peninsula Drive (US 1 or I-95 to Port Orange exit. East on Dunlawton to Atlantic Ocean, then south six miles) 32127. Phone: (386) 761-1821. www.ponceinlet.org. Hours: Daily 10:00am-6:00pm (fall/winter) and 10:00am-9:00pm (summer). Admission: $5.00 adult, $1.50 child. Online coupon.*

This is a fine example of a restored maritime museum. Standing 175 feet tall, this lighthouse is the second tallest in the U.S. and the tallest in Florida.

203 steps to the top - inside it looked like a giant snail shell...

Complete with its original lighthouse keeper buildings, it is the only lighthouse in Florida that is recognized as a National Historic Landmark. Begin in the woodshed which is now the video room. The museum houses many nautical artifacts, educational exhibits and a rare Fresnel Lens exhibit. The staff here are known as Fresnel Lens expert restorers. Running the lighthouse was a family job. The kids had to take a boat to the nearest school. An invigorating (yet nice-paced - a landing is on every 22 steps) climb to the top of the 203-steps is rewarded with breathtaking views of the area's coastline. On a clear day, you can see all the way to Cape Canaveral. To commemorate your visit, make time to scour their wonderful gift shop for souvenirs.

Exit - 220 (east of I-95)

MERRITT ISLAND NATIONAL WILDLIFE REFUGE

Titusville - State Route 402 (Drive east on SR406 over Causeway. 3.5 miles east of town) 32782. Phone: (321) 861-0667. www.fws.gov/merrittisland/. Hours: Refuge roads and trails open daily from sunrise to sunset. Visitor Center: Monday-Saturday 9:00am-4:00pm, Sundays also in winter.

The refuge, which shares a common boundary with the Kennedy Space Center, contains more than 500 species of animals (including 21 listed as endangered or threatened). You can find both freshwater and saltwater environs...even sand dunes. The best times to visit the refuge are winter, spring and fall. November is peak bird watching season as white pelicans and peregrine falcons migrate along the coast. Look for Loggerhead sea turtles nesting in May and bald eagles return each September. A manatee viewing platform located on the northeast side of Haulover Canal is the best spot to see manatees.   Interpretive panels are available at the platform to provide information about these endangered species. While you watching, make plans to hike a trail, or paddle a canoe.

DIXIE CROSSROADS SEAFOOD RESTAURANT

Titusville - 1475 Garden Street (I-95 exit 220, east 2 miles to corner of Dixie and Garden) 32782. Phone: (321) 268-5000. www.DixieCrossroads.com.

Ever had Rock Shrimp? Well, this place (at least the owners) invented a machine to process these hard shelled shrimp found fresh in these parts. All of their entrees are offered with seasonings including:
Old Bay, Key West, Caribbean Jerk (our favorite), Garlic and Salt Free. We strongly suggest a combo and be sure it includes Rock Shrimp! Start with great, hot corn fritters or let the kids color or go out and feed the fish. All their shrimp is fresh from the ocean, not ponds. Oh, and the fish on the Kids

Menu (shrimp, fish or clams) or a hamburger or chicken nuggets, served with fritters, french fries, beverage and chocolate pudding for only $2.99. Lunch and dinner daily. Plan on only spending $13.00 for over 20 entrees (includes fritters and one side). Bigger appetites and combos with enough to share are around $25.00-$30.00.

🍽️

Exit - 215 (west of I-95)

JUNGLE ADVENTURES

Christmas - 26205 East Highway SR 50 (7 miles west of the interstate, stay on SR 50) 32709. www.jungleadventures.com. Phone: (407) 568-2885, Toll-free (877) 4-AGATOR. Hours: Daily 9:30am-5:30pm with 4 shows daily at 10:30am, 12:30pm, 2:30pm, and 4:20pm. Admission: $23.95 adult, $12095 senior (60+), $16.95 child (3-11). Online coupon.

Jungle Adventures is a 20-acre park and wildlife sanctuary that has been in operation for over 30 years. Just look for "Swampy", the world's largest alligator sunning himself along side the road. Jungle Adventures is dedicated to "eco-tourism," a unique experience for close encounters with native wildlife. Each visitor has the option of enjoying the park at his or her own pace. You may spend as much time in the park as you prefer, however, the average stay is about three hours. They offer a wide variety of programs and tours dealing with Florida native history. The tours and shows each run four times a day, with no overlapping times so guests can be sure to enjoy each and every show at their leisure. Watch as huge alligators come to Feast at the Gator Feedings (their jaw power is a site), take a relaxing ride on the Jungle Cruise, take a trip back in time through the Native American Village, hold a baby alligator in the Wildlife Show, and stroll through the park and see many animals including the endangered Florida Panther.

Exit - 215 (east of I-95)

KENNEDY SPACE CENTER VISITOR COMPLEX

Titusville (Merritt Island) - State Route 405 (SR50 and then follow signs right to it) 32922. Phone: (321) 449-4444. www.KennedySpaceCenter.com. Hours: Opens daily at 9:00am. Closing times vary according to season. Closed Christmas and certain launch days. Admission: Maximum Access Admission is $50 adult, $40 child (3-11). Note: Before or after your guided tour, you'll want to check out the many scheduled programs on site. Maybe take in a space IMAX film or an

Astronaut Encounter where you come face-to-face with a real astronaut every day during a half-hour, interactive forum. Fork out some extra bucks ($16.00-$23.00) and have an eventful and yummy Lunch with an Astronaut. Ask a real astronaut what life in space is like. What do your senses experience after lift off - some describe it as a train wreck!

A space theme park - not with rides, but with many visual and 3D attractions. A must-see experience, this tour can begin or end as guests go on a narrated, video-supplemented bus tour of Kennedy Space Center. While traveling to launch pads and rockets, you might see a shuttle being moved to its launching pad. The first stop is the Observation Gantry, where guests enjoy a panoramic view of Kennedy Space Center, rocket launch pads and the Space Shuttle launch pads. Buses then drive

Have lunch with a real astronaunt!

by the Vehicle Assembly Building (VAB) where the Space Shuttle is stacked for launch, as well as the Orbiter examination area. The second stop is the Space Shuttle Atlantis Center. Begin in the giant themed-park atmosphere of a simulated mission control room. In the final moments of the presentation, with exhilaration, the Shuttle jets off with a huge powerful thrust. You walk out and behold a marvelous scene. Just to stand beneath the 36-story Saturn V moon rocket invites awe and it's a blast walking through re-creations of modules used as part of the International Space Station. A great souvenir is the photo op shot of weightlessness (additional fee, but worth the curiosity it invokes). Want to feel a more extreme simulation? Try The Shuttle Launch Experience. Using a custom-designed motion platform as well as multiple video screens, advanced audio effects and special effect seats, the attraction promises to re-create the sensations of blasting into earth's orbit. Back at the main center, the ever-popular Rocket Garden is outdoors featuring several rockets from the past and "climb-in" Mercury, Gemini and Apollo capsule replicas. What are Robot Scouts? Meet the fun robots who take you through a simulated training program assignment with the first to explore new space - robots in space. The younger ones can play in the Children's Play Dome soft play space rocket park. Through all the fun, you'll actually learn about air, gravity and thrust. This was our favorite way to learn about space.

Exit - 215 (east of I-95)

AMERICAN POLICE HALL OF FAME & MUSEUM

Titusville - *6350 Horizon Drive (I-95 exit 215. East on SR50 to SR405. SR405 east) 32780. Phone: (321) 264-0911. www.aphf.org. Hours: Daily 10:00am-6:00pm. Closed major holidays. Admission: $13.00 adult, $10.00 senior/military & $8.00 child (age 4-12). Law enforcement FREE. Internet savings coupon.*

The Nation's first museum, attraction and memorial honoring all police. This educational attraction offers thousands of items on display such as a crime scene, gas chamber, electric chair and a forensics learning area and several interactive displays. Walk through Auto Alley (from scooters to the future); Wild West stockade; Crime Lab -DNA, fingerprinting and composite drawing; Crime & Punishment area with a real jail cell; and the Kids Discovery and Dress-up area where you try on uniforms and then design your own badge. Other photo opportunities include sitting on police motorcycles or the backseat of a squad car, a jail cell chair, and even Daddy or Mommy sized dress up clothes. Kids who love reading detective novels will engage here! Kids who are a little mischievous might straighten up!

VALIANT AIR COMMAND WARBIRD MUSEUM

Titusville - *6600 Tico Road (Exit 212 (SR 407) to end; Turn right (East) toward Kennedy Space Center on SR 405) 32780. www.vacwarbirds.org. Phone: (321) 268-1941. Hours: Daily 9:00am-5:00pm. Admission: Adults $20.00 adult, $18.00 senior & active military, $5.00 child (4-12).*

More than 35 vintage war planes, including Flying Tigers and C-47 Transports, are maintained in top flight condition as tours breeze by eras of military aviation form Sopwith Camel bi-plane days through the P-51 Mustang hardships of World War II.

Exit - 205 (east of I-95)

HOLIDAY INN CAPE CARIBE RESORT

Cape Canaveral - *1000 Shorewood Drive (A1A exit South ports, billboards and signs will guide you there) 32920. Phone: (321) 799-4900. www.ihg.com/ holidayinnclubvacations/hotels/us/en/cape-canaveral/ccvcv/hoteldetail.*

Immerse yourself in a Caribbean setting suited to families. A beach and water lifestyle theme is seen throughout the complex. Rooms and spacious suites are decorated with tones of green, orange and yellow...and bright. We loved the large kitchen table - booth style. All suite units come with a full kitchen and utensils. Bring your own food, coffee, etc. or try the Surf Grill with casual Caribbean gourmet selections - most everything grilled. One warning, once you start roaming the property, be aware that your kids are not going to want to leave the property to site-see. Start with the surfing mini-golf, pool, Lazy River, waterslide, children's outdoor playground, and unique rooftop basketball and tennis courts. And, that's just outdoors. Indoors, look around the corners and plan some playtime Children's Play Center (giant soft play), a video arcade and 50+ seat movie theatre with selections shown nearly all day. Still want to more activity? Activities are planned for families all day, every day beginning at 10:00 or 11:00am. From Surfing lessons, scavenger hunts, dance lessons, beach theme bingo, musical chairs and crafts to fee-paid Pen Pals supervised crafts, munchies, pizza and movie nights.

Exit - 202 (east of I-95)

BREVARD MUSEUM OF HISTORY & NATURAL SCIENCE

Cocoa - *2201 Michigan Avenue (I-95, Exit 202 E. to Clearlake Rd. Turn W. on Michigan, proceed 1/2 mi. to museum) 32926. www.nbbd.com/godo/BrevardMuseum/. Phone: (321) 632-1830. Hours: Wednesday-Saturday 10:00am-4:00pm. Closed most major holidays and some weekdays each summer. Admission: $5.00-$6.00 (ages 5+).*

The Brevard Museum of History & Science traces the area's history from the days of the woolly mammoths to space shuttles. See a simulation of an archaeological dig of the 7,000 plus year-old Windover burial site. It's a bizarre collection, including swarms of honeybees and Indian trading beads, reflecting the pioneering period of the Space Coast while 22 acres showcases three ecosystems and a butterfly garden, outside. A hands-on science Discovery center complements them all.

Exit - 201 (east of I-95)

ISLAND BOAT LINES

Cocoa Beach - *500 Cocoa Beach Causeway (Rte. 520) (on the Banana River) 32931. Phone: (321) 302-0544. www.IslandBoatLines.com. Tours: 2 hour tours $28.00 per person. $2.00-$5.00 off for children, seniors, and military. (Discounts online). Babies in arms are FREE, unless full boat, per US Coast Guard. Soft Drinks & Water available. Passengers are welcome to bring personal food on board. Reservations are absolutely necessary.*

Three daily eco-tours on the "Miss Florida" and "Sunshine" pontoon boats depart from various locations throughout the Space Coast immersing visitors into the nature of the area while they glide alongside dolphin fins and manatee "footprints." A special trip through the Locks of Port Canaveral provides up-close excitement seeing the cruise and Navy ships, submarine base, Space Lab and US Coast Guard Station. Regardless of your choice, your family will have the opportunity to see herds of Manatees, flocks of Birds and playful Dolphins.

Exit - 191 (east of I-95)

BREVARD ZOO

Melbourne - *8225 N. Wickham Road (just east of exit 191 off I-95) 32940. Phone: (321) 254-WILD. www.brevardzoo.org. Hours: Daily 9:30am-5:00pm - No admissions after 4:15pm. Admission: $16.00 adult, $15.00 senior (60+), $12.00 child (2-12). Note: Brevard Zoo is handicapped accessible with wheelchair & stroller rentals. FREE parking, snack bar, gift shop, picnic tables.*

The only Zoo in the United States with on-site kayaking and an educational Zoo School, the Brevard Zoo includes a 7,000 square foot educational complex "Paws On," "Animal Encounters" and "Wild Encounter tours." Newer exhibits, like "Expedition Africa" place guests in the wilds of Africa during nose-to-nose meetings with exotic animals. Here, you can hand-feed giraffes, kayak through the man-made river, ride the train through a lush savanna or explore an aviary of African and Australian birds. Up close to the giraffe, you'll notice their gorgeous brown eyes with glamorous lashes, a wet nose and a long faded purple-pink tongue. Alligator and Crocodile demonstrations are at 3:30pm every Wednesday, Friday, and Sunday and can be seen from the bridge to Wild Florida. River Otter feedings are at 2:00pm every Tuesday and Saturday at the otter habitat in Wild Florida.

Treetop Trek is an exciting new outdoor adventure where visitors experience nature in a whole new way - high up in the trees. Have fun moving tree to tree and challenge yourself with varying degrees of thrilling elements such as tightropes, crab walks, jungle bridges, nets, and best of all, zip lines.

Exit - 156 (east of I-95)

CAPTAIN HIRAM'S RESORT

Sebastian - 1580 US 1 (2 miles north of Rte. 510) 32958. Phone: (772) 589-4345. www.hirams.com.

An adorable dockside property with two restaurants serving seafood and steaks. Try Captain Jim's Famous Crab Cake or anything with grilled shrimp. All of their food is so flavorful. The resort also features shops, a marina and a Key West Inn (some suites have bunk bed rooms for kids). Lunch and dinner with moderate Florida seafood prices.

RIVER KING CRUISES

Sebastian - 1606 Indian River Drive (1590 US 1) (depart Capt. Hiram's Marina, 3 miles north of SR 512 by making left onto Indian River) 32958. Phone: (772) 589-6161. www.hirams.com/river-king.htm Admission: $29.00-$32.00 adult, $12.00 child (3-9). Tours: Daily in winter. Closed Monday & Tuesday (mid-May thru mid-December). Snacks and cold drinks available. Rest room facilities.

The Captain welcomes you aboard the River King and takes you on a journey into the Treasure Coast's scenic waterways. The whole way out and back, you are treated to lots of eco-facts. Every creature sighting includes a run-around watch by all sides of boat. Learn about pirates and gangs on the water years ago. Watch the playful antics of resident dolphin and manatee on one cruise (10:00am Manatee & Dolphin Watch). The Captain guarantees she'll find a pod of the gentle creatures and they slowly maneuver the boat so that you can watch them cavort in the water. Often, you'll see pods (families) working as a team to catch fish for breakfast. Cruise the Sebastian Inlet where the ocean meets the Indian River and around the state park's tidal pool and campground. (Daily except Sunday, 2 to 2.5 hours long). The 1:00pm Sebastian River Cruise takes you along the narrow banks of the jungle river where you might encounter alligators, turtles, raccoons, dolphins and a wide variety of water fowl. Manatees seek out the warm, shallow waters of the Sebastian River during cooler months and often surface next to the boat.

(Daily, 2.5 to 3 hours). The 4:00pm Pelican Island Cruise takes you to Pelican Island, the first National Wildlife Refuge in America, where thousands of birds roost, particularly in winter (peak months are November-March). (Daily, 1.5 hours, doesn't run in summer)

MCLARTY TREASURE MUSEUM

Vero Beach - *13180 North A1A (CR 512 to CR510 all the way to Inlet, left onto A1A, at Sebastian Inlet State Park) 32963. www.atocha1622.com/mclarty.htm. Phone: (772) 589-2147. Hours: Daily 10:00am-4:00pm (last video shows 3:15-4:00pm). Admission: $2.00 per person (age 6+). Note: The observation deck outside is shaped like one of the wrecked ships - very clever and adventuresome feelings surface in this environment.*

The McLarty Treasure Museum is located on the actual site of the 1715 Spanish Plate Fleet salvaging camp (look for a diorama that visually explains this through the reading of a crew member's journal). From the 1500s to the early 1700s, Spanish explorers mined or stole vast amounts of silver and some gold in the mountains of Mexico and South America. These precious metals were made into coins and ingots and then brought back to Spain in wooden sailing vessels. The fleet encountered a large hurricane along Florida's coast and sank on the shoals between Cape Canaveral and Stuart. In the early 1960s, the wrecks were rediscovered and salvage operations began. The video explains much of this and certainly engages your curiosity. The artifacts the crews recovered are on display including gear from the galleons, weapons and TREASURE! Now that you're trained in what to look for - go out and explore those beaches - people still find treasure washed up on a weekly basis!

MEL FISHER'S TREASURE MUSEUM

Sebastian - *1322 US 1 (CR 512 east to left on US 1) 32958. Phone: (772) 589-9875. www.melfisher.com. Hours: Monday-Saturday 10:00am-5:00pm, Sunday Noon-5:00pm. Closed in September. Admission: $6.50 adult, $5.00 senior, $2.00 child (age 5+).*

Mel Fisher and family became famous when they became treasure hunters. Mel spent most of the 1990s successfully salvaging the 1715 Fleet, which sank off the Treasure Coast. They then moved towards Key West in search of the Atocha, a 1622 shipwreck estimated to be worth 400 million dollars. Mel's daughter, Taffi, wanted to relocate here and start a museum. The site now houses a working conservation laboratory and museum which displays a vast array of artifacts salvaged from the Atocha, the local 1715 shipwrecks, and other shipwrecks. A window from the museum overlooks the lab so visitors can view ongoing conservation of newly salvaged artifacts before they are displayed in the "recent recoveries" case. View a video presentation featuring Mel's expeditions, too.

Exit - 156 (east of I-95)

ENVIRONMENTAL LEARNING CENTER

Vero Beach - *255 Live Oak Drive (CR512 to CR510 to beaches, on Wabasso Island between Vero & Sebastian along the Indian River Lagoon) 32963. Phone: (772) 589-5050. www.elcweb.org. Hours: Tuesday-Friday 10:00am-4:00pm, Saturday 9:00am-Noon (extended to 4:00pm in winter), Sunday 1:00-4:00pm. Admission: $5.00 general, children 12 and under are FREE.*

This non-profit nature center on a 51-acre island site develops programs and activities to encourage discovery of nature. They use hands-on exhibits and elevated boardwalks for nature strolls; eco-excursions such as Family birding trips via pontoon boat, wagon rides in a preserve, and beach walks; Lagoon Nights sleepovers and weekly canoe excursions. Kids can touch mystery boxes, make bird tracks, try to be an ibis digging for sand crabs, or identify dozens of birds, seashells and coral. Often, Junior Interpreters are standing by in the Wet Lab exhibit area with a scavenger hunt, live hermit crabs, and other nature activities. Did you know near the high tide watermarks is where you'll find the most interesting treasures? A walk out to the lagoon may warrant a dolphin sighting. On your way onto the boardwalk, take a gander at the giant surprises sitting under the Wet Lab. What will the Gulf Stream bring up next?

PELICAN ISLAND NATIONAL WILDLIFE REFUGE

Vero Beach - *510 Wabasso Causeway (CR 512 east. Right on US1 S. Left on Wabasso, southern end of Archie Carr Wildlife Refuge) 32960. Phone: (772) 562-3909. www.fws.gov/pelicanisland/. Hours: Daily 7:30am-sunset.*

Designated as the first National Wildlife Refuge by President Theodore Roosevelt, the waters and wetlands of Pelican Island National Wildlife Refuge form a complex ecosystem. Over 90 species of birds live within the refuge (including, of course, pelicans!). West Indian manatee, green sea turtle and loggerhead sea turtle. Other wildlife include raccoon, bobcat, marsh rabbit, opossum, river otter, dolphins and many varieties of neotropical and resident songbirds. Visitors are welcome to enjoy year-round bird watching, guided boat tours, kayaking, canoeing and sport fishing within the waters of the lagoon. An observation tower is now available to the public for "birds-eye" viewing from the Centennial Trail boardwalk.

Exit - 147 (east of I-95)

OCEAN GRILL

Vero Beach - *1050 Sexton Plaza (A1A to Rte. 60 east to waterfront) 32960. Phone: (772) 231-5409. www.ocean-grill.com.*

Originally high on a sand dune, the site now sits right on the water as storms and hurricanes have removed much sand and the dunes. A true ocean-side eatery remains. Lunch weekdays and dinner nightly (fine dining but very casual environ). Fresh fish, duck and grilled shrimp are their specialty. Their coloring and games kids menu includes basics plus fish, shrimp or steak for kids (average $8.00). Try a sharktooth sundae for dessert.

DISNEY'S VERO BEACH RESORT

Vero Beach - *9250 Island Grove Terrace (A1A north of town) 32960. Phone: (772) 234-2000 or (800) 359-8000. www.dvcresorts.com.*

Make yourself at home among the old world architecture of spacious Vacation Homes and stand-alone beach cottages. This beachfront location with a pool (Mickey-shaped w/ Pirates Plunge pool slide and a giant lighthouse slide), two restaurants (and poolside take-out), a game room, supervised programming, babysitting and a daily list of community hall activities really make a family want to stay awhile. Enjoy organized board games, scavenger hunts, arts and crafts, card games and table-tennis, play some pinball, rent a bicycle or sporting equipment, play some tennis, get a massage or sign up for a selection of bike tours, bird watching expeditions, nature hikes and evening campfires. Challenge your kids to a round of miniature golf or take to water sports offered from catch and release fishing to snorkeling. All rooms have a full kitchen or a kitchenette and TV/VCRs. Cook your own specialties in your room or at one of the grills located throughout the resort. Mom doesn't want to cook? Try Sonyas or Shutters - both have kids menus with petite size portions of the adult selections so the kids feel grown up (mostly steak, seafood and basic American fare). If you need to wait a little for seating or food, they offer a scavenger hunt to complete at the table and in the corridors near the dining hall. Kids can order Shirley Temples and they get a cute dessert with kids meals. Every Saturday they have Disney Character Breakfasts with Goofy and Max. Adults, try anything steak or seafood and be sure to save room for the Celebration dessert. This place is definitely Disney and all Crew Members are super sweet! One of our favorite beaches and kid-friendly resorts to play, go shelling and relax in spacious comfort.

Exit - 138 (east of I-95)

NATIONAL NAVY UDT/SEAL (FROGMAN) MUSEUM

Fort Pierce - *3300 N Highway A1A, North Hutchinson Island (take SR 713 east to US 1 south to left on A1A east) 34949. www.navysealmuseum.com. Phone: (772) 595-5945. Hours: Tuesday-Saturday 10:00am-4:00pm, Sunday Noon-4:00pm. Admission: $8.00 adult, $4.00 child (6-12).*

Located on the same beach where the first U.S. Navy Frogmen trained in 1943, this museum serves as a tribute to the Navy's underwater demolition teams of World War II and the present Navy Sea, Air and Land Teams (SEALS) displaying many artifacts from Navy combat missions. View uniforms and diving gear indoors but outdoors is the fun place for kids. Maybe a dozen military vehicles are along the long entrance walkway and yard. Look for boats or a Huey helicopter - many very stealth looking for secret missions. How long can a Frogman hold his breath? What training does it take and how special is it be one of this elite force?

Exit - 131A (east of I-95)

MANATEE OBSERVATION AND EDUCATION CENTER

Fort Pierce - *480 Indian River Drive, downtown (SR68 east, crossing over US1. Follow signs, across from the Fort Pierce Utilities Power Plant) 34949. Phone: (772) 466-1600. www.manateecenter.com. Hours: Tuesday-Saturday 10:00am-5:00pm, Sunday Noon-4:00pm (October-June). Summers only Thursday-Saturday. Admission: $1.00 donation per person. Tours: Boat Tours for Manatee Observation are Tuesday-Sunday 10:30am, 1:00pm and 3:00pm. No 10:30am tours on Sunday. $20.00 adult, $15.00 child. Senior discount.*

The manatee is one of Florida's favorite residents. You can view these gentle giants and their offspring in a natural habitat protected hereby the local community. Guests can also tour the butterfly garden, view a replica of a natural spring and climb an observation tower to look at the Indian River. Inside, there are aquariums, a digital lagoon tour and fish displays. Manatee were near extinct years ago. During the winter months, manatee seek out warm water in natural springs and outflows of power plants where they congregate in large numbers. With no natural enemies, loss of habitat is their biggest threat. Manatees generally only produce one calf every 3-5 years and the calf stays with the mother for its first two years (the reason you see many mother/child families). Mature manatees can grow up to 13 feet long and weigh 3500 pounds.

Exit - 131 (east of I-95)

FPL ENERGY ENCOUNTER

Hutchinson Island - _6501 South Ocean Drive (A1A), Jensen Beach (on South Hutchinson Island between Ft. Pierce & Stuart at St. Lucie Nuclear Power Plant) 34983. Phone: (772) 468-4111 or (877) FPL-4FUN. www.FPL.com/encounter. Hours: Monday-Friday generally 10:00am-4:00pm. Closed Major Holidays. Admission: FREE. Note: Turtle Walks every Friday night in June and July. Educational lecture at dark, followed by a night-time walk on Hutchingson Island to witness turtles lay their eggs._

St. Lucie - An Inside Look

You walk in and are greeted by the pirate parrot "Hutch." Hutch invites you on an Energy Treasure Hunt (be sure to get your treasure hunt swipe card). The parrot directs you through the hands-on displays that explore the wonders of energy. How do we get electricity? In the 30 interactive displays, you take a self-guided tour of exhibits such as a model of the containment building of nuclear reactors and you can even be in command on the controls as you raise and lower the control rods of a simulated reactor. Kids can simulate splitting the atom, play computer games, generate electricity on a treadmill and play with a huge, enclosed Energy Roller Coaster. Watch a cute movie entitled "The Amazing Chain Reaction" which uses cartoon dominos to show how nuclear energy is formed. Visitors can also walk next door to Turtle College. View dioramas of giant turtle moms nesting and baby turtles hatching. "This place is so cool" was the comment from our kids -an excellent nuclear energy unit study - for credit - or just for fun. We all learned something new.

SMITHSONIAN MARINE STATION AT FORT PIERCE

Fort Pierce - *420 Seaway Drive (east end of the PP Cobb Bridge on South Hutchinson Island in South Causeway Park) 34949. www.sms.si.edu/SMEE. Phone: (772) 462-FISH. Hours: Tuesday-Saturday 10:00am-4:00pm, Sunday Noon-4pm. Admission: $3.00-$4.00. First Tuesday of every month is FREE! FREEBIES: ask for (or print off ahead of time) worksheets you can use to play games while visiting the museum. Under Educational Opportunities.*

This center features the Smithsonian Marine Ecosystems Exhibit. Six living exhibits each feature a unique marine ecosystem: Caribbean coral reef, Oculina coral reef, sea grass, mangroves, as well as the fish and organisms found in these habitats. These exhibits are supported by aquariums ranging from 500 gallons to 3,000 gallons that showcase a microcosm of each ecosystem and animal life found in the lagoon and ocean. Can you find the hidden flatfish? What new juvenile species have joined the seagrass bed? As an erosion prevention educator the exhibit displays the deep root system of the mangrove as well as a simulated tide cycle to demonstrate erosion prevention in action.

Exit - 129 (east of I-95)

TREASURE COAST BEACHES

Fort Pierce - *34949. Phone: (800) 344-TGIF. www.visitstluciefla.com or www. floridastateparks.org/fortpierceinlet/. Admission: $6.00 per person.*

Located in the heart of Florida's Indian River Citrus district, St. Lucie County is known as the Grapefruit Capital of the State. Comprising Fort Pierce, Port St. Lucie, and Hutchinson Island, visitors to the area find spectacular barrier islands boasting 21 miles of beautiful beaches, some of the best surf and deepwater fishing in the State, and centuries-old shipwrecks which attract divers from around the world. Beach access is about every mile (EX. AVALON STATE PARK). One can spend the morning fishing, swimming, snorkeling, or horseback riding on the beach and the afternoon at attractions in the area. Nature lovers love the many parks and recreation areas which offer a diversity of wildlife from river otters to bird watching. Shorebirds are best observed at FORT PIERCE INLET at low tide, and Jack Island, which allows only foot traffic, is best known for birding in the early morning or late evening. One of the most unique wilderness spots is Savannas State Preserve, the last freshwater lagoon system existing in the State of Florida.

Exit - 126 (east of I-95)

OXBOW ECO-CENTER

Port St. Lucie - *5400 NE St. James Drive (4 miles on Midway Road. Right onto St. James Drive for 1.7 miles) 34983. www.stlucieco.gov/erd/oxbow/. Phone: (772) 785-5833. Hours: Tuesday-Friday Noon-5:00pm, Saturday 10:00am-5:00pm. Admission: FREE.*

Oxbow Eco-Center offers a rare glimpse of "the real Florida" - a place where geologic history comes alive walking the boardwalked trails of floodplain forest, sandy soils, pine flatwoods and ancient swamps and wetlands. The Center houses an Exhibit Hall and Discovery Room, which invite you to use all your senses, touching various artifacts of nature, listening to bird songs, and seeing some of Florida's native reptiles. The centerpiece exhibit takes you on a journey down the St. Lucie River, one of the most diverse rivers in the state, with more species of fish than any other river in Florida. You will experience a unique view of the underwater world, where you'll encounter dozens of fish species, including 20 different replicas of fish, several turtles and crustaceans, and even a life-size manatee with her calf.

Once a month they offer Family Nature programs that feature different aspects of the miles of boardwalk, bridges, observation towers and informational kiosks winding through nature without disrupting it. Most all of the property offers self-guided walks, too.

Exit - 118 (east of I-95)

SAVANNAS PRESERVE STATE PARK

Jensen Beach - *9551 Gumbo Limbo Lane (take exit east until you reach Jensen Beach) 34957. Phone: (772) 398-2779. www.floridastateparks.org/savannas/. Hours: Daily 8:00am-sunset. Admission: $3.00 per vehicle. Miscellaneous: The Education Center is located in Port St. Lucie, two miles east of U.S. 1 on Walton Road. It's open Thursday-Monday from 9:00am-5:00pm.*

Freshwater marshes or "savannas" once extended all along Florida's southeast coast. Stretching more than 10 miles from Ft. Pierce to Jensen Beach, this preserve is the largest and most intact remnant of Florida's east coast savannas. A good place for visitors to start is the Environmental Education Center where they can learn about the importance of this unique and endangered natural system. Kids will love the new live animal exhibits. Picnic tables are available near the center.

Canoeing, kayaking, and fishing in the wetlands are popular activities. Over eight miles of multi-use trails provide opportunities for hiking, bicycling, and horseback riding. When we have ample rain and the marsh is chock full of life, canoe and kayak programs, offered on Wednesdays and Sundays, will usually be sold out. When there is drought, the marsh dries up and life changes drastically for its usual residents. Visitors can finally use their 12-mile trail system without getting their feet wet. Guided walks and canoe trips are available by reservation.

Exit - 101 (east of I-95)

FLORIDA OCEANOGRAPHIC COASTAL CENTER

Stuart - 890 NE Ocean Blvd. (located on Hutchinson Island across from Stuart Beach. Follow signs north to Stuart, then Hutchinson) 34996. Phone: (772) 225-0505. www.floridaoceanographic.org. Hours: Monday-Saturday 10:00am-5:00pm, Sunday Noon-4:00pm. Admission: $12.00 adult, $6.00 child (3-12). Educators: Many activity sheets (PDF) are available on the Teacher & Student Resources page. FREEBIES: some of the Educator sheets are also games like word search you could print and play in the car on the drive.

The 750,000-gallon Game Fish Lagoon, aquariums, touch tanks, stingray tank, and children's activity pavilion has interactive exhibits on mammals, sea turtles, manatees, animal tracks, and a discovery table complete the multitude of hands-on tables and tanks here. Plan your visit during the daily stingray feedings, guided nature walks and boat tours.

SEABRANCH PRESERVE STATE PARK

Stuart - 4810 SE Cove Road (SR 76 north to Palm City. Access to the park is from S.R. A1A near the VFW parking lot) 34997. www.floridastateparks.org/seabranch/default.cfm. Phone: (772) 219-1880. Hours: Daily 8:00am-sunset. Admission: FREE.

Take a leisurely walk through the sand pine scrub, a unique habitat considered "globally imperiled," and most of all, enjoy "the Real Florida." In less than one mile, visitors can see rare sand pine scrub, scrubby flatwoods, a baygall community, and a mangrove swamp. Hikers can explore these natural communities over four miles of trails. New trail markers are in place. Informative, directional signs have been installed on the hiking trails in the park. These trail markers provide mileage remaining to reach the starting point as well as general directions.

Exit - 96 (east of I-95)

JONATHAN DICKINSON STATE PARK

Stuart (Hobe Sound) - *16450 S.E. Federal Highway (I-95 exit 96 east to US1south) 33455. Phone: (772) 546-2771. www.floridastateparks.org/jonathandickinson/ default.cfm. Hours: WILDERNESS GUIDED BOAT TOURS - Departs dock daily at 9:00 and 11:00am, 1:00 and 3:00 pm. Park open 8:00am-sunset. Admission: $6.00 PER VEHICLE admission fee. $15.00-$24.00 fee for boat tours (age 6+). Boat and cabin rentals vary in price. See website. Tours: Visitors can arrange boat tours of the river and rent canoes, kayaks, and motorboats by calling (561) 746-1466.*

This park teems with wildlife in 13 natural communities, including sand pine scrub, pine flatwoods, mangroves, and river swamps. The Loxahatchee River, Florida`s first "Wild and Scenic River", runs through the park. The 44-passenger LOXAHATCHEE QUEEN II (www.floridaparktours.com) takes visitors up the Loxahatchee River to the pioneer homesite of TRAPPER NELSON (2 hour tour focused on natural history sightings). The Loxahatchee Queen II docks at the Trapper Nelson site where passengers are met by a Park Ranger who guides them through the cabins and grounds once belonging to the "Wildman of the Loxahatchee." Trapper Nelson came to the area in the 1930s and lived off the land by trapping and selling furs.

Visitors can enjoy paved and off-road biking, equestrian, and hiking trails. Boating, canoeing, and kayaking along the river are also great ways to see the park. Anglers can catch freshwater fish along the riverbank or from a boat. The nature and history of the park comes to life through exhibits and displays in the Elsa Kimbell Environmental Education and Research Center. The park offers two full-facility campgrounds and a youth/group primitive campground. ATLANTIC RIDGE wet prairie provides a critical habitat for endangered species of plants and animals.

Exit - 87 (east of I-95)

JUPITER INLET LIGHTHOUSE

Jupiter - *500 Captain Armour's Way, Lighthouse Park (I-95 to Indiantown Rd. east, turn left/north at US 1. Turn right at Beach Rd) 33477. Phone: (561) 747-8380. www.lrhs.org. Hours: Daily 10:00am-5:00pm (closed Mondays May-Dec). Admission: $5.00-$9.00 each. Minimum height is 48" tall. No flip-flops or heels allowed. Educators: Lesson plans online under Education/Educators Lesson Plans. Also available are a museum store, Station J Café.*

Jupiter Inlet Lighthouse & Museum offers climbing tours of the landmark 1860 lighthouse. The waterfront Museum in the newly restored WWII Barracks building offers its local history exhibit, Five Thousand Years on the Loxahatchee. Outdoor exhibits include the Tindall Pioneer Homestead & Pennock Plantation Bell. Climb the 105 steps of this newly restored historical treasure on the National Register of Historic Places. From steamships to railroads to the Civil War (lied silent in hopes of preserving it from harm) to modern uses. The first order Fresnel lens is magical to look at.

Exit - 83 (east of I-95)

LOGGERHEAD MARINELIFE CENTER

Juno Beach - *14200 US Hwy. One (head due east off exit ramp. Left (north) onto US1) 33408. Phone: (561) 627-8280. www.marinelife.org. Hours: Monday-Saturday 10:00am-5:00pm, Sunday 11am-5:00pm. Closed all federal holidays. Admission: FREE, donations are appreciated. Note: Park amenities include a guarded beach, nature trails, picnic pavilions. Live Sea Turtle Cam www.marinelife.org/page. aspx?pid=357*

The new campus is comprised of 10,000 square feet of indoor space which will include a visitor center, marine laboratory, sea turtle  veterinary hospital, and learning center. A 3,000 square foot outdoor exhibit 'yard' houses marine turtle rehabilitation tanks, shark exhibit, and a marine touch tank. Exhibits include a giant Leatherback sea turtle, salt water aquaria and displays of local wildlife, as well as educational displays about south Florida's marine environment. The nature center includes a marine-oriented gift and book shop, featuring an excellent selection of children's educational books and unique gift and craft items.

Exit - 77 (east of I-95)

JOHN D. MACARTHUR BEACH STATE PARK

North Palm Beach - *10900 SR 703 (Jack Nicholas Drive) (A1A) (2.8 miles south of the intersection of U.S. 1 and PGA Boulevard on A1A) 33408. www.floridastateparks. org/macarthurbeach/default.cfm. Phone: (561) 624-6950. Hours: Daily 8:00am-sunset. The Nature Center is open daily from 9:00am-5:00pm. Admission: $5.00 per vehicle. Miscellaneous: If you are interested in keeping up with the turtle nesting count, or if you would like to volunteer to help with the turtle program, please contact the staff at the Nature Center and let them know your interest.*

The park is a sanctuary in the center of a major metropolitan area. A unique mixture of coastal and tropical hammock and mangrove forest, this barrier island provides a haven for several rare or endangered native tropical and coastal plant species. The park`s nature center shows visitors why the park is a biological treasure. Visitors may also view a 15-minute video on the park. Visitors can swim, picnic, and surf at the beach; scuba diving and snorkeling are also popular activities. Birdwatchers can see herons, brown pelicans, terns, sandpipers, and gulls. Anglers can fish in the lagoon by wading, kayaking, or canoeing-they can also fish from non-swimming areas of the beach. Whether you prefer kayaking, beach-walking or simply enjoying the quiet tranquility of the undeveloped beach, there is something for everyone. Each spring, comes the arrival of their sea turtle nesting season. Large numbers of loggerhead, green and leatherback turtles nest from early May through late August. Morning beach patrols will check and record the nesting activity of the various species of turtles that return to the undeveloped beach each year.

Exit - 68 (east of I-95)

PALM BEACH ZOO AT DREHER PARK

West Palm Beach - *1301 Summit Blvd. (I-95 exit 68 Southern Blvd. E to Parker Avenue. Turn right on Parker, right on Summit for one block) 33405. Phone: (561) 547-WILD. www.palmbeachzoo.org. Hours: Daily except Christmas and Thanksgiving 9:00am-5:00pm. Admission: $12.95-$18.95 per person (age 3+).*

Over 23 acres of lush, tropical landscaped habitats that are home to over 900 animals from Florida, Central and South America, Asia and Australia. Enjoy the Florida Exhibit, Tiger Falls, Aviary, Children's Carousel, and the newly opened Tropics of the Americas – a multi-exhibit showcase of Mayan culture, animals and horticulture. Come see their stars, baby animals born here, including Caipora and Izel, the first jaguar cubs to be born onsite at the Palm Beach Zoo. Bush dogs, Baird's tapirs, giant anteaters, the Caracol Observatory, Primate Island, suspension bridge and explorer's cave, Amazonian Market Place, and more! Bring your bathing suit and get wet in the Interactive Fountain (changing cabanas available,) enjoy lunch at the waterfront air-conditioned Tropics Café, or shop for gifts of all types and prices at the Gift Store.

Exit - 68 (east of I-95)

SOUTH FLORIDA SCIENCE MUSEUM

West Palm Beach - *4801 Dreher Trail North (I-95 exit Southern Blvd. Head east to Parker Ave. South on Parker, past Southern Blvd to Summit Blvd west tp Drejer Trail) 33405. Phone: (561) 832-1988. www.sfsm.org. Hours: Monday-Friday 10:00am-5:00pm, Saturday 10:00am-6:00pm, Sunday Noon-6:00pm. Admission: $9.00-$12.00 per person. Additional $2.00-$10.00 for galaxy golf, laser or planetarium shows.*

Interactive exhibits show you how to create clouds, generate electricity with a bike, marvel at optical illusions, and build and control your own robot! Natural history exhibits feature "Suzie," a 22,000 year-old mastodon found in Palm Beach County. Also, authentic and reproduction skeletons of whales, sharks and dinosaurs bring history to life. Native and

Galaxy Golf - Putt your way around a universe of obstacles in the 9-hole miniature golf course! Each hole contains a science theme & facts.

exotic sea life from warm waters around the world populate the museum's aquariums (include Touch Tanks). Enjoy a walk around a winding trail of interactive exhibits. This outdoor trail features parabolic whisper dishes, a fossil dig with authentic Florida fossils, dinosaur tracks which tell a story and even an all original turtle-hop game! Exciting laser shows and star shows thrill young and old alike in the Aldrin Planetarium. Touch a 232 pound meteorite or spend a few minutes watching Apollo 14 Highlights while you view a real moon rock brought back on an Apollo mission.

Exit - 57 (east of I-95)

SCHOOLHOUSE CHILDREN'S MUSEUM

Boynton Beach - *129 E. Ocean Avenue (1/4 mile east of Boynton Beach Blvd. South on Seacrest Blvd, 2 Blocks, then East on Ocean Avenue) 33435. Phone: (561) 742-6780. www.schoolhousemuseum.org. Hours: Tuesday-Saturday 10:00am-5:00pm, Sunday 1:00-4:00pm. Admission: $4.00-$5.00 (age 2+). Tours: The Butterfly Garden Tour Includes a true story of how the pioneers rendered the Atala Butterfly nearly extinct; a Search for butterfly eggs, caterpillars and chrysalis; collecting scientific data and more. Educators: Lots of .PDF format quizzes and tests online under Education/Teachers Guide. FREEBIES: printable worksheets, flashcards, games and puzzles to play en route are online on the Education/Teachers Guide page.*

Children learn about Florida's vibrant history through hands-on interactive exhibits. Begin your experience at the Schoolhouse museum by relaxing and enjoying an exciting ten-minute introductory film about Boynton Beach History. Dozens of actual photos embedded into this refreshing, upbeat show set the tone for the fun and learning to follow in the galleries. Step back in time and see for yourself how South Florida grew. Get a ticket at the train depot, pack up a suitcase, and take a ride on the Orange Blossom Express. Dress up like a conductor or a train passenger, ring the bell, shovel coal into the steam engine or read about trains while traveling in the passenger car library. Through imaginary play students and parents together learn about Palm Beach County's rich cultural heritage. Four main exhibit areas, Time Travels, Family Farms, Water World and Main Street provide props and dress-up clothes for children to imagine themselves as Florida pioneers. Photos and wall displays in every area explain the historical characters and places that inspired each exhibit.

Exit - 52 (west of I-95)

LOXAHATCHEE, A.R.M. NATIONAL WILDLIFE REFUGE

Boynton Beach - *10218 Lee Road (I-95 north to FL 806, turn left heading west about 7.5 miles to FL7/US441 and turn right. Travel north 3.1 miles to Lee Road) 33473. Phone: (561) 734-8303. www.fws.gov/loxahatchee/. Hours: Park open sunrise to sunset. Visitors center open Wednesday-Sunday 9:00am-4:00pm except winter holidays. Admission: A fee of $5.00 is charged to private vehicles entering the refuge.*

Loxahatchee National Wildlife Refuge is home to the American alligator and the endangered Everglades snail kite. In addition to being a home to wildlife, the refuge offers many recreational opportunities. Walking trails, a canoe trail, bike trail, boat ramps, fishing platform, observation towers, butterfly garden, and a visitor center are available. The virtual air boat Tour is a highlight of the Everglades Exhibition. Please take your seat and stay seated during your trip. As you begin to move, the seats and floor vibrate, you feel the breeze blowing from the screen in front of you as your boat skims over the water. You are not on a ride at Disney World or on a real air boat ride in the middle of the Everglades. You are about to experience a virtual Airboat Tour. Not quite all of the 147,392 acre refuge is Everglades habitat. A four hundred acre cypress swamp is the largest remaining remnant of a cypress strand that once separated the pine flatwoods in the east from the Everglades marshes. A boardwalk into the swamp gives the visitor a chance for an up-close swamp experience without getting his or her feet wet.

Exit - 44 (east of I-95)

GUMBO LIMBO NATURE CENTER

Boca Raton - *1801 N. Ocean Blvd (A1A) (Palmetto Park Rd. east to A1A, north) 33432. Phone: (561) 338-1473. www.gumbolimbo.org. Hours: Monday-Saturday 9:00am-4:00pm, Sunday Noon-4:00pm. Admission: Suggested donation of $3.00.*

Seawater is pumped directly into large outdoor aquariums filled with representatives of native marine fauna. Indoor and outdoor classrooms, interpretive displays, aquariums, a sea turtle Rehab Center, visual presentations, a butterfly garden, a 40-foot high observation tower, an elevated boardwalk through the hammock and mangrove communities offer unique opportunities for environmental education. Rare and endangered species such as the manatee, the brown pelican, the osprey and sea turtles can often be observed on or from the facility. Coastal relics like a shell midden from the Pre-Columbian Indians and Pond Apple trees from the original freshwater body (known as the Spanish River) can be seen. A cannon and anchors have also been found on the shore of Red Reef park. All these assets give Gumbo Limbo a unique blend of living history.

Exit - 39 (west of I-95)

BUTTERFLY WORLD

Fort Lauderdale (Coconut Creek) - *3600 W. Sample Road (in Tradewinds Park) (exit at Sample Road and head west. Enter into Tradewinds Park on the south side of Sample Road, only a quarter of a mile west of the Florida Turnpike) 33073. Phone: (954) 977-4400. www.butterflyworld.com. Hours: Monday-Saturday 9:00am-5:00pm, Sunday 11:00-5:00pm. Admission: $24.95 adult, $19.95 child (3-11). Discount coupons online. FREEBIES: download a variety of children's books and coloring books online on the Butterflies for Kids page.*

One of the most unusual "zoos" in the world, the Butterfly World is dedicated to the study, care and display of astonishingly beautiful butterflies from all over the globe. The site includes a farm, where the delicate creatures are raised, several aviaries where 1000s of butterflies fly freely, a tropical rain forest, hanging gardens, a museum, a hummingbird exhibit, an English Rose Garden, a Secret Garden and a gift shop. You'll also find fish, lorikeet and insects here. The butterflies are best in the morning until about 3:00pm, so make sure you arrive early.

Exit - 31 (east of I-95)

MAI KAI POLYNESIAN REVUE

Fort Lauderdale - *3599 N. Federal Hwy (take Oakland Park Blvd. East to US 1. on US 1, 5 blocks north of Rte. 816) 33308. www.maikai.com. Phone: (954) 563-3272. Hours: Restaurant open Daily (except Mondays) at 5:00pm for dinner. Show Times: (Dinner served before the show): Tuesday-Friday at 8:00pm; Sunday and Saturday 7:00pm; and 10:00pm again on Saturdays. (Times may vary with season) Admission: Show charge: $10.95 per person. Children under 12 years old enjoy the show at no charge. Dinner Kids Menu (average $18.00), Adult Menu varies but the best value is the package for $45.00.*

What fun! Take a trip to exotic countries without leaving the Florida Coast. The Mai-Kai authentically recreates a Polynesian Village, complete with tiki torches, a thatch roof, gardens, babbling brooks,

so colorful...so fun!

waterfalls and more. Each room reflects a different region of Polynesia. After your South Pacific feast, add the Mai-Kai Islander Revue, performed by Polynesian dancers and musicians in colorful hand sewn costumes. The Samoan fire dance spectacular had the kids in awe! Watch with delight as the brave warriors juggle, twirl and even lick or touch the flaming fire-torches without even a scorch. The ladies competitive drum dance was another favorite. How do they move like that? The Mai-Kai dancers invite audience members to hop on stage and learn some new dance moves. Each child receives a lei and a Polynesian activity book with their kids meal. In addition, the Mai-Kai has a special menu tailored to children's tastes including Captain Cook's Ribs, Society Island Shrimp, Bora Bora Beef and Kon Tiki Chicken. Did you hear your car make thunder as you entered? That's just one of their "tricks" to make guests escape to Polynesia.

Exit - 29 (east of I-95)

PELICAN GRAND BEACH RESORT

Fort Lauderdale - *2000 North Ocean Blvd (A1A) (Sunrise to US-1 North, which becomes Federal Highway. Turn right on SE 17th Street (FL-A1A). Continue on FL-A1A North for about 4 miles) 33305. Phone: (800) 525-OCEAN or (954) 568-9431. www.pelicanbeach.com.*

Guest rooms and Hotel suite accommodations are oceanfront and include private balconies perfect for enjoying the gorgeous beach sunrise or moon glow. Each room is 100% nonsmoking and decorated with a relaxed elegance reminiscent of Florida's grand resorts, yet features modern amenities for a comfortable stay (microwave and mini-frig). Take a ride along the Lazy River or splash in one of two heated pools. Enjoy beachfront dining at North Ocean Grill (kids menu with several selections under $5.00, served on a frisbee) or bask in the warm Florida sun on the large veranda. Grab a scoop at "The Emporium" – old-fashioned ice cream parlor. Or, maybe take a glass-bottom boat tour or boogie boarding day. Underground valet parking and guest can check out board games. A Best Western affiliate - so the pricing is reasonable but the décor is upscale, yet comfortable. Off peak rates start at $99.00 available weekdays. A great place for a family reunion.

HUGH TAYLOR BIRCH STATE PARK

Fort Lauderdale - 3109 East Sunrise Blvd. (head due east on Sunrise Blvd. - off A1A) 33304. Phone: (954) 564-4521. www.floridastateparks.org/hughtaylorbirch. Hours: Daily 8:00am-sundown. Admission: $6.00 per vehicle entrance fee.

The former site of an oceanfront estate, this rambling preserve has woodlands containing the last significant remnant of a maritime hammock (tropical hardwood) forest in the county and is home to several endangered and threatened animals. Visitors can rent a canoe and paddle along a mile-long freshwater lagoon or fish from the seawall. Nature lovers can hike along two short trails and learn about local plants and wildlife while bicyclists and skaters glide along the paved park road. Visitors can access the beach via the pedestrian tunnel under A1A.

Exit - 27 (east of I-95)

FORT LAUDERDALE HISTORY CENTER

Fort Lauderdale - 231 SW 2nd Avenue (head east on Broward, just past the Discovery Museum. Riverwalk, downtown) 33312. Phone: (954) 463-4431. www. oldfortlauderdale.org. Hours: Tuesday-Sunday Noon-4:00pm. Admission: $10.00 adult, $5.00 student (age 7-22)

Located where Henry Flagler's East Coast Railway crosses the New River on Riverwalk, where the city began, it includes three historic buildings, a replica of the first schoolhouse in Broward County and a modern research and collections facility. Old Fort Lauderdale Village is easily recognized with historic markers, a white picket fence, Victorian lighting and landscaping that matches the lush tropical beauty of a bygone era. Guides take you through the 1899 Replica Schoolhouse and the 1907 King-Cromartie House, a pioneer home. They are immersed into the world of over 100 years ago, learning about the history of the original school house and how some children had to walk 1-1/2 miles through the wilderness to get to school.

Exit - 27 (east of I-95)

MUSEUM OF DISCOVERY & SCIENCE

Fort Lauderdale - 401 SW Second Street, downtown (east on Broward Blvd to SW Fifth Ave, turn right. Museum on left) 33312. www.mods.org. Phone: (954) 467-6637. Hours: Monday-Saturday 10:00am-5:00pm. Sunday Noon-6:00pm. Call for showtimes at IMAX Theater. Admission: $12.00-$14.00 (age 2+). Combo ticket *discounts pared with IMAX film. Note: DISCOVERY CENTER - Children seven and under will enjoy this hands-on play and learning center designed especially for them.*

Explore interactive exhibits, experience live encounters with resident animals and learn about Florida's unique ecosystem. See sharks and the largest living Atlantic coral reef in captivity, hang out with bats, be charmed by a 12-foot snake, plus pet alligators, turtles and iguanas. Launch a space vehicle and discover how much force it takes to escape Earth's gravity. Or, take a simulated trip to the Moon or Mars. Check you watch with the Gravity Clock. See sharks and the largest living Atlantic coral reef in captivity or hang out with bats. Listen to the sound and watch the bright lights of a Kaleidoscope or play with Gizmos and gadgets. Outdoors, explore the 11,000 square foot nature trail and learn about Florida's amazing Everglades in the Living in the Everglades exhibit.

INTERNATIONAL SWIMMING HALL OF FAME

Fort Lauderdale - *One Hall of Fame Drive (take Rte 842 east, follow to E Las Olas Blvd one block south on A1A) 33316. Phone: (954) 462-6536. www.ishof.org. Hours: Daily 9:00am-5:00pm. Admission: $4.00-$8.00 per person - active military & children under 6 are FREE.*

Since 1965, ISHOF has promoted swimming, diving, water polo, synchronized swimming, open water swimming, water safety and aquatic art by honoring the great achievements and events in aquatic history. The Museum chronicles feats of famous swimmers and divers, from Esther Williams to Greg Louganis. Located on the ocean side of the complex, the International Swimming Hall of Fame Museum and Exhibition Hall, an elevated wave-shaped building occupying over 7,500 square feet, adorns the entrance to the Hall of Fame Aquatic complex. Johnny Weissmuller's Olympic medals are a part of the world's largest collection of aquatic Olympic medals, pins, badges, diplomas and certificates. Mark Spitz's starting block used to win six of his seven 1972 Olympic gold medals is on view as are over 60 Olympic, national and club uniforms, warm ups and swim suits. The first automatic timing machine to determine the results of close races can be seen along with the modern system used today. The visitor may play the role of both the starter and timer in a hands-on tribute to timing automation.

SEA EXPERIENCE GLASSBOTTOM BOAT & SNORKELING TOURS

Fort Lauderdale - *801 Seabreeze Blvd. Bahia Mar Resort docks - 100 yards north of the Jungle Queen) 33316. Phone: (954) 467-6000. www.seaxp.com. Admission: $28.00 adult rider/$35.00 adult snorkeler. $15.00 child rider/$21.00 child snorkeler. Tours: Two trips daily, 10:15am and 2:15pm.*

Discover the underwater world of south Florida. Swim through the clear waters of the warm Atlantic and experience the colorful fish and marine life that lie beneath the surface. To name just a few, you might see French, Grey and Queen Angelfish, Blue Parrotfish, Trumpetfish, and many others. The crew's favorite snorkeling spot, named the Fort Lauderdale Twin Ledges, is located about a half mile off of Fort Lauderdale beach in 10 to 20 ft. of water. The water temperature is warm all year-round making it an ideal spot for snorkeling. For first time snorkelers the crew is more than happy to provide lessons and to make it a pleasurable experience for all. And if you don't want to get wet, you can enjoy the view from aboard the glass bottom boat!

JUNGLE QUEEN RIVERBOAT

Fort Lauderdale - *801 Seabreeze Blvd. (take Rte 842 east to A1A south. located near the Bahia Mar Resort docks) 33316. www.junglequeen.com. Phone: (954) 462-5596. Admission: $39.95 adult/$21.75 child evenings, $14.00-$24.00 daytime.*

Step back in history aboard this sternwheeler that cruises the Intracoastal and New River on day and evening sightseeing cruises. Cruise to an island for BBQ dinner and variety show nightly at 6:00pm. Narrated 3-hour sightseeing cruises are offered in the morning and afternoon. The informative and humorous commentary on your way to the JungleQueen Indian Village on the New River. On the Tropical Isle you can catch a alligator show and see rare exotic birds and playful monkeys.

Exit - 25 (east of I-95)

WATER BUS

Fort Lauderdale - *1850 SE 17th Street, Suite 106A (take Rte. 84 east to US 1 north to right on SE 17th Street) 33316. Phone: (954) 467-6677. www.watertaxi.com.*

See the "Venice of America" via scheduled on-time service Water Taxis. Water Bus is a unique alternative to traditional transportation, providing a comfortable and relaxing way to avoid traffic and congested roadways. Take a ride along Ft. Lauderdale's wet streets and see the sights and sounds of Ft. Lauderdale's waterways. Daily from 17th Street to Oakland Park Blvd. And west to downtown Fort Lauderdale. All day pass is $22.00 adult/$11.00 youth.

Exit - 24 (west of I-95) / I-595 WEST

BUEHLER PLANETARIUM & OBSERVATORY

Fort Lauderdale (Davie) - *3501 SW Davie Road (exit 7 south to Broward Community College, central Campus) 33314. Phone: (954) 201-6681. www.iloveplanets.com. Admission: $4.00-$5.00 per person. FREE for open house observatory nights.*

Explorations through all of space. Enjoy programs that explore the wonders of the Universe. Most of the public programs involve the stars and folklore. Observatory open to Public Wednesday, Friday, Saturday 8:00pm-10:00pm for free.

FLAMINGO GARDENS

Fort Lauderdale (Davie) - *3750 S. Flamingo Rd (Take I-595 West to Flamingo Rd. (Exit #1B) Turn South) 33330. Phone: (954) 473-2955. www.flamingogardens.org. Hours: Daily 9:30am-5:30pm. Closed Mondays, (June-September). Admission: $18.00 adult, $10.00 child (4-11). Discounts for seniors, military and students w/ ID. TOUR BY TRAM: Adults $4.00, Children (4-11) $3.00, Tours: Narrated tram ride through the tropical rainforest, native hammock, wetland areas, and groves. The tour is fully narrated, lasting approximately 25 minutes. Note: Flamingo Café.*

Once a spectacular estate, this Garden is now a refuge housing a free flight aviary, alligators, flamingos, bobcats and injured animals. Rare, exotic and native plants, a 200-year old oak hammock, citrus groves, wetlands and a tropical flowering tree walk balance out the botanical gardens. A nice living example of Florida's natural history.

Exit - 23 (west of I-95)

FISHING HALL OF FAME & MUSEUM (IGFA)

Fort Lauderdale (Dania Beach) - 300 Gulf Stream Way (located next to Bass Pro Shops) (I-95 to Griffin Road Exit 23; west on Griffin to first light (Anglers Ave.); south to Gulf Stream Way; left at Sportsman's Park) 33004. Phone: (954) 922-4212. www.igfa.org. Hours: Daily 10:00am-6:00pm except Sundays Noon-6:00pm. Closed only Thanksgiving and Christmas. Admission: $5.00-$10.00 (age 3+).

The galleries and marina displays here are full of fish. Meet live alligators, too. Start your adventure with Journeys, an exciting cinematic experience that you can see, hear, and feel! Try "on" reels. Kids might like to feed the fish or try the virtual fishing simulator (sport fishing without getting wet). Younger ones like the Discovery Room where kids dress up and "fish" from a fun boat. Along the Wetlands walk, you might find iguanas, lizards and birds amongst the mangroves. In the Hall of Fame, you'll find the world's largest life-size collection of fishing world record holders. Some are stationed as photo ops so you can go home and tell some fish stories about your big catch!

Exit - 21 (east of I-95)

ANNE KOLB NATURE CENTER

Fort Lauderdale (Hollywood) - 751 Sheridan St. (West Lake Park) (take route 822 east to signs for West Lake Park) 33019. www.broward.org/parks/westlakepark/pages/annekolbnaturecenter.aspx. Phone: (954) 926-2480. Hours: Rentals daily 9:00am-5:00pm. Park open daylight hours. The park is closed Veteran's Day, the Day after Thanksgiving, and Christmas Day. Admission: An admission fee of $1.50 per person for individuals over age five is in affect on the south side of West Lake Park on weekends and County holidays. There is no gate fee to enter the north side of the park, but there is a $1.00 admission fee to visit the park's Exhibit Hall.

Over 1,500 pristine acres of wilderness and mangrove wetlands are minutes from the beach. Visitors can enjoy a variety of activities including hiking, biking, canoeing, fishing, tennis and racquetball. There are abundant nature and canoe trails with wildlife viewing areas, an exhibit hall and observation tower. Sports equipment rentals and narrated boat tours are available at the marina (extra fee). The Fishing Pier Trail leads to two piers that overlook the

Intracoastal Waterway.

The center's striking, contemporary exhibit hall includes a site map of the complex's three-mile preserve, the Living Crossroads theater (a 10-minute closed-caption video program), and a series of interactive and static displays (including a stocked 3,500-gallon aquarium) that vividly portray and explain West Lake's mangrove ecosystem and its importance. Visitors then proceed to the Eco-Room for an engaging hands on investigation and an eye-to-eye view of the animal residents. An elevator or stairs takes you to the top of the center's 68-foot observation tower that offers a panoramic view of the mangrove wetland and coastline.

Exit - 2D (east of I-95) / I-395 EAST

MIAMI CHILDREN'S MUSEUM

Miami Beach - *980 MacArthur Causeway (MacArthur Cswy toward Miami Beach. Exit right at Watson Island) 33132. www.miamichildrensmuseum.org. Phone: (305) 373-5437. Hours: Daily 10:00am-6:00pm. Admission: $18.00 general, $14.00 Florida resident. Note: Subway restaurant on premises. Rock climbing wall, extra fee. Educators: Pre & Post Visit activities and crafts downloadable at the Education/ Pre & Post Visit link.*

This space includes 12 different galleries and many bilingual displays. The Museum features interactive exhibits including a miniature supermarket, television news studio, cruise ship and a giant sandcastle slide. Permanent interactive exhibits include The Castle of Dreams, Bank, Health & Wellness Center, Pet Central, Safety Zone, Supermarket, Television Studio, Meet Miami, the Sea and Me (especially for children under five), Ocean Odyssey, Everglades Park, Ports of Call: Brazil, Port of Miami, Cruise Ship, All About Art and the World Music Studio. Something very fun to do is the simulated firetruck ride and fire. Kids use virtual and hands-on equipment to maneuver through crowded streets to a big fire where they have to safely put it out! MCM is one of the ten largest children's museums in the country.

SOUTH BEACH DUCK TOURS

Miami Beach - *1661 James Avenue (I-395 exit 2 north to Venetian Cswy - departing from South Beach - located between Lincoln Road and 17th Street) 33139. www.ducktourssouthbeach.com. Admission: $32.00 adult, $26.00 senior (65+), $18.00 child (4-12). Tours: Daily 10:00am-4:00pm, departing on the hour. Best to make reservations.*

FLORIDA

A 90-Minute Land & Sea Adventure aboard amphibious vehicles touring famous Miami landmarks before a dramatic "SPLASH DOWN" into beautiful Biscayne Bay for a close up look at the many homes of the "Rich & Famous" on Star Island (Gloria Estavan, the cat house, or Miami Vice). This is the unique way to explore Miami by land and sea aboard a vehicle equipped to do both - the "vesicles" that look like ducks on wheels. Yell hello to J Lo or sneak a peek at the many famous art deco or cruise ship shaped buildings. As you glide through downtown Miami and South Beach, your guide quacks on about landmarks and encourages you to interact with the locals...

Captain Jenny helps the boat climb out of the water...

Next thing you know, you're quacking along. For the kids (and extroverted adults) this is sure to be a highlight of your stay!

ISLAND QUEEN & BAYSIDE BLASTER

Miami - *Bayside Marketplace, waterside (I95 to I-395 east. Exit at NE 2nd Ave/ Biscayne, continue straight. Make right on Biscayne, then left on Port Blvd (NE 5th St), stay on right) 33132. www.islandqueencruises.com. Phone: (305) 379-5119 or (800) 910-5119. Admission: $26.00 adult, $19.00 child (4-12). Tours: Island Queen: Daily 11:00am-7:00pm, departing each hour, on the hour. Bayside: Weekends 12:30pm-8:30pm every 2 hours on the half hour. The tour lasts 1.5 hours. Beverages and light snacks available for purchase.*

- **ISLAND QUEEN**: Sit back and relax as you go on a bilingual narrated sightseeing cruise along scenic Biscayne Bay. See Miami's spectacular coastal sites; including the beautiful downtown Miami skyline, the Port of Miami, Brickell Key, Fisher Island and the celebrity filled islands of Miami Beach known as Millionaire's Row?

- **BAYSIDE BLASTER**: Ride aboard the Bayside Blaster! Race through beautiful Biscayne Bay to the celebrity-filled islands of Miami Beach known as "Millionaire's Row." It's the adventurous way to see Miami's spectacular coastal sites.

JUNGLE ISLAND

Miami - *1111 Parrot Jungle Trail (take I-395 east/MacArthur Causeway to first exit after the bridge-Jungle Trail, follow signs) 33132. www.jungleisland.com. Phone: (305) 2-JUNGLE. Hours: Daily 10:00am-5:00pm. Open until 6:00pm on weekends. Admission: $34.95 adult, $32.95 senior, military & student w/ ID, $26.95 child (3-10). Parking is $7.00 per vehicle. Educators: Lesson Plans for two different subjects (along with activities) are online under the Education/Teacher Resources icon. Note: you cannot use your own camera to take photos - they charge per picture (packages start at $19.95) for their service.*

Open since July 2003 on Watson Island (close to resorts and cruise ship terminals), the theme park is home to more than 3,000 exotic animals and 500 species of plants. Here visitors enjoy animal stage shows, one-of-a-kind interactive aviaries, plant nurseries, jungle trails, ape and monkey exhibits, a petting farm, as well as world-famous parrot shows, a new Serpentarium and Jungle Theater, an Everglades Habitat and more. All of the shows featured un-caged animals performing. Jungle Island offers memorable opportunities to: feed birds, fish and flamingos; interact with roaming trainers and animals; and, take photo-ops with some rare animals and exotic birds. Introduce yourself to the largest cat in the world, Vulcan, their 900-pound tiger. Volunteer to feed Mama Cass, the world's only trained Cassowary (the most lethal bird on Earth). She'll eat an entire apple in one gulp! This is nice, but some families opt for less expensive zoos - having more exhibits for the money. The Jungle has a lot of shady areas, new buildings and exhibits, and an inflatable slide (call to verify if slide will be operating wet or dry).

Exit - 1A (west of I-95)

CORAL GABLES' VENETIAN POOL

Miami (Coral Gables) - *2701 De Soto Blvd. (continue south onto US1. Right on Bird, right on Granada) 33134. Phone: (305) 460-5357. www.venetianpool.com. Hours: Generally Tuesday-Sunday 10:00am-4:30pm or 11:00am-5:30pm year-round. Open Mondays in the summer. Admission: $10.50 adult, $6.00 child (3-12). Significantly Reduced rates November-March and for city residents. Children under 3 are NOT admitted to the facility.*

These historic Venetian Pools were formed from a coral rock quarry in 1923 and fed 820,000 gallons of spring water daily. Considered one of the world's most unique and breathtaking municipal swimming pools, the non-chemical water provides a nice break from the chlorine and salt water, and the beautiful coral rock keeps the water nice and cool even in the summer sun. There are two waterfalls, coral caves and grottos. Hailed as one of the best destinations for families by locals, the Venetian Pool is a great alternative to the beach for family fun in the sun.

FAIRCHILD TROPICAL BOTANIC GARDEN

Miami (Coral Gables) - *10901 Old Cutler Road (US 1 to SW 42nd Ave/LeJeune Rd. Turn left and drive south to roundabout. Take 2nd right onto Old Cutler Rd for 2 miles) 33156. Phone: (305) 667-1651. www.fairchildgarden.org. Hours: Daily 9:30am-4:30pm except Christmas. Admission: $25.00 adult, $18.00 senior (65+), $12.00 child (6-17). Fairchild admission includes a narrated tram tour, offered hourly, plus admission to the Conservatory and Whitman Tropical Fruit Pavilion at no additional charge. Miscellaneous: Garden café and gift shop. Right next door to Fairchild is Matheson Hammock Park, which features a toddler-friendly lagoon style beach, perfect for a late afternoon dip.*

The 83-acre botanical garden boasts extensive collections of rare tropical plants including palms, cicadas, flowering trees and vines. Children can enjoy a naturalist treasure hunt, identifying various plants, insects and animals as they wander the lush, expansive grounds. Take a narrated tram tour past tropical fruit, sunken gardens, lily ponds and an outdoor rainforest. Or, go at your own leisure on winding paths and overlooks.

Exit - 1A (east of I-95)

MIAMI MUSEUM OF SCIENCE & PLANETARIUM

Miami (Coconut Grove) - *3280 S. Miami Avenue (I-95 to Exit #1A/SW 25 Road, stay in the right hand lane and follow the signs) 33129. Phone: (305) 646-4200. www.miamisci.org. Hours: Daily 10:00am-6:00pm. Closed Thanksgiving and Christmas. Admission: $14.95 adult, $10.95 senior (62+), child (3-12). Ticket price includes entrance to all museum galleries, planetarium shows, and the wildlife center.*

Traveling and permanent exhibits are largely geared toward children exploring subject matter from dinosaurs to the properties of physics. Be Heart Smart or go into the Vital Space Immersion Theatre. Live science demonstrations and theater shows daily. (laser shows every 1st Friday of the month) Daily planetarium shows point out the stars of the season, while the Wildlife Center houses rare birds of prey and reptiles.

MIAMI SEAQUARIUM

Miami (Key Biscayne) - *4400 Rickenbacker Causeway (I-95 to Key Biscayne exit, then take Rickenbacker Cswy. From south, take US 1 to Rickenbacker) 33149. Phone: (305) 361-5705. www.miamiseaquarium.com. Hours: Daily 9:30am-6:00pm. Admission: $39.95 general, $29.95 child (3-9). Parking $8.00. Rickenbacker Causeway toll $1.25. Miscellaneous: Food outlets and gift shops are available throughout the park. Also offers popular swim with the dolphins program and feeding sessions with sharks and manatees. The two-hour program lets visitors slip into a wet suit and enter the world-famous Flipper Lagoon for an up-close encounter with dolphins.*

See Dolphins & Killer Whales in the water at the same time...

This place gained notoriety as the location for filming of 1960s hit TV show Flipper. Indeed, "Flipper" still has his own daily show at the Seaquarium, as does Lolita, the killer whale. Laugh with the island adventures of Salty, the Sea Lion. It's the place where moray eels lurk in coral reef caverns, where shiny schools of exotic fish dance through underwater seascapes, and it's the only place where you will see the graceful beauty of four Pacific white sided dolphins combined with the awesome power of a three ton killer whale. Another popular show, the Flipper Dolphin Show, takes place at the Flipper Lagoon, film location for much of the popular 1960s television show of the same name. Brave the "Splash Zone" if you dare. At the Manatee exhibit, guests come face-to-face with Florida's state marine mammal through poolside and underwater viewing areas. The manatees featured are part of the rescue and rehabilitation program at Miami Seaquarium. See Nile Crocodiles fed at Discovery Bay, and the new Salty's Pirate Playground, too. The shows are close together so you can watch them all without running from show to show. At this magical park, dolphins "fly" and whales can "walk"!

BISCAYNE NATURE CENTER / MARJORY STONEMAN DOUGLAS

Miami (Key Biscayne) - *Crandon Park, 6767 Crandon Blvd. (take I-95 or US 1 to the Key Biscayne Exit-Rickenbacker Cswy plus 4.5 miles) 33149. Phone: (305) 361-6767. www.biscaynenaturecenter.org. Tours: Marine exploration trips are scheduled at low tide only. Trips require advance reservations. Schedules online under Family Outings. FREEBIES: A printable book to read and color (Our Living Coral Reef) is online under Kids Only.*

The center offers hands-on marine exploration, coastal hammock hikes, fossil-rock reef walks, bike trips, local history lectures and beach walks to aquatic tourists. The display room has aquariums teeming with aquatic wildlife, sea turtle demonstrations, and stories about the Tequesta Indians while you can observe artifacts from archeological digs. Three walking paths and a bikeway meander through exotic flora leading to a north beach area where low tides expose a fossilized rock reef, offering a view seen on only one other location in the world. On Seagrass tours, a guide will brief you about the abundant sea life, then lead you waist-deep into the warm, salty water to see for yourselves. You'll run a net through the thick seagrass and be amazed at what critters you'll find. Sea urchins, sea cucumbers, pipefish, spotted slugs, blowfish, spider crabs and tiny fish just might fill the nets. Even tiny octopus or exotic puffer fish (the one's that bloat when they're stressed) may be seen. The critters, of course, are not harmed. They are returned to the sea grass. For $10, this is one of the best, cheapest deals in town. Your kids may not want to leave.

Exit - 1A (east of I-95)

BARNACLE HISTORIC STATE PARK

Miami (Coconut Grove) - *3485 Main Hwy (exit east almost immediately onto S Bayshore Dr. heading south a few blocks) 33133. Phone: (305) 446-9445. www.floridastateparks.org/thebarnacle. Hours: The Barnacle is open to the public 9:00am-5:00pm Friday through Monday with guided tours at 10:00am, 11:30am, 1:00pm and 2:30pm. The park is open Tuesday through Thursday for group tours with advance reservations. The park is closed New Year´s, Thanksgiving and Christmas days. Admission: $2.00+ (age 6+). Please use honor box to pay fees.*

This beautiful house with a whimsical name dates to a quieter time. The Barnacle, built in 1891, offers a glimpse of Old Florida during The Era of the Bay. Situated on the shore of Biscayne Bay, this was the home of Ralph Middleton Munroe, one of Coconut Grove´s most charming and influential pioneers. Munroe's principal passion was designing yachts. In his lifetime, he drew plans for 56 different boats. A walk through a tropical hardwood hammock leads to the house. Regularly scheduled tours provide a glimpse of what life was like in the wilds of Florida.

PINECREST GARDENS

Miami (Pinecrest) - *11000 Red Road (exit onto US1 continue south to SW 57 Ave. Head south to gardens) 33156. Phone: (305) 669-6942. www.pinecrestgardens.com. Hours: Daily 9:00am-5:00pm. Open later summers.*

This 22-acre site sits on property once owned by Parrot Jungle. The Gardens include winding paths past a botanical garden, petting zoo (open several times daily), miniature donkeys and alpaca, a butterfly exhibit, a Cypress Slough, Sausage Trees, Turtle Island and the delightful Splash-N-Play Water Squirt Playground. There is a $3.00 admission fee for the water playground and park.

BILL BAGGS CAPE FLORIDA STATE PARK

Miami (Key Biscayne) - *1200 S. Crandon Park Blvd (I-95 to the Rickenbacker Causeway, all the way to the end) 33149. www.floridastateparks.org/capeflorida. Phone: (305) 361-5811. Hours: Park open 8:00am to sundown. Admission: $8.00 per vehicle. Tours: Lighthouse tours are at 10:00am and 1:00pm, Thursdays through Mondays. Tours are FREE. Miscellaneous: Complete your perfect day with a sample of authentic Cuban Cuisine or fresh seafood at the Lighthouse Café by the beach or Boater's Grill overlooking No Name Harbor. The café is open seven days a week, 9:00am until sunset, and the Grill is open seven days a week from 9:00am-8:30pm (Sunday through Thursday) and 9:00am-9:30pm (Friday and Saturday).*

This historic lighthouse, built in 1884, is located on a very scenic beach at the southern tip of Key Biscayne. Be ready to ascend the 109 steps to the lighthouse watchroom and enjoy the view of the beach, Miami and Biscayne Bay from the top, view a short movie, and then tour the Keeper's Quarters. Visitors come to the park to sunbathe, swim, and picnic on over a mile of sandy Atlantic beachfront. Biking and kayaking are also popular activities. Anglers can throw in their lines from the seawall along Biscayne Bay for some of the best shoreline fishing in the region. Walking and bicycle trails wind through native vegetation.

FLORIDA

Curious About <u>All</u> That
Each State Has To Offer?

Our family has kid-tested 12 states and visited over 5000 places!
Discover more exciting adventures in your favorite region. Visit
www.KidsLoveTravel.com *today for complete details.*

Explore places where you can "discover" oil & coal, meet Ben Franklin, or watch your favorite toys and delicious, fresh snacks being made. Over 800 listings in one book about Pennsylvania travel. 9 geographical zones. 264 pages.

Discover hidden history, forgotten islands, secret messages and decorative "decoys". Search for the best harbor havens, Chesapeake crabbing, and brilliant beaches. Over 600 listings about Maryland travel. 6 zones. Includes Washington, DC Area. 264 pages.

Discover where ponies swim and dolphins dance, dig into archaeology & living history, or be dazzled by world-class caverns and a natural bridge. Nearly 700 listings in one book about Virginia travel. 6 zones. Includes Washington, DC Area. 280 pages.

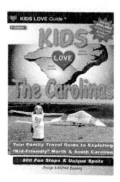

Explore places where you can seek out pirates and real treasure, fly like a bird on the Outer Banks, explore castles and strange houses, Learn of the "lost colony" and Mayberry, and more! Over 800 listings in one book about North & South Carolina travel. 10 geographical zones, 272 pages.

Explore hidden islands, humbling habitats, and historic gold mines. See playful puppets, dancing dolphins, and comical kangaroos. "Watch out" for cowboys, Indians, and swamp creatures. Over 400 listings in one book about Georgia travel. 6 geographical zones, 264 pages.

Search for real pirate treasure and hidden castles or "fly" into space. Explore the best places to meet manatee, swim with sea lions, dance with dolphins, nestle into nature, or wiggle in the waves. Over 600 listings in one book about Florida travel. 9 zones. 288 pages.

For updates & travel games visit: **www.KidsLoveTravel.com**

CPSIA information can be obtained
at www.ICGtesting.com
Printed in the USA
LVOW03s2220140417
530760LV00001BA/10/P